Political Corruption in Transition

A Skeptic's Handbook

D1605785

Political Corruption in Transition

A Skeptic's Handbook

Edited by
Stephen Kotkin and András Sajó

CEU PRESS

Central European University Press
Budapest New York

Published in 2002 by
Central European University Press

An imprint of the
Central European University Share Company
Nádor utca 11, H-1015 Budapest, Hungary
Tel: +36-1-327-3138 or 327-3000
Fax: +36-1-327-3183
E-mail: ceupress@ceu.hu
Website: www.ceupress.com

400 West 59th Street, New York NY 10019, USA
Tel: +1-212-547-6932
Fax: +1-212-548-4607
E-mail: mgreenwald@sorosny.org

ISBN 963 9241 46 6 Cloth
ISBN 963 9241 47 4 Paperback

Library of Congress Cataloging-in-Publication Data

Political corruption in transition: a skeptic's handbook/edited by
Stephen Kotkin and András Sajó
p. cm.
Includes bibliographical references and index.
ISBN --ISBN
1. Political corruption--Europe, Eastern. 2. Political
corruption--Europe, Eastern--Case studies. I. Kotkin, Stephen. II.
Sajó András
JN96.A56 C67 2002
364.1'323'0947--dc21
                                        2002005660

Printed in Hungary by
Akaprint

Table of Contens

INTRODUCTION

PART I: Understanding and Misunderstanding Corruption

PART II: Corruption as Politics

Contributors

Erhard Blankenburg has (since 1980) been teaching sociology of law and (for some time also) criminology at the Vrije Universiteit, Amsterdam. He earned his M.A. at the University of Oregon, a Doctor's degree at Basel (Switzerland) and a Dr. Habil. at Freiburg (Germany). After teaching sociology and sociology of law at Freiburg University (1965–1970), he served as consultant with the Quickborn Team, Hamburg until 1972 as senior research fellow at the PrognosAG Basel until 1974, at the Max Plank Institute, Freiburg 1974/75 and at the science Center, Berlin until 1980. He has published widely on comparative legal cultures, police, public prosecutors, civil courts, labor courts, legal aid and mobilization of law.

Virginie Coulloudon is now based in Prague as Director of Regional Analysis and Associate Director of Communications for Radio Liberty. She was an associate of the Kathryn W. and Shelby Cullom Davis Center for Russian Studies at Harvard University, where she directed a research project entitled "The Elite and Patronage in Russia" and a seminar on "Power and Corruption." She received her Ph.D. in History from the École des Hautes Études en Sciences Sociales, Paris. She is the editor of *The Power of Corruption* (Boulder, Co., 2002), and the author of *La mafia en Union soviétique* (Paris, 1990), one of the first non-fiction books on Soviet organized crime.

Diego Gambetta Ph.D., F.B.A., is reader in sociology at the University of Oxford and Fellow of All Souls College. He is the author of *The Sicilian Mafia. The Business of Private Protection* (Harvard University Press, 1993), and the editor of Trust: *Making and Breaking Cooperative Relations* (Basil Blackwell, 1988).

Elemér Hankiss is professor emeritus of political science at the University of Budapest. He previously taught at several American and European universities (Stanford, Georgetown, Central European University Institute, Florence). Among his books are *East European Alternatives* (Oxford Clarendon, 1990), *Proletár Reneszánsz: Tanulmányok az európai civilizációról (Proletarian Renaissance: Consumer Culture Re-visited)* (Helikon, 1999), and *Fears and Symbols:*

An Introduction to the Study of Western Civilization (Central European University Press, 2001).

Paul D. Hutchcroft is an associate professor in the Department of Political Science at the University of Wisconsin—Madison. He has written on Philippine politics and political economy, as well as on the politics of corruption, and is the author of *Booty Capitalism: The Politics of Banking in the Philippines* (Cornell, 1998). His current project, "Deciphering Decentralization: Central Authority and Local Bosses in the Philippines and Beyond" (forthcoming, Cambridge University Press), analyzes central-local relations in the Philippines in historical and comparative perspectives.

James B. Jacobs is Warren E. Burger professor of law and director, Center For Research in Crime & Justice, NYU School of Law, where he teaches criminal law, criminal procedure and criminology. He is the author of *Is Gun Control Feasible?* (Oxford University Press, 2002), and the co-author (with Frank Anechiarico) of *Pursuit of Absolute Integrity: How Corruption Control Makes Government Ineffective* (University of Chicago Press, 1996).

Lena Kolarska-Bobińska is a professor of sociology. She graduated from Warsaw University and spent two years at Stanford University and Carnegie Mellon University on a post-doctoral Ford Foundation scholarship. From 1970 until 1990, she held various posts at the Polish Academy of Sciences, Institute of Philosophy and Sociology, following which (1991–97) she served as the head of the Center for Public Opinion Research, Poland's largest public opinion institute. Since 1977 she has been director of the Institute of Public Affairs, a non-partisan think-tank. The author and co-author of more than ten books and 150 articles, she has at various times worked as an advisor to the World Bank, the Government of Poland, and the President of the Polish Republic.

Joongi Kim is a professor of law at Yonsei University's Graduate School of International Studies, where he serves as the chair of the International Trade and Finance Program. After private practice at a Washington, D.C. law firm. he entered academia in 1995, when he first joined the faculty of Hongik University. He received his J. D. from Georgetown University Law Center. His research primarily focuses on corporate governance, corruption and international trade.

Stephen Kotkin teaches European and Asian history at Princeton University, where he also directs the Russian studies program. He is the author, most recently, of *Armageddon Averted: The Soviet Collapse, 1970–2000* (Oxford University Press, 2001), and co-editor (with Bruce Elleman) of *Mongolia in the Twentieth Century: Landlocked Cosmopolitan* (M.E. Sharpe, 1999).

Tokhir Mirzoev is a Ph.D. student in economics at the Ohio State University. He received his M.A. from the Central European University, where he wrote a thesis on the economics of trust and social capital.

Mark Philp is head of the Department of Politics and International Relations at the University of Oxford and is a fellow of Oriel College. His essay was written during a period of special leave (1999–2000) made possible by a British Academy/Leverhulme Trust Senior Research Fellowship. His books include *Godwin's Political Justice* (1986) and *Paine* (1989). He is the general editor of *Godwin's Collected Writings* (1992–3) and has written widely on issues in contemporary political theory, including several papers on political corruption. He is currently engaged in a book on political conduct.

Vadim Radaev is a professor, chair of economic sociology, and vice-rector at the State University—Higher School of Economics, in Moscow. He has published five books, including *Economic Sociology* (1997, in Russian) and *Formation of New Russian Markets* (1998, in Russian) as well as more than 100 papers in such journals as *International Sociology, Economic and Industrial Democracy, Problems of Economic Transition, International Journal of Sociology*. His current research interests involve economic sociology, the sociology of entrepreneurship, and the informal economy.

Quentin Reed lives in Prague, where he works in the Open Society Institute's European Union Accession Monitoring Program, focusing on corruption. He completed a doctorate on privatization, corruption and control in post-communist countries, with reference to the Czech case, at Oriel College, Oxford in 1996. His thesis earned the 1997 Political Studies Association Walter Bagehot Prize for the best British dissertation on politics and public administration. He has been an advisor to the Supreme Audit Office of the Czech Republic, and a reporter at the

Prague Business Journal. For the last few years he has written *Business Operations Reports* for the Economist Intelligence Unit, and served on the Executive Board of Transparency International Czech Republic.

András Sajó is professor of law and chair of the Constitutional Law Institute at the Central European University in Budapest. He was the founding dean of Legal Studies at that University. He has published several books on constitutional and socio-legal issues, including *Limiting Government* (CEU Press, 1999). His honors include the Hungarian Academy Book Prize in 1986 and serving as the Blackstone Lecturer at Oxford University. He is a member of the Hungarian Academy of Sciences.

Endre Sík is professor in the department of Sociology at Eötvös Loránd University (ELTE) and a senior advisor to the Hungarian Central Statistical Office. He has published extensively on the social analysis of economics, including problems of reciprocity in transactions, invisible incomes, network capital, and the various shades of markets. His current research is directed at households' economic behavior, immigration and refugees in Hungary, the informal economy, and social capital.

Daniel Smilov teaches at the Legal Studies Department of the Central European University, Budapest, and is a consultant on anticorruption and administrative law issues to the Constitutional and Legal Studies Institute affiliated with the Open Society Institute, Budapest. He is completing his D.Phil. thesis at Jesus College, University of Oxford, His current research project focuses on party funding and campaign finance, covering fifteen countries in Central and Eastern Europe.

Ákos Szilágyi, a poet and translator, teaches literature, media theory and Russian cultural history at the Department of Aesthetics at Eötvös Loránd University, where he founded and co-directs the Hungarian Institute of Russian Studies. He has been a contributor to the research programs and publications of the Korridor Political Research Centre for several years, and has published on the Russian avant-garde, the totalitarian culture of the Stalin era, "negative" utopias, and the appeal of sovereignty. His books include *Les Mondes d' Andrei Tarkowsky* (1987, with Kovács András Bálint), and *Star Boris und die Starewitschi* (1999), as well as others in Hungarian.

List of Figures

List of Tables

Kolarska Bobińska

Smilov

Mirzoev

Preface

In May 1999, the Shelby Cullom Davis Center for Historical Studies at Princeton University and the Open Society Institute held a jointly sponsored two-day workshop on corruption. That event was followed by a joint international conference at the Central European University (CEU) in Budapest, between October 30 and November 6, 1999. This volume brings together a selection of the papers presented and discussed at the workshop and especialliy at the conference. Whereas the Princeton workshop—the culmination of a year–long series of weekly meetings—was by design relatively compact, the Budapest conference had a large number of participants, including students of the CEU. Coverage of the so-called transition countries was broad and comprehensive. But not all of the presentations and commentaries from both events were based upon written papers. In any case, this volume of essays does not strive for comprehensiveness (which in fact would have necessitated several volumes), but to facilitate conceptualization of the issues. The present collection seeks to put corruption back into the social relations of specific systems and of the transition, but without becoming relativist or revisionist.

Accordingly, we investigate understandings or misunderstandings of corruption, corruption as politics, and the multiple contradictory effects of corrupt practices, particularly for the 1990s and the countries that emerged from Soviet-style systems. It would be utterly uninteresting, not to mention wrong, to deny that various forms of corruption occur in the former socialist countries. However, healthy doses of skepticism about what is happening and how corruption is being measured or characterized would seem useful. Collectively, these essays offer a multidisciplinary, non–economistic, non moralist approach to corruption in societies undergoing transition from socialism. The basic approach of most authors in this volume (many of them "locals" concerned about corruption in their own society) is that corruption should be understood as part of a broader web of social relations, which form part of the exercise of political power. We emphasize the centrality of political or government corruption: indeed, corruption is primarily political. However, political or government corruption is not simply about corruption in the public/political sphere, or about bribery in governmental offices and parties. Rather, corruption becomes political in the sense that it is the political structures themselves that enable and often necessitate corrupt practices. To put the matter another way, corruption can be seen as a betrayal of public trust by officials; it also constitutes patterns of behavior dictated by the basic operation of government and political structures, further encouraged by the transition.

The essays that follow indicate that understanding corruption in transition contexts within broader social developments enables us to view corrupt practices as incidents of rational behavior, or at least as behavior generated by powerful incentive mechanisms. Frequently, long-standing patterns, from minute favors to big-time connections, satisfy genuine social and political needs, but in the transition, and in the harsh light shone by open and competitive media, these patterns become systemic corruption. What is being transformed? What is being exposed? Corrupt transactions can be seen as a function of other illegal or even legal social transactions. For example, corruption serves as a form of protectionism. Most commonly, corruption is embedded in clientelistic structures, which are typical in transition countries, irrespective of their varied history, economic development and geographic location. At the same time, however, "corruption" has emerged (once again) as a language of politics, both internationally and domestically, especially where not only a specific ideology (communism) but also the very notion of ideology has been discredited, and "the market" has been offered as an organizing principle for politics. While anticorruption programs have been forcefully suggested or ostensibly required of countries by multilateral agencies professing a reform or neo-liberal agenda, vociferous anticorruption campaigns have been used as vehicles to power for local critics of neo-liberalism (which exists more in the critique than in practice). Neofunctionalism meets post-modernism?

The editors would like to thank the staff of the Central European University Press for managing the book project. An anonymous referee for the press offered many valuable suggestions. Dr. István Szíjártó helped coordinate the large Budapest conference. We would also like to express our gratitude to professor William Jordan, then Director of Princeton's Davis Seminar. In the editing and final preparation of the volume, the coordinating role of the Davis Seminar was taken on by Princeton's Liechtenstein Institute for Self-Determination (LISD), for which we would like to thank the LISD Director, Wolfgang Danspeckgruber. The LISD program manager, Tyler Felgenhauer, did some of the technical editing and the index. Above all, the editors would like to offer their heartfelt appreciation to the many presenters of papers not published and to the other participants, including Robert Darnton, Susan Rose-Ackerman, David Witwer, Gary Gerstle, Errol Meidinger, András Cieger, András Gerő, Malgorzata Fuszara, Jacek Kurczewski, István János Tóth, Árpád Kovács, Károly Bárd, Dániel Szabó, Piotr Korys, Zoltán Szente, Marek Lajtar, Viktor Ukhvanov, Josip Kregar, Helen Darbishire, Henry Siegel, Pavel Frić, István Szikinger, Inna Čabelková-Piven, Leslie Holmes, Elizabeth Barett, Valdas Bartasevicius, Vytautas Dudenas, Michael Gallagher, Adam Czarnota, Michael Kopanic, Juliet Gole, Péter Hack, Helen Sutch, Marijana Trivonpvic, Ivar Tallo, Wladimir Tolz, Yuri Y. Boldyrev, Natalya Gevorkyan, Sergei Pavlenko, Nodari Simonia, Farid M. Habiev, and Bohdan Krawchenko.

INTRODUCTION
Clientelism and Extortion: Corruption in Transition
András Sajó

Corruption in Eastern Europe is decidedly misunderstood and is, to some extent, enveloped in myths. An elementary failure of understanding helps explain the preponderance of misdirected policies in the region. In particular, four key issues warrant close examination.

1) Corruption in Eastern Europe is structural in the sense that it is part and parcel of the region's evolving clientelistic social structures. An analysis of corruption cannot be divorced from an understanding of clientelism.

2) Clientelistic structures in Eastern Europe are related to the previous communist nomenklatura, but the way actual socioeconomic developments are unfolding creates levels and forms of state-centered clientelism distinct from those of earlier regimes.

3) Anticorruption policies are, in part, a response to characterizations of the region by those outside the region. Postcommunist states are often said to be saturated with corruption, steeped in clientelism. This view is a frequently recycled theme of the Western press and is dutifully amplified by the East European press, which wields it in partisan struggles. Exaggerating the problem and exploiting it for political purposes has triggered inappropriate legal reactions and moral crusades. The ritual affirmation of how corruption characterizes the postcommunist state has solidified into a stereotype, and it fosters a spiraling delegitimation of the new democracies. The public's misperceptions about corruption and government sleaze are partly the consequence of this simplification. That the public's understanding of corruption is conditioned, even warped, by Western categories does not mean that no corruption exists in Eastern Europe, only that how it is perceived is not always the result of genuine endogenous factors. Were it not for the drumbeat of external criticism, corruption would not be construed as an acute social problem, at least not in East Central Europe.

4) The success of constitutional democracy in Eastern Europe depends in large measure on society's values, such as meritocracy. Political morality requires transparency to be effective, but "morality" and transparency depict, perhaps misleadingly, a corruption and clientelism that undermine the faith of an increasing number of citizens in the promises of a demo-

cratic state based on the rule of law. The rule of law and the struggle against corruption and favoritism have an inherently problematic relationship. The public's belief in, and allegiance to, the rule of law is fragile, for the whole concept was parachuted into Eastern Europe. It is alien to most of the local political cultures, acquainted as they are with only the primacy of surviving by mutual social favors. Those seeking to combat corruption and favoritism with the rule of law, moreover, have been profoundly disappointed. The rule of law inhibits swift and decisive action and is seen in the region as a formula for passivity or as an impediment to a successful crackdown on corruption. In truth, the rule of law is protective of the status quo, not radical or transformative, and, as a result, it does contribute, in many instances, to the institutionalization and normalization of clientelism and corruption. While transparency is widely recognized as a preventive remedy to corruption, it is also seen, sometimes, as a burdensome transaction cost that impedes the region's economic development. In addition, hasty measures initiated by moral crusaders and by the political rivals of the current winners in the game of corruption erode the fundamental preconditions of the rule of law and perpetuate, as well as enhance society's acquiescence in police-state tactics.

Corruption and Clientelism Distinguished

Moral crusaders and lawyers with do-gooder inclinations tend to approach corruption in a vacuum, oblivious of its social context. In a number of countries, however, corruption is an endemic bacillus; it belongs to a family of social interactions—not all of them healthy, but not all dangerous or life-threatening, either—that, taken together, can be loosely classified as clientelism. It is in this particular context that East European corruption needs to be considered.

Corruption is a well-established notion, at least in one sense: we all know that the experts will never agree on any single definition. In some respects, the problem of contemporary corruption is that its definition almost always reflects the moral opprobrium of outsiders. Just as corruption in southern Italy has traditionally been a matter of northern perception, so corruption in Eastern Europe is, in part, a function of Western perceptions. The globalization of communications and information has made such external labeling virtually inevitable.

One of the most often-cited definitions of corruption, that of Joseph LaPalombara, is misleading when applied to Eastern Europe. He classifies as political corruption any act performed by officials when departing from their legal obligations in exchange for personal advantages.[1] In Eastern Europe, however, "corrupt" officials often do exactly what they would have done under the law anyway. (The degree of discretion at their disposal is a different matter.) Second, and this is true not only in Eastern Europe, officials may depart from rules out of a sense of loyalty and without any personal gain or quid pro quo (this is often the pattern in cases related to party financing). Finally, governmental sleaze is often completely legal but still unethical, for instance, the taking of a vacation in Madagascar and claiming the trip was intended to study how that country's public administration operates. Such forms of behavior must obviously be included in the catalogues of government corruption.

But what is clientelism? In Roman law, clients were liberated slaves or immigrants who sought the protection of a patrician paterfamilias. They were dependent on the head of the family, as were all the other members of the household and, in exchange for protection, they were expected to render services. In contemporary political science, clientelism has assumed a generalized meaning. It is now seen as a network of social relations where personal loyalty to the patron prevails against the modern alternatives of market relations, democratic decision-making, and professionalism in public bureaucracies. Client–patron relations are frequently invoked in explaining social relations in Latin America, and the concept is increasingly used to explain developments in other societies experiencing "distorted" processes of modernization.

Clientelism and corruption are different notions. Clientelism is a form of social organization, while corruption is an individual social behavior (where you are your own client, trying to play patron to yourself) that may or may not grow into a mass phenomenon. One can imagine clientelism without corruption, although the two often go hand in hand. In the postcommunist context, the two phenomena seem fused at the hip. To say that postcommunist clientelism presupposes or generates corruption is to imply that corruption has become a foundation stone of the region's emerging clientelist social structure. I will call this phenomenon "clientelist corruption." Clientelist corruption is a form of structural corruption, which should be distinguished from discrete individual acts of corruption.

In Eastern Europe, clientelism—in interaction with various forms and levels of corruption—is becoming a stable form of social organization.

Clientelistic corruption pervades all areas of public life, although favoritism might be more important in public life than pure corruption. The feeling that governments are sleazy is inevitable. The omnipresence of governmental sleaze reinforces the impression that both public and private action (such as favoring the admission of certain students over others at a school) will be reasonably understandable only within a clientelist setting. Under postcommunist conditions, corruption and other services rendered within the patronage system become social actions in the Weberian sense. In the eyes of observant citizens a public action will always fit into a clientelistic scheme; this is the context that gives social meaning to otherwise haphazard events (such as the outcome of a public tender or a government position paper advocating exclusive executive responsibility for privatization). Attributing meaning to an action by defining it as clientelist corruption is rational, all the more so since the outcome of the social action cannot be explained in terms of market rationality or bureaucratic professionalism.

The preceding analysis leads to the conclusion that, to the extent that clientelism is present in postcommunism (discussed below), corruption will fulfill a social function. The normative question that one has to ask, in seeking any policy alternative, is this: What are the socioeconomic consequences of corruption? In the 1960s it was fashionable to follow Samuel Huntington and Nathaniel Leff's view that, in the early stages of a country's modernization, corruption is an efficient social (economic) action.[2] Furthermore, in developing democracies, corruption is democratic. It offers opportunities to those who, because of protectionism, would otherwise be excluded from participation in the process. Their thesis is seductive in the current East European context. Whenever a civil servant is bribed, the costs are paid by the party who is truly the most interested in the civil servant's decision, rather than by the general tax-paying public. The party offering the highest bribe in the privatization of a firm, so the argument runs, is the most efficient investor, but this thesis presupposes that the bribing bid is undistorted. Given that political actors are involved in the decision-making processes, this assumption may not be valid unless the free market in bribing extends to the political decision-makers, too. Of course, if the barriers to entry (such as special protectionist rights and permits) are few, then there are fewer opportunities for corruption.

Gains in efficiency through corruption can also benefit people not doing business with government. When illegal and legal immigrants bribe the authorities for residence permits, their payoffs ease their entry

into an overprotected labor and service market. There are, as well, striking similarities between postcolonial and postcommunist societies
(nation building in the shadow and aftermath of an imperialist legacy is
one), but the applicability of the Huntington–Leff approach to postcommunism stumbles, in the East European context, due to high literacy
rates, relatively consolidated parties, and integration into the world economy. Moreover, there is growing criticism of the claim that corruption
can be efficient.[3] Corruption's economic advantages appear only in the
short-run, while its destabilizing effects on the political regime are undeniable. It may well be in the interest of transitional societies (not only in
terms of efficiency) that a natural-resource-development license be given
to the group that gives the largest bribe or has the best political patrons
if, and only if, the company pays its taxes and wages. The problem is that
we face here ubiquitous as well as endemic corruption: once the protégé
gets his license, he will arrange through the same patronage system to be
exempted from tax payments. This is close to what we see in classical
feudal patronage: the feudal lord gave protection to his client against both
legal and illegal exactions by authorities. Moreover, protectionist national (domestic) clientelism may discourage foreign investment, which is
essential to modernization, even as domestic client groups accuse the
international investors of foreign domination and exploitation.

Whatever the theoretical value of corruption in modernization, in Eastern
Europe or elsewhere, even if it smoothes the operations of an underpaid
bureaucracy, mostly it perpetuates the influence of political, party-centered,
client–patron structures over the distribution of resources. In Hungary, for
example, broadcasting frequencies are allocated by a board composed of party
commissars. The board members are expected to allocate frequencies impartially, and, indeed, they may not be interested in personal gain. What matters
for them is to grant licenses to those who seem to offer loyalty to the political
party that nominated them and may nominate them again in the future.

Increased Opportunities for Clientelistic Corruption
under Postcommunism

While the communist past proved decisive in the early formation of clientelistic corruption in Eastern Europe, it will not necessarily determine its
future. What is perceived as corruption is, in part, a function of funda-

mental economic adjustment processes. Even if there were no tradition of nepotism and corruption, the ubiquitous opportunities for corruption under communism explain the perceived high degree of corruption now. By opportunities, I mean not only the level of governmental redistribution of assets and services but also the legal and administrative circumstances of this redistribution. Laws are written in ways that enable insider dealing, and, therefore, in the eyes of outsiders, immediately create an aura of impropriety, unfairness, and corruption. What cannot be explained by the transition opportunities is the structure used for these unfair transactions, hence the importance of the clientelist networks.

One could rightly add, of course, that the opportunities are not simply given by nature: they are created or shaped by those who set the rules. After all, the model privatization of British Telecom (copied in Italy, France, and even Germany) occurred in a setting that excluded clientelism and bribery: stocks were floated on the open stock exchange, and all citizens had the opportunity to buy. In Eastern Europe, however, the vast majority of citizens simply lack the financial resources to get in on the privatization process. The voucher-share schemes in Russia, which formally entitled all citizens (and the employees of firms, in particular) to ownership rights, became the new patrons' source of power. However, we still lack a structural explanation.

The way that loyalty within the clientelistic networks operates is explained partly by the nomenklatura legacy and partly by the institutional structures in which that legacy functions. For example, both civil servants and private service providers might be interested in the continued maintenance of state-sponsored social services, where personal (and party) loyalties prevail and determine exchanges rather than where open markets determine outcomes. Both are interested in operating state monopolies. It is the surviving governmental institutions and the new ones succeeding them that have become the rallying point for the former nomenklatura and their clients. Such governmental institutions include social security (insurance) plans, public radio and television, national security, public education, and health care. The nomenklatura's headstart advantage remains unsurpassed. This rule applies even in the Czech Republic, where the disqualification of former communists was the most radical. Those who possessed relational network capital became the new patrons of postcommunism, and, although they now have other forms of influence at their disposal (such as money), they are interested in preserving their powers as patrons, with control over (and access to) monopolistic government services. All this presupposes that the government remains the key service provider and the most important economic decision-maker.

The level, nature, and future of corruption and clientelism depend very much on the ways in which national property has been privatized. The privatization processes were not a happenstance of history and geographic location but a function of the structure of the economy and of the interrelations of economic actors. In this regard, a comparison of Hungary and Russia is most useful. Since 1989, both countries, albeit to different extents, have tried to surpass and liquidate their predecessor regimes through the rule of law and by constitutionalizing freedom. In both countries, especially after the collapse of the traditional Communist Party elite, it was decisive that the only surviving, all-encompassing organized force that remained active was the state, with its huge, underpaid, and incompetent bureaucracy. (Following communism's collapse, as part of the Hungarian espousal of the rule of law, these bureaucrats were rechristened "civil servants.") In Hungary in 1990, and to a lesser extent in 1994, the parties that won government power offered public-service positions to their clients and benefits to these clients in the form of access to special government services. More importantly, the emerging governments acted as clients, in their turn, of the patrons who helped these governing parties win elections.

Many analysts describe Russia as a country where surviving elements of the former nomenklatura have maintained an intimate relationship with the government (executive) bureaucracy. This network developed into systems of clientelistic structures in the games of privatization, governmental subsidy, and the formation of public bodies. There is increasing competition among these clientelistic structures. In comparative terms, it is remarkable how much more the Russian patrons were willing to keep the national economy under domestic control. The price Russia and ordinary Russians paid for this behavior was the stunning decline in the country's GDP. Russia created a "closed commercial state" in the sense of Fichte's *Der geschlossene Handelstaat*. The patron-bosses in Russia managed to protect the Soviet legacy of the closed economy in an increasingly open world market, exploiting all the advantages of national monopolies. For Hungary, with its complete dependence on the world economy, the Russian strategy of self-closure was out of question. In Hungary, everyone who wanted to become rich had to make use of his/her networks in a rapidly opening economy, but even in Hungary they had to make use of, first of all, the good offices as well as the services of the state and its bureaucrats, hence the opportunity for sleaze.

At the early stages of privatization, as there were no alternative social networks, the nomenklatura associated with government bureaucracies (and the newly elected political elite) seemed to be successful in the new and different socio-economic environment. Very soon after, however, the patrons had to choose different strategies. Privatization required investment, particularly foreign investment, and the states that were capital- and resource-poor, such as Hungary, could not afford to pass by these investments. At this point, fundamental differences emerge. Russia had oil, and so it had no need to buy it on the world market. Besides, the masses were comfortingly inert. When the slightest danger of competition emerged in Russia, as it did in the banking sector, foreign banks were practically expelled, notwithstanding serious international repercussions. In Hungary, on the contrary, concessions were given increasingly to foreign (and domestic) banks, as the banks were gradually taken over by foreign investors. In Russia, the public administration seems to operate in conformity with the wishes of its patrons; the patronage system emerged out of the ruins of the nomenklatura.

But Hungary's needs left it defenseless in the face of the West. In 1989, there was no intellectual or moral desire to resist the West. As the other Central European countries, Hungary wanted to Westernize itself institutionally and was willing to copy the West's rule-of-law system as well as its democracy, in one form or another. In the power vacuum of 1989–90 there were no prevailing forces to oppose this Westernization. Perhaps because Western institutions were copied in an institutional void the foundations for a relatively stable party system took root. The electoral and party systems operated in line with their Western models, which resulted in campaign-financing excesses. A need emerged to cover election expenses and to compensate those who were loyal to the party but often lacked sufficient funds. To be sure, this generated ad hoc clientelistic structures. In countries like Hungary, where there are lots of state assets to be distributed, it was and is easier to satisfy the clients than it is in the West. Access to government jobs—the traditional form of patronage—was secondary to such opportunities.

Still, the clientelism surrounding the political parties, when combined with the efforts to maintain the distributive powers of the state, resulted in less clientelism in Hungary than in Russia. In Hungary, actors outside the nomenklatura network got involved early on in the scramble for resources. Locals were successful in creating their own interest-enforcing corporative structures. Foreign investors and their entourages emerged in partnership or competition with former nomenklatura networks. The bar, the chamber of notaries, and the churches used Parliament to push through their parochial interests. (To what extent corporatism engenders its own distinct form of public sleaze is a different matter.) However, even these corporatist structures presuppose the central distributive role of government. The chamber of pharmacists and the (often foreign-controlled) drug industry are both interested in government-subsidized medicine. It is highly relevant who controls politics; it follows that investment in parliamentary elections makes perfect sense.

The Making of Bad Reputations

The analysis thus far suggests that corruption is structural in the sense that it is a natural consequence of the use of power in a clientelistic regime. The shortcomings of the economic and governmental systems in Eastern Europe cannot simply be labeled as "corrupt." These systems have their own clientelistic logic, serving purposes beyond those corruption itself would advance. The clientelistic network provides a viable form of social organization where other networks and forms of social organization are nonexistent or at least underdeveloped. Relations within the power elite are particularly open to patronage. As other forms of social organization did not exist when communism collapsed, it was both obvious and inevitable that clientelist networks would survive and become the core for future relations, notwithstanding the inefficiencies of the resulting give-and-take that corrupts the morale of democracy and the logic of the market.

The departure from the logic of the free market that governmental patronage exemplifies is so obvious that it is nearly impossible to resist the stereotypical characterization of Eastern Europe as corrupt. It must be added that this accusation seems to be only a special application of a global trend related to the internationalization of the economy. Similar comments were made of Italy by the other members of the European Union and of Japan by Americans, when investors sought entry into their domestic markets in the holy name of free trade and ran headlong into

protectionist barriers. The faster globalization advances, the more likely
are such criticisms and the exposure of some corruption. The countries
under attack eventually come to share the free-market rhetoric of their
attackers, and gradually they impose transparency rules on themselves.

The successful imposition of the "corruption" stereotype on East
Central Europe is somewhat curious, as Western governments (with the
exception of the Nordic states) are resigning or at least losing elections
exactly because of electoral corruption and illegal party financing. In the
not-so-distant past, countries such as Japan and South Korea were considered by many as admirable examples for Eastern Europe; yet both had
thrived for decades on systematic political corruption. The family-corpo-
rate conglomerates that have historically supported the state in Asia can
be compared to the style of clientelism seen today in the Russia. To call
the transition economies "corrupt" remains, however, a therapeutic
means of preserving Western self-esteem, of maintaining its sense of
moral superiority. The cheapest form of such therapy consists in disdain
for "the countries in the East." The noninitiated perceive only ad hoc
immorality, the way the illegal exchange of government favors for
money seems to pervade all relations, but the structural regularity—the
bureaucratization—of these exchanges, the impact and the place of the
transactions in the everyday functioning of the transition economy and its
political spheres, remain hidden.

The difference between Eastern and Western Europe is not that
between a robust and a corrupt public morality. It is neither the "Balkan
culture of corruption" nor the "destruction of morals by atheist communists" that makes the difference. The difference lies in the pattern of
opportunities. In systems where the economy is functioning in a transition to a free and open market there are, simply speaking, incomparably
more opportunities for corruption. The postcommunist states inherited a
central allocative role, and privatization is carried on in the state sector as
part of the political process. The routine application of anticorruption
policies remains, at best, only in its formative stage. Opportunity here
means more than huge supply where there cannot be sufficient resources
to supervise adequately the procedure. Opportunity means that the transactions are deliberately designed to be non-transparent. At present the
clientelist structures have every interest in maintaining the lack of transparency. The confusion is increased by the introduction of some stylistic
features of the rule of law, which make the fight against corruption more

difficult. Even if neither nepotistic traditions nor a culture of corruption had developed under communism, countless opportunities would still exist now, and these current opportunities account in large measure for the corruption we observe.

Moral disdain may be justified even if it originates in countries where the milk of nonexistent cows is routinely subsidized. It is certainly telling that, although East European governments have had to resign for reasons of dubious party financing, this is not a matter of major public concern. Nor are there serious or persistent criminal investigations in this area. It is even more telling that successful prosecutions of governmental corruption and illegal party financing are rare and that corruption and governmental sleaze are not crucial issues in electoral campaigns. Public opinion seems to acquiesce in the morass. Of course, this is true mostly in cases where entrenched interests are not offended and there is no blatant abuse of power, but this is exactly the case in the transitions of Eastern Europe. In the most notorious opportunity for corruption, namely privatization, none of the bidders has a preexisting right. Structural uncertainty impedes the development of moral condemnation. Generally, moreover, the authorities are not always clearly abusing their powers. When the mayor of a city issues an order (in the best French tradition) providing housing for himself and his employees at the state's expense, he is authorized to do so by the municipal council. Once again, the validity of that delegation of competence is not clearly objectionable, although the delegation imposes no clear rules on the mayor. Empirically, although corruption as a social problem was seen in the last decade by more and more people as "very serious" and even reported personal corruption experience increased, this did result in normalization of certain corrupt activities, though it had an impact on electoral choices (e.g. 1998 Hungary; 2001 Poland).[4]

There is not enough hard evidence concerning the level of corruption in the East compared with the West. The level of actual corruption is simply nowhere known. As mentioned above, the public's beliefs are conditioned by facts and relations other than actual verified cases of corruption. If so, whence comes the image of corrupt postcommunist countries? After all, as a form of structural corruption, most social actors tend to normalize it. Why do the postcommunist societies fall prey so easily to the label of corruption imposed on them by the West? Western "experts" rely on anecdotes and so-called "surveys." These "surveys" are often based on hotel-lobby chats with disgruntled businessmen, which are frequently conducted by journalists and "experts" who generally do not speak the local language. (In this case, the chat is called an "interview.") The reports remind one of the descriptions of South American Indians written by Jesuit missionaries. As there was no communication and understanding, the Indians were seen and depicted as savages. The objections of Western observers concern what they regard as "barbarous" situations, where the national bureaucracy is distributing governmental services and assets. All efforts by the locals to deny the allegations turn out to be futile and are from the very beginning doomed to fail. The national image makers follow the policy of stupid politicians: they accuse the media, or they repeat that the only problem is that the national authorities did not communicate their message well; that they failed, for example, to explain that the privatization process is eminently impartial and transparent.

How Constitutional Democracy Contributes to Political Corruption

In Eastern Europe, at least to some extent, political corruption is a consequence of modern participatory mass politics under conditions of soap-opera consumerism. Winning elections in a democracy is expensive. Elections and party financing are increasingly subject to restrictive rules, and the demand for more campaign spending is growing. Hence a turn to illegality becomes almost inevitable. At the same time, in a democracy, majority rule and legislative supremacy foster a somewhat arbitrary definition of political morality. So long as the distribution of electoral booty is provided for in the democratic legislative process, the moral high ground from which to refuse these practices is missing. In Eastern Europe, the state has at its disposal many assets and other resources to "exchange." Therefore, illegal campaign contributions may have greater returns than in the U.S. or Western Europe. The way these assets are used is given legitimacy in standard democratic terms. After all, the revolutions of 1989–90 occurred in the name of democracy. The revolutionary rhetoric of 1989 is like that of President Andrew Jackson. In the name of democracy Jackson promised to terminate the partisan rule of the previous administrative establishment, which operated a "tyranny of the elite" over the people. In 1829, he institutionalized a spoils system in the name of revolutionary democracy. "Let the democratic process prevail," which in practice meant: it is up to the people to determine who will get the people's money, including their bribes.

This asset-distributing conception of democracy sounds attractive in an era of democratic legitimation, but it contradicts fundamental ideas of professional, nonpartisan public administration. Political leaders today, and not only in Eastern Europe, are saying, "if the people don't like the way we reward our loyal supporters, which is in the interests of the nation, they will replace us in conformity with the rules of democracy." Free elections thus justify the system of favoritism and distributive robbery. This results in a generally shared political ethic of normalized clientelistic corruption and self-dealing, formulated perfectly by the former president of the Hungarian Ice Hockey Association: "If we, in the interest of hockey, take thirty percent [of the taxable revenue generated by the games], this is okay, but to take eighty percent, this is pure and simple theft."

Free elections will turn into authorizations for moderate pilfering of the public purse. The principle of temperate kleptocracy assumes a sustainable yield; that is, skimming is permissible so long as it allows future political elites to have their own feast. (Because not all assets are taken away, there is enough for further reproduction of national assets.) The citizens may acquiesce in such arrangements, but they will hardly develop loyalty to a political regime that operates under such rules. This will make the political system vulnerable and will rapidly increase its maintenance costs, as officeholders will increasingly have to replace loyalty and voluntary obedience to the law with reliance on bribes, force, and even perhaps violence.

Paradoxically, even the rule of law, the self-imposed straitjacket of postcommunist countries, has hastened the normalization of governmental sleaze. It is the legitimacy of law that makes it possible to turn morally dubious dealings and practices into legally tolerated, and, therefore, politically feasible ones. It is the legitimacy of democratically created law that provides a salvus conductus to behavior that would otherwise be reproachable. These legitimating possibilities of legislation have been exploited fully under postcommunism. In this way dubious legal standards may supersede and even displace the evaluations private morality might otherwise apply to the public sphere.

The power of postcommunist legislation reflects the public's lack of experience in market affairs. There was no experience that could serve as a basis for judgment in these areas, as the whole phenomenon of market exchange was nonexistent under communism. For example, the "property" of the Communist Party existed outside the law, and this made it illegal in the eyes of the population, at least after the collapse of the communist power structures. However, when the new democratic parties seized the old communist parties' assets through legislation, this was presented as being perfectly legitimate. Similarly, there is no place left for criticism once legislation, supported by all parties, approves in a procedurally correct way the financing of political parties from the state budget. Even where such financing is without transparency and without preconditions (as to the use of the subvention), it is sheltered by the legislative process and is immunized against any public criticism. The public is without norms in this regard anyway, and without mechanisms of self-defense. Once party financing by the state has been formally legalized, people become uninterested in the lawful looting of the budget. The factory of law is capable of lending respectability to its own solutions. At least it enjoys public indifference to its privileges. Thus does postcommunist legislation put to sleep the moral sense.

Successes and Failures of Anticorruption Measures under Postcommunism

Elections and party financing are increasingly subject to restrictive rules, and the demand for more campaign spending is growing. Hence a turn to illegality becomes almost inevitable. There might even be a sincere wish on the part of the government to create the impression that there is no sleaze. If one looks at legislation and the attempts to enforce the law in the East Central European states, it is obvious that serious efforts are made to create the deontology needed to attract international investment and to develop the rule of law in line with shared national programs of integration into the West. These efforts remain, however, within the orbit of creating appearances that are "adequate" for some kind of Western acceptance. Anticorruption measures will serve propaganda purposes, while remaining the means of interelite fighting, unless efficient and influential social forces emerge that have a real and lasting interest in government transparency and in terminating sleaze which is exposed by such transparency. The openness of a country to the world economy is not sufficient. At this point in time, there is no credible scenario that would curtail the clientelist systems. Booty distribution through parties or neocorporative formations will therefore continue to flourish. Given the communist legacy, postcommunism tends to be egalitarian, which means that envy is the supreme public virtue. The electorate will never agree to a highly paid civil service, which, in any event, is unaffordable given the sheer size of the state bureaucracy. For its part, this immense public bureaucracy, through its institutional influence, resists all efforts at downsizing. The semiprivatization of public services, which allows for the transformation of civil servant status into private employment, thus permitting radical increases in the salaries of managers and middle-level employees, continues the tradition of dependency on the state.

The Emergence of Extortion Regimes in Transition Societies

Certain socio-political systems rely on social structures that enable extortion. Positions of public power are created in a way to maximize opportunities for extortion. From the perspective of those who are under the control of public authorities the problem is not corruption: extortion is. Likewise, in a clientelistic society corruption might be a routine and regularized transaction, which is just a functional side effect of the given social organization. For example, it would be misleading to describe in terms of corruption a situation where the elected political power holders grant (through proper legislation) a major highway concession or frequency concession to their supporters and others, who are personally related to the powerholders, in exchange for ten per cent (or more) going into party coffers and/or to those leaders who do not benefit otherwise directly from the transaction. Even the core legal element of this venture, namely embezzlement, does not fully describe the story, which is simply a certain mode of exercise of power. As is understood in this context clientelism allows the transfer of money or other advantages to government officials or party coffers without any specific quid pro quo. The distribution of favors is done at a different level and illegal payments become a matter of expression of loyalty.

Kaufmann suggested that, where corruption is rampant, regulations will become deliberate tools and custom-made opportunities for rent seeking.[5] The efforts to normalize corrupt practices in the transition states may develop into "state capture." State capture is defined as "*shaping the formation of the basic rules of the game* (i.e. laws, rules, decrees and regulations) through *illicit* and non-transparent private payments to public officials."[6] Hellman and his co-authors are primarily interested in the influence of firms on government when they apply the above quoted concept of state capture. Such influencing, however, is to a great extent made possible within the pre-existing clientelistic relations, where the writing of the rules of the game is carried out by a government (and a government bureaucracy) that operates as a patron to a clientelistic network. Understandably, the Hellman et al. model puts more emphasis on the influence originating from firms, where in a way the regulators are the clients. This might be true in case of certain larger firms. However, given the importance of state structures in transition societies, it is more the case that, by seizing the state through politics, the dominant government forces (party elites) will enable/reward/protect their clientele through properly written regulations. In addition, the regulations are often written in an open-ended way, without pre-assigning the "winners." The rules simply enable corruption in the future. From a socio-political perspective state capture is defined as shaping the basic rules of the game to the detriment of the common good, favoring one's own clients.

In the escalation of corruption, the next stage is the one where regulations are created not simply to enhance opportunities for corruption but for *extortion*. This is what happens in many postcommunist and post-authoritarian regimes. A milder version of this is described as "enabling constraints." Here arbitrariness is institutionalized in a rule of law system. Such enabling played an important role in "suboptimal" privatization. However, systemic or planned regulatory extortion goes beyond simple governmental maximization of corrupt opportunities. In conditions where investment and other development initiatives are simply designed to increase corruption, participation is motivated by profit, and therefore, to a great extent the transaction is voluntary. In the case of systemic regulatory extortion, however, especially in that of vital government-provided services such as health, safety and security, the regulation is written, and the organizations are designed in a way that facilitates extortion of bribes from those who are otherwise entitled to, and/or dependent on the services provided (or sanctions withheld). The centrality of politics in developing extortion opportunities is such that even everyday corruption is facilitated or even dictated by the needs of the political operation of the society. For example, it was the given form of political domination, certainly related to the shortage of economic resources in the transition countries that allowed and even necessitated extortion practices by the police. Police extortion is what translates into corruption.

In the clientelistic network of illegalities (often referred to as stealing the state, parasitism) corruption plays a secondary, instrumental role.[7] It operates simply as the form of dividing the booty. Once corruption might have been a market-entry-facilitating instrument, but illegal payments (even in the form of a ransom payment) serve to guarantee the maintenance of existing market positions which depend on state support. In the well-established clientelistic state where dependence on state bureaucracies is institutionalized, extortion may become pivotal *vis-à-vis* briber induced corruption. The regulatory system is enacted to create opportunities to extort bribes. Official sanctions (the possibility of their application) are used to extort the ransom money or other goods such as loyalty. In certain postcommunist regimes there is a lack of relatively state-independent social forces. "Civil society" is nearly nonexistent. Here the chances of reproducing sultanistic regimes are particularly good. A sultanistic regime is created to siphon off public goods. The state fails to provide means of subsistence to its servants and instead it provides the monopoly of constraint. The power of constraint is used to extort bribes in order to gain a decent living. In certain post-Soviet states the combination of a lack of a decent salary and access to punishment result in the transformation of police power into taxing power.

Policemen, customs officers and many other civil servants are expecting to be paid for their services by the service beneficiaries, as the state is not paying them adequately. These expectations slip into extortion. Moreover, the superiors expect their subordinates to provide them with a constant influx of revenue; that revenue is the shared extorted ransom. For example, drivers, if stopped on the street, are supposed to pay a bribe to the police, irrespective of their compliance, or not, with the law.[8] Once the bribe was used to avoid tickets. The "original" corruption created the psychological and organizational conditions for switching from corruption to extortion, especially where the superior of the officer expects that ransom be extorted from the citizens and shared with the superiors. All this is closer to pre-modern forms of state organization than to modern public bureaucracy. The more sultanistic the regime, the more misleading it is to discuss these forms of extortion in terms of public trust betrayal.

This takes us to the heart of the problem: for reasons of clientelism or other social interdependencies, social-political systems operate systematically in a way to provide opportunities for clientelistic enrichment (including extortion opportunities). These systems become particularly predatory among conditions of socioeconomic transition, because transition offers an unusually high level of opportunities for poorly regulated and monitored transactions within a very short period of time. The speed of simultaneous events limits all forms of social control in the technical sense: even if some actors would like to exercise control using the opportunities created by democracy and the rule of law, the necessary resources are not available. Of course, the control opportunities are further diminished in the name of speeding up privatization, as happened in Russia with voucher privatization, or in Hungary and the Czech Republic where control over privatization was first taken away from Parliament, and then, to some extent, even out of the public sphere, defining the Privatization Agency as a private company with all the secrecy of a private corporation.

It is in this context that "corruption with theft"[9] occurs, but in the process of the "stealing of the state," corruption is only an auxiliary technique for the officials to steal and defraud. The decisive element of the transactions is that of theft, embezzlement. Quite often embezzlement is perfectly legal; the laws are written to enable such acts. (Similar techniques exist in consolidated democracies, such as bankruptcy bordering on the fraudulent). Once again this indicates the inadequacy of the corruption-centered analysis. Even if the emerging system will be "corrupt," it is not corruption that is decisive. In terms of social deviance (systemic anomie) it is basically irrelevant whether the illegality occurs in the form of bribe or fraud, though it may have different impacts in terms of social multiplication. In "corruption with theft" the kickback offered in exchange for access to state assets at discount price is, in reality, a division of the booty: the official is not in the position/is not willing to take the assets himself, and so he finds an accomplice, a receiver. Anecdotal evidence indicates that, except perhaps in the very early stages of privatization and other mass distributive processes in the transitions countries, government officials actively sought partners, or went/had to turn to existing patronage networks in order to become rich at the expense of the public purse.

At this point extortion emerges as a crucial characteristic of political corruption in transition countries. Noonan, in his often-quoted definition refers to a bribe as "an inducement improperly influencing the performance of a public function meant to be gratuitously exercised."[10] In post-communist (and many other transition) societies the public trustholder has the power of threat. The threat concerns primarily exclusion (e.g. from lucrative transactions), but also, in the web of illegalities, involuntary "inclusions" (e.g. prosecution). Given the importance of extortion in certain corrupt systems, it would be appropriate to shift the focus from corruption studies to an empirical review of political systems in terms of being opportunities for extortion.

It is clear that a clientelistic system has interests in maximizing extortion opportunities, as these opportunities can be distributed among the clientele. Further, and more importantly in a system of extortion, the patron's power is increased as he can offer shelter against extortion. Ironically, to the extent that extortion replaces random corruption in new democracies, one could see here a perverse sign of gaining national strength. After ten years of development some postcommunist transition countries are no longer more responsive to randomly offered petty bribes of adventurist foreign investors. The emerging local elite is capable of setting demanding conditions. The transition process amounts to a history of learning in the sense that government actors who in the early years were bribed by the apparently much more resourceful investors on the cheap, very soon learned the value of their position and used it for extortion. This, of course, made the investors particularly angry as they perceived this as a departure from pre-established, very favorable terms of doing business.

To the extent that extortion primarily intends to guarantee rule observance, the economic damage in transnational investment cases may be less detrimental than in standard corruption cases where allocation is distorted by definition. Extortion may illegally increase the price of services, but this serves only as a certain correction of existing market imperfections. If the contribution to the ruling party serves only to be honestly considered in the otherwise fair bid, than the money transfer may just correct the insufficient public funding of political parties or public officials. If the policeman extracts a bribe from a driver and, in exchange, no legal action is taken against the driver where there is no ground for it, the officers simply tax, on a random basis, the car owners for public safety reasons a function not adequately compensated from the public budget. A similar "consumer tax" is imposed on the actual consumers where police extorts money from shop owners for actually providing them safety (promising that they will actually patrol the street where the shop is located.) A further example with, perhaps, fewer problematic moral overtones is "tipping" in the public health service (see *supra*).

Of course, while many instances of extortion resulting in rule observance may just bring the price of the service closer to its market price
(where the service price is distorted by government) the injustice of the
system and the indirect moral damage are obvious. The indirect moral
damage, among others, is that the political system will become delegitimized and bribery will spread to other spheres of life. One can assume
that, where that extorted bribe only serves that the rules be observed by
the extorter, there will be no rule violation (corruption), but there is
always an increased opportunity to blackmail the extorter into rule violation the next time. The perverse confidence and trust among accomplices
may develop on the basis of shared illegality. Extortion is different from,
not better than, corruption. One has simply to realize the analytical difference between the two. This distinction is useful both to understand the
place of corruption and other wrongdoings in the functioning of transition
societies and for purposes of anticorruption strategies. In case of rule-
observing extortion (in particular in the unlikely case that extortion did
not develop into a network of rule-breaking corruption), one can develop
strategies based on the common interests of the public and those who
would like to obtain the government service and are subject to extortion.

The corruption enhancing interactions, the institutionalized betrayal of
a declared public trust and the emergence of regimes of extortion are
made possible in Eastern Europe by the weakness of a big state. The
weakness is manifest in the successful mass disregard of public order.
The most common forms of state weakness include mass tax evasion,
various forms of non-compliance with the law, and free riding.

Bureaucracy plays an important role in the weakness of the state and
in the speedy resulting development of rampant corruption and the perpetuation of corrupt practices. The bureaucracy is inherited from the
communist past, too numerous, underpaid and not adequately trained or
qualified for services necessary in a competitive world. It is vulnerable to
corruption partly because as Rose-Ackerman (1978) states, its decision-
making process is sequential, fragmented, hierarchical or disorganized.
These features are, however, only partly to be explained by the past and
the lack of resources: the corruption facilitating, decision-making system
is deliberately maintained or developed in order to reinforce the private
use of state power, to increase the chances of "stealing the state." Once
again, one should look beyond grand political and economic concepts of
democracy and market. The specific post-totalitarian nature of public

bureaucracies (lack of public commitment, instrumentalism, high levels of uncontrolled discretionary power, low salary and related underqualification) are crucial. The result is what Stephen Holmes describes as a weak state.[11] The nature and the enabling of the bureaucracy of the weak state are crucial factors.

Governmental and bureaucratic actors of the weak state are to some extent dependent on corruption. Whenever the state tries to implement its rules, corruption will be the way out from the perceived illegality. The corrupt exchange will become institutionalized, and the non-observance of law (depriving the state of her revenues and assets) is carried out on the basis of bribes paid in advance for letting the illegality go unnoticed. The relationship between the public authority and the thief is one of mutual extortion. Indeed, it might be in the best interest of those who control the state to keep public institutions in such inefficient conditions.[12]

The concern about the emergence of corruption in the founding moment of a new political regime is that it tends to aggravate. As Jean Tirole indicates, where there is widespread corruption this will become the dominant strategy in the future: corruption will ratchet up "and does not subside even after the generations that have committed the original sin have by and large disappeared."[13]

The consolidation of democracy may mean in Eastern Europe that patron-client networks will increasingly coincide with formal lines of authority. This enables the state to yield more predictable forms of corruption. Predictability contributes to system rationality and hence it has better chances of becoming established in a market rationality mimicking system. It is not corruption but predictability that matters from the perspective of rational market actors.

PART I

UNDERSTANDING AND MISUNDERSTANDING CORRUPTION

Broadly speaking, the political morality in Western rule-of-law systems across the nineteenth century was based upon the assumption that corruption is immoral. (Of course, this did not hamper immense political corruption, e.g., the Panama and Suez Canal cases). The prevailing mood was, however, one of "geographical morality."[14] Corruption seemed prevalent, even inevitable, not everywhere but in certain societies, especially in the West's colonies and other less developed parts of the world, where even gentlemen were entitled to be involved in corruption. "[T]he temptation," two scholars have written, "to identify corruption with alien societies, with the other, has always been irresistible."[15]

Beginning in the 1960s, however, such an avowedly moralistic approach came under challenge by social scientists.[16] The antimoralistic social science view of corruption emphasized cultural relativism, repudiating a universal understanding of corruption. Social scientists stressed the "unavoidable character of corruption at certain stages of development and the contributions of the practice to processes of modernization and development."[17] Without ever fully eliminating moralism, this social science approach acquired many followers over the next two decades. "It was heresy in the 1960s and 1970s," writes Ivan Krastev, "to believe that a global anticorruption policy package could be designed and that it could be offered to Nigeria, Russia, Mexico, and China at the same time."[18] By the 1990s, however, such packages were commonplace, and a predominant moralism about corruption had returned with a vengeance.

Many explanations can be offered for the renewed moralism in the treatment of corruption, that is, for the shift from corruption studies (promoting comprehension) to anticorruption studies (promoting eradication)—the end of bipolarity and of the cold war freeze, developments in the world economy and international trade, the efforts of business lobbies, the new global reach of the media and the popularity of "investigative" or scandal journalism, activism on the part of judges and prosecutors, expectations (and disappointments) about the end of communism and so on. A plethora of economically oriented studies appeared, seeking to show how corruption "distorts" business (far fewer studies have focused on how business, including much-hyped foreign direct investment, corrupts government).[19] Gone are anthropological notions of cultural relativism, invocations of which are seen as apologetic and major obstacles to corruption fighting. Gone, too, are most arguments that corruption can have beneficial effects, or perform indispensable functions.[20] In their stead we have sweeping condemnations, based upon sweeping definitions of corruption.

These definitions, this revived moralism, these basic understandings and misunderstandings of corruption form the subject of Part I of our skeptic's handbook.

●

What is corruption? In his invaluable research handbook on the subject Arnold Heidenheimer pointed out that "any attempt to analyze the concept of corruption must contend with the fact that in English and other languages the word *corruption* has a history of vastly different meanings and connotations."[21] Such an irrefutable observation may appear to render attempts at a definition worthless. That is not the case for Diego Gambetta, however, who proposes a core definition of corruption, at least for *analytical* purposes. At a minimum he introduces a welcome clarity by underscoring that corruption need not be unethical, inefficient, or illegal.

Pre-empting predictable objections flowing from obvious differences among cases (different legal systems, cultures, political practices and norms), Gambetta suggests that we need a sense of type simply to calculate such differences. The richness of his many-sided tour de force pivoting on the centrality of trust cannot be easily summarized. Readers will decide to what extent he succeeds in his definitional enterprise aimed at a narrowing of the coverage of the term "corruption"—footnote 30 stands out as worthy of further discussion in this regard—but at least one major implication can be highlighted here. Much of the understanding of corruption seems to depend on a sense of rules and their violation, implying that the absence of clear rules is a akin to a condition of being "pre-corrupt." In other words, "corruption," no matter how widespread and endemic, can be seen as a perverse achievement—a stage when, at least, there are rules and violators of those rules can be identified (and punished). Otherwise, if there are no rules or no enforcement of rules, everyone is a rule violator and thus everyone is corrupt, meaning no one is "corrupt," since the concept presupposes the existence of many people who are *not* corrupt. Given that Gambetta's work may indicate that corruption as such can only occur in a fully functional, regulated, law-based market society, there is some irony in the fact that the countries in transition have come to be seen as corrupt by definition or in essence. Yet, even in countries that fall far short of a law-based system, people living there engage in disputes about whether this or that behavior (patronage, for example) is corrupt.

At first glance, Mark Philp's essay on abuse of public office seems to run counter to Gambetta's position. Instead of a trans-national, trans-historical definition, Philp emphasizes that the norms of public office vary, but he further suggests, echoing Gambetta, that when such norms are unclear, multiple, contradictory, or contested, then corruption becomes hard to identify, let alone to combat. Philp's real target appears to be democratization, which he explains can weaken authority and the legitimacy of political institutions, thereby enhancing corruption. In that regard the transition has had a notable impact on the proliferation of corruption because of the deleterious impact it has had on public office and political life more generally. Philp implies that the market, which would seem to be both unavoidable and desirable, offers no "solution" at the level of institutions—on the contrary, it makes matters worse (at least initially). All of this appears to place the reader, like the citizen of a former communist country, in a box: how to struggle against corruption when the transition itself is greatly abetting it? Philp suggests that any anticorruption programs ought not to be the retail equivalent of one-size-fits-all (or one-size-fits-no-one, as it usually turns out), but closely tailored to local conditions. Who does the tailoring? When the problem is the state, can we look to the state for solutions? Who are the stakeholders in a revamping and defense of the norms of public office? Whence and how were such norms developed in the West and, what if anything, does that teach us?

•

Jim Jacobs provides some answers, at least to the latter question, but his answers do not seem very encouraging. Reprising his book (with Frank Anechiarico), Jacobs stresses that corruption can never be eliminated, only controlled, and that corruption control in the United States has entailed formidable costs. Others may want to stress the costs of not controlling corruption, but Jacob's point, too often overlooked, is not a call to inaction or a rationalization, and it has far-reaching implications. Simply put, anticorruption campaigns, however justified, may not result in increased social good. There is a trade-off, which is not easily measured, and at some point the costs of further corruption control simply begin to outweigh the potential benefits, undermining economic growth and good government. Jacobs argues that much of the public administration in the U.S. is a product of anticorruption campaigns, of scandal politics that are entertaining but also, in an important sense, crippling. To be sure, much of the rich empirical material that backs up his assertions is inevitably missing from this brief essay, but his call for caution on corruption eradication emerges forcefully, even in schematic form.

Concerned about the loss of responsiveness in favor of "efficiency," Jacobs writes passionately of the need for good government, by which he seems to mean good people going into government. He suggests that we can have both responsiveness and a considerable degree of efficiency provided we do not let the latter eclipse the former. Thus, he sees patronage not as a pejorative, but as a way to enhance involvement (participation) in government. He does not address the processes by which anticorruption charges lead not to administration reform but narrower political goals, such as, for example, the weakening of unions by businesses. But Jacobs does makes clear that addressing corruption is a political not a technocratic problem, no matter how important may be the technical work in preparing legislation and regulations. Finally, mention of the case of unions (or businesses lobbies) reminds us that "civil society," too, can be deeply corrupt, yet the role of civic groups and public opinion in the U.S. anticorruption movements cannot help but stand out. The same can be said for the activist U.S. judiciary. In the balancing between "efficiency" and "fairness," however, where is the line, and who draws it? Rigidity and the pursuit of absolute integrity are costly, but what is flexibility and tolerable corruption?

•

Clarity about the U.S. experience has great value in part because unsubstantiated notions (implicit and explicit) about the U.S. experience have been readily transferred to transition countries. One vehicle for such transfer has been the infamous Corruption Perception Index (CPI) introduced around 1994 by Transparency International (TI), an NGO. TI's openness about the methodology behind its CPI is impressive but also opens the index up to critical analysis, a task taken up energetically by Endre Sík, who greatly amplifies previous critiques. In the past TI has adjusted its methodology in light of criticism. Whether Sík's demolition effort will have any perceptible effect on the production and influence of the TI index remains to be seen. The lure of a standard of measurement—of something akin to the inflation rate or GDP, readily comparable across borders—remains very powerful.

Perception-based indices and research are, Sík notes, just that—perception. Much is at stake, however, because corruption is no longer a matter of bad behavior, like bribes, but of bad societies—those that score poorly on the CPI. At the same time, what is summarized in "perception terms" as a "high level of corruption" in a given country is, at best, a lumping of various forms of wrongdoing. The fact that many things are morally wrong, Sík suggests, does not make them identical. In the economic or political sense, furthermore, a country or its government might be very corrupt (national assets being misallocated) without much public perception or knowledge of it. In such corrupt countries vigorous anti-corruption policies are in place, because corrupt power holders are keen to maintain their monopoly on corruption. The neo-moralism developed around perception indexes not only confuses different social phenomena but also contributes to the exacerbation of these phenomena. Notwithstanding the fact that *perceived* corruption is a one-sided indicator, once the powerful perception index is presented as an *objective* indicator of a country's comparative moral value, the index acquires its own dynamic. It will inform both the domestic political agenda and the way countries may treat each other. In the end, it is hard to escape the conclusion that corruption perceptions are greatly deepened by frustration with the results of transition, especially the economic depression and accelerated infrastructural decay. One of the simplest, all-purpose "explanations" of the "failure" of transition has been "corruption."

•

Admittedly, perception indices were designed to attract attention, and thus a response, which they have managed to do. Moreover, no one should get the impression here that the assumption of a universally shared understanding of corruption is impermissible for the very reason of being universalistic. On the contrary, there can be no sympathy for the approach of those who claim that in a given society certain transactions which are called "corrupt" elsewhere, are simply part of the local social code. (These views are common among politicians who try to defend practices from which their constituency benefits in their respective countries.) Even if the code of certain societies emphasizes the importance of gift-giving, including public transactions, it is clear that such gift rules do not rule out the concept of impermissible levels of gifts or a disregard of public duties. A gift culture does not exclude either the concept of public trust or the breach of rules in exchange for impermissible advantages.[22] Furthermore, because of increased intra- and intersocietal communication and exchange, the chances of a universal understanding and condemnation of actual practices have increased. Nevertheless, there is an element of false universalism in the currently prevailing understanding of corruption based on corruption perception. Social and policy reasoning along the lines dictated by the logic of a corruption-perception index isolates a simple component of a multifaceted social phenomenon. Simply put, what the accounts of perceived corruption generally do not grasp is the social nature of corruption in a given society. Here is where Paul Hutchcroft's contribution comes in, a broad-based essay that extends the findings of his study of banking in the Philippines, the country for which the term "crony capitalism" was coined.

According to Hutchcroft, an effective dictatorship, like South Korea in the 1950s and 60s, entails the centralization of authority, and therefore the centralization of corruption. The consequence is a greater degree of rent deployment and a lesser degree of rent seeking, enabling relatively "more positive" (or less detrimental) outcomes from the standpoint of development, including a relatively stable social and political environment that did make reinvestment into the development system attractive. Hutchcroft offers Korean examples that indicate that the corrupt preferences were related to productive investment. By contrast, in formally democratic post-Soviet Russia the environment has been unpredictable, and embezzled state assets ended up being siphoned out; in the more stable Central European markets there has been more reason to reinvest (especially as the continued corrupt networks guaranteed very high returns). Elsewhere, Hutchcroft, quoting John Waterbury, refers to Morocco, where "endemic and planned corruption . . . serves only one 'positive' function—that of the survival of the regime." One could add that between 1815 and 1914, the U.S. had the world's highest growth rate—and utterly corrupt politics. Of course, to contradict the notion that corruption always distorts or inhibits economic development is not to suggest that corruption always facilitates economic development. Over time, the world system shifts, and what works in one period (and for one region of the world) may bring different, or even diametrically opposed, results later, in other parts. Context matters enormously for all generalizations about corruption and economics. Moreover, Hutchrcoft reminds us to look beyond, or rather deeply into, the number and ask what kind of growth?

In the ever-growing literature on rents, which has left behind dependency theories, the common remedy for corruption is usually more market and less government (with little power of resource allocation, e.g. licensing). But Hutchcroft presents a summary of trenchant criticisms of the rent-seeking literature, pointing out that even a minimalist bureaucracy is capable of grand corruption. Thus *merely* shrinking bureaucracy is not an answer to corruption problems, at least not in most cases. What probably matters is the nature (structure and resulting ethos) of the public bureaucracy. In certain countries very extended government provided public services operate without substantial corruption in these sectors. (One thinks, for example, of public education in most West European countries: these huge sectors are generally corruption resistant, in part because they are large enough and, therefore, there is no need to buy one's place into the system.)[23] Nor does privatization usually resolve deeply rooted dilemmas: a public service is first privatized to cronies, and then the privatized company will receive subsidies or win public tenders, giving rise to a parasitic relationship based on corrupt relations between "entrepreneurs" and state bureaucrats. Hutchcroft suggests that rent seeking (made possible whenever the state restricts the operations of the market), corruption and clientelism should be built into an eclectic theoretical framework. In that regard (and many others), the postcommunist experience, for all its specificities, is not unique.

Corruption: An Analytical Map[24]

Diego Gambetta

Can we identify a specific social practice that we can justifiably call "corruption," and, if so, what are its distinct analytical properties? Given the multiplicity of definitions found in the literature and the considerable confusion over what exactly we should understand corruption to mean, this question, which forms the object of this essay, has neither a straightforward nor a formalistic answer.

In common usage the word "corruption" and its ancillary terms "corrupt" and "corrupting," carry several meanings, three of which seem to me to be the most relevant. First, "corruption" refers to the degradation of agents' ethical sense, to their lack of moral integrity or even to their depravity. Certain motives or character traits of an agent can thus be called "corrupt" in this sense and "corrupting" may be called the negative effects that derive from the actions prompted by these motives and characters on other people's motives and characters, and indirectly on their social customs or institutions.

Next, "corruption" generically describes an array of *social practices,* regardless of how these are motivated, which either emerge from, or bring about, a state of degradation in certain institutions. In this sense, the meaning of the word does not focus so much on the moral failings of individuals as on the social premises and consequences of their behavior.

Finally, some such *practices*, such as bribery or kickbacks, are themselves called "corruption," not so much because of their premises or consequences, but specifically by virtue of their own features.

There could be nothing particularly worrying about this multiplicity of meanings were it not for the fact that they become entangled not just in common parlance but in the scholarly literature itself. A powerful source of confusion, for instance, derives from the conflation between the last two meanings, namely between the premises and consequences of certain practices and the properties of the practices themselves. In the literature, "corruption" is often applied to forms of wrongdoing—such as kleptocracy, patronage, white-collar crime, and organized crime—which, while they thrive in corrupt institutions and may have corrupting consequences, differ from corruption as a practice in critical ways. Not all practices that have corrupting effects or which spring out of social degradation can themselves be accurately deemed to be cases of corruption. Here I will try to show that corruption understood as a *practice* is a *sui generis* phenomenon with specific properties that distinguish if from other forms of wrongdoings that may have corrupting effects, and that demands to be analyzed in its own right.

In so doing I explore in depth how corruption, especially corruption as a market, differs from other violations and how forms of corruption differ among themselves. At the same time, I will try to weed out some redundant distinctions found in the literature, showing how these can be reduced to basic analytical attributes.[25]

The properties that I have in mind are *behavioral* and *relational*. They are properties of agents' strategies when dealing with one another under certain constraints and rules that govern their actions. They are neither properties of social systems or of institutions, nor those of individuals' characters and internal states.

Furthermore, I will be searching for invariant features that make corrupt practices recognizable across times, countries and domains. I will also try to keep the defining features separate from legal, ethical and efficiency considerations, which are often entangled with them. While, of course, these are of relevance in order to analyze how corruption works and to motivate and legitimate the fight against it, they are orthogonal to the analytical definition of the phenomenon. As I argue in the concluding section, even though most corruption is illegal, and morally and economically wrong, there are corrupting acts that would be hard to regard as unethical. There are also forms of corrupt exchange that, while illegal, increase economic efficiency; and yet other instances about which the law of the state says nothing and yet corruption occurs.

The aim of this article is likely to be met by a relativist objection, voiced in virtually every discussion of corruption, and worth confronting without delay. Since the notion of what is legitimate or legal varies from country to country and time to time, the definition of corruption, it is argued as if it were an obvious inference, must vary accordingly, and there cannot be one for all. In one country, for instance, electoral donations to parties are against the law and are thought of as bribes. In other countries it is not so, and under certain conditions they are acceptable. In yet other countries matters are controversial. In Italy the socialists argued that the bribes they took were for their party rather than for personal gain, and that, since there is no other way for them to finance their electoral campaigns, donations should be legalized. There is no question that people wrangle over rules, and much interesting work can be done on the shifts of what counts as corrupt in one place and not another.

To infer, however, that a stable definition of corruption is therefore out of reach conflates variations in the content of an action with variations in the type of an action. Even just to be able to detect variations in content we must logically possess a prior notion of type. The behavioral properties presented here refer to the *type* of actions that can be regarded as corrupt. That what counts, say, as private property in any one domain shifts from place to place and time to time does not affect our basic understanding of what private property is. Analogously, what is deemed as constituting the institution of marriage varies widely across different normative and cultural systems, but that does not prevent us from detecting the *same* phenomenon through its different incarnations.

Here I try to make a similar operation possible for corruption by trying to improve the conceptual clarity of what exactly we mean when we call a practice corruption. The main purpose of this exercise is that of thereby improving our chances of achieving cumulative results across different studies and disciplines, and of developing a robust understanding of how corruption works.

The Standard Case Defined
The Agents of Corruption

Even the simplest episode of a corrupt exchange has a richer texture than a simple market exchange. First of all, it involves three agents rather than two. I shall call them the truster (T), the fiduciary (F), and the corrupter (C).[26] T may be an individual, such as an employer, or a collective body, relying on the expectation that people in certain positions are bound to follow given rules. F may be anyone who agrees to act on behalf of T— a single voter or an entire government department, a journalist or a prison guard. C is anyone whose interests are affected by F's actions.[27]

Above all, a corrupt exchange is richer in terms of the relationships between these agents. In a nutshell this is how the standard case of corruption can be described. C wants certain resources that F is *not* supposed to deliver to him, given the conditions of his relation to T. Examiners are not supposed to reveal the questions to candidates before the exam. Goalkeepers are supposed to do their best to prevent rival teams from scoring goals. Spies are supposed to work for their country. Students, rival teams and enemy countries, respectively, gain if these fiduciaries violate their duties. Offering a bribe to F is one way to achieve that.

The standard corruption case does, however, have the features of a market exchange. Both F and C freely choose whether to exchange and do so if they both expect to be better off as a result. In the standard case no pressure is applied by F to force C to pay a bribe to F, or by C to force F to accept a bribe (the case in which F applies pressure is considered in the section "Two Other Forms of Corruption"). It would be a neat little market except that it has one victim, T. If they decide to exchange, F and C jointly cheat on T. Rules are clear and everyone involved knows what F should or should not do. F is bribed by C *to violate the rules* in C's favor. Thus, by definition, corruption is not a Pareto improvement, as T is worse off, even though F and C are better off.

Corruption of any conceivable kind assumes the existence of a system of rights and consequent expectations under which T, if not the owner has at least a legitimate claim to regulate the allocation of the resource in question, whereas both F and C are excluded from its control. If the coveted resource belonged to F then F would be free to sell it to whomever he likes, and C would be a buyer rather than a corrupter, and, if it belonged to C, he could just seize it without anyone's permission. This assumption does not, of course, pertain to the notion of corruption alone. It is required to define all property violations and, thus, the notion of a market exchange itself. Rather than simply grab something, one can either *misappropriate* or *buy* it, only in so far as it does not belong to one in the first place.

Corruption as a Breach of Trust

A corrupt exchange between F and C can occur if, and only if, a certain relationship between T and F pre-exists. The best way to describe this relationship is in the context of a *basic trust game* between T and F (fully defined in Bacharach and Gambetta, 2000).

T accepts the entrusting of some resources to F, if T expects F to serve T's interests rather than F's 'raw' self-interest. (The interests of T may be altruistic and coincide with the public interest.) Here I do not discuss why T trusts F. It is just the case that T sometimes believes that F has some trustworthy making property. This can be because of how much T pays F, how easy it is for T to monitor and enforce F's performance or how F's character is. These conditions are irrelevant to the definition, even though they are crucial for understanding how corruption works.

T and F agree on a set of rule-bound actions, a_r, which F must perform when allocating the resources entrusted to him. The agreement rules out another set of *wrong* actions, a_w. The basic preference ordering of T over the outcomes is naturally that $a_r > a_w$. In the typical case a_w will also be worse than 0. This implies that, if T's expects F to do a_w, T is better off not to deal with F at all.

(In some situations T's preferences may be less stringent and a_w may still be better than nothing. This implies that if A chooses to do the wrong thing T gets a sub-optimal rather than a disastrous result. It obtains if, say, A picks a corrupt candidate for the job, but if no other candidate would have done better than the chosen one (everyone is corrupt), *and* if it is better to have someone in the job, albeit corrupt, than no one at all.)

To distinguish willing breaches of the rules from accidents or misunderstandings, F must know T's preference ordering namely $a_r > a_w$. Furthermore, corruption amounts to a breach of trust if T and F both know that T's acting in the way T does by trusting F gives F the opportunity to do a_w. Were it not for T's trust in F, F would not have the opportunity to act corruptly. In the typical case T and F must also know that if F chooses to do a_w T is worse off than if T had not trusted F in the first place (Bacharach and Gambetta, 2000). Corruption is one way in which F breaches trust by doing a_w.

A football team (T) recruits a goalkeeper (F) if, and only if, T expects F to do his best to keep the ball out of the team's goal net. If, say, T expects F to accept bribes, from opposing teams, T does not recruit F. F, in turn, can accept bribes if and only if, he is recruited. The relationship of trust between T and F gives F the power over the resources that interest C. If this relationship were not to exist F would have no opportunity to act corruptly. By acting corruptly, F trades away resources entrusted to him by T. This feature obtains in all forms of corruption. In order to have anything to sell to C, F must be believed by T to be his trusted agent.

Other agents' welfare may further depend on the expectation that F will do a_r. Citizens expect juries to deliberate according to the evidence. Fans expect players to fight for their team. University trustees expect selection committees to pick the best candidates. The mining firm's shareholders expect the prospector not to reveal new mineral sites to competing firms, and citizens trust Amnesty International to include, without exception, all countries that, to the best of their knowledge, deserve to be included in their annual list of human-rights abusers. Typically, therefore, the game between T and F will be nested in other trust games, in some of which the truster becomes the fiduciary.

Not all trust relations between T and F, however, provide an opportunity for a corrupt market. To do so they must negatively affect the interests of a third party. In the standard case that I am considering here, C prefers F to do a_w, which benefits him more than a_r. C wants what, under the rules that bind F to T, C cannot have. T's desired outcome clashes with C's interests if F does a_r. The interests of C and T are opposed. Consider a journalist who writes the truth about C's misdemeanors; a civil servant who gives a public contract to the best applicant rather than to C; a committee which denies permission to C to market his harmful medicine. All these rule-governed actions are bad news for C. C has the reverse preference order of T: he wants F to do that subset of a_w instead of a_r, which benefits or does not harm him.

Corruption as Mimicry

The breach of trust that goes with corruption is shrouded by an act of deceitful *mimicry*. F relies on T's belief that F is his agent even though F is covertly working for C. One may think of it in this way: suppose a mobster would like to be acquitted by a judge. He could kidnap the judge and replace him with an impersonator. However, it is simpler to try and bribe the actual judge. The corrupt judge looks like the same old judge, even though he is not a judge at all but a payee of the defendant. He mimics his role without the additional burden of having to mimic a person, as an impersonator would have to do.

For a corrupt exchange to succeed from C's viewpoint, mimicry has to work long enough for the good exchanged to be consumed successfully by C, before T can do anything about it. There may be, say, secrets that are of use to an enemy country even if it becomes known that they have been sold as soon as they have been sold. The discovery of a corrupt exchange will not, in this case, detract from the value of the resource that C bought from F. However, in most circumstances, when F's corruption is unmasked, T can counteract the consequences and make sure that little or no benefit accrues to C. F cannot thus reveal himself to T as the agent of C, or else the very commodity he is selling evaporates. T would terminate his relationship with F and when feasible invalidate whatever C obtained from F. By losing his position with T, F will not be able to practice further corrupt exchanges. Mimicry must successfully persist for F to be able to continue being corrupt in his position. A corrupt F typically acts as a double agent and mimics his own position for some time.

In cases of systemic corruption, when corruption is rife and everyone knows and accepts that at least some of it will occur all the time, mimicry becomes thinner and mutates into generalized hypocrisy. Everyone will pay lip service to the rules that everyone knows are systematically broken.

One Strategy in a Set

C can employ a number of strategies other than bribery to induce F to act in his favor, notably intimidation and deception. F may reveal his country military's secrets out of gullibility or threats rather than greed or lust. A referee can grant a nonexistent penalty because fooled by a player's acting skills or bullied by the fans rather than because he is bribed. A culprit can threaten a judge or fabricate false evidence to get acquitted. A prison guard can allow jailed mobsters to use mobile phones out of fear rather than of corruption.

Conceptually, therefore, corruption is part of a larger family of strategies; it is one option in a set that can be employed to persuade F to do a_w. Also, it is not an exclusive option, in that it can occur in combination with intimidation and deception. C can threaten a reluctant F into accepting a bribe. If F accepts, this does not make it less of a case of corruption but less of a free exchange. F's payoffs are altered by C not just by offering the bribe but by promising retaliation in case the bribe is not accepted. The extreme case consists of C just threatening retaliation while offering no bribe at all. In this case the threat of violence, which forces F to do a_w, is a pure alternative to corruption.

Modeling corruption choices therefore requires the identification of both the feasible set of strategies open to C to alter F's actions and the decision mechanisms that govern C's choice of one strategy over another. C's decision to choose corruption over other alternatives generally depends on whether C expects that there exists an amount of some currency (π^*), which C is able and willing to pay if the benefit he expects, is sufficient to reverse F's payoffs (such that $a_w + \pi^* > a_r$) and motivates F to do a_w. Whether this obtains, and F accepts an offer, depends on whether his payoffs are modifiable by C's offer. He may reject because the bribe is too small relative to the cost he incurs by doing a_w, or because of integrity: there might be no amount of any currency for the sake of which F is prepared to violate his duties to T.

The Motives of Corruption

F may do a_w instead of a_r for a variety of motives, not all of which involve an exchange with C. Some motives, such as laziness or resentment against T, do not even require the intention of benefiting C. F can also do a_w because he holds values or dispositions antithetic to T's interests. A soldier may refuse to shoot civilians even if they did not bribe him or a judge may acquit a defendant of theft because the culprit was starving even though the law makes no allowance for that. In 1946, a customs official allowed Isaiah Berlin to take out of the Soviet Union prohibited books by Anna Akhmatova out of awe: he noticed they were personally inscribed by her. Many British agents who worked for the KGB betrayed their country because they were communist, not corrupt. An Italian judge of the Court of Cassation acquitted many Mafiosi by not upholding the verdicts of lower courts on technicalities. He did that not because he was bribed, or at least not only. He did that because he believed that the Mafia is an independent "ordinamento giuridico," a legal system unto itself in which another system, that of the state, enjoys no legal right to justify its "intrusion."[28]

Doing the wrong thing may also be used as a signal of one's power in the eyes of an interested audience. A principal who, against the rules, succeeds in promoting an incompetent agent over more competent ones to a higher position and goes unpunished, shows his clout, his ability to deliver despite the rules that bind his actions. The incompetent agent benefits without bribing, since he is merely an object in F's signaling ploy.

These cases of wrongdoing may qualify as corrupt in the sense of being practices, the consequences of which may be corrupting of morals, customs or institutions, but do not qualify as a corrupt exchange, for they come about regardless of C's bribery, even though C may benefit. Corrupt outcomes can thus coincide with outcomes motivated differently. Interestingly, therefore, the key to identifying corruption must lie in *the motive* that persuades F to do a_w. It does not so much involve identifying an outcome as beneficial to C as evaluating the motives of the action that brought that outcome about. *There has to be an exchange between F and C such that C's bribe to F is the motive for F to do a_w.*[29]

When Fiduciary and Corrupter are the Same Person

A special case occurs when F = C, a case in which the same person or collective unit of self-interest covers both roles. Suppose F is entrusted to allocate school places or public contracts according to merit. If F sells school places or contracts regardless of merit to C the case fits the definition of a corrupt exchange. Suppose now that F, in his capacity as parent or moonlighting as a contractor, does the same for his offspring or himself. We are naturally inclined to understand this as a corrupt practice, of the nepotistic variant, namely bestowing benefits on one's kin and friends. However, even though F violates T's rules, self-serving or nepotistic corruption misses two key features of a corrupt market. There is no bribery involved, and thus the bribe cannot be what motivates F to do a_w. Nepotism, in the strict sense at least, occurs regardless of whether one expects to be paid. The outcome of the violation itself *is* the 'payment' to F, in terms of satisfying F's self-interest, vanity or affection. Furthermore, this case does not require any particular action on the part of C, other than just being who he is. It can occur without a corrupter, that is. In nepotistic corruption C may be unaware of the way in which certain beneficial outcomes occur, and in certain instances, C may even be opposed to receiving special treatment from F and this may be forced on him.

Monopoly over the Rules

The elements of corruption spelled out above are as yet insufficient to disentangle it from other kinds of fraud, which also seem to fit the definition. Suppose T lends his bike to F while on holiday, and F sells it and pockets the gain. Is F being corrupt? T entrusts a resource to F on the understanding that F will look after the bike on his behalf and not sell it for profit. So the description suggests a positive answer. Intuitively, however, we know that this is not a case of corruption. F is a swindler and in breach of T's trust, but he is not acting corruptly. Suppose now that T were to 'lend' some political power to F, and F gave it away to C in return for a bribe, in what way would this case differ from that of the bike? Is the difference merely illusory and due to the triviality of a bicycle relative to the importance of political power?

A key condition for corruption to become a relevant option is that the cost of reaching a permissive domain where the rules that prevent C from obtaining what C is after do not obtain, must be more expensive for C than corrupting someone in the domain in which C resides. One may buy hard liquor or cigarettes in another state at times or ages when in one's own the law prevents it. In so far as an expedition to the permissive state is more costly than corrupting a store dealer in one's own state, corruption makes rational economic sense.

The most important instance that in practice satisfies this condition fully occurs when T has the *monopoly* over the allocation of the resource that interests C, if in other words there is no alternative domain in which C could go to satisfy his interests. If no one else is entitled to deliver what C wants, and only T can, by virtue of whatever system of rights assigns the exclusive control over the resource to T, then the cost of finding an alternative permissive domain can be described as infinite. One cannot buy a favorable verdict from a competing court or obtain a valid U.S. passport from another nation. A teenager cannot buy alcohol legally anywhere in the United States, and adults cannot buy alcohol legally in certain hours or days of the week.

One, by contrast, can normally buy a bicycle from many sources with no need to bribe anyone to bend a rule. (If C offered to pay a bribe, when cheaper options are available, to obtain what he wants, he would be foolish. If F asked a bribe in that situation he would either fail, since C would refuse, or, if he did succeed, it would have to be because he fooled C into believing that a bribe was necessary.)

Notice that the monopoly over the rules of allocation does not imply the monopoly over corrupt acts. There may be several agents privy to the information T wants to be kept secret, and they may even compete in the corruption market to sell it to C. What counts is that any F who has control over the resource is bound by the *same* rule.

In practice the existence of a monopoly over the allocation rules is what creates most corrupt markets. This is essentially why much corruption occurs in the public sphere, which works on the basis of universal rules not supposed to be for sale, and which protects the common good often at the expense of private individuals' interests. These features make the public sphere a rich pool of opportunities for corruption. The same conditions can also occur outside the public sphere, however, thereby making the distinction between public and private sphere, which is empirically relevant and analytically redundant.

Not only can corruption occur in the private sphere, the rule itself whose respect is corruptly sold need not even be opposed to the market logic. The rule can be of the form "behave as in a market." A private auctioneer, bound to sell T's goods to the highest bidder, for example, acts corruptly if he accepts a bribe for failing to do so. The *respect of the rule* rather than its content is what should not be on a market, given the terms of the agreement that binds F to T.

The Price of Violating Rules

Is the monopoly over allocation rules enough though? Suppose that T is the owner of the only surviving Ferrari Pininfarina 202 GT 1946 and (unlikely) decides to lend it to F. F then sells it to C who wants precisely *that* model on which T has the monopoly, in the simple sense that he owns the only existing car of that model. Is F being corrupt? That depends on what exactly C is buying and F selling. For corruption to obtain there must be a price knowingly paid and received *for the violation of the rules* that bind F to T.

One can construe cases in which the sale of the Ferrari is undertaken without a specific price being paid by C or, if paid, without C knowing anything about the fraudulent source of the car. F can sell without a specific incentive to breach his trust with the lender. If the owner of a liquor store sells in forbidden hours at the *same* price he sells during opening hours, he must consider that profit sufficient to break the law. Only if F tells C, "I cannot really sell you that, but, if you pay 10 percent extra, I'll do it," or if C entices a reluctant F by saying: "I'll pay extra if you sell me the booze," a corrupt transaction occurs. Also, C does not necessarily need to know that, by buying the Ferrari, he is contributing to defrauding T. F may fool him into thinking that he is acting under T's instructions, or F may pass himself off as the owner and, if C knows the fraudulent source of the car, C is more likely to be a fence rather than a corrupter. A fence is in a sense the opposite of a corrupter: he requires a discount to compensate for the risk *he* is taking to buy stolen goods rather than being required to compensate for the risk the seller takes. In cases of this sort, we may have wrongdoing that amounts to theft, fraud, receiving stolen goods, but not corruption.

In conclusion, the *corrupting act* by C consists in freely offering to pay a price in some currency to compensate F specifically for a violation. The *corrupt act* by F consists in exacting a price for that violation. Both acts make rational sense if, and only if, C cannot obtain the desired outcome legitimately, or more cheaply, otherwise. Finally, for corruption to obtain, both parties must know that they are violating an allocation rule set by the relationship which exists between T and F and that the bribe is the price C pays to persuade F to infringe it.[30]

Two Other Forms of Corruption
The Price of Sticking to the Rules

The standard case, of which I have eviscerated the defining features above, covers a large share of actual cases, which both the scholarly literature and the common parlance dub as 'corrupt'. In much literature, however, corruption is understood as involving a different component, namely extortion. In his monumental book on bribery, for instance, Noonan (1984) defines a bribe as "an inducement improperly influencing the performance of a public function meant to be gratuitously exercised" (p. xi), (even though his examples cover other types as well). Actual examples are not rare. Passport applications can become stuck at the bottom of the pile. Garbage collectors can 'forget' your house unless you bribe them. A film producer can ask you to be nice to him if you want the part, even if you are the best actress for it. A share of Italian corruption that emerged from recent investigations was of this kind. In order merely to be considered for a public contract, firms had to pay kickbacks to political parties: it was a 'pay to play' policy. The Lockheed affair, as described by Karl Kotchian, one of its protagonists, was also a case of this kind: "(. . .) the pledge of money was like the admission to a ball game and if you didn't pay the admission, you were not even qualified to participate in the game" (Noonan, 1984, p. 671).

Here C, whom we shall label C* to distinguish him from the agent in the standard case, wants something that *he is supposed to receive* from T, but which F can artfully refrain from delivering, unless C* pays him a bribe. F puts pressure on C* who, unlike the previous case, is a victim of extortion rather than a corrupter seeking to obtain something he should not have. F asks to be bribed for *sticking to the rules*.

This case differs from the standard one. C* here pays extra for what he should get free of that charge. Also, in this case F initiates the exchange by issuing a threat while in the standard case matters are symmetrical and C and F both have an incentive to exchange and are free not to do so. This case no longer retains the feature of an ordinary market.

There is another fundamental difference. In the extortion case, T's and C*'s interests are not opposed. C* wants a_r just as T does. F, by using his discretionary power, chooses whether to refrain from doing a_r and damage C*. If C* yields and accepts to pay, the outcome will still look the same which T wants, a_r. This should decrease the chances of detection and, hence, increase the attractiveness of this form of corruption. On the other hand, if C* refuses to pay and F's threat not to deliver is carried out then the outcome is a_w, which T does not want, but here T and C* can join forces against F while they would not in the rule-violating case.

A final difference is that, unlike the standard case, the monopoly condition is very likely to extend to F and not just to T, or else the extortion would not work. C* must be constrained to obtain what is due to him from one source only. If one F denies C* something only if C* cannot get it anywhere else the pressure to pay grows. If there is more than one F who can supply what C* is due, if one official denies it, one can go to the next official in the hope he is not corrupt.[31] Except in cases in which C* cannot afford searching for the first honest official and opts for bribing, corrupt extortion is possible only if all Fs are corrupt *and* collude to keep T in the dark about their corrupt activities.

The Price of Improving on the Rules

There is a further form of corruption often mentioned in the literature, which differs from both the standard and the extortionate case. C' wants something that he is supposed to receive from T via F but upon the quality of which F has some discretion. A citizen is entitled to receive his passport if he satisfies the prerequisites and the passport office is supposed to supply him with one. If the office has discretion over the time it takes to hand the passport out, a corrupt office may charge extra to citizens who want their passport in one week rather than in six months.

C' is the victim of a low-quality service provided by T, and F is bribed *to act outside the rules* rather than against them, as in the simplest case, and provide a better service. This form of corruption thrives on inefficiencies and ill-defined regulations. In the acting-outside-the-rule case the resource offered to C¢ is of low quality and F can privately agree to supply a higher-quality version. Economists refer to this case when they claim that corruption can increase efficiency. Under the circumstances, C' may be unhappy but still better off by paying for a *better* service than he would otherwise receive.

In this case T may be indifferent and allow a private market to develop on the side accepting *de facto* an increase in F's compensation extracted directly from customers. This may have its attraction in that it maintains a façade of equality and universality of treatment while silently allowing differential rewards and better allocation of resources and efforts. This form of corruption can thus occasionally be stable.

However, this case of corruption tends to unravel by being legalized or to collapse into either or both other forms of corruption. T may prefer to cash in the extra income directly and openly by legalizing differential services at correspondingly differential costs, thereby neutralizing the opportunities for this kind of corruption. For instance, in the U.K., if one wants a passport more quickly one can legally apply for this and pay a higher fee, or in Russia people can legally pay for extra police protection.

Furthermore, while the better service can conceivably come at no cost to others, in many cases this is not so. Even assuming that inefficiencies are not artfully manipulated by F in an extortionate way, this type of corruption can easily generate negative externalities: in order to provide a better service for those who bribe, F ends up offering a lower quality service to those who do not. A better service for some may thereby imply a breach of, say, the rule 'first come first served' and thus amount to the first case in which someone obtains something he is not supposed to have, in this case jumping the queue.

Those who do not pay, on the other hand, come under pressure to pay just to keep up. Even if F says nothing, they will be subject to an objective extortionate pressure. If everyone ends up bribing, everyone ends up paying extra for what they should have for free as in the extortionate case. One pays simply in order not to be stuck at the end of the queue. This effect undermines whatever efficiency corruption might have injected, and simply increases the cost of the service for everyone to the advantage of F who pockets the gain.[32]

Further Distinctions and Complications

The three forms of corruption defined above, especially the standard and the extortion case, represent the elementary forms of the phenomenon. They emerge from different situations and interests, and must therefore have their own distinctive dynamics. By spelling out their properties and their differences we can be clear about what, minimally, for each case we need to model in theory, and research in practice, to understand how corruption works.

Composite Cases

In reality, there is, however, a host of more complex cases in which those forms merge with each other or with yet another form of wrongdoing. Especially if we introduce competition among Cs and among Fs the plot thickens. For instance, if F plays with both C* and C at the same time, F can threaten C*, who deserves the resource, by saying that C, who does not deserve it, is prepared to pay him a bribe. F threatens to do the wrong thing to extract from C* a bribe to do the right thing. Not only does F have the option of which form of corruption to engage in, but he actually uses one to make the other more likely.

Or consider "Corruption with theft" (at the expense of T), a notion introduced by Shleifer and Vishny (1993): a state official may charge C *less* than he should if he applied official tariffs for a given service, and keep *all* the money without passing any to the state. The official breaks the rule and C is happy to connive with him in exchange for a lower total price. "I have to charge you X, but I can charge you only Y < X, and thus give you a discount you shouldn't have, if you help me to defraud the state." The bribe here is paid by C in terms of complicity and compensated by F in monetary form by a discount.

There are also instances in which the standard and the extortionate case become indistinguishable. If there is competition among many Cs, for instance, F can in principle choose to reward someone who offers the highest bribe or the best guarantees of behaving reliably. The rewarded agent may or may not be whoever should have been selected according to the rules. If C deserved the reward under the rules, then he is subject to extortion—he is paying extra for something he should obtain for free. Else we are in the rule-violating case, and C pays for something he was not entitled to receive (with the excluded top candidate as the further victim). However, not even that much is known in some cases, for often C's relative position is unknown unless one compares it with the other competitors' qualifications. So one does not even know whether one is bribing for something one should or should not get, and the difference becomes irrelevant. This may in the end never be known, for it may be against agents' interest to work it out or make it known. This form of corruption is not, however, very stable for it can create dissatisfaction, and those who rightly or wrongly feel victimized can respond by unmasking the ploy or by colluding with each other.[33] It often requires intimidation to be sustained, which ultimately drives other competitors out of the market.

The family tree of corrupt practices is widely ramified and grows entangled with other vegetation—such as fraud, theft, intimidation, or collusion, but precisely because of this complexity, knowing the properties of corruption of elementary forms—those forms that cannot be reduced to simpler ones—is essential to make one's models and research take into consideration the necessary distinctions.

Distinctions

Our conceptual map provides the opportunity to clarify how corruption as a practice differs from other phenomena. Some of these one may wish to call 'corruption' in terms of their consequences on the fabric of society and its institutions, but still they differ from the practice that we can call 'corrupt' and the market that derives from it.

Theft. Casting corruption within a basic trust game and its 'positional obligations' allows us to distinguish it from crimes that violate natural rights, such as theft, in which everyone is bound to respect universal obligations. A theft can be construed as having one direct victim, the person whose property is stolen, and an indirect one, namely the law and all those who trust others to respect it. Thieves, in the ordinary case, are not agents of the victim, and the victim does not choose to deal with them. Nor are they agents of the law in any strict sense. The victim is simply hit while going about his business, as it were, under the general expectation that his life and property should be respected. It does not make any difference if a third party commissions a theft. For corruption to obtain, T must entertain specific expectations with respect to F, and F must undertake to comply with them.[34]

Fraud. There are cases in which F abuses his position with T, such as when F defrauds T in various ways, say, by embezzling the funds of his employer, making private use of office resources or charging higher prices to unaware customers to pocket the difference. Even though this qualifies as a fraudulent breach of trust, F acts by and for himself alone rather than for a third party. These cases, however, do not amount to a corrupt market, as there is no exchange with a third party that compensates for the violation. For instance, Shleifer and Vishny (1993) define "government corruption as the sale by government officials of government property for personal gain." If a policeman secretly sells confiscated drugs this would count, according to this definition, as corruption. This seems to me a case of fraud, namely theft of state property and abuse of trust at the same time, and not one of corruption. One may choose to call this 'corruption' generically, but corruption proper is more specific in that it has to do not so much with seizing goods for oneself or for sale to others as with selling one's failure to comply with T's rules.

Patronage. The discretionary or arbitrary allocation of resources over which someone has full control—such as an absolute ruler or a wealthy person—does not qualify as corruption (although someone behaving *as if* he were a patron when in fact he is bound to T's rules, does qualify as corrupt). Here we have only two agents, one who is in a position to make the rules according to his whims, or the other who simply does not follow any rule, nor is bound to do so, and allocates rewards at his discretion to the other.

Kleptocracy. This is the obverse of patronage in that punishments rather than rewards are meted out arbitrarily by agents who are not bound to a T; we find practices as petty as extortion and as grand as kleptocracy. These are predatory activities by which racketeers or a state and its incumbents tax subjects aggressively *and* arbitrarily, with little or no relation to the services they supply.[35]

Selective incentives. In an interesting paper Goda (1999) describes how Hitler during the war showered his senior officers with monetary gifts designed to sustain their loyalty. This he calls 'bribery'. However, here we have only two agents—Hitler and his officers—rather than three, and Hitler, an admittedly rather *sui generis* truster, was paying his officers-trustees to do what they were already supposed to do for him in any case.

Organized crime. Contrary to a common view, the practice of corruption is not the defining feature of Mafia-like groups. These are best seen as agencies that supply protection to illegal transactions. Mafia protection is supplied in many different markets, without necessarily involving the market of corruption, and corrupt exchanges occur all the time without Mafia protection. When available, however, Mafia protection fosters corruption by lubricating the corrupt exchange between F and C; by strengthening illicit cartel agreements, which have to rely on corruption to function properly. On the other hand, when widely available, Mafia protection *competes* with corruption in that it provides people with an alternative option to persuade F to do a_w, namely intimidation, thereby lowering the price of corrupt acts (Gambetta, 1993, 1997).

Conclusion

Readers interested in the big picture and in historical synthesis may think that there is not much to gain from dissecting the notion of corruption in such detail as I have done above and providing a conceptual map of the main forms of the phenomenon. Since corruption depends on the existence of clear rules of conduct, if these happen to be obscure, shifting or controversial we may find that the definition becomes inapplicable—as if, for instance, there are conflicting sub-rules, all of which comply with T's general rules. The governor of a central bank can raise or lower interest rates, and justify either action as the most beneficial to the common good by invoking different economic policy principles even under the same economic conditions. The fact that Wall Street will be advantaged in one case and the exporters in the other, is no evidence that he is colluding with the beneficiaries. A pervasive case of the sort—that invariably yields disputes and charges of corruption—is urban planning. Whatever one does, someone will gain and someone else will lose, and in many cases alternative plans are justifiable on different grounds.[36] In these cases we lack a clear distinction between a_r and a_w, even in principle. Here corruption tails off into conflict of interest and disputes over principles while a_w loses focus oscillating between what different groups consider against their interests.

An even greater difficulty occurs if the expectations of T are inchoate, and may be given sharper focus by F's activities. This is especially so in politics where those we trust also help shape our expectations of the character of this trust and of the nature of their responsibilities. Elected politicians are bound to implement their electoral promises on behalf of voters, but on issues outside the electoral manifesto, politicians can vote as they like and claim reasons of principle even if secretly otherwise motivated. The positive analysis of corruption is here toothless as there is no set of T's interests and rules which is not partly defined by and given substantive content by F's behavior.[37]

The study of conflicts over rules is at least as interesting as that of how people flaunt them. Yet, to exploit these instances to claim that the exercise of defining corruption is thereby futile is to miss the point. Clearly, in countries of merry promiscuity there is little use for the notion of marriage; or where goods are common property there is little use for the notion of theft. However, it certainly does not follow that these notions are therefore useless in the countless circumstances in which marriage and property are regulated. Even where local *mores* make notions such as property, marriage or corruption inapplicable, one still needs them to measure the degree of contrast from the usual case.

The advantage is not just that we know what we are talking about when we speak of corruption. By being clear over the notion of corruption we gain generalizability, and thus the possibility of comparing instances of the *same* behavior in different times, countries and domains. This we can achieve by relying on the behavioral and relational elements of the definition. In so far as we can trace the three main characters and their positions relative to each other then, *mutatis mutandis*, nothing prevents us from identifying the same *type* of corrupt episodes in ancient Greece, Tsarist Russia or modern Britain, in the private or the public sphere.

Morality, Efficiency and Legality

The generalizability of the notion is further enhanced once we consider that, as I mentioned at the outset of this article, the morality of motives, the efficiency of outcomes and the legality of rules are not, contrary to much literature, necessary elements of a behavioral understanding of corruption. True, many, perhaps most, forms of corruption are unethical (because the rules it breaks are perceived as fair), inefficient (because it thwarts the optimal allocation of resources), and illegal. Still, corruption need not be so. Let us briefly consider each in turn.

Wanting a bribe need not be motivated by strict self-interest. In countries where the extended family matters and there is a strong sense of family altruism, *rejecting* a bribe is seen as selfish and disapproved of. One would subtract additional income to the other family members with whom bribes are divided 'merely' for the sake of one's moral principles. Familism provides a normative system that favors corruption, while individualistic societies may paradoxically provide no such normative justification to act corruptly, for one is more transparently doing it for self-interest alone.[38] Analogously, corrupt agents, when caught, have claimed that they were doing it for the sake of their party, rather than to line their own pockets.

Paying a bribe, too, is not necessarily motivated by self-interest. One can do so to enhance the welfare of someone else. Wittgenstein paid Nazi officials to spare his sisters, and Lincoln instigated the bribery of some members of Congress in order to achieve the required majority to pass the Thirteenth Amendment. Thorny moral issues of this kind often arise in case of bribery of informants in enemy countries in times of war; and in case of bribery of foreign officials by home corporations in competition with other suppliers, as in the Lockheed affair (Noonan, 1984, pp. 455 and 686).

Altruism, however, does not coincide with morality. Taking a bribe for familial altruism or party's sake may still go against the common good. Similarly, an action can be morally justified and self-interested at the same time. Had Wittgenstein paid to save himself rather than his sisters I doubt we would consider that immoral. The corrupter is morally objectionable only in so far as T's goals are not so. If we consider what F is supposed to do to comply with T as morally objectionable—predatory, unjust and cruel—we may consider the corrupting act as the lesser of two evils. The man in Kosovo who paid one thousand marks to a Serb paramilitary to spare his life was protecting himself from an act that we cannot regard as in any way justified. There are instances in which we can be morally justified to exploit the corrupt motives of others. Most corruption does, however, tend to break rules that are considered to be fair or lawful and it is of major concern for the functioning and legitimacy of institutions because of that.

The position of the corrupt fiduciary is, by contrast, *always* of dubious moral standards in one respect: F invariably breaks trust. The breach can be more or less severe depending on how willingly F entered a contract with T. Still, even a conscripted soldier who accepts a sum of money to let someone free is doing that for gain rather then because he objects to T on moral grounds. He does the right thing for the wrong motives. (Or, if we deem wanting to make money as not a bad thing per se, he does it for at least an unprincipled motive, in that, if someone paid him even more to shoot the civilian, if money were all that mattered to him, he would do it.)

Also the element of mimicry makes corrupt fiduciaries despised even by corrupters: "There is one thing worse than a crook," Al Capone is supposed to have said, "and that is a crooked man in a big political job. A man that pretends he is enforcing the law and is really taking 'dough' out of somebody breaking it, even a self-respecting hood hasn't any use for that kind of a fellow. He buys them like he would any other article necessary for his trade, but he hates them in his heart."[39]

The relations between corruption and economic efficiency are similarly complex. In the standard case F and C are both better off at the expense of T and the outcome is not Pareto optimal. In some cases, however, T's economic payoffs and ideological or moral preferences diverge. Economically, it may be the case that, even for T, $a_w > a_r$, while ideologically T's preferences are reversed. This means that T binds F to act on inefficient principles, as was the case perhaps in the USSR distribution system. In these cases corruption—especially if there is competition among agents—could bring about a better resource allocation than compliance, and thus increase total welfare. In this case T is a victim because his principles are violated rather than because he is made materially worse off. In this instance corruption (and hypocrisy) can more easily become universal—everyone pays lip service to the official will, while no one abides by it—as it does not undermine the resources on which it thrives. Overall, from a sheer materialistic point of view, the outcome is worse than one created by efficient rules and no hypocrisy, but, once there are inefficient rules, it is still better than one produced without corruption.

An analogous reasoning applies to the illegality of corruption. In so far as the rules that govern the allocation of certain resources are inscribed in the law, corruption is of course illegal. This obtains both directly or indirectly. A law can, say, rule that a judge cannot sell a verdict, or that an agent cannot sell whatever he has agreed not to sell in a legal contract. There are also agencies, however, which are not under the control of the law in which corruption of the standard type does occur. Consider the following true story: D's father has a food-producing firm. He labels his goods 'kosher', even though they are not. He thinks that the label attracts even gentile customers for they think it is purer and safer food generally. How does he get the right to use that label? He has a rabbi visit his food plant once a year. On that day alone, the whole process is arranged in such a way as *to look* 'kosher'. The rabbi gives his seal of approval, and gets a large donation in return. The rabbi is supposed to follow certain rules when deciding whether food is 'kosher'. He is an agent of these rules that are universally upheld by the community of other rabbis and are in turn trusted by Jewish and gentile consumers alike. According to my source, the rabbi knows what goes on but does not care. Playing on the ambiguity of motives, if challenged, he can claim that he was duped by D's father.

In most states there is no law that sets out the conditions under which a good can be declared 'kosher' (which is different from a law saying that one should not deceive customers by displaying false information.) The rabbi's act, therefore, rather than illegal is just improper with respect to the rules of his own community (even though the use that the food producer makes of it may be illegal).

Some Empirical Predictions

Finally, by inference from the features of the definition, we can generate a number of empirical predictions about the emergence of corruption and the opportunities for its detection.

Corruption is parasitic on the existence of trusting relations; corruption corrupts first and foremost the trust between T and F, and, by implication, between T and whoever else trusts T's rules of allocation. It follows that *the greater the number of trusting relations, the greater is the potential for corruption.* A society that is more corrupt in absolute terms is not, therefore, necessarily worse than a society that is less corrupt, in that lower levels of corruption may result from fewer opportunities and greater lack of trust rather than from good behavior. Conversely, it also follows that corruption has an upper limit, for, if lack of trust is pervasive, the opportunities for corruption must eventually cease to exist. This limit is purely notional and offers little consolation since beyond *that* "threshold the whole fabric of society may start to unravel" as it may have been the case in the decline of ancient Rome (see Elster, 1989, pp. 270–271).

For F to engage in extortionate corruption a number of conditions must obtain. F must enjoy a certain amount of impunity and be sheltered from T's intervention. Alternatively, he must be sufficiently threatening to discourage C* from informing T; or C* must be in some predicament such that he cannot afford to waste resources reporting F's wrongdoing. *The level of lawlessness, lack of proper supervision, intimidation and collusion required tend to be high for this form of corruption to emerge.* There is, however, a certain amount of petty extortionate corruption that involves small bribes and high cost for C* of informing T. C* may thus accept to pay as it is not worth the bother

That *motive,* rather than just outcome, distinguishes corruption from other forms of wrongdoing has some interesting corollaries. First, it makes corruption harder to unmask. Agents can play on the uncertainty and justify their actions by claiming error, intimidation, or even alternative principles in order to pass off corrupt acts as something else. *The opportunities for doing so are greater the more error-prone or generally turbulent a society is.* At the same time, the relevance of motive in establishing a case of corruption makes the identification of corruption particularly susceptible to interpretation and thus to beliefs about other people's dispositions. *The more people are prone to believe that other people are corrupt the readier they will be to classify dubious outcomes as corrupt.* In turn, this is at the root of the self-fulfilling nature of corruption, for *the more widespread is the belief that corruption is rife, the greater is the incentive to engage in it.*

The opportunities of detecting corruption are inversely correlated with the opportunities of mimicking trustworthiness successfully. If there is a clear and observable distinction between the outcome of a_r and the outcome of a_w F can only exploit the multiplicity of motives and causes that bring about a_w. In other words F can construe a_w as the result of some mistake rather than of bribery—not all goals are the result of a corrupt goalkeeper—but cannot really pretend that a_w is a_r, for failure is observable regardless of motive. We may not know *why* the goalkeeper has let the ball in, but we often know whether he has made a mistake. If that happens often enough, the goalkeeper would he out, whether or not he failed because he was bribed. Mimicry has a low "natural" limit and so does corruption. A corrupt act has an unavoidable cost for F and this constrains his actions. One can only fail a limited number of times or else T will relieve F of his position.

In other situations there is a clear distinction between a_r and a_w, but it may be arduous to know in practice which is which. We expect an art expert's opinion on the authenticity of a painting to be based on good evidence of authorship, but non-experts find it arduous to form an independent opinion on the quality of the evidence and thus on the expert conclusions. That is one reason why the opinion of more than one expert is often sought. Still, there are constraints in this type of situations too. One is inconsistency: a judge can acquit because he is corrupt, but if he then sentences another defendant to jail in a similar case, his actions become suspicious.

In yet more insidious cases, the observable outcome of a_w does not differ from that of a_r, and the evidence of wrongdoing is simply not available for independent scrutiny unless one of the parties reveals all. If a teacher leaks the exam questions in advance, chances are that he will not be detected. Mimicking is thus easy and corruption can continue undetected for long periods of time. T's best chance is to devise a number of indirect strategies to prevent cheating. As Schelling suggested, the agreement between T and F may have to be expressed in terms of something observable, even though what is observable is not the intended object of the bargain. One may have to pay (. . .) a salesman a commission on sales, rather than on skill and effort; to reward policemen according to statistics on crime rather than on attention to duty; or to punish all employees for the transgression of one. And where performance is a matter of degree, the bargain may have to define arbitrary limits distinguishing performance from non-performance; a specified loss of inventory treated as evidence of theft" (Schelling, 1960, p. 44).

An analogous device in the case of teachers and exams could be to expect a pyramid in the distribution of marks. If all students get 'A' there may be something wrong that may not necessarily be corruption; still, if marks are well distributed this at least ensures that corruption has not spread beyond individual cases.

Political Corruption, Democratization, and Reform
Mark Philp

Defining Political Corruption

This paper examines a series of problems associated with analysing and controlling corruption in the process of democratization, with special reference to political transition in Central and Eastern Europe. It takes for its point of departure a definition of political corruption that centers on the abuse of public office. This is relatively uncontentious.[40] The paper then turns to examine the conditions under which public office can function with some autonomy, and the impact on this functioning which democratic transition can have. A common assumption in the literature is that increasing democracy provides the basis for enhanced political legitimacy, increased access to decision-making processes, and greater accountability. In practice, however, democratization can weaken the authority and legitimacy of political institutions, it can open the system to more extensive forms of corruption, and it can turn mechanisms for the formal and political accountability of the political system into highly politicized weapons whose effect is destabilizing. Whether or not these consequences accompany transition depends on a wide range of factors, only a few of which can be examined here. Instead, the paper outlines a set of distinctions that can help clarify the nature of a state's corruption problems, together with a series of suggestions as to how different types of corruption may be targeted.

Core cases of corruption involve four key components:

1. a public official (A), who, acting for personal gain,
2. violates the norms of public office and
3. harms the interests of the public (B),
4. to benefit a third party (C) who rewards A for access to goods or services which C would not otherwise obtain.[41]

Activities which meet all four criteria are corrupt, although there are also many cases where only three of the four elements are present but where we are justified in claiming that the action/relationship is corrupt. It is contestable whether kleptocracy requires a third party benefiting, yet few doubt that such a regime is corrupt. Similarly, the rewards to C may be something C has a right to, but where the public official levies a tax on access. Alternatively, the public official may act to avoid certain costs, rather than to incur certain benefits, or may act in pursuit of political rather than personal gains.[42] We should also distinguish between A-led and C-led types of corruption: in the former the public official imposes the terms on C (from extortion to informal 'taxation'), in the latter the relationship is reversed (from bribery to systematic subversion of the political domain). We can also recognize different types of mutual corruption: cases where the exchange is equivalent and the parties are equal (as in market transactions); cases where the exchange is asymmetric but the parties are equal, as in 'blat'; and cases where the exchange and the parties are unequal, as in patron–client systems.[43] The public interest component may also be weak: the bribed policeman may in fact end up acting in the public interest. What remains central is the construction of public office which identifies the character and extent of, and the responsibilities associated with, the relationships between A, B and C.

There is an understandable desire to provide a definition of corruption, which allows comparative judgments to be made but if there are differences in the norms of public office between states, comparison becomes invidious. The incidence of corrupt rule breaking and prosecutions for corruption will be a function of how extensively corruption is legislated against and how assiduously it is prosecuted. The difficulties become still greater when we face contrasts between stable Western democracies and less democratic societies in which strong patrimonial, patron–client, tribal or communal traditions determine access to political power and shape its exercise. Rather than assessing the latter by standards of the former, we should be asking whether the system has a conception of public office, what the parameters of that conception are, whether those in public office act within that understanding, and (more speculatively) whether that conception is adequate to the tasks and challenges which face the state. Where there is no recognition of a need for a political order, with its associated public offices, formal rules of conduct and sense of the public interest, the fact that distributions and allocations take place on non-political criteria, does not mean there is corruption. Allocations within families rely on other principles, but that does not make them corrupt. It is political corruption only where a political order, with an accompanying understanding of public office and a distinction between responsibilities of office and the interests of office holders, which expresses the aspirations of some significant part of the culture, is subverted by individual or group activities, which violate that understanding and obscure that distinction.

Difficulties in identifying corruption arise from ambiguities in the identification of public officials, their roles, and the rules governing their official conduct, and from the fact that each criterion is intelligible only against the background of a political culture in which there are shared norms and rules governing the conduct, both of public officials and of members of the public in their dealings with these officials. However, a further dimension which needs emphasis is that political corruption is predicated upon the existence of political rule: politics involves the exercise of public office and this implies *rule*— an ability to order the social, political and economic order through the authoritative prescription of rules, backed by the necessary legitimacy and, where necessary, coercive resources. Political corruption is only one way in which political rule is subverted, and we need a sharper appreciation of the point at which obstacles to political rule are appropriately understood as corrupt.

Political Autonomy, Democratization, and Legitimacy

Public office may be exercised well, it may be corrupt, or it may be rendered ineffective by a range of other factors. It is essential to distinguish these cases to underline the fact that political corruption implies that the state more generally, and an individual office-holder in particular, has some power, the exercise of which can be subverted. We can follow Adam Przeworski's account of state autonomy and distinguish two questions in relation to political institutions:44

     a. Are those in public office able to choose the goals of state activity?
     b. Can those in public office realise their goals and objectives once these are chosen?

We can distinguish four state forms on the basis of these two criteria:

Matrix 1

		CHOOSES POLICY	
		YES	NO
REALIZES GOALS	Yes	(1) Autonomous	(2) Instrumental
	No	(3) Embattled	(4) Irrelevant

The matrix helps us see when the state might cease to exercise an independent causal impact on the inputs and outcomes of the political process. In three of the four cases, political rule is subverted. In one of these cases (2), corruption may be a common means of subversion—namely when the state becomes instrumental to the pursuit of sectional goals or interests which cannot be legitimated through the political process or by the norms and rules for the conduct of public office. In the embattled state (3), the political system is unable to implement policies because of overwhelming economic and social conflict or disruption. In the irrelevant state (4) we are dealing with a façade of political rule which has no independent impact on either policy making or implementation. This state is a limit case for the existence of a political realm distinct from the social, in the sense that political life is doubly heteronomous: the officials of the state are incapable of determining policy and of implementing it. We may find such cases in very early stages of political development, but we may also find them in puppet regimes, where the ruling elite is hostage to extra-state forces, usually some foreign power, but where the capacity of the state to ensure compliance with policy so determined becomes compromised through some combination of a general demise of public legitimacy and a loss of control over, or a dissolution of, the coercive apparatus of the state. We may also find such cases where the grip of, the norms governing relations between those in office and the public is so weak that the rules are completely ineffective.

Autonomy is a matter of degree. In most modern states the choosing of goals and their realization takes place within a wide range of constraints. These may be built into the structure of political office, or they may be obstacles to the exercise of office owing to the existence of countervailing 'external' forces and pressures. The former do not compromise political rule, but they limit its remit and resources, and in different states political rule may be more widely or more narrowly delimited—compare the constraints placed on their Presidents by the American, French and Irish constitutions. Countervailing forces external to the structure of public office include economic constraints, the international situation, public opinion, and interest group activity. We must also distinguish structural (or 'hard') constraints from 'soft' constraints (because potentially negotiable) which arise from the agency of particular individuals, groups, or other states. In any state these various elements will have some impact on the policy process, but the central issue is how far they determine the outcome of the process, so that the institutions of political rule and public office play an essentially subordinate role, and how far their impact is itself governed by political activity and public regulation. In democratic states, in contrast to autocracies, the number and range of these group pressures can be very considerable. Indeed, one paradox associated with democracy is that it offers the promise of popular sovereignty while simultaneously opening up states to a very wide range of legitimate influence, which can drastically curtail the scope for autonomous political agency. Indeed, if we follow Linz and Stepan's definition of democratization we can see that, in at least one sense, democracy opens up the political process to influence from a dramatically increased range of sources.

Democratization requires open contestation over the right to win control of the government, and this in turn requires free competitive elections, the results of which determine who governs. (Further . . .) A democratic transition is complete when sufficient agreement has been reached about political procedures to produce an elected government, when the government comes to power that is the direct result of a free and popular vote, when this government *de facto* has the authority to generate new policies, and when the executive, legislative and judicial power generated by the new democracy does not have to share power with other bodies.[45]

That is: firstly, that democratization involves a change in the selection process for political office from a regime in which government is not determined by the popular vote, to one in which it is. Secondly, however, the appeal to *de facto* authority involves insisting that the democratized political process exercises ultimate authority in the policy-making process and in the exercise of power within the state. Democratization, then, requires both that there be democratic politics, and that the democratic political process rules within the state.[46]

Offe suggests that democratization must also involve consolidation ("or [equivalently]'institutionalization'"), which has a vertical and horizontal dimension.

Vertical . . . consolidated systems are those (in which) . . . every actor's decision making is constrained by higher-order, decision-making rules, i.e., rules which are not at the disposition of the actor himself, but to which the actor can refer as a license for, or legitimation of, his own decision making.

Horizontal differentiation (concerns) 'the degree of insulation of institutional spheres from each other and the limited convertibility of status attributes from one sphere to another.[47]

The first criterion might be taken as specifying the relationship between *de jure* and *de facto* authority, indicating that there is consolidation when the political institutions within the state exercise the latter within the constraints of the former. Vertical consolidation is certainly not unique to democracies, and might be thought a component of all political regimes, insofar as they are political (as when the actions of kings come to be considered as restricted by the responsibilities of the crown). The second criterion is more complex. It looks more like a causal condition for secure consolidation, rather than a criterion of consolidation itself. However, a comment by Offe in an earlier paper suggests why we need to recognize horizontal differentiation as providing distinctive problems for the modern, liberal-democratic state. Most crucially, the commitment to the protection of private property, both individual and in the means of production, distribution and exchange substantially restricts the means a state can use to achieve its ends and opens it up to a much wider range of legitimate influences. As Offe puts it: "In making and implementing policy, the political system can only make offers to external, autonomous bodies responsible for decisions. Either these offers are not accepted, thus making the attempt at direction in vain, or the offers are so attractive in order to be accepted, that the political direction for its part loses its autonomy because it has to internalize the aims of the system to be directed."[48]

A central problem for sustaining the independence of politics in liberal-democratic states, on this account, is that it faces an equally autonomous realm of civil society in which groups have every interest in blocking state interference and in seeking to direct the state's activities to serve their own ends. The more autonomous a state becomes, the greater the interest which groups in society have in influencing its activities—pushing it in an instrumental direction.

Transitions can complicate both political agency and its corruption. Both transition and consolidation involve the development and institutionalisation of authoritative norms of political office and political responsibility. When there is consolidation, political corruption arises where public officials evade these norms. However, where the old political order has lost its legitimacy and the new remains unconsolidated, it can be difficult to identify corrupt activity, because the norms of public office are unclear, contested, or otherwise undergoing rapid change. In the transitions which took place in Eastern Europe, there were a number of factors that partly eased and partly exacerbated this situation. Following Offe,[49] we can recognize that the predominantly non-violent (and non-military) character of the transition left the old elite with some residual credit and legitimacy and meant that no single group had the legitimacy to impose a new order. The weakness and ideological diversity of the counter-elites led to uncertainty over both what was to be jettisoned and by what it was to be replaced—an uncertainty which was intensified by the double and often triple character of the transition: political, economic, and national and territorial. We should also follow Offe in recognizing that the universalist pretences of the old regime led to a considerable mistrust of politics among the population, which left them ill-prepared for democratic participation or for trust in politicians in the transition period. We do not have, then, regimes, in which one comprehensive order is overthrown and replaced by another (one might doubt how far that is ever really possible), but ones, in which some residual legitimacy attached to the old political forms and some of the old political players, where there was no systematic alternative elite or ideology available, where a rapid process of decision making and constitution-, institution- and market-building was needed, and where (in some areas) nationalist agendas rapidly became more significant than practical, political or economic agendas.[50] It should also be emphasized that in many areas of economic activity the previous regime had created incentives which forced both private citizens and managers in the productive sector to rely extensively on the black market and on a series of forms of 'grey' corruption, in order to obtain basic necessities and to meet targets. The strategy for most people suddenly exposed to the full economic costs of the previous system, was to make the most of opportunities for covert exchange. Similarly, management of the political system by the ruling elite relied heavily on patronage networks and covert forms of reciprocity. Despite the universalist and collectivist ideology of communism, it ended up with a set of highly individualist practices of self-protection which, in a period of rapid political and economic change, inevitably led many with practical responsibility for assets to invest their energies in securing their position in the new order. Each of these factors acontributed to undercutting the emergence of a consolidated democratic system with clear and adequate norms and rules for the exercise of public office.

In democracies we can distinguish three components of the political process: the competitive contest for public office; the exercise of public office—*qua office*—in the formation of policy; and the execution and administration of policy, governance and law. In a democracy all three components may be vulnerable to corruption, but in transition, the inheritance from the past inevitably accentuates the vulnerability and threatens the establishment of new practices and the achievement of vertical consolidation. States in which corruption has been rife in the formation of public policy and the exercise of public office—more broadly, states in which the exercise of public office has been subordinate to patron–client relations, kinship structures, patrimonial or communal relations, or even straight monetary exchange—are likely to experience extensive corruption during democratization, and subsequently, because they require a transformation in public conception of the responsibilities of public officials, not just a different process of selecting them. The institution of democratic elections may exacerbate the problems, by rewarding those able to muster coalitions of support (always easier for those with past experience in office and the patronage system), and by subordinating policy making to the need to secure electoral support. Clearly, some responsiveness to the electorate must be a condition for democracy. However, there are forms of alliance with electoral forces which themselves threaten to undermine the independence of public office—such as the courting of majoritarian ethnic, class or religious interests with the prospect of securing ascendancy over a minority.

One factor which makes a substantial contribution to democratic political agency is the ability of those who exercise political power to appeal to the formal standing of their office to justify resisting the demands of groups and interests and to impose constraints on the way such demands are made within the political process. That ability rests on the recognition of the legitimacy of the appeal and of the standing of public office by the political culture. Where there is such recognition democratic political rule is dramatically enhanced—hence Offe's account of the vertical dimension of consolidation in which "every actor's decision making is constrained by higher-order decision-making rules." Although the requirement for legitimation places constraints on what politicians and public officials can do, securing legitimation also buttresses their capacity to act—not least because it substantially reduces, in the specified areas, the range of pressure to which they may legitimately be subject, while increasing the willingness of groups to comply with the outcomes of the political process.

Loosely, legitimacy may attach to a) a person or party, b) a policy, program or set of outputs, or c) an office, set of procedures or constitutional order.[51] Vertical consolidation implies the priority of the last group over the second and the second over the first (and within these groups the later terms over the earlier). A democratic system has a very low level of consolidation in so far as that order is reversed. In a consolidated order, the state is able to justify its activities by reference to norms for the conduct of political office, which are recognized as legitimate by groups and interests in society (at the very least by those upon whose practical support those in power rely).[52] For a state to have legitimate authority, it must act in accordance with rules, norms and principles which command (to some extent) general recognition within society—and where they command this, not because (or only insofar as) they serve the interests of those in society (or some portion of them), but because they are recognised as having a validity which constrains the pursuit of those interests in certain fundamental ways, coupling rights of representation with certain responsibilities. Political corruption implicitly rejects the legitimacy of the political process. It is successful only where it compromises the exercise of authority, and it is at its most damaging where it systematically subverts the authority and legitimacy of the state, resulting, in extreme cases, in the collapse of the state's capacity to rule politically.

Legitimacy facilitates political rule: for politics to have some causal role, it must achieve a degree of autonomy from the various interests and forces within (and without) the state, and it is critical for this independence that the norms of political office and the ends of politics (the resolution of conflict, the public interest, or the common good) are recognised as constraining both the way that interests are presented and the range of interests it can be expected to further. Vertical consolidation is evidence of legitimacy, and it also enhances political authority and autonomy. Where these norms are subverted by the search for covert influence, by decisions which circumvent the rules and which cannot withstand publicity, or by rules and criteria which systematically favor some groups or classes over others, political rule becomes a tool for individual or group conflicts, displacing the norms of office and subverting the distinctive character of political rule.

Subverting Public Office

The independence of the democratic political process may be compromised by groups or individuals subverting the electoral process, and/or taking control of policy making and/or blocking the state's implementation of policy.

Matrix 2

		METHOD OF SUBVERSION		
		ELECTORAL SUBVERSION	CONTROLLING POLICY	BLOCKING IMPLEMENTATION
AGENT OF SUBVERSION	INDIVIDUALS	Bribery, campaign funding, buying votes	Inducements and threats	Non-compliance/ free-riding
	FACTIONS/CLASSES	Electoral malpractice	Patronage/ class rule	Non-cooperation/ class war
	BUREAUCRATS/ELITE	Raising entry costs, exploiting access to TV, Media, etc.	Autocracy	Elision of formal controls
	FOREIGN POWERS	Funding of status quo or subversives	Exploiting dependency or venality	Covert support for one or more of the above

This is neither exhaustive, nor especially subtle, as a categorization, but it helps us see the range of different forces that may beset a state. The classification also helps us to identify the main areas of concern for political corruption by providing a framework within which we can identify the extent to which political rule is systematically subverted in the interests of some individual, class, or organization, or by some external source. As we have seen, there are complex issues involved in describing such activity as corrupt. I want to discuss two. The first applies the definition of political corruption to the matrix to ask how far all these forms of activity might, in a consolidated democratic regime, be recognizably corrupt; but the second raises the problem of states where a critical level of political viability has not been crossed.

Broadly speaking, individual actions which subvert the electoral process or attempt to gain control over policy or decisions by the use of illegitimate inducements or threats, will count as corrupt wherever a public official is involved, and where we can establish the triadic relationship, the illicit and personal gains to both sides, and the violation of public rules. Much the same can be said for the activities of factions or classes—not least since a sufficiently stiff form of methodological individualism will reduce collective to individual agency. The situation regarding foreign power is similar, if more complex: similar, because it can be subjected to the same methodological reductionism, but more complex because of the various forms of influence which foreign states may seek to exert, the range of motives for accepting foreign support on the part of those holding public office, and the relative absence of a formal set of rules and norms in the international arena.[53] Where the gains and costs are publicly legitimatable it is not corruption, but there may be cases where the receipt of support cannot be publicized, and yet where the support does not affect the ends or activities undertaken by the state.[54] Clearly, there is much murky water here, and it is crucial to assess the character of the gains made by those who accept funding—personal and private gain is corrupt, public and publicizable gain is not, but certain forms of political or 'institutional' gain (as Thompson's work suggests) may be much closer to corruption. All of these cases are best understood as C-led cases of corruption, in that agents outside the formal institutions of the state seek to influence public officials through the use of incentives and/or threats. In contrast, bureaucrats and members of the political elite provide cases of A-led corruption where they impose extra costs on C. It is difficult to distinguish such cases from straightforward cases of fraud, since in both there is a clear violation of public trust, together with private gain, but no third party who benefits. One possible distinction is between cases where the responsibilities of public office provide opportunities for illicit gain—as in theft and fraud—and cases where the powers of public office are exercised over others to levy gains. But this distinction is suggestive rather than hard and fast. More complex still is the case where the gain sought is simply to sustain ascendancy—this being typical of the extra difficulties associated with A-led corruption: i.e., it becomes harder to keep clear the distinction between the interests of the individual, his/her duties as an office holder, and his/her institutional interests and objectives.[55]

The dimension of the table, which is less immediately relevant to the analysis of corruption, concerns the final column—namely, the ability of individuals to block the implementation of policy. The one exception involves cases where the very individuals who are responsible for the implementation of law (the bureaucracy or political elite) are those who subvert its application to themselves. Again, this may lack certain elements of the four-fold criteria for corruption (most likely the identification of C), but at its extreme it can involve the corruption of the entire political system. In contrast, tax evasion, mass forms of non-compliance or disobedience, civil unrest, and free-riding, all weaken the capacity (and/or indicate a weakened capacity) of the state to rule but they do not necessarily corrupt the institution of public office. Indeed, in such cases of public non-compliance, we are dealing less with cases of corruption than with a lack of legitimation of the political process by those subject to it and a lack of vertical consolidation. At the extreme, where the activity is undertaken openly, with no sense among those who undertake it that their behavior is illicit, then the more plausible conclusion is that the political order lacks sufficient consolidation to deliver political rule. Short of that point, we will find cases where non-compliance is found in some, but not all areas of the state's activity— but, again, these indicate the failure on the part of the political system to secure legitimation across some sphere or spheres of its activities, rather than corruption. It is a paradox of corruption that, understood in these terms, it is parasitic on the existence of legitimated public office and political rule—so the stronger our sense of the political order, the stronger our sense of the character of corruption. The weaker these institutions are, the more difficulty we have in identifying practices as corrupt, and the more we must fall back on counter-factual arguments to the effect that the state could cross a threshold into effective political rule were it not for the systematic influence being intentionally exerted by some group, which undermines that prospect because their interests are better protected by keeping the state weak and ineffective. Social disorder which makes political rule impossible is not necessarily a sign of corruption, nor indeed is the persistence of tribal, caste or familial forms of social organization the presence of which systematically excludes the possibility that a political order rooted in mass public legitimacy will emerge. The cases become more complex where familial, caste, tribal and patron–client forms of social order co-exist with political forms: where the primary allegiance to the group precludes the development of vertical consolidation and the recognition of the binding character of the norms and practices of the political process, and where groups colonize the political system by occupying its offices without accepting the legitimacy of its rules and procedures, it becomes difficult to say that political rule has crossed the necessary threshold of effectiveness, and thereby difficult to claim that it is corrupt.

Transition in Central and Eastern Europe has in general involved a dramatic upheaval in the character of political life and the associated conception of public office: it has opened up the political system to a wide range of new political, international and financial pressures; it has introduced contestation into the process of political selection where there is little in the public political culture to ensure that electoral competition is well regulated, transparent, and fair; it has dramatically extended the state's need for legitimacy (by reducing its capacity to rely on coercion), and this has often been coupled with economic crisis as market forces are introduced into these highly protected economies; and it has both tarnished people's confidence in political office, and created systems in which political office is much more reliant for its authority on the confidence that it can inspire among the public. That there should be political corruption in these societies, on this analysis, is hardly surprising. The problem is to see a way forward.

Controlling Corruption

This discussion suggests that we need to be clear, in tackling political corruption, where the impetus for corrupt activity derives from and in what domains it takes place. Is it C- or A-led, or is it mutual? If mutual, is it an exchange of equal values or an asymmetric exchange? If C-led, are we dealing with individual cases, or systematic activity by groups or classes? If A-led, are they isolated cases or part of a more general pattern? If mutual, is this an extension of exchange patterns which are widespread elsewhere in society? Does the activity aim at the electoral process and the filling of public office, or at controlling policy within the political process or decisions within the administration (including the allocations of burdens, such as taxes and rates, or benefits, such as licenses or contracts), or at eliding the formal controls on public officials and members of the political elite? How securely is the political system legitimated, and how far is its activity blocked by non-compliance among the wider population? What impact does this have on the way the state acts, and especially on its ability to retain its capacity to rule and on its relations with enforcement agencies within the state, such as the police and army? Also, where is the most systematic weakness in the state—and from where does it stem? It is possible, for example, to see the Colombian judiciary as especially susceptible to corruption and thus as a major obstacle to effective political reform. It is, however, also plausible to see the judiciary as systematically undermined by a variety of political and extra-state forces, such that, even if judicial reform were forthcoming, it would be systematically undermined.[56] Similarly, is police corruption relatively free standing or is it systematically linked to political forces in the state?[57]

These are reasonable questions, and ones which need to be answered prior to tackling corruption, since the precise form and context of corruption will affect assessments of what remedies might be appropriate. In choosing between norms, incentives, penalties, scrutiny systems and demands for transparency or tolerance, we must fit the medicine to the patient. I want to suggest a range of factors that need to be considered in giving this homily a more precise and useful form.

(a) *Incentives:* Economic models of corruption mostly assume that the way to reduce corruption is to reduce the incentives to break rules, by increasing the costs of being caught, by increasing the cost of the activity itself (making it more difficult), or by decreasing the opportunities. However, seeing things in cost–benefit terms assumes that the agent's orientation towards rules is such that they are to be followed or broken in accordance with a calculation of rational self-interest. Yet, it is plausible to think that market exchanges would not be sustainable if such a calculus were applied to market rules and the systems of rights which underpin them.[58] The issue, then, cannot be wholly reduced to providing the right incentive structures for people's interests, since some of the time we want to change the baselines from which agents calculate how to act.[59] Indeed, it is wildly ambitious to try to establish a system of cross-checking interests which can ensure that both the principal actors and those responsible for rewarding or penalizing their behavior act to sustain the political order while also acting maximally in their own interests.

(b) *Motivation:* Simply because behavior can be categorized under a single term, such as political corruption, does not mean that this behavior is identical in form or motivation. That it has a single term derives from the fact that its various forms have a similar impact on public office—but that does not mean that every act is similarly motivated. It is true that the common view of corruption as involving *the substitution of private for public interests* strongly suggests self-interest-maximizing trumping demands for self-restraint in the public interest, but the criterion is much better expressed as *the substitution of one set of norms and values (which may, but need not be, self-interest maximizing) for those which identify the responsibilities of public office*. Familial duties, ethnic or religious loyalties, fidelity to friends, norms of reciprocity, machismo values of risk taking, and so on, may all serve to displace the norms of public office for an individual or groups of individuals.[60] We need to examine whether the corrupt behavior in a particular case derives from, or is endorsed by, some alternative framework of norms. Where, literally everyone is corrupt there is room to doubt whether there is a political order. This might be because some other system of value is subscribed to, or because conditions are such that people are struggling for survival in a situation of chaos and we need to understand them as acting to protect themselves as best they can. In neither case is it persuasive to talk of political corruption since (by hypothesis) a political order is not viable. If corruption is relatively rare, then we may well be dealing with individual cases of self-interest maximizing rule-infraction. However, between these two extremes we are likely to find a large number of cases where, albeit to greater or lesser degrees, alternative norms and commitments make corruption an accepted (because in part acceptable) component of people's lives. Where this is the case we need to grasp what is motivating people if we are to change the way they behave.

   (c) *Motives and incentives among corrupters:* The more that corrupt activity derives from individual incentives *un*attached to group norms and a broader motivational frame, the easier it is to deal with. Any political system has a few bad eggs, every system needs checks and audits, and public officials need to be clear when contacts with the public overstep acceptable bounds, but, if we are dealing with isolated cases the costs are likely to be fewer, and detection and prosecution easier. In contrast, the more that embedded corrupt activity is within a society's broader social or cultural mores, the more difficult it is to deal with—because there will be more things to change, more and better organized resistance to change, and less legitimacy attaching to those who promote the changes. This is the more so to the degree that holders of public office share these mores. In such cases it becomes increasingly difficult to say that corruption is A- or C-led, since there can be a very high degree of collusion between the actors, and a sense that what they do is legitimate. The more widespread this sense, the more difficult it is to identify a point in the political system that could act authoritatively to signal that the activity is unacceptable.

(d) *A- and C-led:* The suggestion that we can distinguish corruption which flows from individual maximising as against that which follows group norms is formalized in the following matrix and related to whether corruption is A-led or C-led. This helps generate an account of different types of corrupt activity and of the different strategies which might be appropriate. Thus, a clear code of public ethics which might help increase public officials' awareness of the boundaries of acceptable behavior is more appropriate when we are dealing with C-led corruption on an individual scale, although it might also help to sustain awareness of the margins in C-led group cases.[61] Where we are dealing with officials with expressly corrupt individual or group agendas, subscriptions to basic courses in Public Ethics will be low, as will their effectiveness.

Matrix 3

| | | CONTROLLING CORRUPTION | |
		INDIVIDUAL INCENTIVES	GROUP MORES
AGENTS INSTIGATING CORRUPTION	**A-LED**	(1) Type: soliciting payments *For A:* transparency, audit, formal controls, penalties and education *For C:* multiplying options, access to complaints process	(2) Type: "taxation," extortion *For A:* intra-state conflict between reformers (R) & A *For C:* R seeks legitimacy, public educ'n., increases public expectations
	C-LED	(3) Type: bribery, backhanders *For A:* code of ethics, internal accountability & transparency *For C:* clear and distinct rules and penalties	(4) Type: protection, appropriation *For A:* protection plus limiting discretion at interface with C; insulation of decision process. *For C:* special police powers, infiltration, aim to weaken and divide group

Cell 1. Isolated cases of soliciting payments are not systematically destabilizing of a political system, although particular scandals may rock governments, and they are, relatively speaking, easier to tackle. We assume that in such cases the agent is influenced by certain incentives. To deter such behavior we can try to increase the actual and probable costs of obtaining these benefits, by increasing transparency through audits and formal con-

trols, and by increasing penalties for corrupt activity. We can also work to develop a tighter public service ethos amongst public officials and politicians, so that there is clearer collective condemnation of corruption and a clearer sense of the responsibilities of public office. We can also make it easier for C to resist corrupt solicitation for benefits, or more costly for C not to resist. In the former case, where C is weak and is seeking access to a public service to which there is some entitlement, but where A imposes a levy on that access, we can weaken A's hand by proliferating the points of access for C and strengthening C's access to complaints procedures. In cases such as bidding for contracts, where C stands to gain by the corrupt payments A solicits, we can increase the cost of such activity by allowing prosecutions for collusion and sentences which include the confiscation of assets and withdrawal of tendering rights or rights to conduct business.

Cell 3. When the impetus for corruption lies outside the formal political system, with individuals using bribes and backhanders to gain access to, and control the exercise of political influence or decision making in the public administration, corruption control can follow a dual strategy of strengthening the collective ethos of the public service and the political elite by education, through the development (in association with those involved) of codes of ethics which help individuals think through the limits of propriety concerning their contacts with the private sector, and by ensuring that there is public accountability for decision making. At the same time public campaigns to clarify official codes of conduct (and the corresponding norms for citizens), together with clear penalties for attempted bribery, including those listed above for C under Cell 1, reduce the incentives for such activity.

Cell 4. The situation becomes more complex when the state faces groups and communities which repudiate the norms of the political system, seeking to subordinate the exercise of public office, where possible, to their particular interests (thus rejecting 'vertical integration'). Again we must distinguish cases in which groups effectively resist or seek to block political activity and cases where there is an attempt to suborn public office so as to serve their particular ends (these being more clearly cases of corruption). The problem the state faces in the first case is one of legitimacy and political integration—which is not to say that the problem is tractable, since, where it grows out of, or into, movements for ethnic autonomy or national self-determination, the results can be extremely bloody. We move towards the second case insofar as the groups in question acknowledge the political order (that is, they do not deny its legitimacy or seek its transformation) but seek to turn it to their own individual and collective ends. Mafia-type activity may take this form, as may corrupt business cartels and labor unions, or various types of 'old-boy' networks. To tackle these more organized forms of corruption, we need to limit the control that any A has by virtue of his/her position. By limiting discretion and making more transparent the decision-making processes, C is deprived of the prospect of private and privileged access to the point of decision making. We may also need to strengthen the powers of those responsible for the criminal investigation of such activity. Needless to say, proposals will run up against liberal concerns about the protection of individual rights, and the nature of the tradeoff between these concerns and the strengthening of policing powers will depend on the scale of the threat to public office, and the ability of the state to secure legitimation for more obtrusive methods of investigation.

Cell 2. In each of these three cells (1, 3 and 4), the strategies recommended rely on the presence of a central authority with judicial, disciplinary and police powers capable of authoritatively establishing rules for political conduct and of enforcing them. The more individualistic the patterns of corruption, the greater the likelihood that the state will have the necessary power and authority. In cell 4 the issue is how far the state is able effectively to regulate activity within all social domains, which asks a question about the limits of its *de-facto* authority, rather than about its coherence as a body. In this last cell (2) one unique problem is that it can become difficult to see, insofar as the A-group mores become widespread, which institutions within the state could have the capacity authoritatively to act to regulate the activities of other institutions in the state. Of course, this problem is not always present. Corrupt police forces (LAPD, NSW) may be relatively isolated from the political system, which may then use controls external to that organization to attempt reform—which is not to say that success is guaranteed[62] but the higher-up the corruption goes, the more widespread it is, and the more customary it is, the greater the difficulty in creating a platform for reform and the greater the problems associated with creating institutions to implement that reform. One scenario is that accusations of corruption become a weapon used by reforming political movements against the status quo, but a disadvantage of this is that the very language of corruption can become devalued because it becomes linked to the search for political advantage. A related possibility is for the reform movement to work to raise public expectations of political office through political education, etc. But the viability of such strategies depends heavily on whether they are able to secure the cooperation and compliance of key public institutions such as the judiciary and the police.

Cells 1–4. Cell 2 raises, in an especially acute form, a problem which, while it affects all societies in transition, is especially acute for the post-communist regimes of Central and Eastern Europe, which have carried over from their previous regimes weakly institutionalised respect for the rule of law, a tendency to over-ride administrative regulation by ad hoc decision making directed by those in power, and an extremely weak civil society which provides few collective resources for challenging the activities of the state. The resulting polities have poorly protected property rights coupled with weak judicial systems, and a general pattern of politicians and public servants using the powers and economic resources of the state for their own benefit. Moreover, in many Central and Eastern European societies one major legacy of the past forty to fifty years has been to entrench an extensive mistrust of political leadership—understandably so, but each of these elements contributes to the undercutting of the conditions necessary for a group, individual, or institution taking the initiative in corruption control. Indeed, an increasing problem in these countries is the adoption of a rhetoric of corruption into the partisan programs of politicians and political parties. Instead of there being a programme directed against corruption based on a political consensus, the rhetoric of corruption is used to destabilize and delegitimate the activities of one's political opponents, and where there is a lack of consensus as to what counts as corruption and strong imperatives to engage in ethically dubious horse-trading to build political coalitions, it is not difficult to tarnish one's opponent's reputation, even if there is little or no subsequent attempt to substantiate the accusations judicially. Reform, then, seems to rely on the presence of institutions and political actors who can sustain a position of some neutrality, impartiality and authority; yet, the upheaval associated with rapid multiple transitions, coupled with a legacy of anti-politics, renders this prospect extremely unlikely. In the crudest terms, to reach such a position of influence it is extremely difficult, if not impossible, to avoid acting in ways which leave one open to accusations of corruption.

(e) *Motives and incentives among the corrupted:* Interestingly, we tend to think of public officials and office holders as becoming corrupted by others either within or without the state—so that C-led corruption is seen as corrupting public officials.However, we do not think of people outside the state who become directly or indirectly implicated in A-led political corruption as themselves corrupt. Crudely, the justification for the asymmetry is that public officials who act corruptly, whether at their own instigation or that of others, cease to be reliable officers of the state, whereas there is a much less strong sense of the formal public role of subjects or citizens. One way of tackling A-led corruption is to try changing this rather weak standing which citizenship and is responsibilities have within the state—by public education, and by tightening connections between rights and responsibilities. One possible benefit of this approach is that it raises a sense that responsibility for corruption is widely shared—whereas many corruption campaigns tend to leave citizens convinced only of the fundamentally corrupt character of the political system, which increases the incentive to engage in corrupt activity.

(f) *The victims of corruption:* The above matrices do not consider the victims of corruption, yet they can play an important part in its control, although this is affected by how individuated they are—that is, whether the cost of a corrupt transaction is linked to a cost incurred by some particular other individual(s)—and how directly they are affected. A public official who is bribed to divert a service intended for B to C, imposes a cost on B—although B is not necessarily aware of this: corrupt contracting and queue jumping by bribery may impose costs on B without B's knowledge. On the other hand, while the state may proclaim that it offers a particular social benefit to those who meet the criteria (such as housing), it may be quite plain to members of that group that what matters is not your position in a queue so much as who you know in the housing office. Cases where B incurs costs unawares may need different strategies than cases where B is aware, or has some sense, that she is not being treated justly. In the former case, one way forward is for the political system to increase the probability that B will be aware when his just claims are trumped—by making clear what people's entitlements are, publicizing waiting lists and criteria for queue jumping, and by limiting discretionary powers in public administration. The clearer people are about what they ought to be receiving from their public servants, and the broader the range of countervailing actions which are possible against perceived injustice, the thinner becomes the ether in which much corrupt activity thrives. The range of these actions can be specified as follows:[63]

(i) *Seeking alternative sources of allocation:* A postmaster who tries to 'tax' his pensioners' benefits when they are cashed has limited success because of the range of alternatives open to them—other post-offices, banks, and so on. The greater the transferability of the entitlement, because of the variety of state offices within which they can be claimed, or because of the variability of the entitlement, the less easy it is to 'tax' corruptly or to withhold. Similarly, low cost 'exit' options on the part of recipients diminish the potential for extortion.

(ii) *Protected formal countervailing action against perceived injustice*—which may include institutionalizing complaints procedures, the provision of financial support/legal aid for those making complaints, the facilitating of media investigation and publication of such claims and so on. It is also possible, in addition to strengthening the recipient's arm, to render the public official's role more transparent—by identifying the responsible official and the superior officer, and by making the complaints procedure favor the client. Of course, where one wants the public service to ration the delivery of goods, and where there will inevitably be difficult and complex decisions to make—we often face a trade-off between empowering the client and making the task of the public service increasingly impossible, but short-term schemes which facilitate the complainant, might have long-term benefits without these costs.

(iii) *Playing the Game:* It is always possible for those who are victims of injustice to respond in like coin: to meet corruption with corruption. In some contexts this is simply a matter of: "If you can't beat them, join them," but, formally speaking, the thing to note is the hypothetical—"If you can't beat them . . ." We can understand many such instances as stable, but sub-optimal, Nash equilibria. This means, we have a situation in which A's strategy (X) is the best response to B's, and B's to A's, and A's to C's, and C to A's, etc., but where the outcome for each is less good than could be achieved if each played a different strategy (Y), the difficulty being that, to reach Y, some players have to adopt Y, and doing so renders them vulnerable to costs imposed by those who pursue strategy X. Being honest when all around are knaves is costly, despite the fact that we might all be better off if we were all honest. So a state might take the position that it will systematically underwrite the costs of those who act well while increasing the penalties for corruption, thereby reducing the incentives to act badly and destabilizing the equilibrium (as with witness protection programs used to break cycles of corruption where the costs of defection are otherwise prohibitive. Again, however, a lot will depend on how entrenched is the corruption and what enforcement mechanisms are available to those engaged in corruption. A protection racket which can target those who take the state's side and inflict high costs, with a high symbolic value, *pour encourage les autres,* will seriously weaken the attractiveness of the state's offer.

Although focusing on enhancing victim strategies is a promising line of inquiry, it clearly works best where there are direct, individuated costs rather than indirect, generalized ones. It also works better where those incurring the costs are educated, articulate, and well-resourced, and where there is a strong form of centralized authority able to guarantee the security of those who complain and able to impose penalties on those found engaged in corrupt activity. The more group-based and A-led the corruption is, the less likely is it that any element of the state will have the resources to counter it.

(iv) *Institutional Pluralism:* I have not sought to catalogue the lines of division which may exist between the different actors within the political system, and which may influence the incidence of corruption: politicians, party apparatchiks, civil servants, local state officials, members of quangos, the judiciary, police, armed forces and so on. Clearly, it matters that we get clear where the problems are most acute in any particular state, since these will help indicate what resources might be left within the state to tackle them. However, in addition to these resources internal to the political system, political and economic transition also set up (albeit often very weakly) the potential for a context of institutional pluralism within the broader society. In the West governments are subject to scrutiny from a range of sources in civil society, such as universities, research organizations, newspapers, think-tanks, ICACs, NCCLs, advice agencies and so on. This panoply of institutions provides a context which militates against systematic forms of A- and C-led corruption (although it certainly cannot guarantee its absence—nor can it ensure the absence of more individualized forms of corruption). They are also a way of further limiting the state's freedom of action, by articulating countervailing interests, even as they offer the prospect of increasing its authority insofar as they serve to confirm its legitimacy. They are, then, an essential component of vertical integration, but they do not emerge of their own accord, and there are difficulties in the state playing a founding role in them or in continuing to finance and protect them (least compromising their independence).

This is one reason for valuing the role which international agencies can play—in establishing such agencies, funding them, and publicizing their activities. However, those agencies must themselves recognize that their success will depend on the sensitivity which their offices demonstrate towards the local conditions and practices of the states in which they act. One area in which Western agencies have often shown a lack of sensitivity is in their willingness to supply a lexicon of corruption to political forces in transition states which, rather than assisting in the process of cleaning up government, has simultaneously armed political groups with a resource that they have no incentive to use responsibly and has further weakened the legitimacy of these states both domestically and in the international community. On both fronts, this weakened status exacerbates the problem of tackling corruption, because it reduces the legitimacy and autonomy of the state, and increases everybody's incentives to adopt a strategy which is maximally self-protecting—thereby reducing the resources with which to tackle the problem while increasing its size. Moreover, a great deal of Western economic advice is directed to opening up the often grossly inefficient industries of Central and Eastern Europe to the full force of market competition, as if the market will provide, by its own logic, a sound basis for liberal democracy. Yet, in the vast majority of cases industries will compete very poorly with Western economies, with the result that these countries face a significant period of debt, falling living standards and economic hardship. Those conditions, however, are hardly conducive to the creation of clean politics and administration or to the establishment of a independent judiciary able impartially to oversee the implementation and enforcement of the legal framework for the market and civil society.

Dilemmas of Corruption Control*

James B. Jacobs

There are surely lessons to be learned from the massive investment the United States has made in fighting corruption, especially since the Watergate scandal in the early 1970s. Because of its resources and politico-legal capacity to implement new laws and policies, the U.S. can be thought of as a laboratory for policy experimentation in anticorruption control. Nevertheless, as we shall see, since there has been hardly any evaluation of the *U.S. anticorruption project*, it is difficult to reach confident conclusions about what works and does not.

Let me summarize the argument at the outset. The Watergate scandal involving President Richard Nixon stimulated an outpouring of outrage about governmental corruption. Corruption became a more salient political issue, so that political opponents sought to define each other as, in one way or another, corrupt, while they claimed to be above reproach in every respect. Our normative expectations for official conduct increased dramatically and perhaps unrealistically. Federal, state and local governments invested heavily in diverse anticorruption controls.

One consequence has been a much more scandal-sensitive politics, whose implications for American democracy are not clear. Another consequence, and the one highlighted in Frank Anechiarico's and my book, *The Pursuit of Absolute Integrity*, is that government has become less effective and less efficient because many anticorruption controls tend to reinforce the pathologies of bureaucracy. What we have tried to show is that corruption controls entail costs, and that, in some cases, these costs outweigh any benefits as measured by reduced corruption. The challenge, of course, is to find the optimal type and amount of corruption controls; as we shall see, this is no easy task.

The Always-Expanding Definition of Corruption

Ironically, we are the victims of our own moral crusade. Our ambitions in the area of corruption control are constantly increasing. Over the

---

* This essay draws heavily on the research and ideas developed in F. Anechiarico and J. B. Jacobs, *The Pursuit of Absolute Integrity: How Corruption Control Makes Government Ineffective* (Chicago: University of Chicago Press, 1996). The book also contains an extensive bibliography on the U.S. scholarly literature on corruption and corruption control.

course of the last half century and especially since the "Watergate" scandal, the concept and definition of corruption has steadily expanded. (Undoubtedly, this also has something to do with the 1960s protests against authority and the traditional style of politics.) More types of officials' public and private conduct are labeled corrupt. There are more corruption offenses on the books (e.g. anti-gratuity laws; conflicts of interest laws), and more expansive interpretations of traditional corruption-type crimes (e.g. punishing violation of existential right to honest government under mail fraud statute). The campaign finance laws, in effect, have defined America's traditional electoral politics as corrupt and have turned every political candidate into a potential criminal. In the field of corruption, law and especially criminal law, is seeking to change mores rather than reinforce them. There is a widening gap between law and reality.

Not only is the official behavior of government officials under scrutiny, but so is their private, even sexual, behavior. Evidence of Senator Gary Hart's adultery, drove him out of the 1982 presidential election. President Clinton's relationship with Monica Lewinsky brought him to the brink of impeachment. Whether Governor George W. Bush experimented with illicit drugs a quarter of a century ago is a constant issue in the 2000 Presidential campaign. American politicians and top administrative officials must now be holier than Caesar's wife—*over the course of their entire lives* there ought not to be drug use, adultery, cheating or questionable financial dealing. Given such unrealistic expectations of public and private conduct, it is fairly easy to expose public officials as flawed, tainted, and corrupt.

All sorts of corruption controls have become popular since Watergate. In the area of public contracting we have widespread "reform" in the guise of the lowest responsible bidder system. In the personnel sphere there are laws and rules outlawing patronage appointments (i.e. appointing people to public position on the basis of personal or political ties), and promoting whistle blowing (reporting the wrongdoing of colleagues and superiors). In the field of administration complex accounting procedures, comprehensive audits, and inspectors general have been instituted. Even law enforcement agencies have been mobilized, especially federal, for the investigation and prosecution of state and local public officials.

The Disadvantages of Corruption Politics

It is generally recognized that a corrupt political system leads to a dispirited and alienated citizenry and to all sorts of inefficiencies and distortions in government operations and services. However, a political system that is hypersensitive to corruption can produce the same results. We often hear that "all politicians are corrupt" or that "the system of campaign donations makes the whole political system corrupt." The consequence may be for a large percentage of the citizenry to disaffect from political life and to view the government as illegitimate. This is a problem even in stable democracies such as the United States, where voter turnout is very low and suspicion of government increases. It becomes harder to recruit capable people into government service because government service is not respected and some prospective appointees fear unfairly becoming the targets of special prosecutors and Congressional inquiries. Weak support for government means insufficient support for competitive government salaries; again, recruitment and retention suffers. Under such conditions it is hard for the government to mobilize support for important social initiatives.

Countries going through a political transition from dictatorship to democracy may be especially vulnerable to too much corruption and too much anticorruption ideology. Where "getting ahead" has long been seen as suspect, successful people may immediately be suspected of being corrupt. If a large segment of the population defines the governors and the government as corrupt and illegitimate, they may be receptive to demagogues and extremists. There is also the danger that corruption becomes an excuse for foreign governments and banks not to invest in the developing nation and an excuse for putting off or canceling much needed political and economic steps. The point is that an expansive definition of corruption, that leads to labeling of many or most government officials and government programs as corrupt, may well undermine democracy while having little impact on reducing hard-core corruption.

Obviously, the Watergate investigations weakened the U.S. government severely, at least at the time. Indeed, for many months the Nixon administration could hardly act at all. There was certainly no possibility of implementing legislative or foreign policy initiatives. Perhaps it could be argued that the Watergate scandal in the long run strengthened democracy and the national government, but did it? Or did it lead to scandal "pay-back" politics, whereby every future president's life, in and out of office, would be scrutinized for moral flaws which, when found, would undermine the legit-imacy of his administration? Clearly the long investigation into possible corruption by President Clinton in the so-called Whitewater development weakened his presidency, and the exposure of sexual immorality almost destroyed it. For many months the U.S. government was paralyzed.

The Costs of the Anticorruption Project

Corruption is not just a crime problem, it is a political and public admin-istration problem. A corruption scandal can trigger a political and govern-mental crisis. It can topple governments even in stable democratic coun-tries. Good government groups, the media, and the political opposition demand that governmental units do all in their power to prevent corrup-tion, and they hold high officials responsible for corruption that occurs on their watch. At the height of our intolerance for corruption any amount of corruption is considered unacceptable, a blight on the record of the admin-istration, the agency, and managers up and down the chain of command. Lately "zero tolerance" has become a slogan associated with "quality of life" policing in NYC and elsewhere. It indicates increased attention to low-level offenses that might have escaped much, if any, attention before. However, no one really expects that disorderly street behavior will be reduced to zero. No one will hold the police department responsible if some instances of disorderly street behavior occur; nor will the police department go through a public hand wringing and catharsis if it appears that street prostitution, public drunkenness or graffiti still take place. To take another example, the police department and the department of trans-portation may launch a multi-faceted campaign to "stop drunk-driving," but they will not be excoriated when it turns out that some drunk-driving continues or even if drunk driving remains unaffected by the campaign. More likely it will be the drunk drivers who are vilified for their anti-social personalities and weakness for drink.

Compared with other crime-control initiatives, anticorruption control is far more extravagant in its public goals. Publicly, at least, the chief executive has to be committed to zero tolerance. It is not enough to prom-ise to punish corruption when it comes to light; it is necessary to demon-strate that precuations have been taken and strategies adopted to prevent any corruption from occurring. We are ideologically committed to corruption-free government; any amount of corruption, even its appearance is unacceptable. Policymakers have to promise far more than can be delivered. They thereby set themselves up for powerful criticism and cynicism if any corruption comes to light on their watch. Ironically, greater commitment to preventing and punishing corruption has not been accompanied by greater public confidence in government integrity. To the contrary, the expansion of the concept of corruption, greater sensitivity to ethics in government, more hearings, investigations and prosecutions have been accompanied by declining public confidence in the integrity of governmental officials.

Because the political costs of corruption can be so high, there is a great deal of attention paid to prevention or at least to the appearance of prevention. Indeed, when it comes to corruption control, the ratio of resources spent on prevention to the resources spent on punishment is probably higher than for other crimes. Thus, unlike most other crimes, government is expected to change the way it does business in order to prevent corruption. Hence, the emergence of an entire panoply of prevention strategies—ranging from procurement and contracting regimes to the inspector-general's movement, to accounting systems and corruption vulnerability audits. Preventing corruption can become an end in itself so that a corruption-free administration is a successful administration, independent from whether important socio-economic and diplomatic problems have been addressed.

It is the thesis of Frank Anechiarico's and my book that the structure and operation of government at the federal, state and local levels can be significantly accounted for by layers of anticorruption reforms that have usually been put in place after corruption scandals. We refer to such staples of government and governing as civil service, procurement and contracting rules, conflict of interest codes and financial disclosure rules, inspector-general systems, accounting and auditing programs, and whistleblower protections, and to strategies such as agency reorganizations, dividing authority, structuring multiple oversights, frequently moving personnel around and undercover integrity testing.

The problem is that these administrative anticorruption strategies all entail costs varying, of course, on how they are implemented. The important point is to question the assumption that every administrative "reform" undertaken in the name of attacking corruption, also serves the purpose of more effective and efficient government. This is simply not true.

Consider the civil service. It was originally seen as a remedy for nepotism and the sale of office. Those who promoted civil service also considered it compatible with, if not a requirement for, governmental efficiency. They did not recognize any trade-offs between corruption control and efficiency. Over the years civil service has become a general anticorruption palliative. If some civil service protection was good, more was better. Non-civil service appointments came to be seen as corrupt, and civil service protection has been extended beyond hiring decisions to promotions and demotions.

Only recently have the dysfunctions of civil service been taken seriously. In many governmental units agency heads cannot recruit, promote or demote their subordinates, at least not easily. They lack both punishments and rewards to motivate the men and women who work for them. Excellent performance cannot be rewarded. Mediocre or even unsatisfactory performance cannot be penalized. This means inefficiency and even paralysis.

To take another example, consider government contracting. The lowest responsible bidding (LRB) system is meant to prevent government officials from awarding contracts on the basis of favoritism, including personal financial interests. Any other procurement system is considered suspect and potentially corrupt, but the consequence of a slavish adherence to the LRB system has produced a procurement system that neither saves money nor prevents fraud. The whole process is often tied up in incredibly time-consuming procedures. Under a strict version of the LRB system, in awarding a contract the government procurer cannot take account of the contractor's past performance on public or private contracts; the only question is whether the contractor's bid is lowest. It does not matter that the contractor did an excellent job in the past; no favoritism can be shown him. True, a hideous previous performance may be enough to label the contractor "non-responsible," but it takes fortitude to trigger the procedures that might produce such a determination. At a minimum it takes a great deal of time and effort to have a bidder disqualified. The LRB system puts government agencies at arm's length from their contractors. The government agency does not enjoy a long-term relationship of confidence with its contractors, as is the case with many private sector companies who develop relationships of trust and confidence with their contractors. Such relationships would be considered suspect and potentially corrupt in the public sector.

Unfortunately, the LRB system has stimulated a different kind of corruption. At least in NYC, contractors tend to bid low and then increase the value of the contract by manipulating change orders, sometimes fraudulently, from harried government-contract managers. The final cost of the contract may amount to several times the bid price. Professor Anechiarico and I found that many NYC government officials suspected all private contractors who bid on government contracts to be potential criminals. Obviously, such a situation undermines effective and responsive government.

Whistleblower protections, which became popular after the Watergate scandal, also illustrate how the anticorruption project imposes costs on public administration. Perhaps the encouragement provided to whistle-blowers by protecting them from negative personnel actions stimulates reporting of agency corruption and thereby deters such corruption, but this is only a perhaps. I know of no evidence. However, a proper evalua-tion of whistle-blowing reforms would have to consider possible costs to public administration. For one thing, some whistleblower protection laws almost presume that government managers will not handle corruption charges properly and, worse, will punish employees who make such charges. This certainly does not enhance the status of public managers or their morale. For another thing, encouraging whistle blowing provides a weapon for disgruntled and poorly performing employees to use against their supervisors. An employee with a grudge against a supervisor or an apprehension of being fired may file a bogus corruption charge and there-by trigger whistleblower protections for himself. Once recognized as a whistleblower, an employee is untouchable. He or she may remain on the job for months and even years while the case is being investigated. His or her continued presence in an agency whose director wished to fire him or her illustrates the impotence of the agency head. Should the outside investigators conclude that a negative personnel action against a whistle-blower was improper and must be reversed, the authority of the govern-ment manager may be seriously undermined.

Trade-off: The Reduction of Corruption

Anticorruption controls can and do have costs for public administration. The question that must be asked is whether those costs are worth bearing. Is it not reasonable to pay a price to reduce corruption? Obviously, the answer is "yes." It is worth some amount of increased inefficiency to reduce some amount of corruption. The question we now must turn to is is how much corruption is reduced by various corruption controls?

Unfortunately, there is an insuperable obstacle to answering this question: we do not know whether a particular anticorruption strategy, or spate of strategies, is "working." Unlike almost all other crimes, we have no data whatsoever on the official corruption rate. How much corruption is there? Is the rate rising or falling? Is there more corruption now than in previous decades? Is there more corruption in one city than in another, in one department than in another? Has corruption decreased after implementation of a set of managerial reforms? Corruption cannot be estimated through the Uniform Crime Reports, based on crimes reported to the police, nor through the National Victim Survey, based upon interviews with a national sample of individuals. It is hard to think of any other crime that so lacks an indicator of prevalence. For example, some estimate of the level of drug trafficking can be obtained by surveys of high-school students and others, drug testing of arrestees, drug seizures by customs officials and police, and changes in retail price. There are no similar or comparable indices of corruption.

Very little thought has been given to how to measure corruption or how to construct a construction rate. For example, should corruption be measured by the percentage of officials who have engaged in any corrupt act a year, decade, or over their careers? Would a better measure be the percentage of official transactions involving corruption? Or the amount of money involved in corrupt events as a proportion of an individual's, agency's or governmental unit's total budget?

Not only do the conceptual and practical problems inherent in assessing the amount of corruption seem insuperable, politicians and government officials have strong disincentives to undertake honest evaluation. The ideal position for an agency, official operation in a country or jurisdiction where there is a great deal of concern about corruption is to have all sorts of anticorruption strategies in place and to have no instances of corruption revealed. Revelations of corruption may subject the administrator to criticism for tolerating corruption. The agency might be engulfed for weeks or months in a scandal, thereby jeopardizing the agency's provision of goods or services. Whether the official could have prevented it or not, he or she may become the scapegoat, i.e., held responsible for the scandal and fired (even prosecuted) to assuage media criticism and public anger.

The point is that we should not assume that administrative prevention strategies, instituted in the name of corruption control, actually limit or reduce corruption. Professor Anechiarico and I have shown that it is precisely those New York City agencies with the most anticorruption controls that have the most corruption scandals. Of course, this does not mean that corruption controls cause corruption, or that corruption controls have no effect on corruption. Since we do not know the underlying corruption no such conclusion can be drawn. Still, our study should serve to caution scholars and policy analysts against drawing the conclusion that highly visible and touted corruption controls mean that there is less corruption.

Optimal Corruption Control

As odd as it may at first sound, there must be an *optimal amount of corruption*, i.e., an amount such that the costs of any further reduction would outweigh the benefits. This truism reminds us that the goal of public administration cannot be the total elimination of corruption. Instead, the goal must be to identify: 1) the most costly types of corruption; 2) the most cost-effective anticorruption strategies.

Not all corruption is equally damaging, and various types of corruption are damaging in different ways. Some corrupt acts just impose financial costs, while others undermine democratic institutions. I would suggest that judicial corruption (the sale and purchase of justice) is extremely deleterious for a democracy because it fundamentally undermines the rule of law. Likewise, election fraud directly undermines the legitimacy of the political regime. Certain types of conflict of interest and patronage may be at the other end of the continuum. Government service may still be well provided, even if it is done so by firms and individuals with ties to the party and people in power. It also seems likely that corruption by high-level officials who are closely associated with the functioning and therefore the legitimacy of the state is far more deleterious than corruption by low-level functionaries. In any event, we need to generate and test, as best we can, hypotheses such as these.

Not all corruption controls are equally efficacious in preventing corruption, nor equal in their impacts on bureaucracy and public administration. The problem is that, even in the United States, we do not know, for example, to what extent certain personnel assignment strategies (e.g. frequent rotation of personnel through assignments), accounting procedures, contracting rules, and whistleblower protections have succeeded or failed in preventing corruption.

We have a better chance of finding out which corruption controls take the largest toll on efficiency. I would hypothesize that accounting procedures and auditing would likely have the most potential for promoting both governmental efficiency and corruption control. It is hard to imagine that an agency could run efficiently without having in place financial controls that allow officials to determine how much is being spent, by whom and for what. Of course, "accounting and auditing" are not self-defining terms. In some agencies that Professor Anechiarico and I studied, accounting and auditing aimed at corruption control rather than at informed management had become burdensome and costly for administrators.

Conclusion

For generations we have implemented anticorruption strategies without any effort or even hope of determining whether the strategies worked. Perhaps the whole point of the exercise is to assuage public resentment, to provide political cover, and to demonstrate that public officials have proper values. If no further scandal occurs in the short term, the political elite implementing the reforms can take credit. If another scandal occurs, the political elite can at least claim that previous anticorruption recommendations had been followed and that everything possible was done to prevent a recurrence.

Every major corruption scandal has produced new anticorruption mechanisms and procedures. At the time, these "reforms" are devised and implemented to satisfy the political demands of scandal politics, without much, if any, regard for their impact upon public administration. Wide-ranging rules on conflict of interest, financial disclosure, "revolving door-ism" are good examples. They may provide political cover, but at the cost of discouraging good people from entering or remaining in government. In certain circumstances we end up with both a corruption problem and a corruption-control problem.

This essay is not a brief for doing nothing about corruption. It is a brief for taking corruption control very seriously, indeed for treating corruption control as a science. At present there is no "off-the-shelf" package of corruption controls that, simply by being sprinkled around a corrupt agency, can make corruption disappear while improving the quality of government services. Practically all corruption controls involve costs and trade-offs. Therefore, they should carry the label "use with caution."

The Bad, the Worse and the Worst: Guesstimating the Level of Corruption

Endre Sík

The proposition of this paper is simple. I suggest as an axiom that it is impossible to measure the level of corruption. Secondly, as far as the existing guesstimation methods and estimation approaches are concerned, there are only bad and worse solutions, and, among the latter, there is one that deserves a special status for being especially bad.

The structure of the paper is as follows: In the first part I classify the basic approaches of the corruption guesstimation techniques.[64] In the second, I illustrate the major types of available guesstimation methods using the most recent results of corruption research in postcommunist countries. In the last part of the essay I argue against a corruption-perception method and for a corruption-proxy method, and outline some arguments why I consider the corruption-perception index (CPI) to be the worst among the existing corruption-perception techniques.

A Possible Classification of the Corruption Guesstimation Methods

The starting axiom of the paper is the assumption that it is impossible to measure the level of corruption. Since there is a general consensus among the scholars in the "measure-the-corruption" business that it is absolutely impossible to measure the level of corruption, I do not attempt to prove this assumption. I only refer to the most obvious and most often repeated reasons, i.e., that there is no commonly accepted definition of corruption and that, as a consequence of the illegal nature of the phenomenon, a certain (unknown and substantial) amount of corruption unavoidably remains invisible. As a result, the actual aim of the following approaches is not to measure the level of corruption, but, with a more proper and humble intention, to find a second-best solution to guesstimate it.

There are two major types of guesstimation methods: the corruption-perception and the corruption-proxy methods. The devoted and numerous followers of the first method claim that there is a positive and strong association between the level of corruption and its perception. The less visible and much less influential followers of the corruption-proxy approach assume that one can reliably measure certain (less hidden) forms of corruption, and that the volume of this "tangible" subsample positively and strongly correlates with the general level of corruption.

In my view, both types of corruption guesstimation rely on proper assumptions. The basic assumption of the corruption-perception method is that people at large (or any of their properly selected sub-sample) can be a reliable source of the level of corruption. The more extensive the corruption, the more ordinary people or experts experience it and are ready and able to express their relevant experiences. As to the corruption-proxy method, it makes sense to assume that the measured part of an unknown volume of corruption is larger (though not necessarily in proportion) in cases when the volume of corruption in general is larger. However, in the third part of the paper I will argue that comparing the two basic approaches, there are good reasons to assume that the corruption-proxy method gives a better guesstimate than the corruption-perception method.

Within the two main types of corruption-guesstimation methods there are major differences in the target population and the research technique (Table 1).

Table 1. Types of Corruption-Guesstimating Methods

	CORRUPTION PERCEPTION		CORRUPTION PROXY	
	INDIRECT	DIRECT	GENERAL	SPECIFIC
General public	Behavioral consistency	Common sense perception	Proxy of the practice in general	Proxy of the practice in particular
Target group	x	Perception of practice		

The target population can be the general public or special social groups of which the researcher assumes that they have special knowledge about the level of corruption, being targets of certain corruptive transactions. The advantage of using the general public is that the estimation will be based on a large and representative sample of the population. The disadvantage is that a certain proportion of the general public (size unknown), having no experience whatsoever with corruption, might be totally ignorant toward corruption and still be asked about their perception. In such cases the result of the perception-based assumption will be a pure artifact of corruption-related myths and media influence. While using corruption target groups as the source of corruption perception, the advantage and disadvantage are the opposite. Such an approach will result in having maximum (though not necessarily honestly expressed) information and minimum and non-representative coverage (since the selection of the target group intentionally focused on a corruption-prone subsample of the general public).

The technique of the corruption-perception method can be indirect or direct. The former uses various substitutes for the perception of corruption, the latter translates corruption into concrete corruptive actions. For example, the level of trust toward state authorities of the general public can be a substitute for corruption perception. We assume in this case that the ordinary citizens behave coherently; therefore, if the level of distrust of the general public toward state authorities is high, the level of corruption might be high as well. This type of corruption-perception research can, therefore, be called a method based on behavioral consistency.

In the case of the direct corruption-perception method we assume that the respondent is able and ready to perceive properly the level of corruption using his/her own experience and the relevant information. In the case of the general public such a method can be called common-sense perception since we assume that they (though having only a vague idea of what corruption is and often having not much personal experience with it) can perceive the level of corruption of the society. In the case of the corruption targets this approach assumes that, due to their own everyday practice, they have ample information about the nature and level of corruption, and that they, therefore, perceive properly the level of corruption around them. This method can be termed the perception of the practice.

The corruption-proxy methods can be based on general or specific proxies. The only difference between the two methods is that in the former the research focuses on corruption in general, while in the latter attempts are made at classifying certain specific situations and/or transactions in which the level of corruption is estimated.

The Level of Corruption in Contemporary Postcommunist Countries

To illustrate the various types of corruption-guesstimation methods I selected recent research to guesstimate the level of corruption in post-communist countries.

Behavioral Consistency

There are numerous examples of this type of indirect corruption-perception research. In the following I selected three different elements of the behavior which can be regarded as proper indirect substitutes for corruption perception.

The first corruption-related element of behavior is the anti-state ethos. According to Tóth (1999), there is a fairly high level of anti-state attitude in contemporary Hungary:

In 1998 42 percent of a representative sample of Hungarian adults fully, and 46 percent mostly, agree with the item that "If one wants to achieve something in life, he/she will be forced to bend the rules." In 1996, 50 percent of a similar sample agreed with the proposition that "There are situations when we have to follow our own rules, regardless of being illegal."

Both previous examples refer to the widespread presence of an ethos allowing instrumental deviations from the state-imposed legal rules—a most fertile soil for corruptive behavior.

The New Russia Barometer (Rose, 1998/a) contains several indirect corruption perceptions related to the incidence of using "connections":

Sixteen percent of the sample said "a definite yes," another 25 percent responded with "it usually helps" to the question "Would you say that to get a house or flat in this neighborhood, most people have to have connections?"

Forty-two percent accepted "definitely," while 50 percent agreed "somewhat" with the idea that "people who are now making a lot of money" "use connections" and 13 to 41 percent had the same opinion on"having foreign connections."

In this case it is assumed that a network-oriented culture is more prone to corruption because

(A) the existing networks offer a low-cost infrastructure to run corruptive transactions efficiently (Sík, 1994/a,b, Czakó-Sík, 1988, Bíró, 1998);

(B) and, under such conditions, the differentiation between favor and bribing, and between a reciprocal gift relationship and corruption is blurred, making both a conveniently flexible moral standard possible and policing very difficult.

Another indirect corruption-perception issue is the level of trust in the institutional setting into which ordinary citizens are embedded:

Twenty-four percent agree "definitely," while 49 percent "somewhat" with the idea a writer once produced: "The harshness of Russian laws is softened by their non-enforcement. Do you think it is true?"

The proportion of those who do *not* trust the institutions governing citizens' everyday life is enormous. For example, 50 percent did not trust the courts. The same applies to the police (60 percent), the local government (61 percent), the Duma (70 percent), the trade unions (70 percent), the private enterprises (72 percent), the record-holders of the political parties (81 percent) as well as the privatization investment funds (85 percent).

The assumption behind trust-related corruption-perception proxies is that the lack of trust in law and law-enforcement reduces the chances of being caught and increases the pressure to corrupt. In consequence, the lower are these proxies, the higher should the corruption perception be. As to the lack of trust, this can be interpreted as an indirect sign of rampant corruption in organizations with which citizens have everyday contact. Moreover, if it is not the corruptive behavior of these organizations which causes the lack of trust, it is likely that such an environment increases the readiness of the ordinary citizen to set up corruptive networks as a coping solution.

Common-Sense Perception

The first version of the direct perception method can be called the situation-specific corruption-perception technique. In this case the researcher assumes that the general public cannot answer corruption perception questions in general terms. The underlying hypothesis in this case is that corruption does not exist in general in a certain society, but can be properly perceived (and therefore recalled in an interview situation) in situation-specific contexts.

The New Russia Barometer (Rose, 1998/a) contains several direct questions to estimate the level of corruption in various situations.

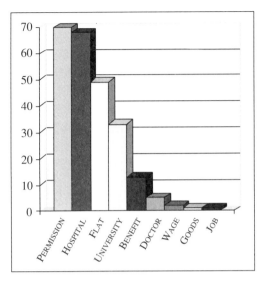

Figure 1. The Level of Situation-Specific[65] Corruption Perception in Russia, 1998
Source: The author's graph from Rose, 1998/a

Figure 1 shows that there are certain situations perceived as "over-whelmingly corrupt," which is very likely close to reality. These are typically situations in which someone wants something valuable and undeserved. The next example (Figure 2) is a comparative version of the previous situation-specific technique.

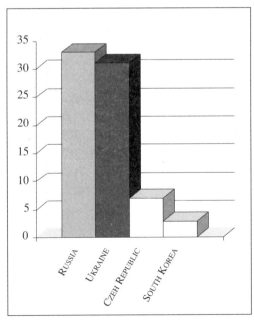

Figure 2. Ratio of Public Acceptance of Bribery Enabling Undergraduate Students to Enter University without Good Enough Grades (Percent)
Source: Rose and Haerpfer, 1998, p. 25.

Another version of the common-sense perception approach is when the focus is on specific transactions within a corruption-prone situation. The most recent example of this rare approach is gratuity (tip-like, illegal payment for special treatment in the health sector) research (Bognár–Gál, 1999). The authors asked the population whether they consider it appropriate to give a gratuity to the physicians or nurses. They broke down this corruption-prone situation into typical transactions (Figure 3)

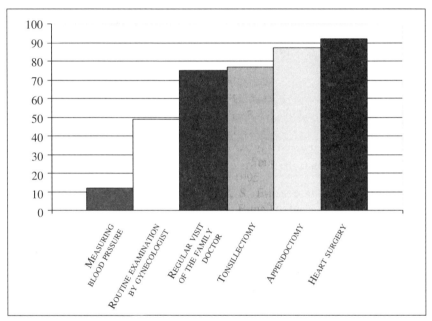

Figure 3. The Ratio of Those Considering a Gratuity as Customary for Various Types of Health Services (Percent)
Source: Author's drawing, the examples were selected from Table 6 (Bognár–Gál, 1999).

The "generalist" version of the common-sense method assumes that there is a general corruption phenomenon which public opinion is able to perceive. Furthermore, this version of the direct corruption-perception technique also assumes that without any detailed definition there is a general "feeling" for the level of corruption and this can be reliably captured by an interview.

The first "generalist" common-sense example is again from the New Russia Barometer (Rose, 1998/b). Thirty-six percent of the respondents answered that "almost every one is corrupt" and 53 percent replied that "most officials are involved" to the question "How widespread do you think bribe-taking and corruption is in the national government in Moscow?" As to the regional equivalent of state authority, at city (oblast) level the respondents said that 18 and 55 percent of officials are corrupt "without exception" or "mostly."

The questions of a diachronic version of the "generalist" common-sense method are the following (both at national and city level): "By comparison with Soviet times, would you say that the level of bribe taking and corruption in Moscow (in this city) has . . .?" The answer was given on a five-digit scale from "increased a lot" to "decreased a lot." At national level, 52 and 21 percent of the respondents, at city level, 36 and 30 percent, selected the "increased a lot" and the "increased a little" alternatives.

This diachronic form of the "generalist" common-sense method was also used in comparative research.

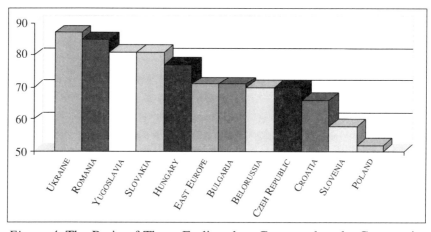

Figure 4. The Ratio of Those Feeling that, Compared to the Communist Period, Bribery and Corruption are More Widespread Nowadays (Percent) *Source*: Rose-Haerpfer, 1993, pp. 32–33.

Perception of Practice

The most likely potential targets of corruption are either the personnel of state authorities (at all levels but mostly at the receiving end of the transactions) or business people (mostly in at least medium-size firms and at the giving end of the transactions).

Vásárhelyi (1998, 1999) analyzes the perception of their fellows among high-ranking civil servants (in ministries, courts, police, public administration, and inspector organizations). Having a job of this kind makes one an expert-target of corruption since (being in a position to give or deny permission, begin or stop investigations, change the rules of the game, etc.) they have an overview of the practice of their subordinates and of the practice of their fellow-big shots.

The author compared the perception of practice of the expert-target group to the common-sense perception of the general public in certain corruption-prone situations (Figure 5).

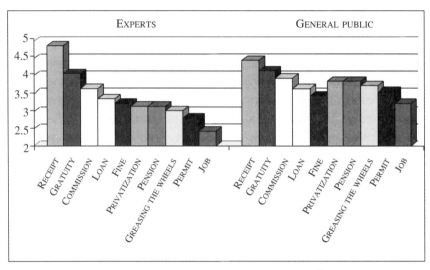

Figure 5. Corruption Perception in Specific Situations[66] by High-Ranking Civil Servants and the General Public (*Scores from 5: "very frequently," to 1: "never"*)
Source: Author's drawing based on Table 3 in Vásárhelyi, 1999.

The general public (i.e., common sense) perceives higher level of corruption in most situations than the civil servants (i.e., perception of practice) do.

Another example of the perception of practice approach is that part of gratuity research (Bognár–Gál, 1999) where the corruption-prone target group, the physicians, were interviewed. A representative sample of physicians was asked to estimate the proportion of patients giving a gratuity in the most corruption-prone situations (Figure 6).

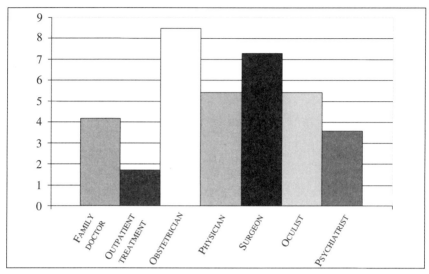

Figure 6. The Likelihood that Patients Would Give a Gratuity to Health
Professionals by Type of Transaction (on a Scale of 0 to 10)
Source: Author's drawing from Table 7 (Bognár–Gál, 1999).

The most widely used and most influential of all corruption perception
methods is the Corruption Perception Index (CPI) produced by
Transparency International. This is a "poll of polls" drawing upon
numerous distinct surveys of experts (and, from time to time, of general
public surveys) on the extent of corruption. The official press release of
the CPI states that this is ". . . the most comprehensive index of perceptions of corruption ever published by the global anticorruption organisa-
tion" (TI Press . . ., 1998).

The standard procedure of constructing the annual CPI (the first was
published in 1995) is to gather together as many (but not less than three[67])
expert interviews (and, occasionally, general public surveys) and, after
converting them into a similar format, compute their average and standard deviation. The annual CPI is a mix of the most recent expert inter-
view-based international evaluations and some sources from the previous
(maximum three) years. The experts who judge the level of corruption in
a respective country are mostly foreign businessmen or international risk
analysts.

The following quotations illustrate the role TI assumes for itself and
for the CPI, and according to all sources, not unsuccessfully.

"The 1998 CPI is a wake-up call to political leaders and to the public at large to confront the abundant corruption that pervades so many countries . . . We hope the publication of the CPI will be an incentive to governments to confront the corruption in their countries. The poor scores received by many countries in the new index illustrate just how serious the global cancer of corruption really is. This has to change . . . directly confronting corruption must be a top priority for most national governments and the international organizations concerned with development, economic growth and human progress . . . Scandalously, and sadly, there are about 50 countries that do not even achieve a score of 5 (half of the maximum E.S.) . . . The CPI scores, with their shocking portrayal of so many countries perceived to be home to rampant corruption, will spur TI to be even more aggressive in mobilizing initiatives to counter corruption world-wide . . . governments that have sought to brush this debate aside can no longer do so, as the whole world sees how their nations rank" (excerpts from the speeches of Peter Eigen and Frankl Vogl, the chairman and vice-chairman of TI, TI Press . . ., 1998).

"... In the last year many leading international organizations, such as the UN the World Bank, the IMF, the Council of Europe, the EU, the OECD, the Organization of American States and the Global Coalition for Africa have articulated anticorruption policies, often with TI involvement. The annual CPI sensitizes public opinion world-wide to the corruption issue, influences the policies of major aid agencies and is a factor in the foreign investment decisions of multinational corporations." (TI Press ..., 1998).

Proxy of the Practice in General

Figure 7 gives an estimate of the spread of corruption in postcommunist societies using a general definition of corruption. There is no effort to define corruption, the respondent is assumed to give a rough estimate about the occurrence of bribery (without any definition or situation-specific illustration) in one year.

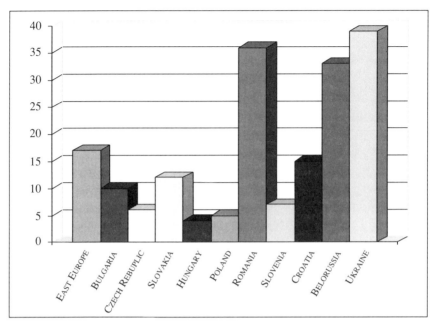

Figure 7. The Ratio of Households with at Least One Member Who in
the Past Year Bribed Someone to Get Things Done (Percent)
Source: The author's computation from Rose-Haerpfer (1993, Appendix
Table 6).

The Proxy of the Practice in Particular

In gratuity research the general public was interviewed about their practices in a particular type of corruption-prone situation, i.e., the frequency
of offering a gratuity to health professionals. On average in one year 26
percent of them claimed to give a gratuity to the family doctor and 15 percent of them to the doctor at the outpatient department.

The practice-oriented nature of this method made the researchers
able to develop a set of questions to describe some characteristics of
the process of gratuity transactions. For example, whether the gratuity
was given before or after the service, (in about 80 percent of the cases
the gratuity was given after the service, i.e., as is the case with standard economic transactions when payment follows the service).

Vásárhelyi (1998) used a direct proxy of practice approach (though with
no time limit and any hint of frequency, and consequently, much too

vaguely to make be useful for estimation) to learn the spread of corruption among potential targets of corruption (high-ranking civil servants). She asked: "Have you been offered a bribe?" Thirty-one percent of those working in the courts, 42 percent of those employed in ministries, 47 percent of the heads of the inspecting offices (tax authorities and financial customs guards), 54 percent of police bosses, and 60 percent of the high-ranking civil servants in the municipalities claimed that they have been bribed.

A more detailed version of the proxy of the practice in a particular expert-target group was the research carried out by TÁRKI in 1995, 1997, and 1998 (Bognár–Gál, 1999). The three surveys covered the major inspector organizations whose main task (or at least one main task) was to monitor, regulate, and inspect the various transactions of the informal economy. The list and major characteristics of these organizations, as well as the number of inspectors covered by the survey in 1998 can be found in the first three columns of Table 2.

Table 2. Basic Characteristics of Inspecting Organizations and Employees

	No. of Cases	Field of Inspection	Job in Budapest (Percent)	University and College Degree (Percent)	No. of Inspections (Monthly Average)	Income* (Monthly, Thousand Forints)
PTSA	107	Parking, street vending, littering	90	5	71	31
HMM	25	Market places, fairs	92	50	20	48
HLI	102	Labor safety and conditions, unemployment benefits, employment regulations	20	74	17	57
GICP	92	Quality of goods, retail practices	13	71	36	56
CANPI	173	Pension regulations	6	15	19	41
HCFG	365	Customs, duties, and trafficking	17	17	14	40
HNPH	187	Economic crime in general	11	85	2	63
TFAO	257	Tax regulations	29	48	42	49
NHIF	252	Sick-pay regulations	7	14	9	40
Total	1510		22	36	22	46

* Measured on a scale. The unit was HUF 10,000, the lowest and highest units being 30,000 and HUF 100,000. The average monthly income was computed with the median of the units.

Acronyms and working terms of the inspecting organizations:

PTSA = Public Territory Supervisory Authority of the Budapest Municipality (from now on street guard);

HMM = Hall and Market Management of the Budapest Municipality (from now on market office);

HLI = Hungarian Labor Inspectorate (from now on labor office);

GICP = General Inspectorate of Consumer Protection (from now on consumer office);

CANPI= Central Administration of National Pension Insurance (from now on pension office);

HCFG = Hungarian Customs and Finance Guard (from now on finance guard);

HNPH = Hungarian National Police Headquarters (from now on economic police);

TFAO = Tax and Financial Audit Office (from now on tax office);

NHIF = National Health Insurance Fund (from now on health office).

The surveys were not representative since, they lack the proper information of the total population of inspectors, so I could not prepare the necessary weightings. Also, a detailed time series analysis was impossible due to the fact that not all organizations were covered by the three surveys. However, due to

- the large number of interviews,
- the fact that that the sample covered the whole country and various social strata of the inspectors,
- and the fact that the average number of inspections was quite large (Table 2),

I assumed the data to be worth analyzing as a rare example of the corruption-proxy method covering a special (never before investigated) group of targets, the more so since this group of officials should be a prime target of corruption. This group is employed by a special subset of Hungarian state authorities, i.e., by those, who (in principle) have a major role in controlling and monitoring a profitable and suspicious, in consequence risk-worthy and hidden, part of the economy. A common characteristic of their occupation is that they have the power over adventurous, risk-taking petty entrepreneurs and wageworkers, willing (and forced) to be involved in unlawful or law-evading activities. The task of the inspectors is to discover and punish the transactions of these informal economy actors. Obviously such a situation makes them the prime target of corruption since their opponents are interested in minimizing the risk of being caught and, in case of getting caught, they are interested in minimizing the volume of punishment. Finally, most of the respondents are field workers, i.e., inspectors working in the frontline, dealing with the offenders and potential offenders directly. This, on the one hand, increases their likelihood for accepting corruption since their monitoring, they being mobile and dealing with a large amount of cases every day, is rather difficult. On the other hand, being ordinary employees, their income is rather low (see the last column in Table 2).

The three proxies I developed to measure the level of corruption were as follows:

- In the past month how many times have you been offered a bribe?
- In the past month how many times have you been offered a gift?
- In the past month how many times have you been threatened?

The first proxy is the most straightforward one and it is therefore the one inspectors would most likely not report intentionally. Therefore I assume that this one offers the lowest estimate among the three proxies. The second proxy offers the inspector a milder version of corruption since I assumed that the low-value presents offered in kind could be reported more easily. The third proxy is an alternative behavior of corruption. In such cases the offender, instead of bribing, tries to fight the inspector.

The first row in Table 3 shows the average monthly amount of the three corruption proxies. Since the practice-oriented nature of the research made it possible, I analyzed the socio-economic characteristics of the process of corruption, i.e. what socio-economic factors increase the probability of corruption. Table 3 contains the averages of the three proxies by the major socio-demographic characteristics of the inspector (those interested in the result of the multivariate analysis of the causes of corruption, see Sík, 2000).

Table 3. Three Corruption Proxies by the Socio-Demographic Characteristics of Inspectors, 1998 (Monthly Average)*

	NO. OF CORRUPTION OFFERS	NO. OF GIFT OFFERS	NO. OF THREATS TOTAL
TOTAL	0.8	0.9	2.0
ORGANIZATION			
STREET GUARD	5.3	3.5	13.5
MARKET OFFICE	(1.8)	(3.7)	(2.7)
LABOR OFFICE	0.6	1.4	0.8
CONSUMER OFFICE	0.2	0.9	1.0
PENSION OFFICE	0.2	0.4	0.2
TAX OFFICE	0.2	0.2	1.4
HEALTH OFFICE	0.1	0.2	0.8
FINANCE GUARD	0.8	1.2	1.2
EDUCATION			
High school	0.9	1.0	2.3
University or college	0.4	0.9	1.5
Income (monthly, HUF)			
Below 30 000	2.3	1.5	6.2
31–40 000	0.9	1.2	1.8
41–50 000	0.3	0.7	1.7
51–60 000	0.3	0.7	0.7
61–70 000	0.6	0.6	1.1
REGION			
South–West	0.3	0.3	0.8
North–West	0.1	0.5	0.7
Central Hungary	0.9	1.4	1.2
Budapest	2.0	1.9	5.4
North	0.2	0.5	0.9
North–East	1.0	1.1	1.0
South–East	0.2	0.5	1.2
POPULARITY **			
None	0.7	0.7	3.2
Small	0.8	0.9	2.4
Medium	1.0	1.1	1.5
Rather strong	0.3	1.1	0.7
Strong	(0.4)	(0.1)	(2.0)

* N = 1237 (those who answered, economic police excluded), parentheses indicate small number of cases (below 50 cases).

** The level of popularity of the inspector's activity in the general public assessed by the respondents on a five-digit scale.

The average of the corruption proxy is about one bribe and one gift plus two threats per month. According to all three proxies, the level of corruption should be higher among the street guards (and much less but still above the average—especially in case of the gift proxy—among the market inspectors), the less educated, less well paid, those working in Budapest. The higher the level of threat, the less the inspector can believe in the popularity of the job.

The Bad and the Worse

If the reader accepts my three suggestions, and if the previous typology of the corruption guesstimation methods makes sense, then the following question should be answered. Which method gives us a more reliable estimate of the level of corruption (if there is any difference between them): the corruption-perception or the corruption-proxy method?

The ultimate problem with the corruption-proxy approach is the underestimation of the "real level" of corruption and it is unavoidable. Moreover, the quantity of underestimation is unknown as well as the compositional bias, which originates from the fact that by definition only an artificially selected subset of corruptive transactions is analyzed. These problems cannot be mended since they are rooted in the immanent characteristics of the proxy approach.

However, since the previous limitations characterize the corruption-perception method as well, and since there are further factors that increase the unreliability of this method, I would conclude that the corruption-proxy method is poor but the corruption-perception method is even poorer.

I owe the reader a brief analysis of the factors which, in my view, makes the corruption-perception method inferior to the corruption-proxy method and which is again unavoidable since it directly follows from the essence of the perception approach:

A—The notion of corruption is very slippery and difficult to define. There are scholars who argue that corruption is nothing but a euphemism for the "public bad" (Gombár, 1998). Being such a soft social phenomenon, it changes its content by time, strata, culture and economic systems. As a consequence, any perception of corruption is questionable since the researcher cannot assume that the respondents interpret the notion identically, and, therefore, their preferences cannot be reliably aggregated.

B—It is a commonplace that the notion of corruption is a politically sensitive issue and this makes it a favorite of the news-oriented media as well. The first characteristic in itself biases the process of perception since the sensitivity and attitude toward corruptive actions are strongly dependent on the political characteristics of the respondent. Moreover, the media coverage of, and their attitude to, corruption in general, and to the concrete corruptive action in particular, distort the process of perception.

This latter aspect of the corruption-perception bias can be especially lucidly shown in comparative analysis. ". . . the data in the Czech Republic were gathered at the time when there were almost daily exposures of scandalous swindles associated with the privatization process, something in which the Czechs had previously had great confidence. This would have affected the public perception of corruption but it does not mean that there is more corruption in the Czech Republic, than in say, Belarus. Belarussians have a rather low perception of corruption because there is no free press, so the corruption there is not publicly known about. Thus, ironically, a free press could actually increase the perception of corruption . . . precisely by doing its job properly." (Wallace and Haerpfer, 1999)

C—The culture-specificity and political sensitivity of corruption also mean that the wording of perception questions is crucial and can substantially influence the answer. To solve this problem there are two bad solutions:

The "generalist" approach is either to have no definition at all and to believe that using an umbrella term (such as bribe or corruption), each respondent would understand the same pile of transactions, and within it, the same composition of the various transactions, or to have very precise wording, which would standardize the understanding, but influence the answer by using specific terms with uncontrolled meaning.

D—The direction of distortion of the corruption-perception method is ambivalent. One can assume under-reporting due to national pride (corruption is bad) or due to bad conscience of those who use corruption occasionally but do not like it (Bíró, 1998), but one can assume over-reporting as well due to hate against those who are corrupt, conformity (assuming that the researcher expects agreement), or general political resentment ("the worse, the better" attitude). Despite its uncorrectable limitations, the corruption-proxy method seems to be more reliable as a source of estimation of the level of corruption than the corruption-perception method, since it has less bias. It is less distorted than the perception method since:

- the misinterpretation of the term corruption is missing (the estimation is based on action-oriented questions and not on attitude or hypothetical situations),
- the political and media influence is less obvious (the pressure is lower if the questions orient on past experience instead of values and hypothetical situations),
- depending on whether it is the corruption-perception or the proxy-method, due to the fact that the notion of corruption is to a certain extent culture-specific and that its composition might vary widely by country, any comparative analysis will be biased; however this bias is again less obvious in case of the proxy method,
- the direction of the distortion is more likely only downward (boasting of being bribed, or a bribe being highly unlikely) and
- last but not least, if one wants more than a proper estimate of the level of corruption, e.g., to do research into the process or socio-economic causes of corruption, then the corruption-perception approach is absolutely out of the question since you cannot ask questions about structure, causes and process and pretend that the answers you get have anything to do with reality. However, using any version of the corruption-proxy approach, you can analyze the composition and the process of corruption (as Bognár–Gál, 1999 did in the case of gratuity) or the factors which increase the level of corruption (Sík, 2000).

As the typology in Table 1 and the further versions within almost all types suggest, there are certain empirical tricks which may improve the reliability of the guesstimation of the level of corruption in case of both the perception and proxy approaches. For example, the more direct and the more situation- and transaction-specific are the questions, the more likely the result will be a good basis for a reliable estimation. Furthermore, the time-series analysis (using the same technique) increases the probability that the reliability of guesstimation will be higher, since not the "real level" of corruption, but at least the direction and relative speed of the change of the level of corruption, can be measured in this way.[68]

The Worst

As I already demonstrated, CPI has a very distinguished status in the "measure-the-level-of-corruption" business. Though CPI is a mixture of various methods, I classified it within the group of the perception of the practice since the main sources of CPI are the expert perceptions. In the following I will argue that there are special characteristics of the CPI, which make it the worst possible alternative among the known guesstimation methods.

(A) Every perception approach by definition is inflexible since perceptions are always mixed with high-inertia stereotypes and often based upon even more rigid prejudices. The way CPI is constructed (using the results of evaluations from the previous three years) artificially increases the inflexibility of CPI. It is of course known by the experts (Frequently . . ., 1998, section "Why are sources from the past three years used . . ."). They argue that this is a way to avoid the unexplained annual oscillations due to a big scandal or a random media influence. This is true but they fail to understand the danger of giving artificial inertia to the CPI by using the same data more than once. They fail to see the danger that this unavoidably leads to the reinforcement of already stereotypical and rigid expert opinions.

(B) The CPI—just as any other expert or target group-based technique does—assumes that the expert interviews which are the basis of estimating the level of corruption of the countries are independent of each other, but such is not the case since independent information is highly unlikely from a self-selected, small and closed circle of experts. The expert community is a small and closed international circle all over the world. Despite the geographical distances, these networks are rather closed.[69] This is why the high correlation the creators of the CPI proudly refer to as the confirmation of the validity of the CPI does not necessarily prove the high level of reliability. Such a correlation can also be the proof of the interrelatedness of the sources, and this problem increases with time since due to the globalization of TI and the standardization and the increasingly mythical nature of the CPI, the expert opinions also become more and more stereotypical. In a way the CPI becomes an institutionalized and globalized form of self-fulfilling prophecy.

(C) It makes a substantial difference whether the experts who evaluate the level of corruption in a certain country are locals[70] or foreigners. Both

cases have special dangers. In the case of the CPI the experts are foreigners. Being a foreigner, increases the chances of

- the lack of familiarity with local customs and language, or what is
  worse, superficial knowledge of them.[71] This situation, combined
  with the self-esteem of being a foreign expert, may easily end up in
  misinterpretation and overestimation of ones personal experiences,
- being suspicious of the locals which may lead to oversensitivity to
  corruption-like gestures and
- meeting with a highly non-representative subsample of the local state
  officials (specialists in foreign relations), members of the business community (multinationals, world market-oriented minority of local business) and seemingly very ordinary citizens (cabdrivers and hotel atten-
  dants, etc.). No corruption perception of a country based on such a self-
  selected sample of corruption-prone citizens can be reliable.

(D) Most of the CPI corruption-perception evaluations come from
businessmen. Being a businessman, one is interested in doing successful
business as quickly as possible. Having limited experience and high time-
and success-pressure, they are likely to use their money (of which they
are likely to have more than the locals) to jump queues and minimize the
time (of which they have less than the locals) of negotiations.

The same is the case with their desire to avoid mistakes in the course
of negotiations (for the sake of sure success they are ready to compensate
for the lack of cultural knowledge). In both cases they are likely to offer
bribes to get by, even in those situations where a local would go on with
more negotiation and would use customary ceremonies and gifts. The
result is more corruption by the expert, which later creates a bad corrup-
tion-evaluation score for the respective country.

Moreover, international businessmen in every country form a small
and closed society. Such expatriate social groups are likely to establish
various clubs, chambers and informal social circles to meet. These meetings serve also as the sites of social chats and business gossiping. Such
occasions are excellent opportunities for reinforcing each other's stereotypes and implicitly for increasing the level of CPI and its inertia.

Finally, there is a hidden assumption in the CPI observation method
that should be questioned. It assumes that the composition of the experts
of the independent sources is similar, but I would argue that the businessmen in a corrupt country might be a self-selected subsample of the

business community in their home countries. Assuming that the corrupt nature of a country was known in advance (and since the development of the CPI, it is almost certain that a businessman or the consultant organization preparing the business-trip knows the CPI quite well), within the business community, businessmen, who are for,or at least can cope with, bribing, are likely to go to such a country.

(E) CPI is the product of Transparency International (TI), and TI has in own vested interests in the CPI and is therefore responsible for the distortion of the CPI. TI is a growth-oriented venture for which success means (among other issues) to measure as many countries for as many years as possible. As a result, TI is interested in increasing the coverage of the CPI and a time series analysis of the level of corruption. Moreover, TI is interested also in proving year by year that corruption is a big problem.

However, the time-series comparison of the CPI is very problematic. The researcher is again aware of it (Frequently . . ., 1998, section "Can data from one year compared . . ."). Still, business is business and, therefore, the TI press release in 1998 talks about the worsening of the situation (see quotation on p. 14) as if the annual CPIs were independent of each other and as if there were no changes in the coverage between 1997 and 1998.

TI wants to become the sole source of corruption evaluation worldwide (see the quotations on p. 14). It considers itself as one (if not the only one, then at least the leading one) of the corruption fighters worldwide in cooperation with every global powerhouse. For them, therefore, corruption needs to be a big and worldwide problem. To achieve this goal they have to have as extensive coverage as possible. This explains why they have sacrificed reliability on the altar of greater coverage. As we have already mentioned, the minimum number of sources to evaluate a country used to be four but since 1998 it has been reduced to three. The result can be seen in Table 4.

Table 4. CPI Average by the Number of Sources

No. of sources	CPI average	No. of countries
3	53.9	21
4	59.3	10
5–8	36.2	14
9	29.3	19
10	35.0	14
11–12	38.4	7

Source: The authors computation from The Corruption . . . (1998).

Compared to the previous year, the coverage has in fact increased by 21 countries. What is even better from TI's point of view is that the average CPI index has increased as well. The reason is revealed in Table 4. The average CPI score of the "newcomers" (based only on three sources) is much higher than the average of the total. This means that TI can express its sorrow that, compared to the previous year, the average CPI has worsened (see quotation on p. 14), but of course, this sad trend increases the importance of TI and widens their media coverage, which might end up in further funds and invitations to highbrow conferences.

Of course, and unintentionally, those countries with more than three sources also fare well since their relative position on the CPI scale improves. It is only the reliability of CPI which is lost since the standard deviation of the countries with three observations is high [higher (1.38) than the countries with nine observations (0.82)]). This also means that the total reliability of the CPI has decreased due to the increased coverage.

This growth orientation of TI explains also why TI intends to relax its restrictions for the sake of increasing the coverage. From 2000, the TI home page will rank every country measured at least once in three years, even if there were no new data (Frequently . . .,1998, section "Will more countries be included next year?"). Of course they intend to make it clear for the users that these countries are not comparable with those with "fresh" data, but we already know what such footnote-like caveats can do when the media wants to refer to a general and fresh index.

The Impact of Corruption on Economic Development: Applying "Third" World Insights to the Former Second World[72]

Paul Hutchcroft

One of the enormous challenges of recent years has been the need to create stronger political foundations for market economies in states that, for decades, very consciously rejected market-based economic models. In the early and mid-1990s, many scholars (particularly economists) were extremely sanguine about the capacity of formerly socialist societies to make an easy transition to capitalism of the "free-market" variety. In 1995, for example, Anders Åslund—briefly an economic adviser to the Russian government—lamented that few Russians "understood that markets *emerge spontaneously* when economic subjects, regardless of ownership, obtain the freedom to trade and become dependent on their own profits."[73] As the years have passed, it has become increasingly apparent that it was, in fact, many of the Western economic advisers who failed to understand the extraordinary difficulty of establishing political and institutional arrangements conducive to sustained economic development. This is not, of course, a new insight: one need only examine Karl Polanyi's analysis of the industrial revolution in England to appreciate how "the road to the free market was opened and kept open by an enormous increase in continuous, centrally organized and controlled interventionism." Contrary to the view of many modern free-market ideologues, Polanyi asserts that "there was nothing natural about *laissez-faire*; free markets could never have come into being merely by allowing things to take their course . . . *laissez-faire* economy was the product of *deliberate* state action."[74] Post-socialist transitions have thus underscored the necessity—and challenge—of building more effective states.

At the core of this challenge lies a major paradox: while strong judicial, political, and administrative structures are essential to the creation and perpetuation of market economies, these structures are woefully undermined if they are themselves permeated by a market mentality. A strong and independent judiciary is essential for protecting property rights and resolving business disputes, yet the judiciary itself will cease to function effectively if it is itself captive to market considerations. It is no boast, in other words, for a country to have "the best judiciary that money can buy." Similarly, political and administrative structures must not be overwhelmed by market behavior if they are to provide suitable foundations for the emergence and endurance of a "free-market" economy; decisions made on behalf of the highest bidder are unlikely to be decisions that best meet national developmental goals.

Some element of particularistic privilege is of course found in all political systems—most clearly in those where corruption and rent havens predominate, but even in relatively more meritocratic states that have been able to harness their civil servants more effectively to the pursuit of official goals. While no "playing field" is entirely level, however, it is equally obvious that landscapes of special advantage vary enormously in shape from one political economy to another: some varieties of unevenness may actually promote economic growth, while other types of rough terrain seem to pose enormous barriers to sustained development. Many Third World states have long provided little but rough terrain and their economies have often suffered as a result. As former Second World states are now called upon to provide suitable political foundations for economic development, lessons from the Third World can offer valuable insights. There are, to be sure, distinct differences between creating stronger political foundations in a post-colonial setting such as Nigeria and in a post-socialist setting such as Russia. At the same time, however, it is significant that Russia has now acquired levels of corruption approaching those of Nigeria,[75] and corruption is commonly given much of the blame for both countries' failures to convert rich natural and human resources into developmental success.

This paper takes initial steps toward building a framework able to explain why a range of related phenomena—variously described as rent-seeking, corruption, and clientelism—may be relatively more compatible or relatively more obstructive to the process of economic development. Although this framework has been developed primarily with Third World examples, it is hoped that its analysis may be of relevance as well to the former Second World countries continuing an on-going transition to market economies. In the course of this analysis, I will highlight how contrasting political settings spawn very different patterns of seeking—and dispensing—particularistic advantage. Moreover, I will seek to demonstrate that the process of creating such a broad framework benefits from an eclectic approach; specifically, it is valuable to draw insights from three literatures, with distinct lineages, that overlap but all too rarely interact: those relating to rents, corruption, and clientelism.

The first section of this paper discusses the utility of drawing on the three major paradigms, and the relative advantages and disadvantages of each in building a broad comparative framework. Second, I propose a preliminary framework for assessing the varying impact of major phenomena described by the literature on rents, corruption, and clientelism, focusing attention on seven elements not fully captured in any one of the paradigms. Together, they examine the variability of the "take" among comparable acts of corruption, the processes by which advantages are allocated, the way in which gains obtained are invested, the manner in which corruption affects the operation of markets, the impact of corruption on a state's capacity to execute a range of essential developmental tasks, the role that corruption may play in promoting or impeding the institutionalization of both state agencies and political parties and the relative presence of factors able to mitigate or counterbalance the prevalence of corruption. The conclusion summarizes key lessons and proposes paths that may be fruitful in further comparative research.

Surveying the Paradigms: Rents, Corruption, and Clientelism

The quest for and allocation of particularistic advantage has long been the subject of academic investigation, but the language and concepts employed in this process of inquiry have varied across time and across disciplines. Each of the major paradigms—rents, corruption, and clientelism—offers important insights to political economists, yet all would be enhanced by a more concerted effort at cross-fertilization. The following is a preliminary attempt to encourage useful hybrids.

The most recent addition to the theoretical repertoire is, of course, the literature on rents that has emerged from economics. The strength of this body of thought is its attention to market processes, and it is not surprising that rent theorists have achieved prominence in an era in which markets are widely praised and governments routinely reviled. Rents are, by definition, created when the state restricts the operations of the market. The processes of rationing foreign exchange, curbing free trade, and licensing some aspect of economic activity—to give just a few examples—serve to create "rent havens" that can be captured by some combination of well-placed businesspersons and bureaucrats. The fight for privilege, known as rent-seeking, encourages "directly unproductive profit-seeking" activities—sometimes legal (e.g, lobbying) and sometimes not (e.g., bribery). Overall, the focus is on "the rent-seeking *society*"; analysis of the specific types of *state* structures in which this behavior most thrives is commonly thwarted by distrust of states in general. Because rent seeking is said to be "directly related to the scope and range of governmental activity in the economy, and to the relative size of the public sector," the solution (as paraphrased by Peter Evans) is self-evident: "The state's sphere should be reduced to the minimum, and bureaucratic control should be replaced by market mechanisms wherever possible."[76]

Indeed, a major problem with the rent-seeking literature is its often strong ideological bias. The majority of theorists are obsessed with demonstrating the negative impact of government on the economy. They view competitive markets as the most socially efficient means to produce goods and services . . . [and] do not treat the effects of government intervention as variable, sometimes reducing and sometimes stimulating social waste.[77]

This bias is best refuted by Evans, who points out that many bureaucracies do indeed possess the capacity to restrain rent-seeking tendencies and promote collective effort among individual officeholders. "Strict adherence to a neo-utilitarian logic," he asserts, "makes the existence of a collective actor difficult to explain and the nightwatchman state [favored by neo-utilitarians] a theoretical impossibility." His analysis of the role of states in economic transformation, moreover, highlights major problems with the assumption that competitive markets "are sufficient to the kind of structural transformation that lies at the heart of development."[78]

Ideological bias aside, there are at least four other major deficiencies with much of the rent-seeking literature. First, even if a bureaucracy is pared down to a minimalist role, it is likely to retain ultimate responsibility for such basic tasks as building infrastructure and providing law and order. As long as bureaucrats continue to be tasked with supplying these goods, there remain "rent havens." In settings where (to quote Weber) individual bureaucrats can easily "squirm out of the [bureaucratic] apparatus," the provision of public goods may bring significant opportunities for private profit. Even in a minimalist state, for example, motor vehicle licensing authorities will potentially be able to extract an extra unofficial sum for a scarce resource, and police may be able to transform their public power into lucrative kidnap-for-ransom schemes. Privatization by no means resolves the dilemma: the process of bidding and negotiating with private companies seeking to build and maintain a road, for example, can provide enormous rent havens easily tapped by those with the most favorable political connections. Because rent theorists have little to say about such post-market-shrinking problems, the solution necessarily shifts away from market remedies and toward the realm of politics and public administration.

Second, the literature on rents generally neglects vitally important political elements of government–business relations. As Jomo and Gomez explain, there are major problems with the presumption that rents will be allocated solely according to market processes—and a "certain irony" that

> the very people who assume that markets have been distorted with the creation of rents also seem to assume the existence of perfectly competitive markets for rent capture involving a fully competitive process. Rent seeking may, in fact, not be very competitive —due to the clandestine, illegal, closed, exclusive or protected nature of rent capture processes—thus limiting rent-seeking activity and keeping down rent-seeking costs.[79]

The allocation is likely to be based not only on the market but also on a range of non-market considerations, including ethnic, regional, party, and old-school ties. Politics, not the market, provides the best clues to these processes.

Third and closely related, is the problem of determining the degree to which rents will be primarily captured by those in the state or those outside the state. This likely brings in even larger structural considerations, based on analysis of the historical development of state–society relations. Within Southeast Asia, I argue elsewhere, the "bureaucratic capitalism" associated with the former bureaucratic polity of Thailand, for example, needs to be differentiated from the "booty capitalism" spawned by the oligarchic patrimonial state found in the Philippines. In the first type of rent capitalism, the major beneficiaries of largesse are found in the state; in the latter, major beneficiaries have an independent economic base outside the state.[80]

Fourth, rent theorists rarely make a clear distinction between whether those who compete for advantage are seeking generalizable policy benefits (as when a exporters' association lobbies for reduced tariffs) or particularistic privileges (as when a family conglomerate bribes customs officials for lower duties on a specific importation, or lobbies congresspersons for the construction of a particular road). Taken together—whether lobbying or bribery, general or particularistic—all are seen as examples of unproductive rent-seeking activities.[81] For a purely market-based standpoint, it is no problem to aggregate such activities into one category; from the standpoint of political economy, however, there are certain disadvantages. Because such distinctions are largely reflective of the degree of institutionalization and differentiation of business interests, they are indeed important to those investigating larger questions of political power and future possibilities of political economic transformation. Moreover, because the relative incidence of bribery versus lobbying has an impact on the character of bureaucratic agencies, such distinctions are important to those analyzing state capacity to promote developmental goals.

As useful as rent theory can be to understanding the allocation of particularistic advantage, its limitations suggest the need to search elsewhere for additional insights. Studies of corruption may have had their heyday in the era of modernization theory, but it is a mistake to suggest that corruption is merely a "primitive" way of conceptualizing rent seeking.[82] It is a distinct paradigm that, over the course of many years, has yielded many important lessons for contemporary analysis. Indeed, it is worthwhile inquiring into why the concept of corruption is often given only cursory scholarly attention—and sometimes eschewed in favor of other conceptual approaches. Because corruption is nearly omnipresent, some analysts seem inclined to treat it as an invariable element of the political economic woodwork; in other words, they are content to note that it exists almost everywhere without inquiring into how it varies in character and impact from one setting to another. Others, have shunned the concept because it is more difficult to compile reliable empirical data on the often shadowy world of corruption (based, quite inconveniently, on the "what is") than it is to construct abstract models of how rent havens are created in the absence of perfect markets (based on the far less troublesome investigation of "what is not").[83] "Primitive" (i.e., early postwar) language, conceptual complexity, and dilemmas of data gathering, however, are no excuses for throwing the baby out with the bathwater.

Corruption focuses attention on the public sector and on the distinction between official and private activity. Nye's oft-cited definition is a useful starting point: "Corruption is behavior which deviates from the formal duties of a public role because of private-regarding (personal, close family, private clique) pecuniary or status gains; or violates rules against the exercise of certain types of private-regarding influence."[84] With this as a starting point, one is able to go beyond the central concern of rent theorists (how states may distort markets) and move into other important terrain as well (e.g., how markets may distort states).

Theorists of corruption, as a group, cannot be accused of any strong ideological bias; on the contrary, one finds enormous variance in how to approach the issue. In the early days of modernization theory, corruption was commonly condemned on moralistic grounds but rarely accompanied by much careful analysis of its precise consequences (not to mention its causes, mechanics, or remedies). Later "revisionist" approaches of the late 1960s found that corruption could, at least occasionally and sometimes systematically, have a beneficial impact on a range of important goals: "nation-building," economic development, administrative capacity, and democratization. Subsequent literature continues the on-going evaluation of costs and benefits.[85]

Such attention to the larger context is at once both a strength and a weakness of this body of literature. On the one hand, it is essential to view corruption as an element of broader political interactions and understand that the prevalence of bribery may have both benefits as well as costs. On the other hand, in the course of achieving breadth there is sometimes a lack of specificity as to which goals are being included in the cost–benefit analysis. Modernization theory's tendency to conflate distinct goals and presume that "all good things go together" spills over into the Great Corruption Debate, as rival camps are at times over-eager to declare corrupt behavior either an overall good or an overall bad. Many scholars who have contributed to this literature, however, are quite explicit as to how costs and benefits need to be evaluated in terms of specific goals.[86]

At the risk of simplifying what is indeed a very large body of work spanning a wide time period—from the earliest distinctions between private and public domains until the present—here are at least four other advantages to building on previous studies of corruption. First, as noted above, the very definition of corruption focuses attention on the character of state agencies, specifically the degree to which any given system reflects a clear distinction between a public and a private sphere. The work of Max Weber not only highlights how polities vary enormously in the degree to which such a distinction is recognized, but also how corruption can have a different impact from one setting to another. Unfortunately, the potential for carrying forth Weber's nuanced comparative analysis of the interaction of politics, bureaucratic structures, and economies has been hampered, in recent decades, by disciplinary over-specialization. Economists tend to treat all states as the same, political scientists rarely devote much attention to bureaucratic structures, and public administration specialists all too often ignore the larger political and structural contexts in which their subject agencies are situated.[87]

Second, the corruption literature almost universally recognizes that corruption can be expressed both according to nonmarket and market factors. Scott explains that

> [a]s ideal types, "parochial" (nonmarket) corruption is a situation where only ties of kinship, affection, caste, and so forth determine access to the favors of power-holders, whereas "market" corruption signifies an impersonal process in which influence is accorded those who can "pay" the most, regardless of who they are. The real world, of course, rarely ever contains such pure cases. The proportion of market to parochial corruption, and hence the pattern of beneficiaries, varies widely among underdeveloped nations.

Modes of payment, he further explains, can be in cash or in kind; in electoral settings, they may of course include delivery of a bloc of votes.

Third, the best of the literature on corruption insists that the concept can only be properly analyzed "within a broader analysis of a regime's political dynamics." Scott's own analysis leads him to suggest that its impact may at times be expected to have a counter-hegemonic influence by promoting the entry of new forces, but its more "normal effect . . . is to cement togather a conservative coalition and hold back or cancel out the effects of growing collective demands." Waterbury concludes that "endemic and planned corruption" in Morocco "serves only one 'positive' function—that of the survival of the regime. Resources are absorbed in patronage and are drained away from rational productive investment."[88] Whether or not other theorists agree with such conclusions, the very tendency to focus on how issues of politics and political power are played out among major social forces can be seen as welcome relief in an era in which the realm of macropolitics is often no longer the premier consideration of political economy.

A final advantage of employing the term "corruption" is that it re-connects academics with real politics and real political discourse. There has probably never been a major political demonstration against rent-seeking, but popular disgust over corruption—the violation of norms based on a distinction between what is public and what is private—has in countless cases nurtured, reform movements, provoked riots, and contributed to the downfall of regimes. As long as corruption scandals dominate the headlines of many national newspapers, it seems a worthy objective for academics to continue to investigate such phenomena.

Further political nuance comes from a third major paradigm, clientelism, which is above all a study of relationships of power. Persons of higher social status (patrons) are linked to those of lower social status (clients) in personal ties of reciprocity that can vary in content and purpose across time. Patron–client ties may or may not be corrupt, but (as John Waterbury explains) "when a patron occupies a public position or extracts favors from those in public positions, patronage and corruption overlap."[89] Conversely, purely market corruption has no element of clientelism: it is a one-time transaction lacking in affective ties. Although concrete empirical evidence may be elusive, it is probable that—contrary to the expectations of many economists—purely market corruption is far less common than other variants of corruption. Power and social relationships regularly interact with everyday market relations; in all likelihood, markets of a corrupt nature—involving the complex interplay of private and public spheres—are even more heavily infused with such ties. Integration of the clientelist paradigm into an analysis of the search for particularistic advantage encourages analysts to go beyond both, the excessive attention to market transactions often found in economics and the legalistic–formalistic approaches commonly found in the field of public administration.

Along with the other two paradigms, however, clientelist literature generally gives insufficient attention to the role of coercion in the search for particularistic advantage. Since coercion plays a major role in certain forms of corrupt behavior (especially in extortion and in the delivery of a bloc of votes), it is important to supplement all three paradigms with careful consideration of the often-prominent role of violence. Scott tends to treat corruption and violence as alternative expressions of political influence (the former "a more peaceful route to influence" than the latter), but in practice the two often reinforce each other in quite effective ways.[90] A New York mafioso, for example, may threaten an uncooperative city official with the proverbial "swim with concrete overshoes" in the East River, or a Philippine influential may utilize state resources (the local police, or temporarily released and heavily armed prison convicts) to strike out at his or her political enemies.

Together, the three paradigms encourage careful analysis of the search for and dispensing of particularistic privilege. Rent literature focuses attention on what happens when state actions distort markets, corruption literature examines how public roles and private influences conflict within state agencies, and clientelism encourages clearer analysis of the relationships of power that permeate states, societies, and markets. The next task is to draw on these eclectic sources and begin to build a larger framework in which to analyze more effectively the very diverse impacts of the allocation of particularistic advantage.

Building an Eclectic Theoretical Framework

In varying settings, it was asserted at the outset, the range of related phenomena variously described as rent-seeking, corruption, and clientelism may be relatively more compatible or relatively more obstructive to the process of development. This paper does not aim to provide a generalizable framework able to explain when, where, why, and how the impact may be more or less positive, nor does it seek to provide a comprehensive new typology of the range of phenomena encompassed by these complementary paradigms. Rather, the purpose is to propose a series of initial questions that may build on previous insights—from eclectic sources—and contribute toward the longer-term goal of building such a framework and such a typology. In other words, it is a preliminary treatment intended to promote discussion and further refinement of ideas.

There are seven sets of questions, I shall propose, that are useful in beginning to assess the differential impact of rents, corruption, and clientelism. It is important to emphasize that the focus here is *the impact of corruption on economic development*; separate assessments of the impact of corruption would be necessary if other goals (e.g., harmonious inter-ethnic relations, democracy, or political stability) are to be considered. Distinct analysis would also be required if one is investigating the causes or mechanics of corruption, or optimal strategies to curb the phenomenon.

1. *Is corruption relatively more variable or calculable?* A key factor in understanding the diverging impact of corruption and bribery on capitalist growth, Weber suggests, is the variability of the phenomena: they

have the "least serious effect" when calculable, and become most oner-
ous when fees are "highly variable" and "settled from case to case with
every individual official." Indeed, if bribery is a calculable element of a
business firm's environment, its impact is no different than a tax; to the
extent that a firm must devote major effort to negotiating each bribe. On
the other hand, there is a high degree of unpredictability in the amount of
time and resources to be expended. Overall, Weber expected that
advanced forms of capitalism relied upon "the rational, predictable functioning of the legal and administrative agencies."[91] If correct, a major
obstacle to the development of more sophisticated forms of capitalist
accumulation is not corruption *per se*, but highly variable corruption.

What sort of polities is most likely to spawn highly variable types of
corruption? Analysis of this question begins with Rudolph and Rudolph's
important distinction between authority (the formal roles conferred upon
individuals in their official capacities) and power (when incumbents pursue "values, interests, and goals of their own choosing that conflict with
those of the administrative structure"). Few would disagree with Scott's
observation, over two decades ago, that "[n]ominally modern institutions
such as bureaucracies and political parties in Southeast Asia are often
thoroughly penetrated by informal patron–client networks that undermine the formal structure of authority."[92] For present purposes, it is
worthwhile building on previous scholarship and examining further two
key aspects of the interaction of power and authority within bureaucracies and parties. First, what are the relative strengths of informal and formal power? Clearly, the formal structures of authority are stronger in
some national settings than others; within any national administrative
apparatus, as well, some agencies exhibit clearer lines of formal authority than others. By definition, the stronger the formal authority relative to
informal networks the less prevalent will be the incidence of corruption.

Second, it is important to examine the process by which the power and
authority interact: do patron–client networks tend to coincide with formal
lines of authority, or do they constitute a competing source of orders and
inducements? Higher degrees of coincidence, I propose, are likely to
yield more predictable forms of corruption; conversely, the greater the
degree of divergence between power and authority, the more variable is
the form of corruption that is likely to emerge.[93] In the former (pre-1980s)
Thai bureaucratic polity, for example, formal bureaucratic authority was
well developed and informal networks of power and formal status over-

lapped to a large degree. In such a system, businesspersons were likely to have a good sense of whom to approach and what to expect from one transaction to another.[94] In the Philippines, by contrast, lines of formal authority are weaker and the disjuncture between authority and power is often quite pronounced. In this loosely structured system, where patrons are as often found outside formal structures of authority as within them, there is likely less regularization of corruption from one case to another. As Rose-Ackerman describes her category "disorganized" bureaucracy,

> the official chain of command is unclear and constantly shifting and the deci-
> sion-making criteria are similarly arbitrary and unknown . . . While corrupt
> bureaucrats may be willing to accept bribes, applicants cannot be sure that
> officials have the power to perform their side of the bargain. Chaotic legal
> procedures increase the *demand* for more certain illegal ones, but if the disor-
> ganization of government is far advanced, no bureaucrats may be able to *sup-
> ply* the requisite certainty even when offered a monetary incentive."[95]

To the extent that this description resembles any given country, busi-
nesspersons (especially those without favorable access to the political machinery) will often find it very difficult to predict the cost, frequency, or results of their bribery of state officials. The basic "rules of the game" will be far more arbitrary, and corruption will have a more obstructive impact on the process of capitalist growth.

2. *To what extent are rents "dissipated" in the course of their allocation? In other words, to what extent (if at all) are resources wasted in
processes that determine who obtains particularistic advantage?*
Analysis of corruption and rents has focused considerable attention on the process by which particularistic privileges are allocated, but has unfortunately achieved little consensus as to the impact of these processes on development. Key elements of inquiry, as we shall see, involve the extent to which allocation is competitive and the degree to which it gen-
erates efficiency.

Many economists—ever faithful to market processes—begin with the presumption that bureaucrats will allocate scarce resources such as licenses and other favors via "competitive bidding among entrepreneurs." Leff argues that within such a system "favors will go to the most efficient pro-
ducers, for they will be able to make the highest bids which are compati-
ble with remaining in the industry." A decade later, Krueger developed a

model that also tends to presume that bidding will be competitive—but came to the opposite conclusion about efficiency. Competition for rents diverts resources toward such unproductive activities as lobbying and bribery, and in the end generates welfare costs for society as a whole.[96]

As discussed above, however, it is quite problematic to suppose that the allocation of privilege will be decided according to market processes. The recognition that rents can be allocated according to either market or non-market processes has led some neoclassical economists to propose— with further irony—that limits on competition might actually yield high- er levels of efficiency. As paraphrased by Mendoza, these economists have argued that since less competition over the allocation of rents is con- sidered less wasteful, "the least wasteful situation is one where an absolute dictator who will brook no complaint will dispense rents as he sees fit." Campos argues that the costs of directly unproductive profit- seeking (DUP) activities will "likely be smaller in an environment in which only a limited elite can acquire rents."[97]

Jomo and Gomez suggest, similarly, that "the existence of rents, in itself, does not necessarily result in rent-seeking behavior." Because "certain political groups, individuals, or institutions usually have much more influ- ence on or even hegemony over the state," some will likely do better than others in the process of securing advantage. Knowing that there is indeed "uneven access to opportunities for rent capture," many parties will not even bother to enter the market. It is thus useful to make an analytical dis- tinction between two broad forms of allocation: "rent-seeking" and "rent deployment." Rents are sometimes obtained by persons or groups that actively seek out the advantage, and in other cases deployed from above to persons or groups who exert relatively little effort. To the extent that rents are deployed rather than sought after, there may in fact be far fewer wast- ed resources in the process of rent allocation than is commonly presumed.[98]

Just as Scott suggests that there are likely few cases of pure "market" or pure "non-market" corruption, so also are there likely few cases of pure "competitive rent-seeking" or pure "rent deployment." A given claimant, for example, might have close affective ties to those who allo- cate privileges, and still have to expend considerable effort and resources to ensure that a) the allocator does not forget to take care of what that claimant thinks is his/her due; and b) this claimant's needs are taken care of before other claimants whose affective ties with the allocator are equally close. In short, both market versus non-market corruption as well as rent-seeking versus rent deployment are best conceived of as continua, across which one finds varying combinations of the two "pure" types.

Overall, we can expect that the centralization of authority and/or power within a political economy will encourage a greater degree of rent deployment and a lesser degree of rent-seeking. Rent deployment, in turn, seems likely to promote relatively less dissipation than rent-seeking and thus have the potential for more positive (or less detrimental) outcomes from the standpoint of development. Despite the considerable attention that these issues have received in the rents literature, however, it is quite likely that other elements of analysis may prove far more important in assessing developmental outcomes.

3. *Once gains from corruption and rents are obtained, how are they invested?* Whereas the previous question focuses attention of the processes by which rents are allocated, this question focuses attention on the purpose to which rents—once obtained—are employed. It has long been recognized not only that one of the "benefits" of corruption may be to promote rapid capital accumulation, but also that one must inquire as to whether the capital itself is invested in productive ways.[99] At one end of the continuum, an entrepreneur invests his/her gains in a high-value-added industry that creates a great many positive externalities to the rest of the economy. At the other end of the continuum, advantages are hustled out of the country and into Swiss banks and Manhattan real estate.

There is no reason to expect that rents sought after in competitive environments will necessarily result in more productive investment than those that have been deployed. On the other hand, in the event that rents are deployed there is no reason to expect that either deployers—or those who obtain rents via deployment—are necessarily going to be interested in promoting productive investment. As asserted above, one must look at the larger context in which rents are allocated. I propose that there are at least three key variables to examine in assessing the productivity of privileges obtained: 1) what are the motivations of those who allocate and obtain privileges?; 2) presuming that rents are allocated in order to promote developmental goals, what is the capacity of the state to enforce or promote productivity criteria?; and 3) how secure is the environment in which a given entrepreneur is operating?

The motivations of those who obtain privileges through competitive rent seeking are likely impossible to evaluate with any precision: some will be inclined to productive investment and some will not. In the case of deployment, however, one is by definition evaluating a systematic effort toward a clear objective. The nature of the objective, however, may have little to do with the promotion of explicit developmental outcomes—and may just as likely be oriented toward clearly political objectives. Such goals may in fact be relatively harmless—or actually promote—developmental objectives, as when privilege is extended to a particular region or ethnic group. In other cases, political goals may have a very harmful impact on the process of economic development, as when a highly unproductive businessperson is given a trading monopoly and extraordinary access to state credit in exchange for building political support for the regime in an important bailiwick. If the deployer is highly dependent on such local powerbrokers for political survival, it is particularly unlikely that developmental goals will figure prominently in the bargain.

Second, when rents are in fact allocated with clear developmental goals, what is the capacity of the state to enforce or promote such goals? In an optimal "rent-seeking" scenario, those who obtain privilege through competitive bidding must invest them in productive enterprise. In an optimal "deployment" scenario, those who give out the rents are not only very skilled in choosing the right entrepreneurs but also quite capable of enforcing strict performance guidelines from those they have provided a particular benefit. Entrepreneurs favored by South Korea's Park Chung Hee, for example, were granted enormous privilege but at the same time forced to meet performance criteria (commonly in the form of export targets). In many cases, however, those who obtain advantages will be able to pursue their own goals—which may or may not be oriented toward productive investment.

The clearest analysis, here again, requires careful examination of the broader configuration of authority and power within which rent allocation takes place. Privilege may be extended to collective interests (a particular region, ethnic group, political party, or military faction) or to far more particular interests (family members, fraternity brothers, golfing partners, etc.). It is necessary to examine the relationship of rent allocators to each of these types of interests. Moreover, one must note that, while in some settings major beneficiaries will be found within the state (commonly top bureaucrats and military officers), elsewhere major beneficiaries have an independent economic base outside the state. Overall, analysis of the ability of allocators to enforce and promote performance criteria requires that one examine such basic issues as the distribution of political power, the character of bureaucratic agencies, and the institutionalization and differentiation of business interests. Questions of enforcement cannot be understood without careful attention to the larger realms of power and authority.

Third, rent recipients operating in a very insecure environment may have little incentive to adopt a long-run strategy in the country where their advantage was obtained: capital flight, rather than productive investment of capital, will likely predominate.[100] To the extent that corruption and cronyism undercut the legitimacy of a regime, of course, they may at the same time undermine the overall stability in which rents are invested.

4. What is the impact of corruption and clientelism on levels of competition and the overall functioning of the market? This question moves analysis from issues of investor productivity to those of market performance: does rent allocation, corruption, and clientelism tend to promote or discourage competition among firms? Doner and Ramsay contrast "competitive clientelism" (in which competition among political elites keeps barriers to entry low and thus fosters business competition) with "monopoly cronyism" or "monopoly clientelism" (in which entrepreneurs can use their access to the state machinery to enforce higher entry barriers and reduce competition).[101] Quite clearly the former can be expected to promote more favorable conditions for capitalist development, particularly where the state lacks the regulatory capacity to ensure efficient performance from cartelized and monopolized sectors.

Second, and closely related, is the need to examine whether corrupt acts provide an end-run around policies that obstruct markets, or whether the acts themselves obstruct the efficient functioning of competitive markets. The first case is perhaps best illustrated by West African cocoa farmers evading laws that require them to sell their produce to state marketing boards, and smuggling their produce to markets in neighboring countries.[102] The second occurs when an anti-trust lawsuit is squelched through bribery of key officials.

5. What is the impact of corruption on the capacity of state agencies to undertake important developmental roles? States have important tasks to achieve in promoting development. Even advocates of a relatively minimalist role for the state, such as the World Bank, assert that

> governments need to do more in those areas where markets alone cannot be relied upon. Above all, this means investing in education, health, nutrition,

family planning, and poverty alleviation; building social, physical, administrative, regulatory, and legal infrastructure of better quality; mobilizing
resources to finance public expenditures; and providing a stable macroeconomic foundation, without which little can be achieved.

To the extent that corruption inhibits the achievement of these vital
foundations of *laissez-faire* capitalism, opportunities for sustained
growth will be impaired. If one expects that promotion of late, late industrialization requires an even more extensive role for the state, quite clearly, it will be necessary to build up an even greater degree of capacity
throughout the bureaucratic appartus. For present purposes, however, it is
possible to confine our attention to the impact of corruption on the basic
political foundations of capitalist growth.

Some argue that corruption promotes development by promoting
administrative responsiveness. "Many economic activities would be paralyzed," wrote Myron Weiner of Indian politics in 1962, "were it not for
the flexibility which *bakshish* contributes to the complex, rigid, administrative system." Huntington concurs: "In terms of economic growth, the
only thing worse than a society with a rigid, overcentralized, dishonest
bureaucracy is one with a rigid, overcentralized, honest bureaucracy."[103]
Others introduce the distinction between "speed payments" (involving
"bribes that *expedite* a decision without changing it") and "distortive
payments" (which "change the decision and contravene formal government policy").[104]

From the standpoint of an individual businessperson or citizen, corruption does indeed grease the wheels of a bureaucracy; to be sure, "honest bureaucracies" can be infuriatingly inflexible to those with a justifiable need to bend the rules, and "dishonest bureaucracies" highly responsive to those who have the means and/or connections to do so. From a
macro perspective, however, it is important to consider the impact of
even seemingly innocuous "speed" payments on the likelihood of a
bureaucratic agency to deliver the services it was set up to deliver. Such
payments can encourage systematic delays, precisely because slowing
things down brings such handsome financial rewards to those in a strategic position within the bureaucracy. Corruption may in some cases be a
valuable "lubricant" to individual claimants, but one must not neglect the
degree to which such incentives build more bureaucratic "toll posts," and
in the end exacerbate delays in the system as a whole.[105]

Moreover, one must assess the longer-term impact of corruption on administrative capacity to perform essential developmental tasks. Theobald asserts that:

> widespread venality, far from drawing together the different departments and areas of the public service, provokes fragmentation, dissension, inter- and intra-departmental rivalry . . . the low levels of morale and paranoia which are typically associated with an acutely unstable work situation...will have very marked consequences for job performance . . . [A prevalence of] nepotism, political patronage and bribery . . . [means] there is little incentive for functionaries to work efficiently or honestly.

While not denying that corruption may have some "positive consequences," Theobald asserts that "it is virtually impossible to confine corruption to those areas where its effects are deemed to be beneficial." Even Huntington, who sees many positive benefits in corruption, acknowledges that it "naturally tends to weaken or to perpetuate the weakness of the government bureaucracy."[106]

Aside from questions of flexibility and capacity one must consider the impact of corruption on government budgets. How much of an expenditure intended to promote certain developmental goals actually ends up being utilized for such purpose, and how much gets leaked to promote private gain? On the revenue side, as well, corruption may reduce the proportion of a given tax that actually ends up in public coffers; taxpayers can bribe the right officials to informally bargain down their tax burden or obtain a formal exemption. Either way, funds are diverted from public to private ends. Leff argues that "there is no reason to assume that the government has a high *marginal* propensity to spend for developmental purposes"; moreover, "when the entrepreneurs' propensity to invest is higher than the government's, the money saved from the tax collector may be a gain rather than a loss for development."[107] This begs the question, however, of whether the private hands that dip in the till will be investing their resources in the provision of public goods essential to the promotion of development. In many cases, even the most basic political foundations of economic development are severely disrupted by corruption: such tasks, for example, as law enforcement, fire protection, and the construction and maintenance of infrastructure. While entrepreneurs may invest some resources in provisioning themselves with these goods (private security guards, fire brigades, and roads), it will be rare for private investors to charitably provide public goods when governments fail to do so. As the World Bank explains, governments must do what markets alone fail to do.

A key question, then, is how much corruption actually reduces public expenditure on developmental goals (whether it be an irrigation project, a road, or a rural health clinic). Wade has provided an exceptionally detailed empirical portrait of how corruption in a South Indian system of canal irrigation impedes developmental goals. Irrigation engineers are able to raise "vast amounts of illicit revenue" in the construction of irrigation works and in deciding how water is allocated; in the process, the "economic well-being of local communities" is often poorly served.[108] Overall, one can expect that five percent diversion of resources from public purpose to private hands is relatively harmless compared to ten percent, and ten percent far less damaging than 25 percent and above.

Within any given country, some elements of the political machinery are likely to divert more resources than others. The actual incidence of corruption may vary, for example, depending on whether one is examining the upper level or the lower levels of a bureaucracy, Agency A or Agency B.[109] Huntington asserts that "most political systems" exhibit a high *incidence* of corruption "at the lower levels of bureaucratic and political authority," and that, as one moves to higher levels the frequency of corruption, may—depending on the country—remain constant, increase, or decrease. In all cases, however, "the *scale* of corruption (i.e. the average value of the private goods and services involved in a corrupt exchange) increases as one goes up the bureaucratic hierarchy or political ladder."[110] Broad judgments as to whether upper- or lower-level corruption will tend to be more damaging to developmental prospects are difficult to make: bribes at the lower level involve less money per transaction, but may well prove more disruptive to the functioning of the overall legal and administrative order. One can presume, however, that corruption will have the most debilitating impact when it is pervasive throughout a system, not only obstructing the provision of basic services through petty corruption at the lower levels but also resulting in large-scale graft at the top.

From one agency to another, as well, there are commonly great variations in the prevalence of corruption and rent seeking. "Unable to transform the bureaucracy as a whole," Evans explains of Brazil, "political leaders try to create 'pockets of efficiency'" in which universalistic norms governed recruitment and an "ethic of public service" nurtured a "clear esprit de corps." Doner and Ramsay similarly call Thailand a "bifurcated state... divided between politically well insulated macroeconomic agencies [including the Ministry of Finance and the Bank of Thailand] and highly politicized line agencies."[111]

Moreover, the character—and hence impact—of corruption can vary according to whether or not democratic institutions are present. While some systems exhibit a clearer demarcation of administrative agencies and parliamentary bodies than others, in general one can say that the presence of representative institutions and electoral competition opens up the system to the influence of a wider array of actors: party leaders, politicians, and at least some element of a broader public. Moreover, electoral systems offer

> noncorrupt channels for influence that simply do not exist in autocratic systems. For a businessman to give money to a civil servant is generally illegal, whereas the same amount given to a politician's campaign fund may 'buy' just as much influence over government decisions but is quite proper . . . The over-all level of corruption (legally defined) is not necessarily lower in party systems, but the party system generally does legitimize certain patterns of influence that could only occur corruptly in a military/bureaucratic system.[112]

Finally, democratic institutions can in some cases provide new incentives for corruption. In his study of India, Wade concludes that "it is likely that elective institutions have amplified the pressures towards corruption and made it more systematic . . . because of the spiraling cost of fighting elections and nursing a constituency between elections." The relationship between democratic institutions and corruption, however, depends on a broad range of political dynamics: at the same time it enables more persons to seek a place at the trough, it can also provide greater influence to those trying to topple the trough.

Despite the analytical utility of locating where resources may be diverted from developmental goals, it is important to recognize how the various parts generally fit together as one single system of corruption. Wade criticizes those who "treat 'administrative' and 'political,' 'high' and 'low' level corruption as distinct and unconnected forms," demonstrating that they are often "systematically interconnected." Theobald, similarly, treats "administrative and political corruption as dimensions of the same phenomenon, as different sides of the same coin."[113]

6. *Does corruption tend to promote or inhibit the institutionalization of state agencies? What is the impact of corruption on the institutionalization of political parties?* In addition to examining the impact of corruption on the capacity of states to perform important developmental tasks, it is also valuable to consider whether certain types of corruption may promote the institutionalization of bureaucracies and militaries. Returning to the discussion above of the relationship between formal lines of authority and informal networks of power, I propose that a higher degree of convergence between power and authority may occasionally promote state institutionalization. In the late 1950s, for example, then-Colonel Suharto was transferred from his post as regional commander for Central Java because of involvement in a "smuggling scheme ostensibly to raise funds for the 'welfare' of his troops." While personal gain was clearly a major factor, Indonesian generals engaging in such economic activities were also motivated to "maintain the functioning of their units and the loyalty of their troops." State appropriations were insufficient to provision adequately the rank-and-file soldiers, and it was wise for patron-generals to share part of the gains from corrupt activities with a clientele located within the state apparatus.[114] Anderson makes a similar point in his analysis of the "morphology of corruption" in post-independence Indonesia.

In most cases the corruption is not chiefly for the immediate personal advantage of the official assigned to supervise a particular sector of the economy (though such an official is rarely in straitened circumstances). The corruption is typically used to finance a whole sub-sector of the administrative apparatus. That is to say there is a system of parallel financing of favored sectors of the bureaucracy through the invisible flow of corruption running alongside the formal salary-structure. The flow, channeled down through an informal pyramid of patron–client clusters on a typical patrimonial model, serves to reinforce the cohesion of such clusters . . . Thus in many sectors, corruption has become an essential element in the stability of bureaucratic organization.

The second consideration is the impact of corruption on the institutionalization of political parties. This question draws on Huntington, who connects the achievement of more institutionalized parties with the demise of corruption itself:

For an official to award a public office in return for payment to the official is clearly to place private interest over public interest. For an official to award a

public office in return for a contribution of work or money to a party organization is to subordinate one public interest to another, more needy, public
interest . . .Corruption thrives on disorganization, the absence of stable relationships among groups and of recognized patterns of authority. . . [It] varies
inversely with political organization, and *to the extent that corruption builds
parties, it undermines the conditions of its own existence* . . . the incidence of
corruption in those countries where governmental resources have been diverted or 'corrupted' for party-building is on the whole less than it is where parties have remained weak.

Historically, he continues, political parties of the West which were initially "leeches on the bureaucracy in the end become the bark protecting
it from more destructive locusts of clique and family."[115]

As Huntington suggests, however, one should not presume that the
mere contribution of money to a political party will necessarily strength-
en the party itself. Just like bureaucracies, political parties combine formal lines of authority with informal networks of power. In some cases,
grants of money obtained via corruption will promote the institutionalization of the party, but in other cases parties themselves are so riven
along the lines of cliques, factions, and personalities that new resources
are unlikely to have that result. Corruption can indeed contribute to the
important goal of party building, but weak parties may endure even when
they are major beneficiaries of corruption. It is important to take
Huntington's observations a step further, and ask why "corruption builds
parties" in some settings but not others.

7. *To what extent is corruption's impact on economic development counterbalanced by other "growth-promoting economic and political factors?"*
Does a political system generate an internal "sense of limits" able to mitigate the extent of corruption? In assessing the impact of corruption on economic performance, it is commonly argued that other factors may insulate
economies—at least temporarily—from its possibly detrimental effects. In
some settings, as MacIntyre summarizes the argument, it seems, that
"clientelism . . . has been sufficiently counterbalanced by other growth-promoting economic and political factors that have enabled strong economic
growth to continue in the face of rampant rent-seeking, or served to rectify
the situation when the cumulative effect of rent-seeking activities threatened to endanger the economy." Among these factors may be large endow-
ments of natural resources, sizable quantities of foreign aid, strong investor

confidence, and the presence of nascent "market-oriented reform coalitions." The basic notion of considering countervailing factors is valid, but, as MacIntyre demonstrates, this line of inquiry tends to raise as many questions as it answers. Indeed, a simple comparison of how Indonesia and Nigeria utilized their petroleum resources and developed investor confidence during the "oil boom" years returns analysis quite quickly to the question of how some political economies are better equipped than others in insulating themselves from the impact of "rampant rent-seeking."

A far more fundamental "mitigating factor" is the extent to which a political system may be compelled to provide its own internal limits, however modest, to the prevalence of corruption. The presence of external threat is often a key factor in encouraging "a sense of limits," explains Scott, and "an elite which enjoys a measure of cohesion and security can develop a sense of its collective, long-run interest." In many cases, however, "limits are virtually absent."[116] To the extent that corrupt practices become culturally embedded over the course of decades or even generations, it will likely be all the more difficult to promote a stronger sense that "enough is enough."

Conclusion

For many decades, scholars have inquired into the impact of corruption, clientelism, and rents on the process of economic growth in the developing world. This paper has attempted to draw very broadly on some of the lessons developed in the course of past inquiry, and contribute toward a framework that can help us to understand better why a range of related phenemona may be relatively more compatible or obstructive to developmental goals. The content of the framework presented here is tentative, but in the process of construction I hope to have demonstrated the utility of an eclectic approach, able to extract valuable insights not only from recent contributions to the topic but also from those made in decades past.

Moreover, I hope to have highlighted how the politics of privilege may vary in both character and impact from one setting to another. Although initially developed for analysis of Third World countries, as explained at the outset, it is my hope that this framework might also be relevant to analysis of former Second World countries as well. Applying the framework to a range of polities—each with its own particular landscape of special advantage—will likely yield very different conclusions about the impact of rents, corruption, and clientelism on developmental outcomes.[117] Admittedly, the model proposed above lacks parsimony; but so, for that matter, have many previous attempts at explaining these issues.[118] Perhaps a narrower or more abstract approach could produce greater simplicity— not to mention more scientific precision; but, in all likelihood, some important aspects of (not surprisingly, complex and diverse) reality would be discarded in the process. For all the efforts that have gone into this line of inquiry in the past, it remains the case that corruption, "a phenomenon which affects administration, politics, business, education, health and a host of other crucial areas of social life . . . has been so little studied."[119]

Future comparative research is necessary to prioritize the elements of analysis more clearly and pursue major issues in greater detail. To the extent possible, it would be useful to develop measures of the variability of corruption, the dissipation of resources in the process of allocating particularistic advantage, and the diversion of budgetary resources from developmental purposes. It is also worthwhile to review the presence or absence of performance criteria across various sectors, and seek to understand more clearly the political processes by which barriers to competition are imposed and maintained. Finally, more research is needed to understand the interconnections of various forms of corruption as found throughout the entire political system, and the structural conditions that may promote (but by no means guarantee) a stronger "sense of limits." As inquiry continues, it is sure to be hobbled by many of the same obstacles that have long plagued the study of corruption. Research can only benefit, however, by drawing freely from the various literatures that have sought to answer, in the past, many of the same questions we are seeking to answer today.

PART II

CORRUPTION AS POLITICS

Bismarck's Reich, founded in 1871, had a reputation, rightly or wrongly, for being less corrupt than its neighbors, Austria–Hungary and (especially) tsarist Russia. Never mind that King Ludwig of Bavaria was paid a colossal bribe, 4.7 million marks, in exchange for agreeing to unification—he claimed he needed the money for upkeep of his castles—or that Bismarck was able to draw upon the fortune of the court and the compensation payments exacted after the Prussian–Danish War, to create a special "Reptile Fund," which he used without parliamentary oversight to gather dirt on socialists and other enemies, pay off journalists (sometimes entire newspapers), and bribe party leaders to join political coalitions. Despite all this, and the fact that it was not only the Nazis who solicited large "donations" from industrialists and the wealthy, corruption in Germany never evolved into a dominant image of the country. Moreover, incidences of corruption came to seem a matter of ancient history. By the 1950s only a tiny handful of West German civil servants were being sentenced for bribe taking (even though tip-of-the-iceberg rumors circulated that enormous bribes had been paid to make Bonn and not Frankfurt the post-WWII capital).[120] In short, by reputation Germany was "clean." Then, however, came the abrupt downfall, in a party-finance corruption scandal, of the political giant and re-unification chancellor, Helmut Kohl. What happened, people exclaimed? Had Germany been utterly corrupt all along?

Erhard Blankenburg's analysis of the great scandals that shook West European political systems, including Germany's, in the 1990s, poses an ostensibly simple question: did corruption increase during that decade, as the attention given to it might indicate, or did a certain constellation of institutions and interests shift, leading to a new intensity of exposé? His answer is indirect, but forceful. Blankenburg observes that in many previous instances, allegations of scandal had not led to charges of corruption, and thus he urges us to consider why and how corruption has been exposed at particular times and places, with consequences often exceeding the aims of those who set the scandals in motion. For the 1990s he points to the increased popularity and remuneration of a certain type of highly competitive, vicious investigative journalism and a new assertiveness on the part of low-level but powerful judges, who together produced a rising scandal industry. Blankenburg gives captivating examples of how the exposure of corruption via scandalization worked and of how behavior that had been accepted as legitimate and normal suddenly took on a new, sinister shading. He wonders, therefore, whether we can possibly discuss an "increase" in corruption when the very definition of corruption and its pursuit underwent profound changes, as a result of politics. For all we know, he suggests, corruption might have decreased during the scandalous 1990s.

Blankenburg focuses on Germany and the "Latin" countries Italy, France, Spain (inclusion of the former pre-empts the usual stereotyping). Space permitting, he might also have taken up the U.K. (the collapse of the conservative party, partly in relation to the Archer Affair), Sweden (the Bofors Affair), or Belgium (incidents of political protection being extended to child murderers), not to mention the EU itself (the scandal-induced resignation of the EU president and commission). Whatever the many repercussions, Blankenburg traces the onset of Europe's exposure culture to the 1970s Lockheed scandal in his native Netherlands, but he notes that, during the cold-war struggle against Communism, West European media tended not to attack domestic corruption systematically. What is particularly noteworthy in his argument is the role of those he views as "small people" employed in the law. Whereas public prosecutors had tended to offer plea bargains, which were often accepted by those indicted on corruption charges to keep their names out of the paper, such an inclination to obtain penalties for state coffers in plea bargains became less in evidence during the 1990s, when prosecutors often failed to obtain convictions or penalties in court cases but gained notoriety for themselves. These members of the middle class, lacking elite club memberships or large salaries, helped push through a corruption revolution, which with the aid of the much-expanded commercial media, radically altered public perceptions of their own societies and politics. That the political titan Kohl could be brought so low so quickly cannot be laid exclusively at the door of the double-dealing Chancellor.

The conclusion appears incontrovertible: "corruption" is not solely a matter of the betrayal of trust, or rule violation, but a social and political phenomenon involving an array of contending interests. Corruption is politics. This is an utterly banal statement, to be sure, but one that bears elucidating. Such is the task of Part II.

•

Corruption, as transition countries know all too well, can be a synonym for an entire socio-economic system, but who recalls that corruption could be synonymous with a system that lifted a country out of extreme poverty? Today's prevailing demonization of corruption, especially among economists, has trouble handling examples of successful "corrupt" economies, like South Korea, where spectacular growth—130-times leap in GNP in just 36 years—took place under acknowledged grand corruption based on collusive bureaucracies and non-competitive *chaebol*. Evidently, not all corrupt structures are alike, or have the same consequences in specific contexts. One may have little sympathy for authoritarianism and corporatism but, historically, the record of free market-based development (or purported free-market development) is not always as impressive as that of "distorted" development strategies.[121] To be sure, the extent to which avowedly corrupt growth was tied to a specific international conjuncture—such that its time has "passed"—can be debated, but one should not read the supposed standards for present-day economic performance backwards. It is, of course, quite right to blame corrupt structures and their resulting inefficiencies for the 1998 financical crisis and much else. Still, the long-term results of corrupt growth were not eliminated by the temporary crisis. All this is the upshot of Joongi Kim's analysis of South Korean clientelism, amplifying this volume's earlier essay by Paul Hutchcroft.

Following the work of others, especially Carter Eckert, Kim locates the onset of *modern* Korean clientelism (a social structure in which corruption flourishes) in the period of Japanese occupation (1910–45). Certain Korean businesses developed special relationships with the Japanese and learned that collaboration could be a guarantee of business success. Korean beneficiaries of Japanese patronage later managed to assume the same clientelistic role under new patrons who gained control over the country, namely the U.S. occupation forces, and the Syngman Rhee government.[122] Such an analysis can be extended beyond the Korean case. "Balkan" corruption, for example, was a learned pattern of cooperation with the Turkish authorities within the Ottoman Empire. In other words, what is labeled as corruption by today's observer was once upon a time an official form of revenue generation: officials were not paid a salary, under the assumption that they would extract (extort) their upkeep from the population subordinated to them. Of course, contrary to the Korean example, the learned pattern of "corruption" became more diffused in some post-Ottoman Balkan societies, and it had different, long-term economic results (judging so far). Nonetheless, the point holds: "corruption" often denotes the basic functioning of political systems, and that functioning can have far-reaching positive as well as negative effects on economic development, not just consecutively but simultaneously.

Against what can be described as an earlier generation's apologetics for South Korean corruption, however, Kim's thumbnail sketch of South Korean economic and political development stresses inefficiencies and unfortunate consequences, but his analysis also suggests that clientelism can facilitate money transfers to government officials or party coffers without an identifiable quid pro quo. Favors and payments may involve network building and expressions of loyalty. This lack of a clear quid pro quo (and, often, the lack of any departure from formal rules) appears to have caused legal difficulties in the criminal process against the South Korean Presidents Chun and Roh. In these trials of top leaders—unique at the time in world practice—traditional standards of bribery were not met. The former leaders were convicted all the same, however, in a kind of retroactive political pronouncement on their epoch for the new times.

•

Shifts in South Korean understandings of corruption have been notable (indeed in 1993 their Supreme Court changed the operative definition of corruption in the law). Whether one regards such changes as an advance or as a reflection of a new political and international conjuncture, such shifts highlight the fact that transition countries emerged when certain understandings of corruption had come to prevail—understandings that had not obtained over the previous several decades. At least for a while, corruption had seemed to work well for South Korea. The same has not been the reality, or the perception, for post-Soviet Russia, the subject of Virginie Coulloudon's essay on anticorruption politics.

Outsiders have not been sufficiently probing into anticorruption politics. Coulloudon's forcefully presented argument is that both Soviet and post-Soviet "campaigns" against corruption were not what they nominally purported to be; rather, they constituted methods of political infighting aimed at discrediting rivals and building personal power networks. She further contends that these campaigns had the effect of further weakening state authority by undermining its legitimacy. To put the matter another way, anticorruption campaigns in Russia seem to grow ever louder, yet corruption seems not to decline; equally important, the real result is a blackening of the state that accelerates the inefficacy of the state, in a vicious circle. For her, the key question becomes who gains control over anticorruption as a political issue and vehicle to aggrandizement? And yet, the same discrediting appears to have happened to the politically motivated anticorruption campaigns: their ulterior motives, too, are being undermined. Scandals continue to play a role in electoral campaigns, especially regionally, and they continue to entertain the public (selling newspapers or advertising time on electronic media), but fewer and fewer people believe in the sincerity of anticorruption campaigns. People have come to doubt the veracity of most public corruption charges, which are increasingly viewed as political not legal. Nonetheless, the stain still often attaches to the target, and, anyway, there seem to be few other ways of conducting politics, and so the game evolves, yet it goes on.

•

Ákos Szilágyi offers a lively, poetic rumination on these themes of scandal-mongering and mutual attack as everyday politics among elites in Russia. Like Coulloudon, he emphasizes that the "fight against corruption" is not primarily about corruption; it is about access to political and economic power, and one of the primary weapons in *that* fight is compromising material, abbreviated in Russian to *kompromat*. Szilágyi concedes that such use of compromising material ("real" and counterfeit) is encountered throughout recorded history, yet he finds a special quality to the post-1991 Russian example. In Russia kompromat became a full-fledged industry, staffed by the enormous surplus of KGB personnel from the Soviet State and fed by a newly unleashed media. At the same time, however, as everyone and every institution in the Russian state was tarred with the broad brush of "corruption," it seemed as if the only clean or un-compromised institution was, ironically, the old KGB (renamed FSB). This at least partly, helps account for the Putin phenomenon: a president emerges from the agency at the core of the manufacture and dissemination of kompromat and the state agency that was the most trusted by the public.

Beyond the example of the renegade former Vice-President Alexander Rutskoi's infamous eleven suitcases in 1993, Szilágyi does not labor over the many cases when kompromat was attempted but did not take hold. Nor does he have space to offer comparisons to other countries where kompromat is either as widely practiced as in Russia

(Ukraine) or not nearly as successful (Poland) which showed that scandal-mongering was far from automatic. Belarus President Lukashenko headed that country's parliamentary commission on corruption (no one else had wanted the job) before his first successful presidential bid (the commission was then expanded and moved into the presidential administration). Thus the particularities of the Russian case remain to be established further, but Szilágyi does indicate that the kompromat phenomenon in Russia was losing steam by the late 1990s. Much of the "action" seems to have shifted to Web sites, a more self-enclosed world. It is not clear if this and other changes constitute, in his argument, a fundamental restructuring of the nature of politics and elite behavior, or simply a tactical shift in an ongoing game. Has the post-Soviet malformation of the Soviet era run its course? Will scandal in Russia become "normal"? Will anticorruption cease to be the central language and mode of politics, replaced by more clear-cut ideological competition and better-organized, defined power blocs? Lurking behind kompromat, it seems, lies the deeply personalized nature of Russian politics—clientelism, networks, and patronage—as well as an enduring sense that politics is somehow never what it seems.

•

To analyze, as Blankenburg, Kim, Coulloudon and Szilágyi do, the anticorruption campaigns and the politics of scandal and kompromat by no means implies the normative assumption that it is all smoke and no fire, or that dealing with (naming) corruption only aggravates the problem. However, given the political role of the corruption moniker, it becomes very difficult, if not impossible, to isolate anticorruption reform from populism or the manufacture of corruption. "'Corruption' means what people think it means, and exists where they think they see it," Arnold Heidenheimer once wrote. His follow-on point was sobering: "The utility of reform efforts must be balanced against the costs and benefits of corruption itself . . . Corruption must be compared to its genuine, imperfect alternatives. We may at times conclude that while corruption entails significant costs and waste of scarce resources, there are few real assurances that its absence would have resulted in better policy and politics."[123] That is not a call to inaction but to hard-nosed realism, differentiation, and more specific targeting.

The more that "corruption" could be defined (and measured) as an economic problem, the more it seemed amenable to policy prescriptions applied in technocratic fashion (without stakeholders)—whether privatization, deregulation, transparency, or the like. The more corruption seemed to be a political problem—indeed an entire system of social relations—the more it seemed congenitally resistant to reform, let alone eradication, and became an all-encompassing "condition" of existence. Conveniently, therefore, the "epidemic" of corruption has afforded both supposedly non-political, missionary work for economists, bankers, and experts, and an all-purpose excuse for their evident lack of success. The decade of the 1990s may ultimately be remembered not as the decade of grand corruption but the decade of a grand anticorruption bacchanalia. A response need not involve a retreat to "cultural" excuse making, but crafting an informed political approach to what is a thoroughly political problem.

From Political Clientelism to Outright Corruption— The Rise of the Scandal Industry[124]

Erhard Blankenburg

Western Europe saw a wave of corruption scandals in the 1990's that shook their political systems. Changes in four arenas help to explain the increased scandalization, in terms of corruption, of what for long had been seen as clientele patterns imbedded in local, regional and national politics.

First, in the political arena traditional ideological party loyalties broke down, and the polarization of bourgeois parties having to defend against the communist/socialist threat disappeared. Election campaigns have consequently become much more dependent on ever new mobilization of voters. Increasing needs of party and campaign financing resulted in giving rise to a new type of "business politicians". Second, the ideological and moral gap that resulted from these political changes was filled by a moral campaign on the part of a few judges and prosecutors, who in Latin countries (Italy, France and Spain) enjoy a strong position in the criminal investigation process. Using preliminary arrests and search warrants in sometimes-spectacular actions against prominent suspects, they managed to stage scandals with high-profile news. In Germany where investigations of prosecutors are more tightly controlled, scandals have been less frequent, but once they broke loose with the help of investigative journalists, they have had devastating effects on the party establishments involved. Even though guilty verdicts could not always be attained, investigations themselves became embarrassing enough to stop the careers of suspects and to let them look for pre-trial settlements. (One could adduce related examples just as readily from Great Britain or Sweden, or from the EU itself, for that matter.)

Third, the increasing competition among mass media and their investments in investigative journalism have helped escalate these scandals. In repeated attempts of creating scandal sensations, the media have developed their own moral entrepreneurship testing innovative fields of moral sensitivity and public outrage. Thus, scandalization became nationally divergent, using sex in some countries, police and terrorism in others, but corruption issues in all of them. Finally, the international business community became increasingly defensive against the trade barriers that corruption networks grant to local and national markets. Free trade on global markets is vitally interested in universalistic and dependable legal rules. It is, therefore, not amazing that the World Bank supports anticorruption drives of organizations like Transparency International.

The upshot from the interplay in these four arenas, each acting according to its own logic, is a remarkable increase of corruption scandals around the world, with particular judicial legitimization in the Latin countries of Europe. It would be impossible to say whether corruption practices have really increased in European politics, as the very concept of "corruption" is constantly reformulated as a social construction resulting from this interplay.

The Use of Corruption Scandals in Political Competition

"If ever you want to damage a competitor in politics, if you think that a generation of politicians has been in office too long, or if you want to set the agenda for politics anew, look for corruption as an instrument of political scandal. In order to be effective, the allegation has to be orchestrated with some potential for escalation. Make a strong bang at the beginning, but be prepared to back up your fire, look to it that you have some powder left for answering counter-attacks and draw the range of your allegations wider, so that your competitors think it better to admit and quit rather than to risk further revelations." This advice could be the text of a handbook for modern politicians—and, even though it has not yet been written, professionals are already following its recipe. They can learn from the worldwide experience in the dynamics of corruption allegations, following the scandals around the bribing practice of *Lockheed* that swept around the capitalist world in the early 1970s. It was the American *Newsweek* which made effective use of the bribe recipients for the political arena at home and—quite unexpectedly—unleashed scandals in the countries of the bribe payers. Among the many prominent politicians affected were the Japanese Prime Minister Tanaka, President Leone in Italy and Prince Bernhard of the Netherlands—all of them found guilty of corruption. Up to then they had been respected figures in their respective domestic arenas, and there was no reason to challenge them for their clientelist behavior, which was simply seen as part of their political culture. In Japan and Italy, as well as in the Dutch royal house, the elites were quite upset that foreign media ostracized them for behavior which in domestic terms had always been taken for normal. The

American magazine in the beginning had a local scandalizing interest, it did not intend more than to claim international rules of competition and fair trade in the weapons industry, but in the end, the Lockheed Scandal shattered a few established political regimes around the world.

We might consider the *Lockheed* scandals as the other side of economic globalization in our days. An originally local scandal of a news magazine escalated to become a global event: the establishment of a universalistic standard of free trade and fair competition as a favorite topic of globalizing mass media. With gobal communication, the *Lockheed Scandal* also initiated standards for the scandalizing of corruption. However, the enthusiasm about globalism should not let us forget the observation of Carl J. Friedrich[125] that, even though the reproach of corruption has been made at all times, the phenomena under charge have been changing persistently from one historical period to the other. Therefore, the attempts are vain to find a universal causal explanation of the occurrence of corruption, such as that by van Klaveren,126 who postulated that lack of moral control of a middle class would be responsible for corrupt practices.

The thesis fits some occurrences which have been perceived as corrupt in their times: for example, the enrichment of colonial officers in the Dutch East Indian Company, which van Klaveren analyzed. It also meets with the facts in France of the nineteenth century when the rising bourgeoisie accused the *Ancien Régime* of forming a closed and corrupt clientele. They claimed the moral standards of the ever-rising bourgeoisie using the normative ideal of correct civil servants who are bound by law as counter-image to the corrupt nobility. However, van Klaveren's thesis does not meet the ambition of finding a common denominator for other historical phenomena, for example, when looking at corruption in baroque times. Forced by history, van Klaveren has to admit the contingency of the concept of corruption when the prominent High Chancellor Francis Bacon was impeached under the accusation of his corrupt court practice; and the bourgeois standards seem entirely turned around when King Louis XIV praised the resources gained from the purchase of high office in court as a means to reduce uncontrolled corruption. It took the French revolution to abolish the legal purchase of office (together with the nobility altogether).

History teaches that the definition of what is seen as corrupt changes with the regimes and especially its oppositions.[127] It follows that, before the analysis of any phenomena of corruption, comes the analysis of those who define it as such. That involves more traps than might be expected. It is far too tempting to look only at those cases where the allegation has been successful in leading to scandal. As is the case with any behavior that is morally condemned, the dark field of outrage without consequences and of allegations without success is by far greater than the highlighted field of full-fledged scandalizing. Any theory of corruption therefore has to give an answer to the difficult questions of non-events: why, at what time, which allegations of which definition of corruption culminated in scandals, while so many others did not.

Scandals come in waves; they announce changes in social and moral moods, often before academic discourses catch up with them. Therefore, it is worthwhile reading them as a moral mirror of the state of political regimes. However, in the frenzy of scandals it should not be undervalued that in order to shatter the legitimacy of an entire regime, there needs to be a fundamental underlying weakness. It takes more serious (mostly economic) calamities before a corrupt system effectively breaks down.

Contemporary Arenas of Corruption Allegations

In the 1990s corruption allegations became a regular instrument of politics all over Western Europe. Corruption scandals shook up politics in Italy, Spain, and France, they swept over the cities of Berlin and Frankfurt, and at the end of the decennium destroyed the monument of fame that the German Chancellor had built for himself with the success of the German unification.

Not that corruption had been new to any of these political systems—it had usually been taken as a normal fact of politics, triggering some cynical gossip at best. The surprise was that a practice that seemed so normal could arouse scandals, that they could effectively terminate the career of politicians and escalate to the breakdown of political parties and their regimes. The explanation has to be sought in the interaction of at least four arenas that each changed independently of each other, but that have interacted. Together they form a new pattern according to which the political game is played.

1) The fall of communist regimes in Eastern Europe ended an era of ideologically defined parties with a firm class basis among their members

as well as voters. Their demise has been observed as an ongoing process since the 1970s, in the Latin countries somewhat later than in the welfare states of Northwest Europe. Solid voter blocks gradually became supporters of single-issue movements changing according to the actual political situations. Consequently, the place of political parties and trade unions polarized along the lines of class, and religious denomination was taken by political campaign organizations, very similar to American party machines. Increasingly, politicians have to collect ever-higher financial support for their campaigns.

Depending on the number and organization of their sponsors they have to pay back in political currency after the elections: not only by fulfilling programatic promise, but also by supplying sponsors with influential positions and prestigious office. In the United States such a "spoils system" is part of the traditional set of rules of democracy, which is only emphasized by the flood of regulations by which Washington tries to make "spoils" transparent. The structural problem of party financing of the American campaigns now reached European countries, which had relied on rather stable, often publicly subsidized, party financing. Politics therefore had become more prone to corruption, and thereby politicians became endangered as victims of scandalization.

2) This scandalization is the job of the media. The increasing competition among an increasing number of media forced them to chase ever-new sensations. Trying to win some advantage by exploiting privileged information over a short time, many political magazines and newspapers have built up teams of investigatory journalists—thereby explicitly following the example given by *Newsweek, Washington Post* and *Der Spiegel* in the 1970s. Since the 1980s television companies and independent news agencies followed suit by investing in long-term investigation projects, sometimes engaging in merciless *papparazzi* fights for successful scandals. The tone of their revelations qualified them as moral entrepreneurs who, by often creative imagination, invent novel allegations, thus simply using trial and error to find out which topics might be suitable to arouse a moral panic.

3) Also, the business community has come under higher pressures of competition, in their case a direct consequence of globalization. Protection of national industries has been an age-old tradition in all highly developed countries with networks of big industry, banking facilities and state guaranteed infrastructures (such as railways, airports or postal

services). At various times there have been reasons for subsidizing, either because labor was in danger (as in mining or steel industries) or because research and development had to be stimulated. Wherever business and politics needed each other, they had formed problem-solving coalitions, which only too often survived the acute crisis and grew into stable clientele structures. International competition in the 1980s and 1990s has shed doubts on many of these protective coalitions between industries and national politics. Global free trade liberalism with its rules in GATT agreements, World Bank conditions and the treaties of European (as well as American or Asian free trade zones) opened the national arenas, forced them to privatize state-run companies. Fighting corruption on the side of bribers as well as of the bribed has been one of the credos of the globalization efforts.

4) New to the game among the arenas is the prominent role of prosecutors and investigative judges. Especially in Latin countries of Europe, but with some imitation effects also in Germany, judicial procedures have triggered major political scandals in the course of their (preliminary) investigations. Remarkably, they have not so much impressed the political class with definite convictions and criminal sentences (even though these might have followed in selected cases), but rather with some of the measures that they took in the course of their investigations. This explains why it first came up among Italian prosecutors and among (what the French call) "small judges" who in their system enjoy extraordinary powers to guide investigations and to instruct police and tax authorities. Judicial activism among them has been explained as the ideology of a young generation of jurists who are less bound up with the bourgeois establishments of the traditional jurists.

Once it attracts the mass media, the legal process usually gains momentum. The media only too gladly use the courts of justice as a stage for scandalizing. The game has to be played with utmost care, however. If media become somewhat careless about unfounded suspicion, they bring active judicial investigators into great danger. Investigative action such as arrests of, or seizures at, the homes and offices of prominent persons easily leaks out to the media. In reaction prosecutors have to be doubly cautious not to perform spectacular measures without gathering substantial proof for suspicion. Once this is achieved, however, their investigations are frequently helped by the media and their pressure on public figures to declare some of their guilt (and to explain away the unproven parts of it), in order to prevent the scandal from growing somehow. The mechanism might also explain why the public does not mind any more that final verdicts often follow much later or get buried under procedural finesse altogether: the process was the punishment.

It is obvious that the four arenas interact. While each of the actors operates according to his own logic, the overall effect is one of rendering scandals a permanent stage for a moral as well as a legal discourse. It is a discourse about the terms under which "corruption" is defined and redefined.

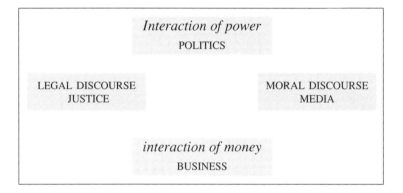

Each of the arenas can be portrayed as a relatively closed system. For our understanding of corruption scandals, however, interactive links are more important than system boundaries. They are at the same time discourses of moral and legal arguments as they are interaction systems by which power is effectuated. Actors can use them interchangeably and try to step from one arena to the other by either judicializing politics or politicizing the arena of justice, instrumentalizing mass media for legitimation purposes or buying political decisions. The arena of justice figures prominently by providing scandals with moralizing symbolism and with the serenity of the law.

Recent Corruption Scandals Which Changed Political Systems in Western Europe

All over Western Europe the interaction of the four arenas explains the increase of corruption scandals in the past years, but it does so in culturally specific ways.

The high art of scandalous theater is to be found in Italy. The "clean hands" scandals *(mani pulite)* began harmlessly, but they triggered the collapse of the entire Italian party system in the 1990s. Mario Chiesa, a petty administrator of a socialist housing corporation and of orphanages in Milan was arrested in 1992 for a charge of embezzlement. Having public housing at his hand, he was well equipped to favor socialist party supporters, securing votes as well as collecting financial contributions for the party in exchange. He was furious, when under arrest, the powerful party boss Craxi called him "a petty mariolo" and subsequently dropped him. Chiesa took revenge by "singing" and involving others in his affair. When the party intervened and tried to get Chiesa out of prison, it was too late. Such attempts only brought the bosses and Craxi himself into focus. To make things worse, their counterattack on the press and on the investigating prosecutors failed. Instead, the affair escalated into a full-fledged scandal. Within a year the socialist party was delegitimized, Craxi fled to Tunisia where he had to stay in fear of criminal prosecution at home. He died in exile in 1999.

Other parties only shortly enjoyed the breakdown of the socialists. Counterattacks brought the scandalizing technique to full swing and extended it to the entire party system of Italy. What until then had been regarded as the normal practice of clientelism was successfully labeled by the prosecution and by the press as "corruption."

The technique of "scandal theatre" made the local prosecutor Di Pietro a national hero, and encouraged imitators throughout the entire apparatus of justice. There was no lack of counterattacks, however: the prosecutors in Brescia investigated Di Pietro, accusing him of corruption and demonstrating thereby the degree of polarization within the Italian justice system, but the procedure against the preosecutor had to be terminated for lack of proof, and Di Pietro tried, temporarily to serve in political office.

At the same time, businessmen who stood under suspicion of corruption entered politics. In an attempt to reform the party system in 1994, Silvio Berlusconi had to give in after a short and promising government period under the pressure of investigations and procedures directed at his own business enterprise. He had to face two verdicts of corrupt practice, fighting them through possible appeals, while a third investigation remains under way. He defended himself with the obvious argument that even a businessman with the most honest intentions, could not help but give in to the extortion of civil servants, tax inspectors and parties to pay the usual clientelistic contributions and outright bribes. According to him, not the briber but the bribee had to be blamed for corruption. His various media support his allegation that the system of justice was experimenting with a "Marxist coup d'état."

With so many allegations and counter-allegations it is no wonder that only a fraction of all investigations lead to a final condemnation. In the course of 2,970 "clean hands" investigations in Milan, investigative judges had taken up 1,063 charges by 1998 and of these a mere 438 led to a verdict in court.[128] The scandals had managed to terminate a few political careers, and had shaken political parties, but it remains doubtful how long their impact would last. By the end of the 1990s parliamentary scenes of verbal, and sometimes physical, polarization cast some doubt on the optimism that the new parties could stand the test of a thorough party reform.

What remains, however, is the fortified political role of the courts of justice, especially of the institution of investigating prosecutors. The scandal theater strengthened the autonomy of justice which (even though already promised in the 1948 constitution) were introduced first in 1958 with the establishment of a *Consiglio Supremo da la Magistratura*. This highest council has successfully shielded the recruitment and promotion of judges from direct intervention by the executive branch.[129] According to the constitution, the autonomy of the magistrates includes prosecutors, who, after the amendment of the penal procedural code in 1989, enjoy the same competence that had formerly been the power basis of investigative judges. The autonomy of criminal investigations more than ever forms the backbone of the definition power of the magistrates, enabling them to act in politically sensitive criminal investigations. It might be considered the price of this political power, however, that the *Consiglio Supremo* itself has not been able to prevent further polarization of the magistrates in politically opposed camps.

France, too, in the 1990s saw a breakdown of political clientelism, even though at first only in the provinces. Justice heroes such as van Ruymbeke, Halpern and others became well-known names in the news in the country itself and beyond. Since 1992 the satirical magazine *Le Canard Enchaîné* has regularly taken the initiative to conduct exposés; since 1994 the most respected daily newspaper *Le Monde* has been listing more than one honored politician every year who was arrested and put on remand. Here, too, investigatory competence is decisive. Because the French prosecutorial office was still hierarchically subordinated under the Minister of Justice, politically sensitive procedures, especially in Paris, were often directed to *nonsuit*. Scandals in the provinces, however, escalated. Since 1997, when the President's office and government entered into open antagonism with the opposing parties, the national taboo on each other's hidden scandalous mines has become precarious: the polarization of the co-habitation of a socialist government with a Gaullist presidency might render scandals possible among the political friends of the President (while he himself remains constitutionally immune from criminal investigations).

Judges, however, are independent in France, and as according to Latin tradition, the criminal procedural code leaves investigatory judges the authority to direct any criminal investigation themselves (which is even emphasized in appeal as the competence of *conseiller*), these have developed a considerable potential for raising scandal. They can order a warrant of arrest and issue a writ of capias, which in the case of prominent suspects cannot remain unnoticed by the media. In defense of their judicial autonomy independent judges and hierarchically dependent prosecutors have been playing subtle games of judicial procedure.[130] In some scandals (such as those around the financial manipulations of the *URBA corporation*, 1991) investigative judges used their right of personal inspection and of issuing a search warrant explicitly in order to shield their investigations against a hierarchical order of *nolle prosequi* by the Prosecutor General. In such cases the support of the media disclosing information that has reached them without open breach of confidence can be a great help in effectuating criminal justice. Even if they are careful not to actively alert journalists (as those above), an implicit degree of instrumentalization of the media cannot be denied. The investigation easily develops into public condemnation. Critics, especially among the suspects involved, therefore raise the allegation of a "coup d'état of the petty judges."[131]

In Spain, Judge Garzon played a similar role as the Italian and French justice heroes. As national investigation judge (*juéz central de instrucción* at the *Audiencia Nacional*) his competence reaches from the war against drugs and other forms of organized crime to fighting terrorism, high treason or crimes against humanity. Scandals under his investigation contributed significantly to delegitimizing the Gonzalez government in 1996,[132] and here, too, the collusion of investigatory judges with the media served inevitably as a means of public ostracism. The ambition of the Spanish judges did not stop at the country's borders: in prosecuting ex-president Pinochet and high-ranking Argentinian generals (in the name of victims residing in Spain), they have triggered a wave of imitations across Western Europe which might lead to the emergence of an international legal order of human rights. Nobody should be amazed that such a breakdown of national sovereignty has called (not only some high-ranking political friends) to the defense of the accused.

The constellation of politically emancipated magistrates opposing the patterns of traditionally clientelistic politics rests in all European countries on social changes among a new generation of judges and prosecutors, which is rendered even more acute by the growth of the personnel of the courts of justice. Latin countries had been accustomed to historically close ties of the representatives of justice to the political establishment: twenty years ago Spanish courts were still dominated by Francoists, the Italian courts were polarized between Christian Democrats and leftist parties, and the French ones closely allied with regional and national elites. The delegitimation of these regimes and breakdown of the establishment elites gave the new generation a chance for establishing institutions of autonomy for the magistrates as a "third power" in the *trias politica*. An expression of their independence is the establishment of Supreme Councils of the Magistracy in all three countries, which reserve the right of recruitment and promotion of judges and of regulating the conditions of their work.

The politics of scandals, however, has always been the privilege of *single* judges and prosecutors, who managed to fight political corruption and tax embezzlement by raising the support of popular morals. The Prosecutor General Bernard Bertossa in Geneva invited the figures of judicial protest of the Latin countries to formulate a common declaration. Their Geneva Appeal of 1995 understands itself as an attempt to form a common front of justice as a moral institution *vis-à-vis* the systems of illegal finance, corrupt politicians and tax-evading business corporations.[133]

In Italy, as well as in France, the scandals of the 1990s were triggered by a new generation of investigative prosecutors and judges who went to law school during the years of student rebellions; in Spain they came into office after the Franco regime. They were more active in using the legal powers that the increased autonomy of magistrates grants them, and they dared to interact with the media. Thereby some of their protagonists gained influence on the political arena. While traditionally prosecution and courts had played a finalizing role in legitimizing the scandalization which other players had set loose, the corruption scandals in Latin countries of the 1990s were often initiated by investigatory judges and prosecutors.

Of course, this evoked a countercharge that these petty judges lack any democratic legitimacy.[134] The more the effective judges play a political role, the more they have to account for standards of legitimacy. Therefore, any policy of active scandalization brings the profession into the arena of politics with its specific dependencies. Only tight control of all investigations and strict secrecy of the allegations would prevent the instrumentalization of judicial action outside the public hearings in the courtroom. How such control can protect politicians for a long time, and how devastating the effects are when they break loose after all, can be seen in the party-financing scandals in Germany that destroyed the reputation of Chancellor Helmut Kohl.

Party financing has been a controversial issue in German politics for more than fourty years. Since 1958 the Constitutional Court (BVerfG) had ruled that tax deductions of party donations unduly favor parties which are backed by financially strong interest groups and corporations, and the political parties started looking for ever-new ways of public financing. It led to direct subsidies for the established parties that the BVerfG had to restrict again by another ruling in 1968, allowing only for "reimbursement of expenses for public functions." This challenged the creativity of the parties to invent a multitude of ways of obtaining public revenues such as a flat sum of DM 2,50 for each vote attained in elections, reimbursement of costs for their parliamentary staff and financing of political education by party foundations. The BVerfG also ruled on the statutory regulation of publication of private donations, performing some drastic changes of mind. From 1968 any donation above DM 600 was ruled due to be published to 1986 when the limit was set at DM 100,000.

The latter constitutional ruling came at the end of the Flick Scandal, which unveiled major donations of a few million DM to the ruling Christian Democrats (CDU) and the Free Democrats (FDP) in exchange for tax exemption on the sale of the industrial imperium. It was triggered by the investigative journalism of the weekly magazine *Der Spiegel*, which in 1981/82 managed not only to launch the scandalous story, but also to survive various counterattacks of blame for breach of privacy and for publicly condemning mere suspects. Especially information that might have been leaked from the files of the Bonn prosecutors was suspected, so that the Federal government launched accusation proceedings against the judiciary in North Rhine–Westphalia (which resorted under a Minister of the Social-Democratic opposition) to disclosing information to the press. However, even though it was evident that information from the judicial files had been leaked, the counterattack remained unsuccessful as no prooof could be found against any of the prosecutors.

Throughout the one and a half years that the scandal evolved, the strategy of *Der Spiegel* was to always hold back some information, so that each attack could be followed by further details of the scandalous story of scandals.[135]

Counterattacks by the embarrassed parties on their political competitors had success, however. In the course of the 1980s the same magazine revealed some of the systems of bribery and collusion of (mostly Social-Democratic) building contractors, housing corporations and their banks that were close to the trade union movement. The series of scandals led to the bankruptcy of huge enterprises of the *Neue Heimat* and of the co-operative banks related to them.

The Flick Scandal and the scandals around the co-operative industries demonstrate that there are quite capable scandal entrepreneurs among the German media, blaming all sides of the political spectrum. The role of the judiciary, however, remained reluctant and largely reactive in Germany. In contrast to their colleagues in Latin countries in Europe, the hierarchy of public prosecutors keep their investigations under strict secrecy and tight control. Of course, not leaking allegations to the media and not accusing before sufficient proof is available serves to protect suspects from being ostracized by the public, which might at the same time seem to be a strategy of safeguarding professional independence. Being bound by statutory law and jurisprudence to the principle of mandatory accusation (*Legalitätsprinzip*), German prosecutors general have managed to keep their office largely out of political controversies. The price to be paid for such professional integrity is that the majority of corruption cases do not lead to conviction in the courtroom.[136]

A few exceptions confirm rather than negate the rule. Activist prosecutors (like StA Schaupensteiner in Frankfurt), who tried to bring local corruption patterns into the public discussion in the early 1990s, had only moderate success: as most of the investigations against local corruption had to be terminated because of lack of proof, the publications turned into a self-inflicted scandal blaming the ineffectiveness of prosecution rather than unveiling the corruption pattern itself.[137] That satisfied the limited goal of the scandal raisers: following a truly legalistic policy, they stuck to the inner-directed aim of enlarging their investigative competence, an aim that they satisfied in 1997 by an amendment of the penal procedural code.

Nevertheless, under exceptional circumstances, strict legalism can also lead to scandals, even in a hierarchically controlled German state such as Bavaria. Only after Chancellor Kohl had left office and his power base was fading was it brought to light that the Flick scandals of the 1980s had only driven his party into even more clandestine illegality. In 1990, the East German election campaigns presented acute financial needs to the party, but the unification also presented special opportunities for receiving money in the course of the privatization of East German industries. The party thus not only continued, but even increased its dubious financing practices throughout the 1990s.

It led to a new outburst of scandal around CDU party financing. The Augsburg prosecutors' office had opened investigations against some lobbyists of the German arms industry in relation to big transactions with party officials of the CDU as early as 1997(at the time the governing party under Chancellor Kohl, although not organized or represented in the State of Bavaria where the sister party the CSU, traditionally dominates). Augsburg prosecutors were competent for the investigations by the mere fact that the main suspect was registered in their district. Investigations lingered on for more than three years, but the very fair and legalistic prosecutor would not close the file, especially as evidence was provided on his request by the prosecution office in Geneva/Switzerland (where, as we have seen, one of the centers of the European anticorruption judicial activists) can be found. It took until November 1999 that an arrest warrant against the CDU finance official (the, by now retired, honorable Dr. Leisler-Kiep) and the suspected lobbyist (Dr. Schreiber) became public. As the latter was in Toronto/Canada at the time, he could prevent his arrest by waging a claim against extradiction by the German judicial authorities. It opened for the media free access to his stories which he disclosed piece-by-piece in order to threaten the German establishment and divert it from pursuing its procedure any further. It was too late. Within the following four months one disclosure after another of illegal financing practices of the CDU was unveiled by the media, by parliamentary commissions and by the disenchanted CDU politicians themselves. It turned the party of former Chancellor Kohl upside-down, destroyed his reputation and brought a new generation of Christian Democratic politicians to the fore.

The Global Dynamics of Scandal Industries

It is evident that each of the scandal stories bears its specific historical and cultural characteristics, but, even though the collaboration of the system of justice with the media underlies national contingencies, it is part of the processes of globalization. The popular, often vulgar, morality of corruption scandals is easily intrumentalized for damaging political opponents, sometimes even for disqualifying them from the political arena altogether. Global learning and imitation have spread ever since the Watergate scandal demonstrated the power of the media in American politics. All over the world, daily newspapers, magazines and television companies have invested in teams for elaborate investigations. Investigatory journalism has produced an complete scandal industry in the past twenty years.

As usual in the innovative race of the contemporary global economy, the United States stands on the frontier of inventing ever-new public drama. However, the political scandals around the sexual adventures of President Clinton in 1998 show that allegations in Puritan America can extend much beyond corruption into issues of sex and crime. Media exposure of what, in most countries on the European continent would be still considered private affairs drew them into the sphere of television soaps and the special investigation initiated by Congress and performed with all of the judicial finesse of adversarial procedures, used the legitimacy and the symbols of a judicial procedure for a manifestly political game.

Imitation effects can even be seen in Russia where the system of all-pervasive corruption is used as an easily mobilized norm trap, which is instrumentalized by all political sides as a weapon against any political competitor.

Back in Soviet days, Khrushchev and Andropov started their reigns with a cleaning of the administration by large-scale anticorruption campaigns. In a system of double-talk, where the planned economy could only be held up by systematically compensating failures through black market exchange, the allegation of corruption could be raised against anybody at any time. The norm trap was used as a regular means of changing leading personnel. Boris Yeltsin used the same technique in 1992/93 when combating the position of Alexander Rutskoi who had been made chairman of the "Interdepartmental Commission for Fighting Crime and Corruption" in October 1992. In April 1993, he took the chair of the commission himself and in August he unexpectedly announced at a press conference that he had given the Moscow prosecutor an order to investigate big-money transactions with Swiss banks by Rutskoi and his clan. Similar allegations against collaborators in the President's office had preceded this step. Alongside the battle around the "White House," which culminated in its bombing by the President's, the power struggles between Yeltsin and the Duma parliament were fought about who could nominate the prosecutor general. As is well known, the group around President Yeltsin won the fight and, thereby, the power of defining who is corrupt and who is not.[138] The element of socially organized construction in scandals around corruption leads to the conclusion that the number of scandals can in no way be taken as an indicator of the real extent of corrupt practices. The opportunity for triggering corruption scandals does not correlate with any measurable degree of corruption but rather with media competition, institutional competence and power constellations in the interplay of the four arenas outlined above. That, however, does not suggest that there were no differences in the "corruptness" of regimes. Despite all difficulties in measuring objectively the extent and form of corruption, there is no denying the observation that there are national (and also sectorial) differences in the degree of effectiveness of corruption networks. According to their global interests, the World Bank, and the International Monetary Fund (IMF) have declared war against corruption, an enemy of international competition.

That leads us to the fourth arena in the above scheme: the business world that increasingly tries to protect norms of fair competition and free markets by sanction impediments. They can count on international treaties that are on their side, such as: the European Community, which terminated many a tradition of national and regional protection by enforcing European merger control and the harmonization of tax and subsidy privileges; the international GATT regulations, which allow national governments to insist on international tenders for national projects, such as the American government invited in the case of Narita airport near Tokyo which had previously been a protected park, the "pork barrel" of high civil servants of the MITI department of commerce and technology.[139] Or they count on the pressures of the World Bank and IMF, which tie their credit facilities, in Indonesia and elsewhere, to conditions by which they hope to end structural patterns of nepotism.

The definition of corruption they employ starts with a simple counter-model to that of a free world market. The frequency of corrupt blackmail such as that of paying bribes to the customs, to public officials and government members, up even to heads of state, can be objectively established by aggregating subjective estimates and observations. That is the clever operationalization of a former World Bank official (Dr. Eigen) who uses surveys among business people about the amount of pressures that they were exposed to for paying bribes in different countries.[140] The index based on the information of bribers on the bribed has been refined considerably by updating and using a multitude of reputation sources.[141] The "hit-list of shame" of the Transparency International Index achieves its effect by worldwide publication in the media. It has gained considerable efficacy by exerting a powerful influence on credit conditions and by withholding the support for investments.

In scientific terms, however, the aggregated experience of business people and journalists remains unsatisfactory as operationalization, because their interpretation depends on the moral and legal context of the respective legal cultures. The transparency index measures first of all the external reputation of countries with respect to bribes for gaining public contracts. It is subsequently complemented by contextual variables such as indicators on the institutional infrastructure of corrupt opportunities and the arenas that could possibly scandalize them. That brings all factors of enabling and of controlling corruption into the picture: the system of party finances, the web of clientelistic personnel patronage and the lobbies of gaining public contracts, the control of auditing units, the freedom of the press and the functioning of democratic checks and balances as a whole. As in the classical writings of Montesquieu and Rousseau, who used the concept of corruption to scandalize the general moral degeneration of their society, the reproach of corruption is used for establishing a countermodel of a better society.[142] In our times the catchwords of Utopia are a free market economy embedded in a civil society of "honest" politics. Deviance from this model can take various forms, but moral as well as legal discourse tries to scandalize them as corruption.

Clientelism and Corruption in South Korea
Joongi Kim

Introduction

South Korea's post-war prosperity has been considered as a miraculous achievement in economic development. Rising from the ashes, in a span of under 40 years, South Korea's drive to industrialize raised the country's per capita income more than 130 times from less than $80 in 1960 to more than $10,543 by 1996. South Korea also became the thirteenth largest trading nation in the world, a member of the exclusive club of the Organization of Economic Cooperation and Development (OECD) and an overall model of development to many emerging economies. Notwithstanding this dramatic economic transformation, however, during the process South Korea also developed critical structural defects in its political system, and consequently its financial system, defects that eventually contributed to its dramatic financial crisis in 1997–98.

Korea has been persistently dogged by a perception that it is plagued by wide-scale grand corruption. In studying grand corruption in South Korea much emphasis has been placed on the collusive relationship between the forces of the political parties and bureaucracy on one side and the large business firms or *chaebol* conglomerates that have dominated South Korea's economy on the other side. This paper will attempt to show that clientelism can offer a means for evaluating the characteristics of these collaborative ties and understanding the near institutional nature of corruption in South Korea. Clientelism can provide a basis for assessing the framework of legitimate political contributions and illegal grand corruption in South Korea.

This paper will first examine the origins of the clientelism-based relationships as they have evolved in the modern history of South Korea. It will in particular focus on patron–client bonds that have dominated the South Korean political landscape. The first concerns the clientelistic association between the large *chaebol* conglomerates and the political parties and bureaucracy. It will review the effects that clientelism has had on political financing and breeding corruption, for instance, during South Korea's economic development. It will also examine the other notable forces of clientelism that have emerged over the years such as those relationships based on regional ties that have played a powerful role in recent South Korean history. Finally, this paper will seek to assess the negative impact which pernicious clientelism has had on South Korea's development, leaving it vulnerable to a host of systematic weaknesses.

Clientelism in Modern South Korea and Patterns of Corruption

As used in this paper, clientelism signifies an excessive reliance by two parties upon a patron and client relationship when conducting public affairs.[143] Under this rubric, which typically arises in politics, exchanges are made to favor private individuals or to benefit certain groups at the expense of the public at large. East Asian countries are supposed to be notably susceptible to these types of reciprocal associations because they are noted for a tradition of reliance on particularistic relationships.[144] Clientelism as described here can be found in many forms in South Korea. The symbiotic relationship between South Korea's party-bureaucracy and the private sector as embodied by *chaebol* interests remains the most powerful example. Woodall refers to this type of patronage relationship as "systematized clientelism."[145]

Some analysts trace the origins of modern clientelism in South Korea to the Japanese occupation (Nam, 1995). During the colonial period between 1910 and 1945, Japanese occupation forces developed special relationships with certain Korean business factions and elements such as landowners and the reviled police to sustain their rule over the country. According to Carter Eckert (1991), it was during this period that Korean businessmen learned that collaboration with the state was the best means to guarantee business success. Hence, some of the seeds of modern clientelism *vis-à-vis* the state were sown at this time. Upon liberation in 1945, the more striking fact remains that the Korean clients who benefited from the Japanese patronage managed to assume the same clientelistic role under the new patrons that gained control over the country, namely the U.S. occupation forces and the Syngman Rhee government.

On top of clientelism, South Korea also retained characteristics of a "corporatist state," in contrast to a pluralistic one. A pluralistic state occurs where law and policy result more from pressures placed on a passive government by various interest groups and is the style of government typically associated with liberal democracies. A corporatist government develops policies on its own and then seeks to implement them through such instruments as corporate entities and its citizenry. Corporatist states tend to be far more interventionist than pluralistic ones. Therefore, given its inherently corporatist nature, dominated by towering patron leaders, the South Korean state was more prone to bestow patronage resulting in even more intertwined bonds of clientelism.

To a large extent, the various forms of clientelism that emerged in South Korea were not merely a symptom but were to blame for the pervasive corruption that existed.[146] According to Kurer (1996), clientelism and corruption are "inseparable twins." Patronage or clientelism that remains wholly within the discretion of the patron does not involve corruption. The problem with clientelism is that it bestows preferential exchanges upon select clients based on personal and private ties instead of using criteria demanded by law, universal principles, or institutional procedures. Clientelism therefore leads to inefficiencies, cronyism and, in its worst form, outright corruption. Obviously, a degree of favoritism is inevitable in all political process. Legal political contributions made to obtain preferential treatment where legitimate political discretion exists must be distinguished. The focus of corruption in this paper will be on benefits that amount to illegal, merit-less advantages that are received solely because of reciprocal payments. Hence, the definition of corruption is limited to bribery-related offenses, typically to bureaucrats, or illegitimate political contributions made to politicians. By nature, patrons and clients, have an innate interest in favoring and, at its worst, replacing the collective good with their own private good. This can be accomplished by overriding required bureaucratic norms and procedures and allocating resources on the basis of political expediency.

This type of clientelistic activity under this setting originates at the political level and emerges as a means to gather political support. Since corrupt activity is typically sanctioned at the highest level by the patron leader in South Korea, its influence has inevitably spread to all spheres of the government and legislature, even including the judiciary. The clientelism that emerged in South Korea will also be distinguished from pure nepotism or cronyism based on mere affection. Corruptive clientelism in South Korea consistently involved a quid pro quo in the form of monetary payment in return for the favors bestowed. While clientelism cannot be viewed as the sole cause or reason for corruption in South Korea, it can offer a means to understand why corruption persists despite South

Korea's development. Over the modern history of Korea various patterns of corruption have emerged in relation to clientelism. The primary clientelistic relationship that will be reviewed has been between the politico-military patrons and private sector clients. Other relationships such as those based on regionalism will also be reviewed in this light.

Political and Military Patrons and Private Sector Clients

1. *Formative Stages of Modern Clientelism: The Rhee Government, Liberal Party and the First Republic (1948–1960).* While not as extensive as in later years, traces of the early beginnings of modern clientelism can be found in latent forms in the First Republic that was established in 1948. Following the devastation of the Korean War the corporatist Syngman Rhee government commenced a program of developing the South Korean agrarian economy. At the same time, in an effort to finance its political operations, the cash-starved Rhee government also began to display patron-type characteristics.

Rhee's patron nature was best exemplified when his government resorted to the sale of public property and real estate. This type of disbursement of public property became a lucrative source of funds, and reportedly 80 percent of government property that was privatized under the early Rhee government was used to support the coffers of Rhee's political machine, the Liberal Party and its factions. As noted by Moon Chung In and Jongryn Mo (1999), the distribution of "enemy property" (*juksan bulha*) that was formerly owned by the Japanese occupiers, was a tremendous source of patronage for Rhee. The Rhee political matrix formed a broad network in bestowing these favors and the primary beneficiaries often consisted of former Japanese collaborators because they were the only ones with the necessary capital to make such purchases and contributions. Rhee, himself a long-time exile, had to quickly establish a political base to support his new Liberal Party while fending off challenges from other rival factions within South Korea, and he had no other choice but to join forces with many of these collaborators.

Other means of conveying patronage under the Rhee government included selectively granting public concessions. This type of patronage became most visible during the major presidential elections of 1952, 1956 and 1960. One of the most egregious scandals indicative of this pattern of patronage occurred in March, 1952 and involved concessions granted for tungsten.[147] Certain designated companies, such as Korea Enterprise, Mijin Company, Namsan Trading, Yongdong Trading and Shinhan Industries, were allowed to receive $ 4 million worth of government currency to be used in the sale of tungsten and purchase of wheat and fertilizer at an official exchange rate of 6,000 won to the dollar. With the black market exchange rate trading at 3 to 4 times this rate, these designated companies could collect a windfall of over 55.3 billion won based on the difference in the exchange rate alone. Furthermore, when the profits from the sale of wheat and the fertilizers were combined, the gains from these concessions totaled a staggering 150 to 200 billion hwan, which amounted to close to 15–20 percent of the government's entire 1953 budget of 982 billion hwan. These colossal funds were amassed by Rhee's political forces during this process to finance the Presidential and Vice-Presidential elections that were held in 1953.

Another episode in the Rhee government that was indicative of the patterns of patronage involved the Defense Ministry's sale of raw cotton received through financing by the Food and Agriculture Organization (FAO) and the Industrial Bank of Korea.[148] Approximately $500,000 worth of raw cotton was supposed to be used as winter blankets and clothing for military personnel. Instead, the material was distributed to seven inexperienced companies on a selective basis. The privileged companies then resold the cotton material at profits of over $1 million, almost all of which were contributed as donations to the ruling Liberal Party. These funds became an important source for the 1956 presidential elections.

Overall, while not extensively, the Rhee government through its Liberal Party gradually developed clientelistic ties through these various means. With its political funding, the Liberal Party dominated government affairs and acted as an oligarchic patron by choosing to bestow upon favored businesses various concessions and procurement projects. Ultimately, this pattern of clientelism reached unbearable levels during the March 15, 1960 election scandal. Some 4.3 billion hwans of industrial bonds and 2.4 billion hwans of agricultural bonds were issued to 52 select companies such as Daehan Cement, Taechang Textiles, Kukdong Shipping and Daehan Textiles, through various banks to raise political funds. These companies purchased the bonds in return for subsequent promises of reciprocal benefits and patronage. Mass anti-Rhee protests eventually ensued. Coupled with charges of election rigging, a spontaneous democratic revolution ousted President Rhee in April 1960.

From a legal standpoint, at this time South Korea did not have a comprehensive law concerning political contributions. The only regulations that existed at the time were the nominal provisions in the Political Parties Law and Election Law. These provisions were ineffectual at this nascent stage in South Korea's political history.

2. *The Emergence of Entrenched Clientelism: The Park Government and the Third and Fourth Republics (1961–1979).* In 1961, Park Chung Hee seized power from the unstable Second Republic in a military coup d'état. Once in power, it was during Park's authoritarian 18-year rule that the more prominent features of the present structure of clientelism were etched into the political fabric of modern-day South Korea. Park's single-minded drive for economic development succeeded to a large extent during his iron-clad rule, but his policies also led to adverse repercussions that were particularly severe in the long-term such as entrenched clientelism, political suppression, cronyism and ultimately a breeding ground for corrupt activity.

Park's assumption of power ushered in the beginning of a two-decade-long economic transformation under authoritarianism. President Park first engaged in an ambitious effort to pursue an export-oriented model of industrialization under which labor-intensive manufacturing industries were strongly encouraged. It was during this stage of industrial development that the massive *chaebol* conglomerates that still dominate South Korea's economy were first nurtured with industrial policy. The 20 largest *chaebol* produced 21.8 percent of the Korean GDP in 1973, 28.9 percent in 1975 and 33.2 percent in 1978.

It was on February 9, 1965, that Korea first enacted its Political Contributions Act. As demonstrated over the years, however, while this law contains admirable provisions and continues to be updated, it has not been effective because most contributions to politicians have tended to be made outside its contours.[149] Nevertheless, the new law did include provisions on the giving and payment of contributions, and had terms on when contributions could receive exemptions from corporate taxes, income taxes and transfer taxes. The Act sought to legitimize payments made by individuals to political parties. Contributions had to be consigned to the Central Election Management Commission who would then distribute the funds to parties. The amounts that were distributed by the

Commission to the parties would be disclosed in the National Register but the identity of contributors could be withheld if desired. If a person wanted these contributions to go to a specific party, they would have to designate two or more parties that had seats in the National Assembly.

During Park's presidential tenure this law was amended in 1969 to the benefit of the leading party. Non-designated contribution funds were distributed such that 60 percent went to the leading party. The remaining 40 percent was distributed to the other remaining parties according to the number of seats they had. Park's ruling party therefore directly benefited. Overall the law was not effective and instead was often abused through its use as a means to put pressure on the opposition parties (Boo, 1991, Park, 1995).[150]

At first, as with the First Republic, the newly established government initially planned to purge the business establishment. These leading business firms were nevertheless recruited into a state-led developmental coalition because they were the only ones capable of filing the government's needs. The Park regime's active intervention in business policy matters based on a corporatist developmental strategy forged a close and semi-permanent nexus between business interests and governmental forces. The combination of a corporatist state actively making, directing and financing the large private sector *chaebol* conglomerates through government-controlled banks established the foundations for the Korean economic miracle of the 1980s and early 1990s. Furthermore, during the Park Chung Hee presidency the symbiotic relationship between party and bureaucratic elites and *chaebol* businesses became a three party alliance or an "iron triangle" with the addition of the dominant rule of the military.[151]

Under this artificial equilibrium, such critical traits as open competition, transparency and disclosure were disfavored and in fact often viewed as impediments. The consequences of this development were that monopolistic and oligopolistic clientelism emerged. In other words, the patronage offered by the Patron State came to be unilaterally reaped by certain clients. The patron-government/party "rewarded" entrepreneur clients who complied with its policies by publicly honoring them and, of course, permitting them to become wealthy. In return, Park's authoritarian government and Democratic Republican Party received legitimacy and political support from the client *chaebols*.

During the early years of industrialization, the *chaebols* primarily served as instruments of state power. The state dominated the direction of industrialization and *chaebols* were compelled to comply or lose their preferential economic treatment. At the same time the state and ruling Democratic Republican Party received rebates. Although, the "iron triangle" consisting of the ruling military, bureaucracy/party and big-business elite was recast several times over the years, the fundamental clientelistic structure remained intact.[152]

First, according to Moon Chung In and Jongryn Mo (1999), from the 1960s to 1980, the government's greatest source of influence over the private sector and the *chaebols* was the control of commercial bank credit. Patronage was granted through investment rates, entry permits, exit regulations, tax incentives, information services, and price and wage controls.[153] The patron-government therefore implemented its policies through the commercial banks that it controlled by subsidizing favored clients through preferential credit, low-interest loans, and various tax incentives.

Park Chung Hee apparently harbored a suspicion of banks and, upon assuming control of the country, put all of them under state control. Commercial banks were all state owned until their privatization in the early 1970s. The government appointed most management officials in banks and the bankers were largely directed as to which strategic industries and companies to lend (MacDonald, 1998). Korean banks became the government's instruments for disbursing credit to clients along favored party lines. If the government favored a particular industry such as textiles or steel, then the banks were guided accordingly to extend credit to those companies preferred by the government. Given this tight control over credit, the government easily dictated the direction of economic policy. Park also began to finance his political funds through sales of government land to these various client entities.

The differences in the patron and client tie during the Park presidency lay in its scope and highly stable nature. Given the extensive reign of Park, the degree of monopolistic clientelism reached a climax. The most natural collusive clientelism involved military procurement contracts. Starting from shipping contracts during the Vietnam War in the 1960s, all phases of military procurement became critical sources of reciprocal funding. More specifically, from the early 1970s it is reported that between 2–10 percent of all construction contracts procured by the government were later redonated as political contributions. This sum amounted to between 0.6 and 3 percent of the government's entire budget. For official governmental loans, in 1969 of the $800 million in loans that were granted, $160 million were returned as political funds to the ruling party and forces. Another example was the 6-billion-won loan given to six major companies in 1965. Of these funds, some 1.5 billion was allegedly pledged to the Blue House, the presidential residence, as rebate money.

By 1972 Park faced growing discontent from opposition parties and alienated non-clients, Park responded by amending the constitution ushering in the Fourth Republic and by imposing further authoritarian measures that further entrenched clientelism. Basic political rights were abridged and dissidents were suppressed. The implementation of the Yooshin Constitution in 1972 led to a change in the power-oriented patronage structure into a more forceful donation-oriented system. The Democratic Republic Party received close to 105 million won per month from the Blue House during this time. The Blue House's unofficial size of expenditures was estimated at 10 billion won a year. It was at this stage that the Political Contributions Act was amended once again. The new Act provided that, in the case of non-designated funds 70 percent would be given according to the number of seats of each party and the remaining 30 percent would be evenly distributed among those bodies that have negotiating status at the National Assembly. This amounted to a nominal change in the legislation.

Finally, the newly founded Korean Central Intelligence Agency (KCIA) also utilized manipulation of the stock market to raise funds for its war chest. This involved, for example, the KCIA forcing the Agriculture Central Cooperative (ACC) to sell 128,000 shares of Korea Electric that they possessed at an enormous discount.[154]

Therefore, it was during the Park regime that clientelism became entrenched in Korean society. Based on Park's activist intervention policy, a powerful patronage alliance between the politico-military and *chaebol* businesses emerged that would dominate Korea for years to come. Through such critical means as banking credit and financing, industrial policy was implemented, bestowing upon enormous preferential patronage upon select clients in the process. This clientelistic structure easily consolidated during Park's 18-year monolithic rule.

3. *President Chun and the Fifth Republic (1981–1987)*. The unstable presidency of Choi Kyu Ha, that followed Park's assassination in 1979, was cut short as a result of a military coup d'état led by General Chun Doo Whan. Chun's rise to power ushered in the Fifth Republic and a pro-

longation of the military elite exercising enormous influence on governmental affairs. The general pattern of clientelism that developed under
Park continued during Chun's presidency, although the change in power
softened the monopolistic patron–client relationship between the
party/bureaucracy and the *chaebol* at least momentarily while those
involved realigned themselves.

As was later revealed in the sensational slush fund trials, Chun collected over 216 billion ($270 million) won from over 42 corporate heads
during his reign.[155] The leading contributors, who were also later charged,
were the chairmen of the top *chaebol* conglomerates who often transferred the funds in private meetings with Chun at the Blue House.
Overall, including various contributions and donations from other
sources, allegedly over 950 billion won ($1.19 billion) was amassed dur-
ing this time. In anticipation of the October, 1987, presidential elections
at the end of Chun's term, for instance, certain corporate heads were
instructed to pay over 17 billion won ($21 million). In return, *chaebol*
conglomerates received a wide range of benefits such as special licenses,
exemption from tax audits and special favors for major infrastructure
projects to gradual dominance of the financial sector.

Disobedient clients, however, received harsh punishment. The most
vivid example involved the "mid-air dismantlement" of the Kukche conglomerate, which at the time was the fifth largest *chaebol* in South Korea.
The Kukche Group was purportedly dissolved because its chairman,
Yang Jung-Mo, refused to accede to demands for political contributions.
In an epilogue to the affair, a telling indication of the clientelistic relations in the Fifth Republic emerged. Hanil Synthetic Fiber, the company
that was later able to acquire six of the former Kukche subsidiaries,
apparently was the company that donated the largest amount for that year,
over 4.6 billion won ($5.75 million).[156]

The funds amassed during the Fifth Republic were collected for projects such as the 1988 Olympic Fund, the New Village Movement fund,
the Ilhae Foundation and the Veterans Support Fund. By 1987 the Fifth
Republic was under tremendous pressure, however, to undo the authoritarian clientelistic structure of power. Opposition leaders and radical students mounted a legitimacy crisis that led to the first peaceful and democratic transition of power in 1987. Numerous reforms were also adopted
that gradually loosened the clientelistic ties such as monetary liberalization, land reform and the adoption of the so-called real-names account

system. Land reform was necessary because through patronage-based favors, many *chaebols* had amassed enormous profits by speculating in real estate, whereas the real-names account system was to prevent the transfer of illicit money transactions.

It must be noted that, during President Chun's rule South Korea achieved staggering economic growth. From 1981 to 1987 the country maintained an average growth rate of 9.1 percent—and this was following a disastrous year in 1980 after Park's death. Its GDP nearly doubled to $136 billion during the same time span. Chun's government also pressed forward in maintaining high levels of enforcement against corruption during the Fifth Republic, especially compared with previous years. On December 31, 1980, before Chun officially was elected president, he also substantially amended the Political Contributions Act. The new act provided that Supporting Committees could be established and that political parties could receive government subsidies. These Supporting Committees could not exceed more than 1,000 members excluding party members and could not fundraise during election periods. The Election Commission was made to distribute funds according to the number of seats of each party. Yet, as in the past, violations of the Act were rarely punished in an effective manner.

4. *Peaceful Transition of Power: The Sixth Republic and President Roh (1988–1992)*. In 1987, Roh Tae Woo, a former military colleague of Chun, was elected president, largely as a result of the failure of opposition political forces to reach a compromise and field a single candidate. South Korea henceforth launched a tradition of peaceful and democratic transitions in presidential power. Therefore, unlike previous presidents, Roh did not have a serious legitimacy burden to overcome at the onset of his presidency.

Nevertheless, as later revealed in the Slush Fund Trials, President Roh was found to have continued previous practices. He gathered over 283 billion wons ($353 million) from 35 *chaebol* chairmen, much in the same fashion as Chun. In total, approximately 140 billion won ($175 million) was collected and used for political funds, 80–90 billion wons ($100–112 million) for party expenses and 210 billion ($262 million) to assist the campaigns of ruling party candidates. Evidence later showed that in the process Roh personally amassed over 229 billion wons ($286 million) in wealth.

One central aspect of the Slush Fund Trial of both Presidents Chun and Roh worth considering is that the payments given were not collected with any specific benefits in mind. This lack of a *specific* quid pro quo made it difficult to apply traditional standards of bribery. This diffused bribery, although it had coercive elements, still offered the bribe-giving conglomerates considerable preferential treatment. Nevertheless, as the Korean courts later found, the payments were made based upon the President's broad range of powers that could influence practically any decision. The courts hence found both President Chun and President Roh guilty under a newly developed comprehensive bribery theory.[157]

As was later discovered, in particular, these funds were later related to such incidents as the Korean Electric construction project, the transfer of the Sangmu Military Base, the development of the Susoo District and the construction of a key navy station. Roh's government therefore appeared to continue the clientelistic traditions that were maintained in the past. Those more critical of Roh's policies suggest that the regime's clientelistic tendencies were blatantly confirmed when the Sunkyong Group, Korea's fifth largest conglomerate, was selected as the recipient to acquire Korea's premier state-owned mobile telephone service.[158]

The Political Contribution Act was amended three times during Roh's reign in 1989, 1991 and in late 1992. In particular the provisions concerning the Supporting Committee and the government subsidy were modified. For instance, National Assembly members and candidates with Supporting Committees were made to elect an accountant for their Committees and report the appointment to the respective Election Management Committee. While these were solid legislative initiatives, the law still remained ineffective because of the lack of proper enforcement.

5. *Completing a Transition to Civilian Rule: President Kim Young-Sam (1993–1997)*. During the 1992 presidential elections, Chairman Chung Ju Yong of the Hyundai Group made a bold challenge to the long entrenched patron–client relationship. Chung established his own political party and ran for president. Although Chung did not succeed, Nam (1994) considers that this turn of events due to Chung's initiative "cause[d] a fundamental change in the South Korean political economy."

When first elected in 1992, President Kim Young-Sam declared that he would not accept any political contributions. In the process he also openly disclosed his property ownership and assets and forced other senior government officials to do the same. President Kim also initiated a critical break from the past when he decided to reform the military and dismantle their clientelistic control. One of his main tasks was to dissolve the powerful and selective military clique called the Hanahoi whose leading patrons were the former Presidents Chun and Roh.

Despite Kim's own personal efforts, he was unable to extirpate the power-oriented clientelistic corruption that persisted around the office of the presidency. His own initial promises notwithstanding, the President's immediate family and followers were later mired in numerous scandals. First, President Kim's own son, who the President relied upon heavily, was later found to have collected 3.2 billion wons from 2 companies. Later, one of Kim's closest aides was convicted for receiving over 1.8 billion wons in bribes, dealing a critical blow to Kim's credibility. The third major incident during Kim's presidency involved the special loans granted to the defunct Hanbo conglomerate. At least 32 ruling party National Assemblymen and bank presidents were accused of receiving bribes to assist Hanbo in obtaining favorable loans. Five Assemblymen were later indicted for receiving bribes and 24 were found to have received these funds as part of election funds, political funds and donations.

Kim's government also commenced a widely perceived political vendetta against the Hyundai Group for Chung's challenge during the election. Hyundai was hit with tax audits and arrests for tax evasion and stock manipulation. This served as a notice, as the Kukche case in previous years, of the possible repercussions conglomerates might face if they improperly challenged the power of the newly established patron. Nevertheless, as the economic prominence of the *chaebols* increased and as the government eased its direct ownership and control of commercial banks, the traditional patron–client relationship that had sustained itself gradually showed signs that it was transforming into a more mutual dependence-based relationship. Many *chaebols* that had a highly dependent relationship with the state in the past were now able to exert considerably more political influence.

Despite some of the problems that the Kim Young-Sam government faced, it does deserve credit for its determination to enhance anticorruption enforcement. It was during his term that South Korea recorded the highest levels of enforcement against bribery-related cases. A sitting cabinet-level minister was arrested for the first time since the Second Republic and for only the second time in modern Korean history. The Political Contribution Act was amended four times during Kim Young Sam's presidency in 1994, 1995 and twice in 1997. In 1994, in particular, the Supporting Committees were for the first time required to deliv-

er receipts issued by the Election Commission when they received contributions of money or goods. Most political contributions however continued to be made by circumventing the law.

Other Clientelistic Coalitions in South Korea

In addition to the grand clientelism associated with the large *chaebol*
businesses and senior levels of government, clientelism in South Korea
can also be traced to dominant political personalities intertwined with
familial, regional, school and military ties. As mentioned previously, the
military elites in particular maintained a solid internal clientelist bond
with their military patrons that enabled them to control South Korean politics for close to 25 years from 1962 to 1987. The general lack of legitimacy of the political leadership until the 1987 election spawned a higher
degree of reliance upon clientelism, and this self-perpetuated the dependent relationship.

Assuming power through a coup d'état, for instance, one of the first
tasks for the former military officers under the leadership of General Park
Chung-Hee was to reorganize the bureaucracy, the political party and
centralize policy-making. Park consistently maintained a preference for
selecting from among those with a military background in filling positions in the party rank and file and the bureaucratic elite. This created a
strong internal clientelistic relation that ironically contributed to his own
demise when he was assassinated by the head of the KCIA, a long time
military supporter and colleague. According to one study, 42.4 percent of
all cabinet-level ministers during the Third Republic had backgrounds in
the military.[159] During the Fourth Republic this proportion remained relatively high at 31.7 percent and during the Fifth Republic, 24.5 percent.

Particularly since the 1980s, South Korea's modern history has been
shaped by another crude clientelistic force, namely divisive regionalism.
Regional-based favoritism and allegiance bred a powerful clientelistic
link that has disproportionately ruled recent Korean history. Those from
the southeastern region of the country called Kyungsang province
became the favored clients, largely excluding those from the southwest-
ern region called the Cholla province. According to Roh (1998),
Presidents Chun and Roh naturally gravitated toward fostering a clientelistic relation with the Kyungsang region, especially because of their

weak institutional background. Unlike the Park regime they lacked a strong military bedrock, having carried out a coup d'état from within the military. Roh (1998) suggests that Chun and Roh therefore had little choice but to develop a patron–client relation with the bureaucratic elite from the Kyungsang region. This marriage of convenience served both parties and can be witnessed in the dominance of the bureaucratic elite from the Kyungsang region during their reign (Roh, 1998: 76).

Another factor that, helped clientelistic ties to consolidate is that, until 1997 South Korea had not had a natural and peaceful transfer of power from a ruling party to an opposition party in its modern-day history. Although the ruling parties have changed names and composition, they have continued to maintain certain patronage-based relations. The "iron triangle" consisting of the ruling military-bureaucracy-big-business elite was recast several times over the years, but the fundamental clientelistic structure remained intact. This also fueled a powerful entrenchment of the ruling party as evidenced by their complete dominance of all political contributions.

This pattern finally ended with the 1998 election of President Kim Dae-Jung who was not only an opposition party candidate but also hailed from the excluded non-client Cholla region. Many anticipate that this transition in power will offer another means to unlock the entrenched clientelistic behavior. It will not only realign forces but also will signify a transition away from the traditional sources of clientelistic inbreeding. At the same time concerns exist that in reaction to the years of deprivation, the new government might be prone to continue the same policies of the past, albeit in their own favor. While signs of these concerns are materializing, it is unclear whether that they will be able to reach the levels of years past.

Costs of Clientelism and Corruption in Korea

According to Klitgaard's (1988) classic definition of corruption, corruption equals monopoly power plus discretion without accountability. The entrenched clientelistic models that developed over the past several decades therefore became a natural breeding ground for corruptive activity. First, the entrenched clientelistic forces maintained a monopolistic power based upon the strong authoritarian rule of such patron leaders as

Rhee, Park and Chun. As pointed out by some observers, corruption flourishes under one-party politics.[160] The dominant power these patron leaders exhibited during their reigns also led to a lack of accountability and, instead, to a wide-range of discretion. Given this monopoly power, there was an inherent lack of political will to pursue reforms and, instead, to maintain over-regulation. Under this model of "elite hegemony," as described by Johnston (1997), the risk of extreme corruption exists because it can become organized and systematic.

In the end, there existed little to prevent corruption other than the political will and moral fortitude of the rulers and bureaucratic elite. President Park on a personal level is reported to have amassed little personal wealth during his reign. While praised by many, this lack of expropriation could have been due to the fact that he did not anticipate his departure and did not have any incentive. Presidents Chun and Roh, unfortunately, offered a different picture, as was revealed in the slush fund trials.[161]

Specific patterns of corruption can be identified as characteristic of South Korea. It appears quite consistently that high-level government officials are more prone to being involved in bribery-related offenses than lower level bureaucrats. This is significant because higher-level officials naturally will have a higher tendency to be involved in grand corruption. From 1972, from when such statistics first began to be collected, until 1997 senior government officials have been consistently involved in more bribery-related cases than lower-level officials.

While economic development continued at staggering levels, and clientelism thrived, those non-clients, in contrast, that were excluded, suffered an inordinate burden. Non-clients that disproportionately suffered include small and medium-sized companies, labor, and those not from the Kyungsang province. South Korea is noted as being one of the only developed countries in the world where medium-sized companies do not provide the primary strength of their domestic economy. This has largely stifled innovation and competitiveness in South Korea's economy.[162] Unlike client *chaebols*, these companies could not secure favorable financing.

Labor also suffered inordinately during this development process. Starting from the Park presidency, for example, wages were also kept artificially low by directly engaging in wage setting. The state's favoritism on behalf of business led to a severe repression of workers' rights. Labor organizations could not enjoy the rights to organize and engage in collective action, could not make political contributions or form a party. All strikes were banned, unions were deregistered and union activists were arrested. Industrial policies heavily favored business leaders who reciprocated by offering generous support.

The Cholla region also was excluded from many development opportunities as well as those talented bureaucrats from that region. These elements all served as enormous costs for the public at large. Public scrutiny has helped bring to light such patronage-type projects such as the Seoul-Pusan high-speed electric train to finance the election and gain favors from the Kyungsang region.

Throughout modern South Korean history in fact many heads of *chaebol* conglomerates have been charged with bribery. Numerous chairmen, including those from the largest ones have even been sentenced. Those that lead the largest conglomerates, however, have consistently escaped actual prison sentences. They have either received suspended sentences "in recognition of their contributions to the country" and almost all of them have received a subsequent amnesty or pardon. This type of immunity not only creates a moral hazard but also fosters distrust.

As Fukuyama (1996) has also observed, strong distrust has emerged as a result of the political and *chaebol*-patronage alliance that has ruled in South Korea. Credibility became eroded as favoritism instead of merit predominated. Wrongdoing often became the norm, and behavior according to notions of public responsibility and trust the exception. Clientelistic behavior eroded by corruption became particularly pernicious because the patrons were at the highest echelons of power. The dominated parties offered little in holding the bureaucratic elite accountable.

From a different perspective, as pointed out by Nam (1995), the guarantee of the patron-state's protection did enable South Korea's *chaebol* to engage in large-scale projects beyond their financial capabilities. Some may claim that notwithstanding the potential corruption associated with clientelism, numerous advantages exist. This structure did help conglomerates to attain enormous size, market share and certain economies of scale. Faster and more efficient decision-making was also made possible. Some argue that, to a degree, transaction costs are saved as a result of efficient clientelistic practices. On the other hand, this structure led to inordinately risky investments such as the spectacular business failures of Samsung Motors, Hanbo Steel, Kia Motors and more recently the Daewoo Group. This clientelistic model, therefore, helped create a critical moral hazard upon which reckless expansion was pursued. The iron-clad relationship also created an environment where opaqueness was promoted over transparency.

Clientelism stresses interpersonal relationships and loyalty over the rule of law. Carothers (1998) declares that South Korea is almost alone in taking the efforts beyond the commercial domain to seriously attack government impunity and corruption, as evidenced by the recent conviction of the former Presidents on corruption charges. The Asian financial crisis highlighted the failure of the region's various rule-of-law reforms to bring transparency and accountability to the dealings of the inbred circles of privileged bankers, businessmen, and politicians. Pressure is growing for more reform, both from within Asia and from the international financial community.

Conclusion

Much of the economic development activity and corruption in South Korea's recent history can be better interpreted through an understanding of the vast array of clientelistic forces that have dominated social relations and politics. Clientelism was an influential feature in Korea's modern development. Clientelism developed in multifarious forms across the social network. Laws such as the Political Contributions Act that sought to regulate some of this activity were ineffective and still remain so. In the early periods, especially during the Park and Chun regime, the military-government patrons dominated the early periods of economic development. During the ensuing Chun and Roh's presidencies an additional facet of clientelism that became pronounced was based on regional ties.

Modern South Korean patron leaders bestowed vast favors of patronage upon the business elite while collecting the funds by which to maintain their political machinery. While development ensued, South Korea paid large costs in the process, not to mention the scores of groups that were unable to gain the favor of the leading political patrons of the time. Scandals of grand corruption still continue, undermining the integrity of the system. The 1998 election of President Kim Dae Jung and the devastating financial crisis mark an opportunity for dramatic change. Several factors are leading to the view that the dominance of entrenched clientelism is weakening. Democratization, a greater appreciation of the rule of law, higher ethical standards and material affluence have weakened clientelistic ties. Increased legislative power, a freer press and wider popular participation enhances the chances for accountability. Corruption appears to be diminishing with authoritarianism's demise. At the same time stronger legislative power is also facilitating new forms of cronyism at the public's expense.

In addition, Kim Dae Jung's election marked the first time that not only a member of the opposition party defeated the ruling forces, but also the first time that a member of the non-client Cholla region assumed power. High expectation prevailed as to whether the new president could refrain from the clientelistic coalitions of the past. While significant efforts were being made at economic reform of the dominant *chaebol* conglomerates, many wondered whether the new government would be able to withstand the same regional-based clientelism of the past that served as a breeding ground for corruption.[163]

Russia's Distorted Anticorruption Campaigns
Virginie Coulloudon

While meeting in Washington in mid-September 1999, the finance ministers of the seven most industrialized countries issued a statement in which they said there was a "critical need" for Russia to "fight corruption" and money laundering.[164] In using such vague terminology without taking into account the structural character of the Russian phenomenon, the financial leaders of the G7 indicated they believed that Russia's corruption problem depended on loopholes in the current legislation. In other words, they believed that should Russia take a series of administrative, legislative and coercive measures, it would be able to rectify its problems once and for all.

The then Russian Finance Minister, Mikhail Kasyanov, responded to his G7 colleagues with the same level of analysis. To reassure the West, he stated that his country had already taken measures "to stop capital flight," meaning that the federal authorities had already started both drafting new laws and using coercion to arrest violators. In so doing, not only did Kasyanov limit the phenomenon of corruption to one particular economic crime, but he also supported the idea that corruption in Russia was not a structural problem. Additionally, by limiting anticorruption measures to law enforcement agencies, Kasyanov indicated that he believed the core of the problem derived from individuals of questionable morals. In May 2000, prior to his confirmation as Prime Minister, he reaffirmed this belief in his address to the Duma, Russia's Lower Chamber of Parliament.[165]

In the months following the August 1998 financial crisis, Russian officials repeatedly promised to "fight against corruption," highlighting the negative value systems of some individuals. They believed that should the Kremlin get rid of a handful of "bad guys," the problem would be settled. In February 1999 then Deputy-Secretary of Russia's Security Council Boris Grushin stated that, "in order to demonstrate the political will to fight corruption, bodies of the executive and the legislative powers should undergo a thorough purge."[166] Fighting corruption is now on the agenda of leaders of all parties in the political spectrum. Yet instead of opening a debate and reflecting on the different forms and functions of today's corruption, rather than providing a complex answer to the phenomenon by simultaneously and structurally reforming bureaucracy, police forces, and the economy, Russian officials focus on individuals only. This moralistic argument is not new in Russia. On the contrary, it has been extensively used many decades, and one may recall the numerous political anticorruption campaigns launched by the Soviet and Russian leaderships to discredit and eliminate political rivals. It is true that the country has adopted a new legal framework specifically designed to fight bureaucratic corruption (bribery) and embezzlement, but the tendency to single out individuals has remained a permanent feature of all the successive Soviet and post-Soviet governments.

Twenty years of anticorruption campaigns aimed at replacing alleged corrupt elements by new civil servants have failed to clean the state structures. It is hard to believe that one cannot find a sincere and non-corrupt political team among a population of 145 million. Surely, there are people of different values who represent a potential alternative elite, but it does not seem to be enough in the Russian context, where even officials of goodwill who were educated in the West have not been able to limit corrupt practices. Thus, successive failures have shown that a proper answer to corruption in Russia should be sought in the complex measures articulated simultaneously around a renewal of political values and a reform of Russia's governance. As Susan Rose-Ackerman has shown, the nature of corruption depends both on the organization of government and on the power of individuals.[167] It is only with this dual approach that one can expect to find an answer to the problem of political corruption.

This article focuses on governance. It aims at highlighting the dysfunctional mechanisms of the Russian government that encourage various forms of corruption to spread. The general argument is that the centralized Russian State—as weak as it is—provides a favorable background for nepotism, embezzlement, and abuses of power. Moreover, anticorruption campaigns generated in this institutional environment undermine the legitimacy of the state both in the eyes of the population and among officials. Such campaigns create a profound problem of confidence in the state structures and thus further weaken the capacity of the state, creating a vicious circle.

Corruption and the Perception of Corruption

One of the main difficulties in examining corruption both under the Soviet regime and in post-Soviet Russia consists in definitions. Ever since Yuri Andropov, who launched systematic anticorruption campaigns in the late

1970s, all Soviet and Russian general secretaries and presidents have emphasized the necessity of eradicating the phenomenon without clarifying what particular phenomenon they had in mind.[168] When analyzing the various aspects of what the Russian state has tried to eradicate, one is surprised to see how different the causes and the forms of corruption are. One could draw a long list of them: from rule evasion and bribe-taking to abuses of power, theft, and insider dealings. More importantly, the meaning of the infringements of the law are perceived differently in different contexts: under the Soviet regime as opposed to post-Soviet Russia, or if motivated by the necessity to survive in an economic and politically hostile environment as opposed to a thirst for personal gain.

Corruption and Centralization—before 1988

Many Soviet experts have emphasized the collective nature of corruption in the Soviet Union.[169] They have pointed out that the system of organized corruption did not depend on the negative value system of a handful of individuals, even when the level of corruption varied, sometimes substantially, from one regional Party boss to another. Rather, the phenomenon was intrinsic to the Soviet centralized economy, an economy that denied private property and constituted a single, colossal public sector. In the strictly centralized Soviet economic system everything was determined by a series of five-year plans drawn up by the state and Party organs. Everyone, from the minister to the chief executive officer at an enterprise, was professionally and politically evaluated according to his ability to achieve the goals of production imposed by these plans. This was also the fundamental criterion of promotion to the upper rungs of the bureaucratic ladder.

Not only did these plans establish targeted output volumes for each enterprise, they also determined the type and the quantity of raw materials the enterprise was allocated. Additionally, they established the type of equipment a plant should receive from which suppliers, as well as to whom and in what quantities it would sell its output.[170] Industrial managers were not allowed to choose their suppliers or their clients. They were also unable to obtain the materials and equipment they considered the most appropriate for their needs. Central planning often led to absurd situations where a manager could not reject inadequate raw materials because he knew he would receive nothing in exchange.

The duty of the Soviet industrial managers was to fulfill the plan at any cost. Not only because this would advance them in their own careers, but also because, if the plan were fulfilled, their factory's workers would receive a bonus that augmented their annual salary by about 20–25 percent. Unable to get the needed materials through legal channels, industrial managers would therefore have recourse to three alternative strategies, all three at that time illegal. Firstly, they would try to strike barter deals with other factories and would, therefore, operate in the shadow economy.[171] Secondly, they would try to negotiate with Party and ministry officials at a lower level of production or "buy" new orders from them. Finally, they would falsify the statistical records or accounts once they made certain that they did not have to fear audits from regional Party bosses and ministry officials.

These three methods forced industrial managers to lure the regional political leadership into their system. To distribute bribes, they needed cash. This cash came from the only source available: salaries. Hence the existence, in the official factories' lists of workers, of "dead souls," fictitious individuals who were regularly paid salaries. This extra money generally ended in "bribery funds," which provided ready cash to ensure the smooth functioning of the factory. This corruption functioned in a chain going all the way up to the ministers.

There is a widespread opinion among Russian and Soviet émigré scholars that the endemic corruption of industrial managers and higher-ranking officials was harmless, given the context of the political and economic system. These scholars argue that, while Soviet corruption was a massive dysfunction of the centralized economy, it nevertheless created a parallel economy, which compensated for the excesses of the Soviet system.[172] William Clark has enumerated some of the positive aspects of corruption in the USSR. In his view, corruption, among other functions, encouraged capital formation, reduced bureaucratic rigidity, promoted entrepreneurial behavior, substituted economic activity for political violence, and attracted quality personnel to government service.[173]

Another specificity of the single-party regime is that it implicitly offered absolute power to all the first secretaries of the Communist Party who could exercise it, limited only by the territory they administered: a specific city, district, or region. The entire state was run by a single vertical executive power, the power of the Party, which exercised control over the economy, the judicial system, and the police.[174] Those powers were also associated with duties: Party first secretaries were responsible for the social stability and the economic achievements of their cities, regions, or republics. This made them prisoners of a system imposed from above. They too had to negotiate the budget of their territory in the Central Committee and often had to resort to gift giving to maintain their position. On a local level their absolute power often led to systematic abuses of power, lawlessness, and arbitrariness. This elaborate system of organized corruption was made possible by a highly secretive state decision-making process and, not surprisingly, by a systematic policy of patronage and cronyism by high-ranking officials.[175]

Whatever Soviet industrial managers' and officials' degree of sincerity was, the overwhelming presence of the Party in their daily lives shaped a specific mentality and attitude which can be interpreted as passive resistance in a "cold war" environment. In this context the enemy or occupying power was the Party, which most of Soviet citizens perceived as stranger to their lives, at once provider and vampire, and to which they nourished a forced respect. In Soviet Russia a clear dividing line separated the Party and the rest of the country.

Transition to a Market Economy—after 1988

It is generally considered that the turning points between Soviet and post-Soviet Russia are the August, 1991, coup and the breakup of the Soviet Union in December, 1991. If these events are the most important from political and geostrategic perspectives, one should consider the law on cooperatives, adopted in 1988 under Soviet president Mikhail Gorbachev, as a watershed in the liberalization of the economy and in corruption.[176] It was then that the Soviet authorities allowed an embryonic private sector to develop. Shortly after this the first decision to create a private banking system was adopted. After seventy years of a controlled and centralized economy, the only organizations with enough capital available for investment in "private" enterprises were the CPSU Central Committee, the Komsomol (Communist Youth) organization,[177] the Ministry of Foreign Trade, and the KGB. They built the most powerful financial institutions, which continued to develop under the Yeltsin regime.[178] The former Soviet ministries in charge of regulating industry were transformed into private corporations with the aim of creating a different industrial apparatus. Both in the financial and industrial sectors, the authorities did not draw any clear line between the public and private sectors.

Corruption inevitably shifted in response to these structural changes. While most of the "economic crimes" of the Soviet regime amounted to bribery, gift giving, and rule evasion, corruption after 1988 became more diverse. It now involves all kinds of deliberate transgression of laws connected with the implementation of the market: insider dealings, misappropriation of public funds and, more importantly, conflicts between state and private interests. Therein lies an interesting paradox that relates to Yeltsin's regime: regardless of the disappearance of the centralized economy and the emergence of privatization, businessmen and industrial managers say corruption under Yeltsin did not, in fact, change in nature and remained state-generated.[179]

In the minds of businessmen and industrial managers what seems to be the cause of the persistence of corruption is less the multiplication of opportunities as a result of the emergence of a private sector than the ongoing perception of the state as the main provider of resources. In the absence of appropriate legislation resource allocation remains in the hands of government officials who are the only ones to decide which strategic enterprises are to be privatized and what the rules of access to them are. Therefore, what industrial managers and politicians who are not part of the Kremlin's entourage consider being corruption is limited to cronyism and insider dealings involving representatives of the executive power. In spite of Gorbachev's institutional reforms to limit the powers of the Party in 1989–1990 and the change of regime after 1991, a dividing line was maintained under the Yeltsin regime, this time between the executive power and the rest of the society. Although corruption took several sophisticated forms under the Yeltsin regime, its main agent—the un-circumscribed executive power—remained largely unchanged from the Soviet era.

The Steadfast Patterns of Russian Governance

No one would argue today that Russia has not developed a political regime and an economy fundamentally different from the Soviet ones. In the economy Soviet President Mikhail Gorbachev imposed the shaping of a monetary system, which led logically to the creation of the first private financial institutions. Reforming the military-industrial ministries and the Gosplan, the Soviet central planning agency, was also of great importance in remodeling the economy. At the political level the decision, adopted in February 1990, to abolish the leading role of the Communist Party (granted by Article 6 of the Soviet Constitution) allowed a transfer of power from the CPSU to the government both at federal and regional levels. To these reforms Boris Yeltsin added a freely elected bicameral parliament, as well as a Constitutional Court, and maintained the freedom of speech. He also continued to develop a market economy with an emphasis on the privatization of state enterprises.

Despite these fundamental transformations, the post-Soviet Russian government has maintained three fundamental characteristics inherited from the Soviet past: an overpowerful executive branch; elite recruitment through cooptation; and an extremely secretive decision-making process. As shown below, these traditional aspects of Russian governance have encouraged systematic bribery, rule evasion, and economic crimes at all levels of the state.

An Over-Powerful Executive Branch

During the first years of Yeltsin's presidency, the institutional vacuum and political confrontation with the legislative branch forced the democrats to rely on the executive power as a vertical chain from the Kremlin down to the regional level. The new team needed a powerful political tool to impose a policy of democratization. Thus, regional governors were appointed directly by the Kremlin. In 1993, a newly drafted Constitution offered the executive power the upper hand over the legislature. The president, as well as governors at the local level, started ruling the country by decree. Although people from Yeltsin's entourage claimed they were unable to democratize the country without relying on a strong executive branch,[180] this political choice led to a new paradox: while political parties flourished, Russia still lacked a competitive system of politics.

Yeltsin's reforms were determined by a policy implemented from above only and left no room for concertation with various political, social, financial, and industrial bodies. During the year 1997, a handful of Russian investors and industrial managers elaborated, outside of the executive power, a complex proposal regarding the deregulation of the Railroad Ministry (MPS), then headed by Nikolai Aksyonenko. They asked for tighter control over the MPS's finances to provoke a drop in transport prices and for the privatization of several "satellite" enterprises. In so doing, they were obviously interested in getting a lucrative—but non-strategic—share of the Ministry's assets. They claim that then First Deputy Prime Minister Anatoli Chubais was so interested in their proposal that he even promised to give his go-ahead, but he suddenly changed his mind and failed to give any explanation to this unexpected U-turn. Whatever Chubais's motives were, the businessmen understood his reaction as a way to give the Railroad Minister sole control over the privatization of his institution. They felt excluded from the privatization process and this fostered a strong distrust towards the state structures in general, and the Yeltsin team in particular.[181]

Obviously enough, the ongoing perception among high-ranking officials that all elements external to the ruling elite and its policy were potential destabilizers did not favor policies based on consensus. On the contrary, it led to the alienation of the state from society and part of the industrial and financial elite. Consequently, Yeltsin's executive power closed down a path toward alternative power and reproduced a Soviet pattern of governance.

This attitude had yet another consequence. While taking personal responsibility for implementing a democratic regime, Yeltsin used the traditional lack of a balance of power and occasionally resorted to non-democratic means. On various occasions, the president gave free reign to the executive power to arbitrarily govern the country, individual regions, and cities.[182] Yeltsin's granting of virtually unlimited power to his allies was a means to carry out his democratization policy in an institutional vacuum, but this eventually led to an unforeseen situation in which, both at federal and local levels, representatives of the executive branch eventually developed quasi-absolute power and eventually stopped obeying the center.[183]

The Russian press usually sees the post-Soviet ruling elite as composed of three political interest groups: the so-called "Kremlin group" organized around the presidential administration; the "government group" led by the Prime Minister; and the Moscow city government group. At the regional level, local oligarchies navigate around the governors' and the mayors' administrations. These groups compete with each other for political influence, in the process using the media they own to discredit their rivals by accusing them of "corruption." What goes unnoticed in the Russian press, however, is that, although they have different political agendas, members of these elite groups share an understanding of the state, which they imagine to be vertical and highly centralized. They also believe that reforms should be implemented from above only and that politics regulate both the financial and the industrial development of the country. It is true that one can find various degrees of sincerity and corruption among members of the same group, and from one group to another, but, maintaining an overwhelmingly dominant executive power inevitably leads to arbitrary policies, various corrupt activities—including gift-giving, insider dealings and misappropriations of public funds—and abusive recourse to coercion, using the pretext of anticorruption campaigns, to eliminate political and financial rivals.

State Policy of Patronage

Under the Soviet regime, access to state resources for industrial managers depended mostly on their good relationship with government officials. This, in turn, generated a sophisticated system of organized bribery and patronage. An interesting characteristic of post-Soviet Russia lies in the persistence of a widely developed policy of patronage, both on the part of the state and among the "non-state" financial and political elite. Today's Russian politicians and industrial managers openly acknowledge that, in the recruitment process of their cadres, they favor loyalty over competence. Most of them argue that patronage is the safest way to avoid recruiting spies from their political or financial enemies and emphasize the necessity to build cohesive groups to survive in the hostile environment of the transitional period.[184] Elite groups and clienteles are formed or dissolved following patterns about which we know little.

Patronage has long been a key element of Russia's political culture and should not be considered as a crime or corruption practice per se. However, this practice has led the ruling elite to a fundamental confusion between the public and private sectors. The state policy of patronage, which was meant under the Yeltsin regime to create a coherent ruling elite, led to the paradox of cronyism in a market economy, where one would expect competition and new rules of recruitment. When they

acquired power after the collapse of the Soviet Union, members of
Yeltsin's entourage created a new team disconnected from the CPSU
Politburo and Central Committee traditional networks, but they did not
break with the former rules of recruitment.

While most of the banking system had already been shaped in the last
years of the Soviet regime, the Yeltsin administration still continued after
two years of the change of regime to support the creation of private financial structures on the basis of government institutions. As an illustration,
one of Russia's most successful banks, OneksimBank, was created in
1993 on the basis of the official bank of the Foreign Trade Ministry
(Vneshtorgbank) and of a former state bank, the International Bank of
Moscow (MMB). Its chairman, Vladimir Potanin, was also co-opted by
the federal government.[185] With the help of the Finance Ministry,
OneksimBank progressively took control over most of Vneshtorgbank's
and MMB's accounts and staff members. Although Potanin's bank was
officially presented as a private establishment, it represented the interests
both of the state and, at the private level, of the Foreign Trade Ministry's
top executives. Shortly after it was created, it became the government's
official agent in a number of financial deals.[186]

Not only has the alliance between financial institutions and politicians
never been hidden, but it has also become systematic from the federal
government down to the city level.[187] An example can be drawn by the
actions of the federal government and their attempt to drastically increase
its revenues. In March 1995, a consortium of commercial banks suggested that they lend the government funds and as collateral take large blocks
of shares in the country's most profitable companies.[188] On August 31,
1995, Yeltsin authorized a version of this plan that came to be known as
the "loans-for-shares" scheme.[189] According to this scheme, the banks
were supposed to inject money into the most heavily indebted enterprises in return for a significant volume of shares. This plan was also meant
to "save the bond market:" the government would be funded but would
not have to sell the shares it held in those enterprises. Thus the aim of this
scheme was to prevent equities from taking a nosedive. The bidders had
no conditions to meet and shares in the enterprises were supposed to be
granted to those banks that would offer the best loans. In view of the
Kremlin's monetary policy, everything sounded logical.

Yet the result was quite different. Only a few bidders—the consortium
members—were authorized to take part in these auctions. All of them had

close links with the federal power. Shares in the companies were given only to the consortium members that had already been chosen by the government to manage the federal budget. Those bidders whose offers were eventually turned down said they feared the outcome of the future auctions would only profit the banks that took part in the "loans-for-shares" privatization.[190] These authorized banks were soon given shares in some of the most strategic enterprises. This was the case in August 1997 when OneksimBank acquired a controlling share in Norilsk Nickel, Russia's main nickel producer. Some commentators argued at the time that the auctions were only a screen to hide the real purpose of the scheme: a distribution of the state's riches to a handful of cronies.

Even though it was obviously not intended to, privatization consolidated the oligarchic structure of power. Russian and Western media have extensively described the role played by the private banks in Yeltsin's 1996 re-election. In return for tax exemptions and greater investment opportunities, Russian bankers offered the incumbent president control over the media. During the year that followed the elections, the banks managed to consolidate their power by funding the government in some of the most strategic areas, including national security.[191]

Until recently, former government officials explained the collusion between the financial and political worlds by repeating that their priority was to implement a market economy and to democratize the political institutions, even if that meant closing the recruitment channels and writing off a potential alternative elite. Increasingly, the popular perception of the Yeltsin regime was that it was nothing but a weak central state ruled by a handful of bankers and industrial managers. This feeling was reinforced by official declarations of federal ministers admitting that it was difficult to struggle against the oligarchs.[192]

This perception that state officials were enriching themselves while in power was reinforced by a genuine policy of cronyism and even nepotism at a ministerial level. In October 1997, one leading Russian newspaper disclosed that officials in the Railroad Ministry had signed commercial contracts with private enterprises owned by their relatives. The press labeled this huge organization the "Ministry of Wives and Sons."[193] Then Railroad Minister Aksyonenko repeated this attitude after he was appointed First Deputy Prime Minister in the governments of both Sergei Stepashin and Vladimir Putin. In September, 1999, with the help of Fuel and Energy Minister Viktor Kalyuzhny, he again used the pretext of the cohesiveness of the team to arbitrarily dismiss Dmitri Savelev, the head of the crude oil pipeline monopoly Transneft. This move, however, had at least two other goals. First, it was meant to ensure that the company would fund the Kremlin candidate during the upcoming presidential election. Second, it was also intended to please one of the oil companies that had supported Kalyuzhny's appointment as Fuel and Energy Minister and Aksyonenko's promotion as the government's second top official. As a result, Savelev, an appointee of former Prime Minister Sergei Kirienko, was replaced by one of LUKoil's top executives.[194]

This systematic policy of patronage on the part of high-ranking officials shows that the state is still treated by them as not only as a major actor in resource allocation, but also as a patron dealing with a select clientele.[195] According to the parliamentarian Grigori Yavlinsky, the state still has the upper hand over most of the country's industrial fabric by placing its own clientele at the head of newly privatized enterprises and keeping ownership rights over the land.[196]

A Secretive Decision-Making Process

In the eyes of the post-Soviet ruling elite, the same politically hostile environment of the transition period justified the maintenance of an extremely secretive decision-making process. This allowed individuals to influence the presidential and government decrees, a specificity that opened the way to endless struggles for power.

According to Janine Wedel, during the years 1992–1996 the Russian "young reformers" often secretly drafted presidential decrees to carry on the government's privatization policy, thus bypassing a parliament dominated by the Communists and their conservative allies.[197] In their defense the "young reformers" claimed that the real incentive behind the lack of transparency was political belief, not personal gain, but in debating whether this secretive collusion between the financial and political worlds occurred by design or by accident, Russian high-ranking officials demonstrated that they were still thinking in Soviet terms.

One of the causes of the numerous capital flight scandals lies precisely in the way the Yeltsin administration chose to implement its political priorities. As we have seen above, the Kremlin team sought to establish a democratic regime with the belief that the end would justify the means, thus choosing to rely exclusively on the executive branch and to recruit members of their team through co-optation. To avoid endless debates with their own legislature and with Western financial institutions, they were also eager to maintain a highly secretive environment.

The Fimaco scandal, which concerns Russia's Central Bank, is a perfect illustration of the transformation of state officials into "ideological kleptocrats."[198] In November, 1990, the Soviet government established a small offshore company on Jersey, named Fimako, and transferred sums to its accounts from the Communist Party coffers. Starting from 1992, Eurobank (a Paris-based subsidiary of the Russian Central Bank, which also took part in establishing the company in 1990) began to control it. Fimako continued to have access to government hard currency reserves, using them to play on the Russian bond market on behalf of the Central Bank.[199] Had it been known in the West, these financial operations could have created serious problems with the IMF, which forbids the currency reserves of the country to be placed on the national market.

Therefore, rather than openly acknowledging the state's dramatic lack of cash and examining various solutions with both the Russian parliament and the IMF, the Kremlin decided to circumvent the IMF procedure. More precisely, this meant turning the loopholes in the Fund's rules to its own advantage. According to IMF Russian Managing Director Alexei Mozhin, one should not talk about corruption in the Fimako case. In his view, the problem is that the IMF simply failed to adapt its own rules to the Russian environment.[200] In July, 1999, the chairman of the Russian Central Bank Viktor Gerashchenko acknowledged that he had authorized hard currency transactions through Fimako.[201] In Gerashchenko's view, this transfer was not designed for personal enrichment and, on the contrary, was meant for the sake of the country's ailing economy. Such a reading of the case is typical of a biased understanding of democracy, which forgets about the democratic regimes' essential elements of governance, such as transparency and consensus.

As explained above, where one would have expected genuine competition and legislative regulation, the Yeltsin regime has seen an ever-growing executive power that has retained the Soviet method of managing the public sector (using arbitrariness and refusing any kind of balance of power). Imposing a state policy of patronage has engendered an oligarchic regime. Keeping financial, industrial, and political spheres under a single locus of control has encouraged embezzlement and repeated abuses of power. In the absence of appropriate legislation, resource allocation has remained in the hands of government officials, who were the only ones to decide which strategic enterprises were to be privatized and what the rules of access to them were. These three patterns of governance have all led to growing corruption and abuse of power. Despite the disappearance of the centralized economy and the emergence of privatization, the Russian authorities never drew a clear line between the public and private sectors.

The Pitfalls of the Traditional Anticorruption Campaigns

Since the late 1970s, several massive anticorruption campaigns have been launched by Soviet and Russian authorities. All of them may have succeeded in installing a new elite group in power, but so far have failed to eradicate corruption. Before elaborating new exit strategies for corruption in today's Russia, one should keep in mind the causes that led to the failures of these campaigns and avoid the pitfalls that the Kremlin has systematically run up against.

Struggle for Power

It appears that most of the campaigns have failed precisely because they struggled against a particular clientele rather than struggling against patronage as a structural flaw.

Whereas the Soviet press under Stalin and Khrushchev often denounced bureaucratic corruption and cases of embezzlement to justify the use of coercion, it was KGB chairman Yuri Andropov who launched the first systematic, anticorruption campaign at the end of the 1970s. Gathering compromising information on Party officials close to then General Secretary Leonid Brezhnev, he suddenly labeled the practices of rule evasion and gift giving that previously had been perceived as management tools as "corruption." His main goal in doing this was to overturn the ruling elite, offering his own faction greater latitude in which to exert control over the Party hierarchy, and to put an end to abuses of power at the local level. Andropov died in late 1983, only a year after having been promoted General Secretary, and before he could implement the structural reforms he had in mind. As a result, his anticorruption campaign has been perceived as a model for achieving power and has been eventually replicated by several political leaders, including Yeltsin, Russian Vice-President Alexander Rutskoi, and many regional governors.

In this power struggle both the law and legal institutions have been a tool in the hands of the executive power. Investigating committees have promoted a moral interpretation of corruption and have helped eliminate undesired networks or groups by qualifying them as "subversive." A cynical interpretation of anticorruption campaigns has easily been found, and key institutions such as law enforcement agencies and the judiciary, as well as intelligence and information channels, were used for the private purposes of certain elite groups. On the eve of the 1999 legislative election a fierce battle broke out between two elite groups vying for power: the Kremlin group and the Moscow city group. Both used the media they owned to publicize the compromising information—true or falsified—they had gathered against their political rivals. This political war was so intense that it soon lost all kind of respectability and legitimacy in the eyes of the public and non-state elites.

Legitimization of the New Team in Power

A new type of campaigning occurred each time a new team rose to power and took over from its predecessor. Under the Soviet regime, which lacked any kind of democratic electoral process, these campaigns were designed to legitimize the new team in power.

During the June 1987 CPSU Central Committee Plenum, Gorbachev criticized the head of Gosplan and other economic officials in charge of the Soviet economy under Brezhnev, so as to justify both reshuffling the ministries and the choice to authorize private cooperatives. Corruption and nepotism, in addition to being considered as negative trends inherited from the Brezhnev regime, were also presented as the main obstacle to reform. "Cases of falsified information, arbitrary action and violation of Soviet laws still occur," emphasized the Central Committee in July 1988.[202] This behavior, as well as the "bureaucratic actions of the ministries" and "the passivity of many Party organizations," was presented as an incentive for structural reform of the political system.[203] Gorbachev and his team needed new blood to regenerate the system. For this purpose, they used the same rhetoric as the late CPSU General Secretary Yuri Andropov, subjecting to public criticism behavior—patronage and nepotism—that they themselves continued to resort to.

Yeltsin repeatedly resorted to this kind of denunciation campaign as well. From the very beginning of his regime, he emphasized the necessity to fight corruption each time the political environment required a demonstration of force, each time he was eager to shape an image of the state's incorruptibility and needed to justify the choice of a new Prime Minister. The Russian president reproduced this pattern in February 1996 when he announced he would run for a second term. He then exposed "corrupt" state officials to reassure the population of the morality of his team five months before the presidential poll. Another objective of these denunciations of former allies and team members was for Yeltsin to direct critics at them and justify the slackening of the economic reforms. Finally, the public accusations leveled against political rivals were also a way to discredit these rivals and prevent them from acquiring power.

Other denunciation campaigns occurred when the country's leadership was anxious to maintain the cohesiveness of the political apparatus on the eve of a strategic political move. By denouncing a handful of so-called "corrupt elements," the political leadership sought, first, to justify a change in policy and, second, to gain the support of the vast majority of state and Party officials who had just been absolved. Putin's state is no exception. Only a few days after the president's inauguration the General Prosecutor's Office raided a private media group known for its political opposition to Putin. Suspicion of corruption, tax evasion, and spying on individuals were used as pretexts for this raid. Officials emphasized the need for order and law enforcement when the victims claimed that the operation was politically motivated.[204]

The Blackening of the State

For Yeltsin, the strategy of building an image of incorruptibility did not work as initially planned. In April, 1992, when he signed presidential decree No. 361 urging civil servants to declare their revenues and announcing a new campaign against corruption within the state structures, journalists reacted with skepticism. Convinced that it was a stillborn operation, they criticized the decree for its lack of a time frame and control mechanism.[205] In the fall of the same year, Yeltsin created another bureaucratic structure to struggle against corruption. This time it was an interdepartmental commission under the aegis of the Security Council.[206] As with the earlier decree, the media eventually accused him of offering a pretext to struggle against political rivals and of focusing on "small fish" to avoid the debate on greater corruption among high-ranking officials.[207] Beginning in 1993, in no instance did Russian politicians let themselves be abused by the successive campaigns against corruption launched during the wrestling match between the executive and the legislative branches. Not only did they not believe these campaigns were well grounded, they saw them merely as a political barometer and tried to guess which side would eventually have the upper hand as to join the right network.

In an article published in early 1993, then Deputy Security Minister Yevgeny Savostyanov complained that everyone, "from parliamentary and interdepartmental commissions to the president and the Supreme Soviet," was combating corruption. "To what result?" he asked. "Almost none."[208] Savostyanov argued that, to make campaigns against corruption efficient, the political leadership needed to launch a debate on the nature of corruption and to adapt the existing legislation accordingly. Yet, instead of pursuing any constructive policy, the government drifted along a different path. Corruption under Yeltsin redistributed power within the state mechanism by attributing greater authority to office holders; it therefore contributed to the weakening of the state's authority.

This systematic split between the official discourse and actual policy contributed to the general political chaos. Soon the successive campaigns against corruption drained any creativity in structural reforms to the state and the economy from politics. Not surprisingly, corruption returned to the center of the debate between the legislative and the executive after the profound crisis of the summer of 1998. But these new campaigns against corruption had the same consequences as earlier: they were now perceived as indicative of the state's impotence in finding a constructive way out of the crisis and as lies progressively were losing all strength. The chasm between discourse and reality was so great that everyone who denounced corruption was now perceived as corrupt himself, eager to use anticorruption campaigns as a means to denounce political rivals and therefore acquire power.

The recurrence of these campaigns at closer and closer intervals has sapped Russia's political life during the transition period. Although corruption problems for the most part have structural causes which lie in the patterns of governance, most of Russia's anticorruption campaigns have focused exclusively on their moral aspect. They have aimed at individuals exposed as persons of low morale, rather than striking at the root of the problem. If some of these campaigns were also designed to prepare public opinion prior to structurally reforming the state and the economy, they nevertheless had identical consequences: paradoxically enough, by aiming at individuals, anticorruption campaigns tarnished the image of the entire state.

Very quickly the Russian state power has found itself caught in a vicious circle: the more struggles it has launched against corruption using the pattern described above, the more it has undermined the reputation of its representatives. State institutions, instrumental as they are in struggles for power, made the executive power appear extremely corrupt and cynical in the eyes of those who remained outside of the state structures. The countless accusations of corruption and the numerous arrests of high-ranking officials unintentionally projected the image of a rotten state rather than that of a clean one. It progressively undermined the legitimacy of the state, even in the eyes of its civil servants.

The more acute the political confrontation with the legislative branch became, the more Yeltsin accused his rivals of corruption. The more the state declared its willingness to struggle against corruption, the more it was forced to fight the negative perception inherited from previous campaigns, and the farther it became from the actual problem. In a stalemate, the state was then bound to resort to even more coercion in order to conceal its impotence.

In conclusion, it appears that analyzing Russia's traditional patterns of governance, as well as the distorted perception of the causes of corruption and their potential remedies, offers invaluable insight to understanding the repeated failures of the government's anticorruption campaigns. Opposite positions on several key issues, such as the role of the state in implementing economic reforms or the need to resort to temporary collusion between politics and economics during a "transition" period, have developed. As a rule, those involved in the Russian state refer to the extremely unstable transition to explain the state's involvement in the economic sphere, an attitude that would be considered a responsible one in a different environment. Seven decades of communism, nevertheless, have biased the perception many non-state elite representatives have of the Kremlin's policies. The Russian media tend now to denounce any government policy as systematically dictated by cronyism and corruption. The executive power, as an extremely close and secretive environment, has engendered a significant lack of confidence among the population, who often qualify today's endemic corruption by the word lawlessness (*bespredel*). Such a biased perception has, in turn, undercut the effects of all state's policies.

It appears that the only way to make the struggle against corruption effective is to break the vicious circle of tarnishing the state by opening a genuine dialogue between the state and society. To restore confidence in the state, the executive power should agree to secure transparency by making its budgets public. It should, first and foremost, have a genuine balance of power, with a truly independent judiciary and legislature. As essential as it is to protect the rights of individuals, it is vital to secure a division of responsibilities among different institutions and groups and to protect alternative elite groups, not only as reservoirs of potential leaders, but also as entities capable of playing the role of a counter-weight in the balance of power.

Overall, the preservation of a Soviet pattern of governance in today's Russia has contributed to the widely shared perception that corruption in post-Soviet Russia has not changed its nature and is still state-generated. As a result, the country confronts a corruption of the state rather than the corruption of a handful of civil servants within the state structures. Anticorruption campaigns as they are traditionally implemented in Russia do little to combat the phenomenon. They cannot be seen as the only means for fighting corruption. If the right exit strategy does not lie in coercion and the replacement of individuals, other means should be sought. The structural reform of the state should respect three basic features that make a democratic regime function: a genuine balance of power and respect for the legislature; elite recruitment based on merit rather than patronage; and transparency of budgets.

Kompromat and Corruption in Russia
Ákos Szilágyi

Perhaps now is the time to say something about the word "corruption" itself. At the turn of the second millennium corruption comes up more and more often. In fact, it not only comes up, it takes root, flowers, and spreads like a weed. We encounter the word "corruption" most often in our interaction with each other. In newsprint, in television reports, in academic conferences, in parliamentary debates, in political denunciations, both within and outside parties, between states, in research institutes, in bars, at the dinner table, among friends, in official corridors—in other words, anywhere at least two people come together. Probably those who most often run into the word "corruption" are those who exist within the reality of corruption—that is, those who represent a link in the corruption chain: the corrupted and the corrupters.

It is not completely clear why we hear so much about corruption and so little about the term "corruption." Perhaps corruption researchers should start their job by scrutinizing the use of the word. Professionals specializing in corruption investigation, journalists who expose corrupt relationships and affairs every five minutes, populist politicians, and moralizing intellectuals often act as if these matters were obvious, as if they were empirically researchable, as if they could be clearly judged, when, in fact, there is hardly any more obscure and elusive, social phenomenon.

At first hearing, anyone would be surprised and prompted to disagree with our claim: corruption exists in the way, at the time, and to the degree that it is openly brought up in conversation or rather—as we shall see—as often as it is exposed. The question actually is in what way, for what reason, by whom and when is the word "corruption" brought up, and what does it actually mean: exposure, moral sermons, threats, blackmail, or purging? Who brings up and how does this come about? Who gives the orders, who is the "judge," who is the "accuser," the "accused," and, finally, who is the "victim"? Is it moral enthusiasm, the political philosophy of public welfare, or rather selfish private interests that motivate the current political verbosity of the theme of corruption? What are the goals and the results: the discovery of the truth, "pure" community life, or blackballing and weakening of the position of a political and/or market competitor? Or is it perhaps all of these things together, so that in this way both public opinion and the desire for power are satisfied?

What kind of discourse is appropriate for talking about corruption? Whom or what do they want to induce to an action or compel toward an action with corruption? Depending on how corruption is brought up, what the discourse is like, it can be a tool of moral purification (i.e., education), of ideological indoctrination (i.e., the legitimation of power and the duping of society), and that of political battle (i.e., of acquisition, division, and maintenance of power). Hence, it is one tool among many, or, as is the case today, one of the most important tools.

It is beyond the scope of this study to make an exhaustive linguistic-sociological or political–theoretical analysis of "corruption speech." I only attempt to analyze the most recent and most characteristic phenomenon of post-modern political discourse, the "language of kompromat," based on the political language richest in this regard, i.e., Russian.

The Kompromat of Corruption

There is no other word in the Russian language that has had a broader career in the past ten years, and that is more often encountered in the press, in parliamentary debates, and in public prosecutors' reports than this peculiar acronym that does not even have Russian roots. After "soviet," "tractor," "sputnik," "gulag," and other delicacies, the newest Russian word begging admittance into the European languages is "kompromat."

Kompromat is a slightly frivolous-sounding abbreviation of the expression *komprometiruyushchii material* (compromising material); at the same time, it is difficult not to hear in the *mat*-ending the music of the thoroughly Russian *mat* (meaning, vulgarities). Ultimately, kompromat can also be understood as a political vulgarity. The meaning of the word—as it is customarily used—can perhaps be best expressed as follows: publicizing, with the intention of compromising someone, data, evidence, circumstances, or documents (or the threat of publicizing such data), using the traditional and reformed journalistic and political genres of reporting, exposing, defaming, and recrimination. The information must be capable of morally and politically discrediting, destroying, keeping in check, or charging with criminal activities a political and/or economic opponent (other possibilities include accusations, house searches, interrogations, arrest, confinement under remand, international arrest warrants, etc.).

We examine the word "kompromat" in the context of corruption speech, as a theme of political language, which is also the language of force.[209] Because—regardless of the factual contents of the kompromat—what the initiators would like to accomplish, and how, by attacking with a kompromat is never by exposing the truth. Kompromat is always directed against the stability of the regime, towards subjecting and suppressing, towards victory at any price. In political speech kompromat is like a rhetorical last word—it plays the "and-that's-the- end-of-it!" role. In the game of politics everyone is for winning. It is not irrelevant, however, who, by what means and how is able to win. Victory is won if one finishes off his/her opponent, and if in the election—fairly or not—one collects more votes. These two kinds of victory match two different kinds of political games, which differ not only in the means they use, but in the sense and purpose of the game as well.

Someone who wants to win by using kompromat, has either run out of political arguments (perhaps he lives in "such a time" in which political arguments routinely do not count, or are not enough for victory); or does not have time (political or business time) to wait for the struggle to be decided on the political battlefield with the permitted tools of political fight and opinion formation. The stakes are, possibly, too high for someone to risk losing, or to risk the struggle not turning out for his/her benefit. Kompromat puts an end to political debate and struggle, because it disqualifies the opponent or at least announces that she is disqualified: she is no longer an enemy. Whoever has at least a little self-respect (and the possessor of kompromat is necessarily such a person!), cannot enter into a legal political fight with an opponent who has lost his political honor. Such a person must flee from the political battle. If he does not want to leave, then he has to be thrown out.

Kompromat can take the form of a challenge: blackmail, provocation, or a declaration of war. Usually, however, it is a response to the opponent's political or business arguments, or perhaps to his success.Either way, it cuts off all normal—political or business—possibilities of interaction. You cannot argue with kompromat, nor can you refute it. There is only one adequate response to kompromat, i.e., counter-kompromat. To this, you can respond with a newer, even more powerful counter-kompromat. Kompromat follows kompromat and thus a war of kompromats (*voina kompromatov*) continues as long as the opponents still have new kompromat in their arsenals, or as long as someone is still left alive on the political stage.

Kompromat and Corruption, Two Good Friends

The fight against corruption, as everyone knows, is declared and continued by politicians, mercilessly and relentlessly, night and day, up to final victory, at all times and with all means at their disposal. However, because of the very nature of the fight, the "fighters," even under normal circumstances, tend to forget about, and abandon, the goal of the political fight (the destruction of corruption) during the battle, and the holy purpose is turned into the tool of a completely different and common fight, the fight for power and bread. The battle is waged no longer against corruption, but against each other, for the purpose of acquiring, influencing, shaking, or preserving political power. As a result, kompromat is a phenomenon of the anticorruption political struggle, in which the political goal is reduced to a tool of the unhindered assertion of private interests and goals.

Kompromat does not achieve its goal when the suspected corruption is verified, resulting in one or two fewer corrupt government officials, politicians, deals, or interpenetrations in the state. Instead, it achieves its goal when, regardless of its verified or unverified nature, it scars, besmears, disqualifies and forces resignation on its "targets"—the minister, leader of a professional union, government head, public prosecutor, tax inspector, newspaper editor, etc. The contents of the kompromat may be true, but that is a side issue. Kompromat is never directed toward the discovery of truth or punishing the guilty. Rather its goal is to pull down the opponent. It is a kind of political manhunt with trained journalists, but in this hunt even the hunter can turn wild at any moment.

It is almost a rule that the more often political actors reach for the weapons of kompromat and the more fatal the possible consequences with the weapon being fired, the greater the actual corruption and the more feeble and illusory the fight against corruption. Kompromat is a phenomenon of the anticorruption political struggle in which the goals of the state—the political community—are degraded to a tool of private interests. The excess of kompromat in political life signifies that the constitutional state is fatally weakened, or is incapable of strengthening itself. The squabbling private interests tear the state into pieces and swallow it up (this is the essence of structural corruption!), with the result that the state cannot fulfil its most important legal protection, tax collection, social, cultural, financial, and security functions. The more often kompromats explode in the political life of a country, the more certain that the corruption is of a structural nature and the rule of law is simply a fiction or a part of the democratic political image.

An economy dominated by the privatized criminal–corrupt–klepto-cratic clans who have privatized the state—that is, the power to act in the name of the state—possesses a kind of political life in which corrupt kompromat is necessary; the continuous reciprocal mud-slinging that exposes the economic deals and interpenetrations, playing a major role in the media war for power, money, and property between the clans. Kompromat is usually confidential information: documents, lists of names, letters, records, contracts, bank statements, recorded telephone conversations, or video recordings—that is, physical evidence—which is secret, or at least not intended for public knowledge. It can also be a reference to some document, conversation or contract which has not been seen or read by anyone, with which the political opponent can throw a politician and/or corrupt client (businessperson, proprietary group) competing for his place and or market share off his path. On the battlefront the political actors (party leaders, ministers, bankers, raw material barons, and media tsars) shoot each other with such documents.

Of course, let us not forget that a kompromat is the refined, or if you like, civilized version of destruction (or threat of destruction) of the business and/or political opponent, rival, or competitor. The unrefined or "raw" version is assassination. Kompromat and assassination are interconnected in this sense, and in the postcommunist decade in Russia they became the preferred technique of conflict-resolution in social-economic life. A huge service industry (private investigation offices dedicated to the gathering of information, private security forces and protection armies, hired assassins, terrorists, provocation services, etc.) took shape for this activity. A genuine kompromat market and killer market have emerged in Russia. The prices in this illegal market are determined by the law of supply and demand, and there they stand ready to satisfy the buyer's every demand, provided the buyer's desires are in conformity with her ability to pay.

Where the constitutional state is weak, the citizens of the state can never feel secure: neither in the physical nor the moral sense, neither on the street nor in their homes, as neither in business life or in the life of the community. Anyone, anytime, can get his own killer or kompromat, be it the president, a government head, financier, media mogul, mafia chief, party politician or journalist. For this reason, everyone who can tries to watch out for his own security—to the extent he can, or to the extent his fears extend. All means are permitted. This is why the ten years following the fall of the Soviet Union have been a chaotic era of the war of private individuals in Russia: *bellum omnium contra omnes*. The death of the old monster-state, the Soviet Leviathan, was not followed, and could hardly be followed, by a new Leviathan, a state associated with civil world order, the creation of a consti- tutional state. It seems that Russia needed ten years of chaos, continuous eco- nomic and social decline, and basic moral decay in order to recognize the civ- ilizing (economic and social) need for a constitutional state that guarantees public security, creates legitimate laws, guarantees equality before the law, and plays by the rules in the economic and political spheres.[210]

The Power of the Media in Accusations of Corruption

Without globalization of the structures of corruption and the power of the media in politics, kompromat could not have developed into such an independent and important tool of political battle. Corruption scandals have always been part of politics and the significance of some of the old political scandals was no less than that of those today. But allegations of corruption ("kompromat war," which is preceded by kompromat collec- tion and/or kompromat fabrication, the threats connected with the intro- duction of kompromats and the appropriate timing of the kompromat, etc.) have so far not been among the most widely accepted and most important tools of political battle technology. Until recently such allega- tions had not been a continuously calculated part of defensive and offen- sive strategies and tactical manuevers; they had not been used as an advertising miracle-weapon against rival products by the image-making companies who create political products for the market of mass culture, and who work alongside parties and party leaders.

Since both the national community and the national states have defined corruption as the central theme of political life, it seems that the breath- taking, monumental, colorful topic of corruption increasingly belongs to the normal working of the political process. With it, one can stop or start the process, take down political opponents or marginalize them, and make converts cheaply and easily. We no longer beat our political rivals with old-fashioned ideological arguments, persuasive force, political schemes, successful programs and effective propaganda, but with the publicizing of proven or supposed acts of corruption.

The goals of politicizing corruption and of publicizing true and imagined acts of corruption are not always the finishing off of a rival politician. Kompromat is often used for bringing into line, rebuking, deterring, and as a last resort, "blackmailing" a politician or political group (clan, party, corporation) in power, or vying for power: "if you make a decision against us, if you don't obey us, if you take away our authority, then you will be in trouble—and it's not your subordinate's, or your wife's, or your daughter's, or your brother-in-law's corrupt affairs that we're going to expose in the press, but yours!" Or in another way: "watch out if you hang out our dirty laundry, because we'll hang out yours!"

Usually, the goal of kompromat is accomplished if the suspicion or accusation of corruption is brought into the open. Kompromat is simply the publicizing of an accusation of corruption. This is the only way that it could become independent and turn into the most important tool in the political battle for power, influence, property, and resources in the last decade. The revving up of the political topic of corruption would hardly have been possible without the achievements of the telecommunications revolution and the increasing influence of the media in politics. At the same time, more than anything else, kompromat is a picture: a picture of persons caught in corrupt activities or under suspicion of corruption. In kompromat the word "corruption" almost comes to life: it becomes "fact." At least that is the way it appears, as if they do not speak about corruption, but instead simply point out: "this is the bank statement," "this is the place where," "this is the tapped phone conversation, in which," "this is the document we have found in the trash pile or dumpster." If the case of corruption is objectified, then the faces and figures only have to be attached: there are plenty of photos and films of all the common characters. The image soaks up almost every sinister context or implication of sensational exposure: the face under accusation of corruption practically speaks for itself. That is, it is distorted, because from now on it communicates corruption. When technical products (photocopies, television pictures, etc.) make corruption visible, or when they present objects posing as evidence and persons considered as criminals to the judges or the viewers, then it is as if they have provided absolute certainty about it to those looking at the pictures. All that is not visible is not interesting—including, of course, the truth. By use of the technically produced picture, kompromat makes the impression of the of the factuality of the kompromat. It does not even intend to do more than that.

Let us take a simple example from the everyday experience of still-influential politician–businessman–media magnate Boris Berezovsky. *Time*: March 1999. *Place* (or rather, *Scene*): ORT, Russia's most-watched, so-called public television station (channel 1), whose majority shareholder is the state, but whose actual boss is the oil-oligarch who controls the board of directors and program production—Berezovsky. *Crime*: the removal from power of the then Prime Minister and would-be president, Yevgenii Primakov, especially considering that Primakov approved of an international arrest warrant for Berezovsky issued in Paris at that time. *Counterattack*: publicized kompromat.

1. The assignment is given: Kompromat must be prepared against Primakov, who became the main enemy during the 1999–2000 election war and also later the main rival of one of the presidential candidates, Vladimir Putin. Primakov, however, is one of the few old-liner Soviet politicians whose political relationships and affairs are not connected to the new-Russian criminal and kleptocratic world. The fact that the believability and credibility of kompromat against him would be slim does not prevent such materials from being introduced against him. Primakov's weak point is else-where: his uncertain past, full of secrets; he was the head of intelligence, the master of secret diplomacy, the man behind the scenes who knows a lot and, according to common opinion, could have been involved in many dirty deals.

2. At the ORT news editorial office, Berezovsky's "inner staff" looks at pictures of Primakov. They come across a strange report about Prime Minister Primakov's visit to a Russian military technical exhibition. In one of the scenes Primakov is holding a bazooka in his hand and joking-ly asks the professionals gathered around him: "and will this shoot through an armoured Mercedes?"

3. On this point the brain trust starts working. Someone realizes that "Shevardnadze's armoured Mercedes, a gift from Kohl, was shot up the other day by a bazooka just like that," although the Georgian head of state, thanks to the armour, escaped harm. In addition, the relationship between Gorbachev's former foreign minister and his national security minister was not ideal. The kompromat is ready, the next day its system and method can be found in *Noviye Izvestiya,* one of Berezovsky's news-papers: "Primakov ordered the attack against Shevardnadze."

4. The same day the evening news report, ORT, refers to the *Noviye Iszvestiya* kompromat (naturally, without mentioning that Berezovsky's

television is referring to Berezovsky's newspaper), but in a manner appropriate for television: while the news anchor is speaking they show the incriminating scene from the six-month-old report, in which Primakov is asking about bazookas in a Mercedes factory. Here the circle is complete: the kompromat is set in motion.

The Privatization of Political Denunciation

Obviously, the post-political language of kompromat did not just emerge out of the blue. It has a long history as that of modern political ideologies. Denunciations of corruption, as political tools of power and territory acquisition were well known and used with master perfection in ancient Rome, in late medieval Western Europe, in Peter the Great's Russia, in the "ancien régime" and then in Jacobin France. Originally, kompromat was one kind of political denunciation, although it was not so named. However, not every political denunciation was kompromat. The difference is especially clear if we compare the Soviet and post-Soviet types of political denunciations in Russia.

In the religious sense people are decidedly corrupt beings—mortal and depraved. This depravity is demonstrated, by the fact, among others, that we are corruptible and can be even further tainted, but beyond the religious sense corruption has a purely political and economic meaning as well. The totalitarian, ideocratic Soviet state considered persons as corrupt, that is, liable to political degradation, having a weak strain, subject to perversion and more or less degenerate. It was not unfounded that this saying went around the state security authorities during the time of Stalin's reign of terror (the golden age of "ideological kompromat"): *Byl bi chelovek, statya naidetsa.*" That is, "Just have the man, and we'll find an article of the law [under which to punish him!]."

On the other hand, in a society in which all actors end up in "complete market" relations with the state-regulated private economy, one is considered as potentially corrupt primarily as a private person (and this includes public servants and politicians as well). Depending on one's place in the system and on the condition of the state, which is to monitor the rules of the game and the laws, everyone is, to some degree, subject to the temptation, inducement, or occasionally even the compulsion to be corrupt. To accept or offer bribes in the interest of private goals, to bypass laws, one should deceive the tax authorities and have no concern for the "common good." Accordingly, the Soviet pattern turns the original corruptibility of the political animal, the common person, against private individuals (from this comes the "vigilance" and "healthy mistrust" which was the most important political-moral requirement demanded of the Soviet citizen), thus being entirely diverted from governmental-political and ideological interests. By contrast, in the post-Soviet version the economic animal, the private individual, displaying his bottomless depravity, fights against other private individuals for the sake of achieving private goals—in both a weak political state as well as in a "wild capitalist" market economy. In this sense kompromat is the privatization of political denunciation, which is enhanced by its content (bio-political and corrupt or criminal exposures) and its mass-culture function (the entertainment industry, media-shows, deconstruction of traditional political thought with magical tools, sub-conscious manipulation).

If it is true that denunciation and informing "naturally follow from the dominant technique of the exercise of power in a society, but at the same time are themselves a kind of peculiar technological structure, which intertwines with many other power techniques woven throughout society,"[211] then kompromat—like the "privatization" of the Soviet-type political informing—is one such peculiar "technology" that corresponds to the techniques of the power-exercising kleptocratic–criminal–corrupt clans, at constant war with each other and maintaining the post-Soviet State, society, property and media under their reign. The autocratic-totalitarian Soviet state's boundless power was not replaced by a democratic constitutional state founded on a division of power and the sanctity of the law, in which power is balanced by a civil society ready and capable of organizing itself. Instead, the old, torn-apart state was revived to an independent life: the unlimited tyranny of its "privatized" parts (or practically speaking, tyranny only limited by the competing parts, the state's property and power sectors: regions, ministries, secret services, the military, custom guards, tax authorities) and the constant war of these private tyrants, a fight to the death against each other. The post-Soviet kompromat is the weapon of this war, the war of the private interests, private properties, and privatized state sectors, the war that does not show mercy or has no moral scruples. No matter what the cost, there is no moral price that the oligarchic clans will not pay for victory, or rather—in the majority of cases "spontaneously"—for the keeping or multiplying of properties, possessions, and money by means of methodical stealing, underground extortion, evasion of the law, and bribery of officials. Of course, compared to local civil wars, bombings, and assassinations, kompromat seems to be a relatively gentle and conservative weapon, since it "only" destroys moral lives, not physical lives. True, the lines between battle styles and weapon types are indistinct and not firm: a kompromat war can at any time turn into an actual war, assassination, or bloody showdown.

The 11-Suitcase Kompromat

In the time following the collapse of the Soviet Union, the goals of kompromat "caught up with" its transformed content. Since then kompromats exposing of private sins are primarily in the service of private interests, regardless of what political significance the action has and regardless of the fact that the moral pathos of the anticorruption fight introduced "kompromat war" into the rhetoric of the both the central powers and the opposition. Kompromat as the most effective tool of political battle, appeared on the stage of Russian political life in April 1993, when Aleksandr Rutskoi, Yeltsin's then vice-president, threatened the President and his circle with his comical, theatrical "11-suitcase kompromat." Naturally, immediately after that a string of "counter-kompromat" came crashing down on Rutskoi's poor head, so that the suitcases, if they had existed at all, never exposed their dark and mysterious depths. Rutskoi's April kompromat, followed by a counter-kompromat, was followed in September by a political checkmate, and in October by a "tank-mat" at the Moscow's White House.

A kompromat war, however, rarely spills over into that kind of anachronistic modern phenomenon—into shooting and the spilling of blood. Over time, the torment, even in this sphere, has become more dignified: that is, today e they do not attack the Moscow mayor's office with tanks anymore. In December, 1999, at the end of the Duma elections, it was not from gun barrels but from the Internet that a destructive kompromat fell upon Luzhkov and his "Moscow family." Luzhkov, Yakovlev, and Primakov, who presumably played a role in the plan to ensure that the suspicions of corruption and money-laundering (Mabetex scandal, Bank of New York, etc.) by the Kremlin "family" be publicized in the West, were then hit by their own nice, big kompromats from the Kremlin, just as Rutskoi had

been in his time. True, we could consider the renewed Chechen war as the
spilling over of the Moscow kompromats into real war. The opposing
sides—both for and against—tried to play the breaking out of war as a
kompromat against each other. The Luzhkov–Primakov camp gathered
material for accusations of "you are the house bombers!" and "financiers
of the Chechens!"; the Yeltsin camp hurled accusations of "you are toad-
ies of the Chechens!" or "bribed by the Chechens!," accompanied by all
kinds of compromising data and documents, on the heads of the Moscow
group and their media-toadies—primarily the oligarch of NTV, Gusinsky.
In the pro-war public opinion that developed in the wake of the bombings
this front of the kompromat war became uninteresting; it was not possible
to influence broad public opinion with this "big kompromat" that pushed
the limits of reality (and even of fantasy).[212] No matter how they tried, the
opposing power groups could not manage to convincingly blame the other
for the bombings. The hysteria united the population in one single desire
that finally someone would come to end this nightmare, no matter from
where, at what price, and completely regardless of who the instigators and
perpetrators of the deed had been—the Chechens, the GRU (State
Reconnaissance), the FSB, the Basayev brothers, Berezovsky, Voloshin,
Kvashnin, Chubais, or all of them together.[213] Terrorist assaults against the
civil population pulled the Chechen question out of the state ideological
sky and onto the ground of private citizens' problems. Whoever took a
stand against the heated campaign (and, indirectly, against Putin) for stopping "international terrorism" and the otherwise existing Chechen ban-
ditism, for the right to life of the state's citizens, for public security, that
is, for private goals (and not as in 1994–1995: "the stopping of Chechen
separatism" and "defense of the territorial integrity of Russia"), no matter
what kompromat he devised, it became unpopular. On the other hand,
whoever stood on the side of the war benefited from the popularity of the
"true cause," even if he did not excel on the kompromat front.[214]

The Kompromat Market

Kompromat is worth money, and not just a little. Money for the one who
is compromised by the documents or information and money for the one
who orders it and uses it in the interests of his own success, business, or
power ambitions. The one who is blackmailed by kompromat pays (in

cash or in some kind of services), as does the one who wants to extort from an opponent or remove someone from his/her political or business course. Until the middle of the 90's, however, we could only speak metaphorically of a true kompromat market, kompromat production, and kompromat trade in Russia. Starting in 1996 the metaphor became reality. If there was a cog-wheel in the market machinery of Russia that made a complete revolution in the last few years, then that cog-wheel would certainly be the kompromat market, along with the wheels of the information market, the money market and the media market, all spinning against each other.[215]

Of course, kompromat is rarely traded in the physical sense, on store shelves. Exposure (or the threat of it) is realized in the mass media, that is, it reaches the consumer through the newspaper, television broadcasts, perhaps even through the Internet. This is also commerce and the press itself is undoubtedly interested in the creation, purchase, and selling of kompromat. The primary transactions take place between the one ordering or directing the kompromat and the one developing or in possession of the kompromat. Kompromat in the physical sense (documents, video recordings, etc.) are first bought, and then it is decided how these objects can be most effectively used. The carrying out of the kompromat (the timing, preparation, presentation, disclosure) is a separate service, which the developer and deliverer of the kompromat never touch; instead it is the work of PR teams, political technicians, and media professionals hired by the initiator of the kompromat.

On the primary market transaction level, kompromat rarely consists of photos or scandalous, and, therefore, entertaining, video recordings; in themselves, these objects have little persuasive power. In the true kompromat market the participants much more commonly buy and sell boring financial documents, reports about the target person's (or company's) financial circumstances, papers regarding taxes, customs transactions, or judicial records relating to the person, copies of private correspondence, items from the dossier of the interior ministry or the secret service, Interpol reports, medical reports and other kinds of written information. Only documents of a confidential or secret nature have market value. The more confidential the compromising information, the more expensive.

The gathering of kompromat is done by companies (security services, protection firms) that explicitly specialize in these matters and do so more or less legally. They are also the manufacturers, deliverers, and sellers of kompromat (intermediaries rarely appear on their own between the ordering party and the seller). Who are the ordering parties? We know that already: on one hand, entrepreneurs, who order kompromats against public officials, their own colleagues, or business competitors and politicians; on the other hand, public officials and politicians, who use compromising information against each other and against entrepreneurs. The actual identity of the ordering party is never revealed. This is the unwritten rule of the kompromat market: the identity of the buyer is taboo. (In principle this taboo, this secret, this confidential information could be the object of a new kompromat. This, however, does not happen often on the kompromat market, since this would ruin the business. Potential buyers would be scared off. If they start to trade in concealing the identity of the ordering party, that itself would lead to the collapse of the market and impossibility of performaing for the buyers), but even if the identity of the buyer remains secret, the carrying out of the kompromat always reveals what was ordered, who was the target, and who benefited from it. It is also always possible to figure out whether the kompromat's "fireworks" or "bomb" blew up or sputtered, or whether, perhaps, it blew up under the bombers because of bad timing or because it was not put together professionally.

The majority of kompromat deliverers and manufacturers emerged out of the dismissed or broken up ranks of those dumped on the street by the KGB and now offering their special expertise to private firms.[216] Most of them found their place in various groups of the financial sector, banks, and security services. Already in 1993 the number of people working in different kinds of private protection enterprises (CSOP) exceeded 200,000. In addition to property protection, extortion control, and assault protection, private secret services also take care of surveillance and information gathering. In a way the whole thing has been simplified: everyone is wiretapped, or at least an attempt is made. Although the placement of "bugs" or tapping a phone is against the law, the secret tools of information-gathering can be obtained on the market without any kind of approval procedure. In place of the state's (Big Brother's) all-seeing one eye and one ear, i.e., the KGB, now there are a thousand eyes and sharp private ears monitoring who does what in secret.

Naturally, the security service professionals know each other well. The state secret service and private services have always maintained informal relationships. Solitary heroes were rare in the profession. The teams that specialized in preparing the kompromat were made up of secret service personnel who, as a "cover," worked in the security services of civil associations, clubs, and commercial firms. According to a high-ranking official of the former KGB, "anything can be ordered or bought from the secret services. They no longer deliver the materials obtained by their operatives [staff] to the judiciary, but rather sell it for cash on the market."[217] One of the most direct and most fatal manifestations of the weakness of the Russian State was the "breaking loose" of the repeatedly reorganized and carved up secret services: until the Spring of 2000 neither the state's financial nor administrative tools were effective for the control of these services, although according to certain signs that I will mention later, a change is expected in this area. Many believe that secret service personnel were attracted to the "kompromat-industry" not just by the money, but because of their wounded pride and a desire for revenge for the destruction of their professional carriers and the moral humiliation which they had to suffer after 1991. The majority of them perhaps reasoned that "the Soviet Union was ruined by the top leadership's betrayal. It is entirely irrelevant to what political trend the 'new masters' belong— they are conspirators against the state and criminals, against whom any kind of weapon is permissible."[218] From this point of view, the post-Soviet kompromat game is also motivated somehow by the state-professional corporation's interests and their fundamental political-ethical position: the more people get their own kompromat, the more obvious the criminal nature of the system and its all-pervasive corruption and indefensibility will be. Consequently, the dissatisfaction of society will be all the stronger. This calculation—considering the 2000 presidential election and society's mood—was not completely unfounded, since not only is the new Russian president (Putin) coming from the former KGB, but a certain number of the most important positions in the state apparatus is now filled by his St. Petersburg KGB colleagues. However, it does not follow from this that a KGB coup has occurred in Russia and that the building of a new police state is in full swing. The formula is a bit more complex than that.[219]

The private secret service agencies producing kompromat maintain a constant, well-run relationship with the state secret services and security services (the interior ministry, defense, customs officials, tax police etc.); they help each other and conduct a kind of "barter-trade" in documents. Usually they are not less technologically capable than the state agencies. Since 1992 the technical tools of the discovery operatives have escaped from of the exclusive jurisdiction of the chopped-up KGB. In the Soviet era, one hand pulled all the strings of the secret service; today, however, a whole line of services is endowed with the right and means to carry out secret surveillance. The whole process of information gathering has become uncontrollable and incomprehensible, and the persons responsible for allowing or creating the leaks cannot be discovered.[220]

Lawyers and investigators also play an active role in trading confidential information, but they are usually not motivated by money. Lawyers usually deliver compromising information to the press (in this case the kompromat is always realized and dramatized in the mass media) in order to exert pressure on the courts or on the investigation,in the interests of their clients. Investigators leak information to the press in order to seek protection by publicity—in order to stop the investigation—in the face of increasing pressure put on them from above. If the goal is not (or not only) the weakening and removal of the political or business opponent, but rather blackmail, then it is not publicity, but the lack of it, which accomplishes the kompromat: the article can be "bought out" of the newspaper or the incriminating chapter out of the book. For example, one of the international firms mentioned in the sensational, mysterious kompromat book written by Anton Surikov (who was the shady press secretary of Yuri Maslyukov, ex-Prime Minister Primakov's ex-deputy) supposedly paid tens of thousands of pounds to remove an entire chapter from it. It is possible that from Surikov's point of view that was the sole point of publishing the book, only 1000 copies of the shortened version ever saw the light of day. The media only gets the kompromat machine running for free if the kompromat is sensational enough or if the organization of the press campaign serves some particular interest of the one of the media magnates. (Of course, the scoop-hunting part of the press would gladly buy kompromat for purely business reasons, since this increases the circulation and, therefore, the advertising income and profit.)[221]

The prices on the kompromat market depend partly on the quality of the goods (the confidentiality, the degree of inaccessibility and the moral-political destructive power of the document) and partly on the fluctuations of supply and demand (during election periods demand grows, which in certain circumstances also drives down prices). Prices can go down when there is some "anarchist" campaign on the Internet, when from somewhere—completely free of charge —a large quantity of kompromat turns up on the net. This stirring up of the kompromat market's swarming anthill may not only be the ironic vengeance of the deeply contemptuous marginalized Internet-intellectuals who watch the political and business games from outside and above ("eat it up and choke on it!"). It may also be a business move, part of the competition battle, if from the outset it is not just a media trick designed to throw off the political opponent/enemy. (During the Duma campaign period two popular "anarchist" sites ruined the secret services' and politicians' business: the *kogot* [claw] and the *slukhovoje okno* [peephole].)

In the article from *Ekspert* mentioned above, one can find a price list from one of the average firms dealing in confidential information. According to it, for official documents that contain potentially comprising information about someone with the rank of deputy minister, without naming that minister or giving details, the starting price is $150 (according to other sources, $500). For copies of documents detailing concrete financial transactions which reveal that the targeted person is engaged in activities which are not completely legal, yet not criminal (presuming that the person is of at least the rank of deputy minister), the starting price is $2000. For documentation that credibly witnesses to the fact that a company or company executive (possibly a bank) is a participant in a criminal business, or that it has connections to mafia leaders or to the justice organizations protecting them, the starting price is $2000. A compromising video-recording of an incumbent regional representative running for re-election to the Duma costs at least $2000; the price for placement of an article in a central media forum exposing a well-known politician starts at $3500. The price of a kompromat directed against the highest-ranking officials is, naturally, even higher.

In the upper circles the only way to keep the peace is to constantly prepare for war, to be prepared to counterstrike, that is, to arm oneself with counter-kompromats. There is a kind of armed campaign going on here, in which all of the actors strive to get ahead of the rest. This race probably reached its high point last year, because the kompromat weapons used in the election war—a huge number of magic weapons—showed that the large clans had reached the extreme in their mutual moral-political annihilation. They went beyond the point past which everyone loses and there is no victory to be gained. That is to say, the kompromat war of the clanized state sectors has reached a kind of stalemate. This indicates that a politician has come into power—namely, Vladimir Putin—who, being the chief and commander of the state secret services, and even in a certain sense their envoy, has access to such a quantity and quality of count-er-kompromat that its use would be equivalent to an atomic bomb attack. Everyone, even the oligarchs, has to give up their right to launch a "first strike" and to start a new kompromat war against each other. In the past year not one opposing political-proprietary group has introduced a kom-promat against Putin, despite their attempts. Considering this, the defini-tion of the power of the tsar, deterrent power, and charismatic power have to be modified in today's Russia: the tsar is one against whom there is no (and can be no!) kompromat, or (which is the same thing), one who can-not be beaten by kompromat. It must have been justified that the quasi-monarchist Aleksandr Tsipko pleaded in his message to the political elite after Putin's appointment as Prime Minister in October 1999: "Take care of Putin!"[222] Protect him from the winds of the kompromat war as well; otherwise, there goes strong rule, the aura of the charismatic hero, and there goes Russia as well. Since, after the kompromat war, everyone had given and received so much that practically speaking, only the morally crippled and dead remained on the political stage, the preservation of Russia depends—at least according to Tsipko—on whether or not it is successful in "distancing and protecting from the kompromat war the politician in whom the operating capacity of the state is currently embod-ied. I speak of Prime Minister Vladimir Putin. . . I do not claim that Putin is a man of unblemished reputation. There was no politician who had to make decisions about the distribution of Soviet property and who could have remained completely pure under the conditions of total privatization and primitive capital accumulation. However, we must overlook Putin's sins for one simple reason: he is fulfilling a calling that coincides with our most personal common interests . . . Completely regardless of what we think of Putin as a person, he is the only one who took the responsi-bility for Russia's fate. I am serious in saying that."[223] So once again the fate of the Russian state and the fate of its head of state have become one. Putin's political death would be equal to the death of Russia. Whoever starts a kompromat against Putin, launches it against all of Russia.

However, there is hardly any reason to fear this in March 2000. The shutting down of the big kompromat war of 1999 in Russia probably commenced the age of kompromat peace. Just as the precondition for the kompromat war was the general weakness of the state, kompromat peace is built on the re-strengthening of the state. This peace cannot be broken with kompromats, but only with terrorist attacks, assassinations, micro-civil wars, in other words, with other kinds of weapons. We are still unaware whether, due the money putsch leading to the collapse of the oligarchy in the fall of 1998 and the kompromat war, which wore down both Moscow and the Kremlin, there remains a power-proprietary clan in Russia with adequate strength and fighting spirit to undertake such a risky endeavour: to run up against the newly built walls of the Russian State waging localized wars, playing the Chechen card again: revolution, or assassination. It is unlikely that the Russian oligarchs, whether separately or collectively, would attempt an informational or financial putsch or uprising against Putin and his associates, but it is also unlikely that Putin's group, as a last resort, would initiate from above a populist revolution against the ten to twenty oligarchs who control the Russian economy, calling to the streets an estimated fifty million people who would be emotionally ready to fight. In each case the risk and the possible loss, the resulting economic and social chaos, are too great for the political groups now holding state power and the oligarchs ruling the economy *not* to seek a compromise and a way out of this acute situation at the negotiating table.

Most people see the essence of a compromise as a so-called "zero solution": the state does not pry into the crimes and corrupt practices the oligarchs committed during the ten years of Russian "primitive accumulation" (after all, that is how they have becamo oligarchs), and the oligarchs accept the new rules of the game established by the state. This means that the legislative and executive power, the prosecutor's office, and the courts are independent of them, that there is no such thing as "equal" and "more equal" before the law; that the legal system can no longer be violated with impunity, that there can no longer be deceiving, killing, stealing, and lying.

Kompromat.ru

The Internet, alongside the written and printed press, plays an increasing role in the transmission of kompromat. The Russian-language kompromat sites can be divided into three groups according to their goals and tools: business–trade, political–moralizing and civil–intellectual (antipolitical or ironic).

The first group contains sites whose goal is primarily commercial, and whose owners want to strengthen their market position by using the

Internet. They offer seemingly free services ("kompromat about every-one in every amount"), but are really just advertising spaces that partly conceal and partly announce the true business goal: the buying and sell-ing of confidential information. The site kompromat.com is the prime example of these. As a foretaste and warning, let us give here a portion of the text which was presented at the opening of their services as a large-scale "intellectual project": Learn about our new project! We have gathered information here that many, more-or-less well-known, persons would like to hide from the public eye. In the current beginning stages of the development of the project we have set up a database from open information sources: from newspapers, journals, and television broad-casts. Every newspaper article lives for one day: it was so—now it is not. "Kompromat.com" is the single site where those articles are always accessible. At any time you can find on this server information about the figure in public life of interest to you, about a politician, business exec-utive, banker, or company. If you have come into possession of infor-mation about such a person or company that is worthy of attention, you may put it on our server. Of course, this does not only refer to persons who are publicly known or who have already appeared on our server. For example, if you were the injured party in your business partner's misdealings, if your partners did not pay back a loan on time, if you were not paid for goods which you had delivered, if you have been the victim of fraud, you can give an account of all of this on this site in order to help others avoid the same problem. The account should be informative, should include all details, numbers, and data. It does not hurt to include copies of the relevant documents. If you find your own name on our server and do not agree with the presentation of the events relating to you, or if you think that you have been slandered, that the information referring to you is false, then you may send your rebuttal to our server. The compromising materials [kompromat—author's note] that we can verify are specially marked (with the exception of those that have already appeared in well-known papers). We also make a note of whether a piece of information has not been checked (or cannot be checked). "Our database is accessible to anyone free of charge. If you need information (including confidential information) about a person or company and it does not appear in our database, write to us and we will do our best to help you. In this case the cost is based on the degree of difficulty of the work and the nature of the information requested. An

English-language version of our site is being prepared for English-speakers. This server is located outside the borders of the Russian Federation and is, therefore, outside the jurisdiction of Russian legislative authority"[224]

So far there is very little information on this site. Its maintainers have hardly even updated it in the last half-year. It is possible that it is not in their interests, or that they cannot handle the pace dictated by intellectual kompromat sites such as <u>flb.ru</u>[225] or Vladimir Gorshkov's "home kompromat library," <u>kompromat.ru</u>.[226]

Among the kompromat sites with overtly political goals I would mention only two. Both opened at the end of last year, in the heat of, and purposes of, the election war. One is <u>ovg.ru</u> (ovg = *organizovannaia vlastnaia gruppirovka,* which loosely translates to "organized powerful criminal groups"). On this site Gleb Pavlovsky gave a political *coup de grâce* on 3 December, 1999, to his already half-defeated Kremlin opponents: Mayor Yurii Luzhkov of Moscow and Mayor Vladimir Yakovlev of Saint Petersburg, as well as ex-Prime Minister Yevgenyii Primakov, the three leaders of the OVR voting block. The first two were accused of the legalization of the "criminal municipal authorities that they created," the latter of protecting those who are repeatedly mentioned as "godfathers" of the Moscow and St. Petersburg mafia. Gleb Pavlovsky is employed as a talented "poli-technologist" in the service of the Kremlin power team, considered the grandmaster of the so-called "black PR" since 1995 (the date of the creation of the FEP, the Foundation for Effective Politics), a matchless conceiver and organizer of political deceptions and provocations, Lebed's first image-maker, the key figure of the 1996 and 1999 Kremlin election staff, the founder of the Postfaktum news agency, the creator and director of one of the Russian Internet's (RuNet's) most popular sites, <u>polit.ru</u> opened <u>ovg.ru</u> during the conclusion of the Duma elections. The essence of this site's personally and morally zealous project recalls the show trials of the Soviet era. The site's webmaster attaches a whole list of criminal charges to an indictment using the tone and language of former Soviet Procurator-General, Vishinskiy. He calls upon his intellectual audience to create a virtual civil summary judgment seat for the condemnation of the two "monsters"—Luzhkov and Yakovlev. In front of this seat the two "criminal mayors" must finally answer for all of their illegal activities for which the legal courts did not find a statute in the criminal code. It is as if <u>ovg.ru</u> wanted to incite a kind of virtual lynching among the politically engaged intellectual masses on the Internet. (Of course this is nonsense, so it would be better to speak in this case of a "lynching game.") Pavlovsky writes this in the sermonizing introduction to his site, justifying its unexpected opening: "We want to make public all information relating to the organizations, activities, and connections of the leaders of the "Otechestvo–Vsia Rossiia" block, and our purpose is to initiate a civil investigation (*grazhdanskoye rassledovanie*) to show how extensively these "publicly respected gentlemen" and "publicly known politicians" are involved in the commitment of actions which the court does not consider crimes, but about which numerous "criminological" hypotheses have been formulated . . . The mafia, known as THE SYSTEM, together with the REGION'S guardian–protector–executioner subclass, is incapable of changing. Therefore, on the basis of the judgment of the federal courts, they must be—and shall be—liquidated, but until then, we, the citizens, cannot sit around just idly waiting for something to happen. We must use every legal tool of self-defense against the mad dogs of the OVR (Otechestvo–Vsya Rossiya)." As revealed by his language, there is no less than a virtual show trial going on here, in which anyone who adequately hates the defendant or agrees with the accusers' point of view can be a witness for the prosecution, that is, a kompromat-deliverer. Pavlovsky continues: "When the punching guys attack the intelligentsia [reference to the fact that one of the FEP's female colleagues was beaten in her own apartment building not long after (post hoc, ego propter hoc) one of Primakov's colleagues invited her to dinner and questioned her about the FEP—author's note], the intelligentsia must use the humble advantage of those who do not agree with the breaking of bones. Putin and Marshal Sergeyev are far away and have thousands of problems in Argun [i.e., the valiant heroes of the Chechen war cannot protect every intellectual who is fond of them, because they are currently defending the country—author's note]. We must act on our own. We live in a free country and we have the freedom to choose the instruments of political self-defense . . . Let us stack up and document all the reasons why we do not like the OVR leaders and why we are afraid of them and let us discuss these reasons." Naturally, this peculiar dramatization of the standard kompromat material (a virtual show trial) is the product of a political moment: a soap bubble, which will be followed in the next moment by a new soap-bubble site.[227] Who now—three months after the elections—remembers ovg.ru?

Kompromat Inflation

The unprecedented eruption of the Russian kompromat phenomenon—as we have seen—in the end can be attributed to the impotence of the Russian State (or rather the social weakness of the free system). On the one hand, there is the birth of the independent secret services and the inpenetrable mesh of state and private services, which form the foundation of the problem; on the other, there is the impotence of the courts and the fact that they are at the mercy of the local and central executive powers, oligarchs, and mafia. In a country in which you can expect almost nothing or almost always only bad things from the state authorities—from state officials, judges, police, governors, and party politicians—everyone tries to take care of their business in their own way. Everything can be bought: kompromat, assassinations, explosives and exploders, secret service agents and Chechens, prosecuting attorneys and judges. Only very rarely does anyone go to court against someone that has compromised them or been compromised. This is understandable, considering that the punishments imposed for slander and libel after a prolonged court procedure are not serious and the suit itself gives yet another opportunity for a lengthy publicized discussion of the kompromat, in effect a secondary realization of it. Since the effect of the kompromat cannot be quenched legally, only the illegal way remains: counter-kompromat or, worse, assassination. The production of kompromat will immediately decrease if the Russian constitutional state is strengthened and if it can enforce the laws, restore or create the independence and authority of the judiciary, put the secret services under unified and legal supervision and strictly control their operating range, the objects of their investigations and the tools permitted in those investigations.

The huge kompromat war that erupted in Spring–Summer, 1999, among the privatized state sectors (raw materials, federal and regional authorities, media, branches of power, etc.) in the midst of Russia's dramatically-paced economic and social decline has reached such a degree that the prospect of general collapse loomed large in everyone's mind. The destitute of Russian society (the great majority), having reached the limits of their tolerance, having been spontaneously left out of the "spontaneous privatization," are prepared to give a free hand and moral authority to the "charismatic heroes" and purist dictator to put an end to the criminal chaos (the "bespredel"), the free theft, the moral inferno. That

Russian oligarchs have currently to face the "tough laws" of a liberal constitutional state and not the "brass knuckles" of some populist dictator is
only due to the fact that, after the 2000 election, the state-building and
order-creating authority ended up in the hands of "westerners" professing
pragmatic and democratic values.

If the almost completely impotent central state of today can regain its
independence, if it can create and implement the legal, administrative and
financial tools with which it could extract the corrupt net of clashing private interests from the power of the state, if it can stop the private wars in
and for the state of the regional barons, raw material oligarchs, mafia leaders, and power clans, then the kompromat war will also come to an end.
The first signs of this are already visible. I think that it is only in this context that we can objectively interpret the initiatives of Vladimir Putin and
his group of reformers: the practical measures, the legislative drafts, and
the strategic development plans, ranging from modification of the federal
arrangement to the abolition of the privilege of the oligarchs to be above
the law and to the breakup of the domination of the oligarchic clans in the
media. From the point of view of the subject of our study, kompromat, the
new amnesty law is of particular interest. According to it, from 31 May
2000 an amnesty is retroactively granted to all who were decorated with a
state honor during the Soviet era or during the ten years of Yeltsin's presidency. Since this group largely covers the post-Soviet proprietary and
political elite, 90 percent of whom were part of the old Soviet nomen-
clatura and the other 10 percent of whom were recruited from among the
new-Russian entrepreneurs, the law in effect means a kind of zero-solu-
tion: no one, neither privatizer nor top official, can be attacked with any
kind of kompromat exposing a crime committed in the past, whether
alleged or factual, verified or speculative, known or undiscoverable.

What Yeltsin and his family received as a privilege in December 1999
from the new (and then interim) President Putin, six months later is
extended to practically all of the ruling elite by the new amnesty law.
(Even Vladimir Gusinsky, the media-oligarch who was arrested on
charges of economic wrong-doing many years ago, had to be pardoned
two weeks after the amnesty law had taken effect, since he had received
a state honor from Yeltsin.) However, we would misinterpret the situation if we saw this law as some kind of "free pass" that the state rushed
to bestow on the new ruling elite instead of recognizing in this amnesty
law, which borders on legal absurdity, the legitimate intention of break-

ing the absurdity of post-Soviet relations. Since almost everyone committed some kind of illegality or crime during the ten years of post-Soviet "primitive accumulation" (among the pioneers of "primitive accumulation" hardly anyone remains alive), since almost everyone was a link in the corruption chain, and business connections reached to the underworld, and since—without risking the collapse of the fragile Russian economy—the new economic elite is "irreplaceable," the only solution is the slashing to pieces of the corrupt–kleptocratic–criminal network and the crushing of the magic circle of the corrupt kompromats. No one should be blackmailed: neither in the state, nor in the business world. With this legal surprise attack, they excised the state, in which there hardly exists an official or politician who cannot be extorted by a kompromat because of some supposed or true corruption, from the oligarchic clans. The amnesty law can therefore be understood as a kind of kompromat market crash. In the summer of 2000, the devalued kompromat masses stand, if not on the streets, at least on the hills of the Internet highway. The various Russian kompromat sites are throwing onto the Internet kompromat collections of private, or semi-private secret services (Gusinsky's Media-MOST, the office of Aleksandr Korzhakov, the presidential bodyguard who was fired in 1996), although until now they have primarily relied on revealing newspaper articles and documents from other communication sources. It is probable that the secret services, especially the FSB, are behind this activity. The collapse of the kompromat market in Russia is, in any case, at the end of the beginning, or the beginning of the end.

PART III

CASE STUDIES AND EFFECTS

Prior to 1989–1991, illicit payments to doctors (mostly ex post facto) were common in communist (free) health care systems. The new democratic governments did not have the courage (or wherewithal) to radically restructure their inherited health care systems. At a minimum, governments feared public discontent related to identifiable transfer costs (i.e., a drastic increase in individuals' contributions). Even when such reforms were proposed, they were derailed by the resistance of elites in the medical profession, who rightly considered the rotten system to be the source of its own privileged position. As there was no essentially government-initiated reform, resources necessary to keep the inherited health care systems operating could only come from semi-voluntary, semi-illegal payments paid by patients to physicians and nurses.[228] Functional necessities, these ubiquitous and highly visible illegal transfers also perpetuated the inefficiencies and irrationality of the old system. Reform of health care, difficult as it will be to implement, would go a long way to altering the public perception of corruption in transition countries, and shifting the focus to the heretofore overshadowed grand corruption in the health sector, namely the corrupt relations between pharmaceutical companies, insurance and doctors. Exploring the differences between petty or quasi-corruption and grand corruption, both for perceptions and experience, is a neglected line of inquiry.

Surveying a half century of corruption experience under Communism and its implications for post-Communism, Elemér Hankiss explains that corruption can be considered as a social pathology, a symptom of systemic dysfunction, a strategy for corroding the system (small acts of rule breaking become cumulative), a strategy of social domination, or a game. In the latter case, he notes that corruption need not be extortion—both parties can enter into a free and voluntary exercise, neither cheats on the other, and they follow rules on how to break the rules, which carries risk and thus imparts a sense of excitement, pleasure, a feeling of power in outwitting the authorities. His essay shades off into psychological analysis and helps us understand how corruption both helped to challenge the monopolistic tendencies of the communist system and prepared people, at least to some extent, for independent social action. Longer-term effects, of course, were not necessarily so benign. Here is where the importance of "tips" in the health care systems comes in. Such payments may be the single most important reason domestically for the high public perception of corruption in many post-communist countries; at least, payments for medical treatment have been the most common everyday occurrence of "corruption"—payments that seem to "confirm" the reports of corruption at the top and the notion that "everybody does it," or "what choice do we have" and other commonplace rationalizations.

Hankiss' Olympian essay and the example of unreformed health care systems indicate the value of having sharply focused discussions and of case studies. That is the task of Part III.

•

Quentin Reed offers a detailed narrative account of privatization in Czechoslovakia and what became, after the 1993 divorce, the Czech Republic (adding Slovakia would have amplified his arguments). He shows that, unsurprisingly, the Czech "clean hands" campaign, a term borrowed from Italy (see Blankenburg), was perforce political not technocratic, and, anyway, the campaign was soon abandoned in order to secure a political agreement on control over parliament. Reed also notes that the privatization process was removed from judicial review by law. Readers will decide for themselves the extent to which neo-liberal ideology served as a prime *motivating* force of the voucher-scheme privatization, or whether understandings of socialism (and hence of what was required for socialism's transcendence) involved certain ideas that may have appeared to outsiders (and even insiders) as superficially resembling neo-liberalism. Be that as it may, one can detect in the Czech example strong evocations of South Korea, where relatively "clean" low-level governance coexisted with massive corruption at the top, which (eventually) imparted a foul odor over the entire country.

To an extent, the high-profile privatizations at the top deflected attention from small and medium businesses, which account for 70 percent of employment in the West and must be the building blocks for sustained long-term economic success in transition countries. The oversight, however, is partially rectified in Vadim Radaev's survey of entrepreneurs in Russia. Radaev collected 227 questionnaires and conducted 96 interviews (first in 1993 and then in 1998), and, under the auspices of U.S. AID, carried out a regional study in 1997 and 1999 in Tomsk oblast (western Siberia). He points out that there were no less than thirty ministries involved in licensing and certifying business activity, and that, for lack of proper financing of their regional branches they adopted the tried-

and-true method of bureaucratic self-financing (*kormlenie*), consisting of both formal "rent" and informal extortion (bribes). Pricing of such "services" proved to be arbitrary and inconsistent (and thus unpredictable for entrepreneurs); worse, the purchased services frequently failed to be delivered. For small businesses, in short, corruption is all too real and deleterious. The fact that much of the activity involved in doing business is not bribes per se but "inspections" and other nominally legitimate procedures makes the degree of corruption difficult to measure, but it does seem to be the case that in Russia "inspections" were double the number in Poland.[229]

That politicians and bureaucrats on the receiving end of payoffs take comfort in the status quo would be unsurprising, but Radaev also finds that entrepreneurs, who might be expected to become an organized group pushing for change, instead "get used to the 'system'." They cry foul— just as many bribe-taking political figures do—yet, if entrepreneurs prove nimble enough, they extract individual privileges and advantages. He investigates primarily the costs of doing business for those already established, rather than the entry costs for new businesses, a constituency that may harbor a different view on toleration or opposition to the institutional and political environment. As for officialdom, it emerges that a powerful element in their views on the relation between business and officialdom is their desire to achieve control and foster dependency. Whether such a dependent relationship on local officialdom also holds for the truly big concerns—such as the energy behemoths—is beyond the scope of Radaev's essay, but the suspicion would be that the dependence works the other way around. The inter-relations between the big firms and smaller ones loom as another topic provoking our curiosity.

•

Radaev for Russia and Reed for the Czech Republic explain the systemic and transition-related aspects of corruption in remarkably similar terms. They both show that corruption occurs (both at the national level in the Czech privatization case and at the local level in the case of Russian business licenses) as a result of a normative system designed to enable people to extort bribes. Frequently, however, it is not money that changes hands but favors. This phenomenon of deliberate creation of opportunities for extortion or favoritism has been well described for

Poland, too. "Major legal bills submitted to the parliament," two analysts have argued, "showed a clear preference for vague laws that delegated important legislative powers to the executive branch . . . This type of legislation creates vast potential for corruption and the promotion of private interests."[230] What is corruption, however, and what is the "normal" promotion of private interests in the legislative process of a democracy? What has been the relationship between democracy and corruption? Does opening up the system (democracy), the widening access to the policy- and law-making process, inevitably expand opportunities for corruption, or at least certain types of corruption? Who pays for democracy, from election campaigns to party buildings?

The study of transition corruption as a phenomenon that is both generated (partly) and exposed (often) by emerging democratic modes of political organization draws our attention to the often neglected fact that a good amount of "transition" is present in more settled democratic systems. Modern mass democracy itself became *per se* the source of some corrupt patterns. The spiraling cost of competitive elections necessitate that party coffers be replenished.[231] It would be, of course, an impermissibly naïve assumption to believe that political elites of modern democracies would be honest but for reasons of electoral campaign spending. Indeed, representative democracy is an expression of the public's *mistrust* in the authorities, in its *own* authorities—hence the desire that political trustholders be elected, supervised, and removed by the people. Representative systems differ greatly in detail, however, as Daniel Smilov demonstrates in his comparative analysis of Bulgarian and Russian campaign financing. He distinguishes between the roles of parties in parliamentary and presidential regimes and between "libertarian" and "egalitarian" rules for party finance. He also points to the importance of NGOs, since parties proved uninterested in more cumbersome rules and regulations.

Smilov argues, based on mid-1990s data, that party finance has been an area of systematic violations of the law, when there has been adequate law, and that the rules have arguably exhibited a strong bias in favor of particular political actors, especially incumbents. The electoral triumph, after his essay's completion, of Bulgaria's ex-king over both incumbents and ex-incumbents upset many people's calculations. It seems that, however advantaged incumbents may be, they are not shielded from public discontent when a strong or unusual challenger emerges.[232] Equally important, the role of parties seemed to be called into question when an individual, dressed up unconvincingly as a party, proved capable of rallying the voting public. There is a need for skepticism about what constitutes, in transition countries (and elsewhere), a political "party" and a party-system. Nonetheless, Smilov's work goes some way toward explaining the relative weakness of Russia's parties compared with Bulgaria's. He also shows how technical decisions about political party-financing mechanisms (and vice versa) have far-reaching repercussions for the operation and stability of the political order. Much the same can be said about public finance systems more broadly.

Understandably, it has proven easier to study the climate of opinion surrounding corruption rather than corruption per se (some might say that the latter and the former overlap to a significant extent), but even in the study of opinion one encounters surprising twists, such as those put forth in the essay by Lena Kolarska-Bobińska on attitudes toward democracy in Poland. Her main preoccupation is the ostensible paradox whereby the people's evident disgust with corruption and politicians did not appear to result in disillusionment with democracy (one thinks of Russia or Ukraine as counter-examples, though it is unclear if we have differences of degree or kind). It is probably fair to say that almost everyone gravely underestimated the institutional challenges involved in transition. Just as the Communists inherited the pre-WWII legal system, so the post-Communists inherited the Communist legal system (with some of its pre-WWII aspects intact), producing a mishmash (Poland passed its first conflict of interest law only in 1992, and implementation has conjured up much politicking). In these unforeseen but logical circumstances, Kolarska-Bobińska finds that society has tended to condemn corruption morally but to accept it in practice, whether out of resignation or expediency, without abandoning belief in democracy, but she worries that toleration for corruption could corrode civic commitments too deeply. In short, widespread perceptions of endemic corruption, even when kept relatively compartmentalized, must be addressed.

•

Corruption in war-torn, impoverished Tajikistan, Tokhir Mirzoev demonstrates, has been very serious, though not the most serious problem in the everyday life of ordinary people. Many individuals claim to be

unable to imagine activities that are possible without bribes, and they
tend not to resist extortion. Relying on the results of a survey that encompassed 201 business enterprises and 521 households throughout the country, Mirzoev details how the specific conditions of transition have
increased certain aspects of corruption. At a most basic level, "decentralization" multiplied the sheer number of bribe-taking institutions. The on-
again, off-again civil war reinforced "clan" (really regional) political
machines. Most often, however, corruption is concentrated at the customs
stations at border crossings, among the gatekeepers to higher education,
in the state health care sector, in the licensing of export/import activities,
in contacts with road police, and during tax and financial inspections
(highly reminiscent of the picture drawn by Radaev for Russia). Mirzoev
concludes on a grim note about the impossibility of eliminating corruption in Tajikistan.

This is not to say that a "successful anticorruption strategy" is an oxy-
moron. History offers examples whereby corruption, as then known,
ceased to be a systemic element. The British Parliament was incomparably
less corrupt in the second half of the nineteenth century than a hundred
years earlier.[233] Even in these long-term success stories, however, corruption is often simply replaced by more restricted forms of rent seeking.
Similarly, corrupt organizations can be "cleaned up," but "success" as
promulgated by the moral-cleaning industry is suspect, since it often serves
only to centralize corrupt practices. Generally speaking, government
efforts to curb corruption presuppose certain conditions that do not exist
everywhere. If one considers, for example, the oft-cited case of Singapore,
one needs to keep in mind that the drastic and apparently successful measures were taken by an essentially one-party government that could compensate itself with very high salaries in exchange for honesty (and loyalty).
Moreover, the Singapore government, insulated from the people, could disregard popular discontent about increased civil service salaries. In the view
of their critics, the measures enabled the government to become a monopolist of illegalities (including the drug trade with Burma). Singapore's anticorruption measures also contravened traditional understandings of the rule
of law (once again, that was not a problem in Singapore for the governing
political and legal elite). Finally, the Singapore government was in a position to dispose of the necessary resources, which may not be available in
transition countries (notwithstanding possible savings resulting from efficient anticorruption measures).[234]

Given the institutional possibilities and limitations in Tajikistan, Mirzoev sensibly cautions against too ambitious a program, suggesting that the aim should be not the chimera of all-out eradication but minimizing the scope for corrupt behavior, whenever possible. He also urges that the efforts to combat corruption be systematic and based upon a long-term commitment, rather than the usual loud and episodic approach. Strategists need to be keenly cognizant of both political context and the hard technical work involved in pragmatic corruption fighting, from auditing and accounting practices to laws on conflict of interest and Amakudari (Japanese for descent from heaven, or how regulators later land jobs in the private sectors they once regulated). It is hard to disagree with Mirzoev's conclusion that world experience indicates that highly emotional hunting down and punishment of bribers and bribe-takers fails to help, and may worsen the prospects for reducing corruption. Policies must seek to involve the lowest feasible costs, and be targeted at the most serious kinds of corruption.

Games of Corruption:
East Central Europe, 1945–1999
Elemér Hankiss

The Background

This paper is partly based on some of the preliminary results of an international pilot project (started in1999), which is being conducted by Gallup Hungary within the framework of the Global Program against Corruption organized by the UN Office for Drug Control and Crime Prevention and the Centre for International Crime Prevention in Turin.

Within this framework, Gallup, in early 2000, conducted four surveys: 1) a victimization survey, including a block of questions on corruption (Budapest, adult population, random sample, N = 1514); corruption in public institutions (national random sample, N = 1839); 3) corruption in local government (employees in five local government, N = 431); and 4) corruption in the sphere of small and medium-type private enterprises (a random sample of managers and owners, N =. 511). The final report will be published by Gallup Hungary (Project director: Robert Manchin; Project coordinator: Regős Rita).[235] The project is being replicated in several Central and East European countries (comparative data were still forthcoming at the time this essay was written).

In addition, Gallup organized a series of focus groups with the members of various professional groups (judges, mayors, journalists, business people, managers of multinational companies, etc.) between December, 1999 and July, 2000. These focus groups were extremely useful and interesting. Participants knew their various fields very well. They raised a great number of important issues. They were familiar with a great variety of corrupt practices and were surprisingly good at analyzing these practices. At the same time, they were rather skeptical about the possibility of restricting corruption but proposed some important measures that, applied step by step, could help.

The present paper is a think-piece based on the author's previous work and on the analysis of the focus group records. Survey results are referred to only once or twice.

The Concept

Corruption is an elusive phenomenon. It is secretive; it has a thousand faces, it exists in a gray zone of social interactions; it is enveloped by social outrage and tacit acceptance; decent citizens may be tempted by it, or forced to get involved in it; people are uncertain as to how to cope with it. Corruption is difficult to define, to state its character unequivocally, to know what other kinds of social, economic, political, moral or other phenomena we touch upon when we interrogate corruption.

Corruption may be considered, and handled, as a social pathology. It may permeate the structures, textures and fiber of a whole society, its institutions, its people's lives and minds. Corruption may also be the symptom of the malfunctioning of a social system, and treated accordingly. The high level of corruption in certain countries indicates that their institutions are unable to adequately perform their role of systemic and social integration. Corruption may also be considered as a latent or semi-latent second system of redistribution which lives on the deficiencies of the first system. It may be regarded also as a survival strategy of people who try to find loopholes in the rigid framework of an authoritarian system. A myriad of these efforts may gradually corrode and disintegrate the system.

Corruption, however, is a double-edged sword. While "grassroots" corruption disintegrates the system, corruption may also be, and often is, a fearful weapon of domination in the hands of those in power. It may be also analyzed as a "game." I shall come back to this aspect of corruption later in this paper.

The Definition

The Latin verb *corrumpere* means to break something. The question to be answered is what is "broken" by the act of corruption. The obvious answer is that the Law is broken; or that a legal rule is broken; a duty is broken; a norm is broken. However, it is important to add that communities and human personalities may also be broken by the practice of corruption. Communities are disintegrated by corruption because it undermines predictability and accountability, reduces social transparency and erodes social trust, and the integrity of the human personality is broken because corruption involves lying, dissimulation, and living according to two (contradictory) sets of standards. Social disintegration and the loss of personal integrity may be the greatest long-term damage done by corruption.

In the focus groups, a great number of cases of corruption were discussed and attempts were made to come up with a definition of corruption. Given the complexity and great variety of the cases, this was a difficult task. Finally, the various attempts boiled down to two definitions,. a shorter and a longer one. The shorter: Corruption is the act of breaking an established system of rules (regulating the distribution of goods) in order to privately profit from this breaking of the rules. The longer: Corruption is an act in which a public official (or another person in a position to distribute public goods or services) breaks the rules of distributing a public good or providing a public service, rules for the enforcement of which he or she is responsible, in favor of a client, by whom he or she is rewarded for this breaking of the rules.

We decided to accept the second definition as a tool to work with. It is not flawless, comprehensive and precise enough. Each of its elements is open to criticism. It can be argued, for instance, that not only public officials may be corrupted, not only public goods and services may be involved in acts of corruption, but an act may be corrupt even if the actor is not rewarded by somebody else. Yet, most of the acts of corruption are likely to be covered by our working definition, particularly the socially most harmful effects among them, and so its use seems to be justified.

Favorable Conditions

There are historical contexts and socio-political formations that are particularly favorable for the generation of widespread corruption. Here are some of them: rigid authoritarian systems that have entered their declining period (East European state socialist systems in the 1980s, for instance); the so-called period of original accumulation and wild capitalism in which a great quantity of public goods and services are being privatized (new market economies in 1990s Central Europe); a ruling elite and a body of public servants who do not feel solidarity with their societies (colonial bourgeoisies and bureaucracies, for instance); the leaders of a bankrupt country who rob their country before the final collapse (some of the East European countries in the 1990s); societies in a period of transition, when the old rules of the game do not function any more and the new rules have not yet crystallized and have not been interiorized by the populace; new market economies in which the idea, the ideology, the myth of an absolutely free market is so strong that any kind of public regulation is labeled as crypto-socialist (Central European countries in the 1990s); a "hybrid society" in which several "organizing principles" work side by side.[236]

In the last category, a characteristic case is a post-colonial society as described by Heidenheimer.[237] In that society the traditional principles of reciprocity and of tribal redistribution interact and clash with the principle of market exchange and the system of redistribution on the nation state level. One of Heidenheimer's examples is a tribal chief who has been nominated a minister in the colonial/national government. To appoint the members of his tribe to all possible public positions is a duty and an act of decency for him in his capacity as the chief of the tribe, but the same is an act of corruption on his part as a minister who should appoint public servants according to merit and not tribal loyalties.

Societies in transition are more or less "hybridized": heterogeneous institutions, regulations and "organizing principles" work side by side and their interaction is not yet clearly regulated. This leads to a confusion in which corruption may flourish. One never knows exactly what is legal and what is not, what is an act of corruption and what is not, offenders cannot be punished because there are loopholes everywhere, etc. As an example, let me show the variety of organizing principles that were at work in Hungary between 1920 and 2000. (Table 1).

Table 1. Organizing Principles in Hungary 1920–2000

1920–1945
Market mechanisms
National economic policy ("planning," control, intervention, allocation of resources, etc.)
Late-feudal oligarchic and clientelistic networks
Central redistribution run by the nation state
1960–1989
The principle of centralized political (re)distribution (political goals)
The principle of centralized economic (re)distribution (to further economic development and safeguard equilibrium)
The principle of centralized social (re)distribution (equality, social security, etc.)
1960–1989
The principle of oligarchic (re)distribution (oligarchic interests)
The principle of clientelistic (re)distribution (the interests of patrons and clients)

Table 1. cont'd

The principle of (re)distribution on the "administrative market"; "bargaining society" (the interests of the institutional players of the economy and politics)
The principle of market economy (business interests)
The practice of informal/popular exchange; the "second economy" ("grassroots interests")
1989–2000
The principle of market competition
National economic policy ("planning," control, intervention, allocation of resources, etc.)
The principle of centralized social (re)distribution

As can be seen, before the Second World War distribution was based on a combination of the market mechanism, national economic policy, centralized social redistribution, and late-feudal, oligarchic and clientelistic networks. When the communists came to power, they forced a system of political distribution on the country; that is to say, distribution was governed mainly by political interests; goods, services, privileges, exemptions were distributed with the intention to reinforce the political power of the communist elite. Gradually, however, other organizing principles started to work as well, so much so, that in late Kadarism (the 1980s), there was already a chaotic interaction of a great number of heterogeneous economic and social mechanisms, and this chaos was, understandably, a hotbed of corruption.

Since 1989, East Central European societies are not more "hybrid" than Western democracies (which all have several distributive-redistributive systems), the difference being only that, in them the interaction of these various systems is still less formalized, less transparent, less controlled. In other words, the rules of the game by which one could judge various behaviors and acts are not established yet. Without such a set of rules the moral and social control that could curb corruption has no solid foundation.

Who Corrupts Whom?

There are relatively simple one-way acts of corruption. This is the case when somebody corrupts a public servant. However, most of the cases can be best described as two-way transactions. Participants are both corrupters and corrupted. Take, for instance, the case of a routine business/politics corruption. On the one hand, a businessman bribes a politi-

cian or a public servant to break the rules of the social distribution of public goods in his (the businessman's) favor, but in the very same transaction a politician or a public servant corrupts the businessman into breaking the rules of fair market competition by granting him advantages over
his competitors. Both actors break their own system of norms, which—
as politicians, public servants, or businessmen—they have accepted and
to which they publicly adhere.

The "second economy" that flourished in the 1960s and 1970s in
Hungary was full of these I-let-you-corrupt-me-and-you-let-me-corrupt-
you transactions. People corrupted the apparatchiks into shutting their
eyes to the expansion of the second economy, while apparatchiks corrupted people into renouncing their rights of free citizens. Both sides
profited from this mutual breaking of the rules: the apparatchiks got
gifts, bribes, and a subservient population, and people got an opportunity to develop their small-scale businesses and achieve a higher standard
of living.

As a case of a three-way corruption, let me give an anecdotal example
again from Hungary in the 1970s. I call it "The case of the bartender." To
wit, in a factory cafeteria it is forbidden to sell alcoholic beverages to the
workers and employees. Nevertheless, the bartender sells alcoholic
drinks, but she also reports the names of her buyers to the manager of the
factory. In return, the manager closes his eyes on her selling alcoholic
beverages in the cafeteria. In this case, first, people corrupt the bartender
by tipping her and prompting her in this way to break the rules of the canteen. Second, the bartender corrupts the manager into allowing her to
break the rules of the canteen, by supplying him with valuable information on her clients. And third, the manager corrupts the bartender into
breaking the rules of civil decency and social loyalty by allowing her to
accept the tips of the customers.

Corrupting a Society

A whole society may be corrupted. People may be bought by those in
power (political, business) to renounce an important public good in their
possession: their right to vote, to choose their leaders, to control those
whom they have elected to public offices, their right to freedom of consciousness and information, etc. They may be bought—and this was the

case in Hungary between 1965 and 1988—by offering them desirable bonuses, by relenting the political and ideological pressure, by letting them find loopholes in the system and build up their small family businesses, by letting them build holiday cottages, travel abroad and so on. This was balancing on the razor's edge between corruption and extortion. If people had not accepted the deal, they would have been forced to passivity and obedience, but corrupting and being corrupted seemed to be a much better bargain for both sides. In the short term it certainly was a better solution. Both sides profited from this deal more than they would have profited from the use of force, on the one hand, and, on the other, passive obedience and resentment.

Dangers

Much has been written about the damage corruption can do to societies. It undermines social trust and the rule of law; it erodes public morality and people's sense of justice; it obstructs the working of the market and distorts the legitimate systems of distribution; it reduces civic responsibility; and so on. It is a dangerous, self-multiplying social–economic–political–cultural mechanism.

A Social Trap

Corruption works like a social trap or the mechanism of the "tragedy of the commons." People enter the game of breaking the rules of their community in order to privately profit from it, but as more and more people "desert" the community, less and less will be the profit of each of them. After a certain point everybody will be in a worse position than he or she was originally, but the costs of jumping out of the game and returning to the rules of the community are so high that the process can hardly be stopped. In the same way, corruption is tempting because it promises each candidate a special advantage over the other members of the community, but the more people enter the game, everybody's profit will diminish and, finally, everybody will pay more for the same goods or services than they originally paid; let alone the fact that the corruption of the social institutions will cause further, perhaps even more serious, damage.

The Fact, or Myth of "Positive" Corruption

There are situations in which corruption plays, or seems to play, a positive role and this makes it even more dangerous. I have already mentioned the example of the rigid state socialist system, whose loopholes (and the corrupt practices related to them) lent a certain flexibility to these economies and rendered them—in a certain respect—more efficient. Or, in the last ten years, in Hungary, for instance, the profit of corrupt officials from the process of privatization may have amounted to billions of forints (and that of their clients to tens or hundreds of billions of forints). However, rapid privatization may have been in the interest of the country and, in this case, one could argue that the price paid in the form of corruption may have been not too high. As a matter of fact, nobody has seriously studied these cases. Nobody has drawn the balance sheet of gains and losses generated by the "second economy" in the 1970s and 1980s, or those of the successful but corrupt privatization process in the 1990s. One thing is certain: the fact that corruption may surround itself with the aura of social profit and respectability confuses people and makes corruption even more dangerous.

Indulgence

People in our focus groups seemed to be more lenient toward corruption than other types of crime. Prompted by a question ("Which is a more serious crime, to get hold of 10 million forints?") they came up with the following rank order, going from the gravest offense to the least serious one: drug dealing, armed robbery, blackmail, accepting a bribe, embezzlement, swindle. Asked to comment on this outcome, they said that they ranked these offenses according to their social dangerousness, and, more precisely, according to: a) the number of actors involved: b) the number of victims involved: c) the presence or absence of violence. With embezzlement there is one actor, there are victims and there is no violence. With giving or taking a bribe, there are two actors, there are no victims, actors participate voluntarily and there is no violence. With blackmail, there are two actors, the victim is forced to participate in the transaction, an innocent person is victimized and there is violence.

Games of Corruption

Corruption has got a certain appeal for people because it may be perceived as a game. Tax burdens are so heavy, red tape is so annoying that even decent citizens may be tempted to outwit the bureaucrats and find some more or less "innocent" loopholes in the system. In this game of tag there are even some rules as to how to break the rules. Like a game such corruption is free and voluntary; there is no coercion in it (as for instance in extortion, or robbery). As in sport, there is a certain risk and excitement. There is also pretense and acting a role: when, for instance, you bribe somebody, you both pretend not to notice the transaction; you play the role of being decent citizens.

The "Neurosis" of Corruption

Strangely enough, even the fight against corruption may generate corruption. Let Hungary again be my example. The media treat cases of corruption superficially but on a daily basis. Grassroots communication is also full of rumors about corruption—so much so, people are saturated with news and rumors of corruption and have the feeling that they live in a thoroughly rotten and corrupt country. This is seriously counter-productive. The belief in the monster of corruption may become a self-fulfilling prophecy. The myth, and fear, of the universality of corruption may further undermine social trust in public institutions and ultimately may obstruct the functioning of democracy. The myth "all the world is corrupt" may serve as an alibi for people to be, or become, corrupt (the devil's argument: "If everybody is corrupt, why should I be honest?"). Suffering from the "neurosis of corruption" people lose their hope that corruption may be restricted and controlled and, as a consequence, they are less willing, and able, to fight corruption. Focussing obsessively on corruption may become a kind of overkill that, instead of destroying, nurtures its object.

In this atmosphere, a kind of general social complicity may evolve whereby everybody forgives everybody for what they all reluctantly do. As a character in a famous Hungarian play formulated it in the mid-1970s: "I excuse them for excusing me for excusing them . . ."—and so on, *ad infinitum*. There is an interesting discrepancy between the general and concrete assessment of corruption in our societies. In Hungary, people have the general impression that corruption is very high in various public institutions, but if you ask those people who have personally been in contact with these institutions, their experience of corruption is—in the majority of cases—much lower than their reputation (Table 2).

Table 2. General and Concrete Perception of Corruption, Hungary (April 2000, N = 1514)

GENERAL PERCEPTION OF CORRUPTION			CONCRETE PERCEPTION
INSTITUTIONS		PERCENTAGE OF CLIENTS	PERCEIVED CORRUPTION
Local councils	37	15	2
Tax Office	31	20	1
Ministries	34	2	3
The judiciary	21	N.D.	0

This discrepancy between the general and concrete perception of corruption is an important warning about the possible damage the "neurosis of corruption" may do in our societies.

What to Do?

In the focus groups we asked our participants—legislators, judges, mayors, journalists, businessmen, managers—to discuss the main causes of corruption and the possible measures that could gradually curb it. I give here a selection of their remarks and suggestions.

Legislation and Legal Reforms

Our participants were rather critical of the process of legislation and urged a new approach to legal reforms. They said that our laws have no consistency; they are "flexible," they can be bent to all kinds of purposes. The bills proposed by the government lose their consistency during parliamentary debates and—in the absence of a strong concept and a strong legislative will—lobby groups are able to build into the final text too many exemptions, special treatments, loopholes. Thus, a new approach to the process of legislation, with a stronger legislative will and more professionalism producing more consistent and transparent laws should be a priority in the fight against corruption.

In 1989 and 1990, during the round-table talks ending Communist rule, and the first month of post-Communism, the emerging new political elite seemed to be practically independent from business interests. Since then, they have lost their innocence. Business interests have encroached upon politics. Attempts at separating the two spheres have failed so far. This situation is one of the main sources of large-scale corruption in the country. A new electoral law, which would solve the financing of the political parties and electoral campaigns, is overdue.

The process of transition has not helped the formation of this strong "legislative" and "political will." There have been too many outside influences pulling and pushing the new, democratic governments in different directions. There have been to many contradictory interests with which the new governments had to cope without having the necessary skills of democratic politics. This uncertainty and confusion created favorable conditions for corrupt practices.

Even if the laws are consistent, institutions are not strong enough, and not dedicated enough, to implement the laws. The passing of special laws that would guarantee the implementation of existing laws should be a priority, but better law enforcement in itself would not suffice. Even the best laws cannot be enforced if the economic and social conditions that would enable the citizens to observe the laws are not given.

There are experts who argue that Western-type rule of law is based on a relatively high material security of the citizenry. In countries where an important portion of the population struggles with the problems of everyday survival, respect for the law is likely to be low. As one of our participants said: a poor country cannot afford the high level of legal and moral discipline of some rich Western countries. Legal deregulation is proceeding too slowly since—in our participants' opinion—deregulation is against the interests of the ruling elite. Deregulation would decrease their political power and weaken their control over economic and social processes. The over-bureaucratized legal system and public administration is a hotbed of corruption. If one needs fourteen permits to have a hotdog stand at a street corner, then corrupt officials fare well, and business suffers. Radical legal deregulation should be a priority in the fight against corruption. People's respect for the Law has been eroded by the fact that the ruling elite itself has ignored the laws and the ruling of the Courts. The Constitutional Court has found the Parliament guilty in not passing certain Laws by constitutional deadlines. The Government has ignored the ruling of the Supreme Court of Justice to pay its debts to the City of Budapest. Several Ministries have ignored the reports of the State Accounting Office. High-ranking public servants have not resigned after having been found guilty, or to be prime suspects, in corruption cases. Raising the moral standard of the ruling elite, prompting them to be exemplary in respecting the law, reinforcing the principle of *rex sub lege* should be a high priority in the fight against corruption.

Focus group participants—with the exception of the majority of businessmen, who were very skeptical and critical—agreed in the fact that there is practically no evidence of judges accepting kickbacks, but some of the judges are exposed to, and some have been unable to resist, the "soft pressure" coming from politics, and the tactics of intimidation from organized crime. The great number of cases of judicial "procrastination" may indicate that most of the judges want to safeguard their integrity and escape from these traps by endlessly postponing trials.

The reinforcement of the independence, and safety, of the judiciary should be high on the priority list.

Lex versus Mores

Focus group participants fervently discussed the question whether the legal or the moral aspects of corruption are more important and whether remedies should be looked for mainly in the field of law, or in that of morality. They seemed to have a penchant for believing that the moral factor could, and should, play the leading role in the fight against corruption. They emphasized the importance of education. One of them went as far as to argue that appointing young men to important positions may reduce corruption since they are not corrupted yet. Several of them seemed to believe in the essential goodness of human nature, or at least in the importance of character and principles. "He who is honest, is and will remain honest," one of them stated.

As may be seen, this discussion was not exempt from a certain naïveté, but the issue itself is important. It would be a priority to study the process in the course of which decent, young, and not too young, men and women are corrupted by their peers, their colleagues, their clients and so on. At present, case studies focus on corrupt transactions between people who are already corrupt. The process of getting "socialized" in corrupt practices is far less known in spite of the fact that information on this process could be essential in the fight against corruption.

Public Service

In another focus group the main question discussed was how the integrity of public officials could be reinforced. Participants were rather sceptical in this respect. Attempts at creating a Weberian "vocational order" of public servants have failed so far. Career paths are not clearly laid out. Salaries of the rank and file are low. Salaries at higher ranks are better than the social average but they are 3, 5, 10 times lower than those of people in the business sector can earn. Temptation is too great. If a traffic cop can get a bribe (for not giving a ticket to a driver) which amounts to his or her monthly salary, he or she should be a hero or a paragon of morality not to accept the bribe. According to our participants, even a 100 percent rise in the salaries of public servants would not do too much against corruption. The uncertainty of their positions is a further factor in undermining their integrity. There are plans to create an elite group, pay them market salaries, and entrust them with eradicating corruption from the public service. According to our participants, these plans are highly controversial. They may backfire and further disintegrate this field. There were participants who argued that local politics is the real hotbed of corruption. Others thought that as far as the number of cases was concerned, local politics was more contaminated with corruption than other institutions, but, as far as the amount of money involved in corrupt transactions was concerned, national politics, and especially the process of rapid wholesale privatization, was by far the front runner.

Would corruption recede with the conclusion of the process of privatization? Participants thought that two new fields would take over the role of privatization: public tenders and the allocation of positions in public administration. This latter point led to a lively debate. According to some participants the government is replacing thousands of public officials with its own people. This process, in itself, would be justified, to a certain extent, by the fact that governments need a public service that they can trust and on which they can rely in implementing their programs. The question is, which layers should be affected by these changes. Only the highest layers (secretaries of state, for instance) or should it cut deeper?

Another question is, how to control these changes. If governments have a free hand in appointing anybody they want, then the dangers of corruption and cronyism are high. Participants lamented that the Law of Public Administration leaves this question practically open. Moreover, the four governments that have been in office since 1989 have resisted any attempt to regulate this field and they have even dismissed attempts coming from the rank and file to issue an Ethical Code or Guidelines for public officials. Participants argued that a system of open competition for all the positions in public administration should be introduced, the sooner, the better. They admitted, though, that years would pass before such a system would function efficiently. The question of whether a tenure system would protect the field better against corruption than a system of rotation and renewals on a competitive basis could not be solved by participants. There are a few fields where positions are already filled by competition, but participants think that in the majority of cases these competitions, are rigged.

In other cases the process of competition leads to absurd situations. At present for instance, the family-doctor system is being privatized and candidates have to apply for these openings, but the competition for good (lucrative) districts is so intense (in a recent case in a district in Budapest, there have been 27 applicants for one single opening), that a rational and balanced selection is impossible.

Citizen's Responsibility

The process of transition has laid heavy burdens on people's shoulders; resentment is high in spite of the outstanding achievements of the country on the macro level and in official statistics. People feel themselves abandoned by the political and business classes, and, as a consequence, citizen's responsibility is low, people do not identify themselves with their country and community. The idea of the "common good" is still vague, or non-existent. In this situation, breaking the rules is not experienced as a serious wrongdoing. It is often considered as a justified act of compensation, an inevitable strategy of survival or even a moral protest against social injustice. Thus, the gradual strengthening of citizen's ethos may be the most important precondition of a successful fight against corruption. Let me mention here a personal experience.

My brother and I were young boys of about eight to ten years, when we visited our grandparents in Budapest. One morning our grandfather took us downtown, showing us around. To go home we took a tram and when we got off, we noticed that our grandfather tore three tramway tickets into pieces. We were puzzled and asked him why he did so. "Because the conductor has not come and has not punched them," he answered. "This was good luck, we saved three tickets!" we replied. "Gentlemen [he would address us in this way whenever we did something wrong], how can you say so! I would not cheat myself!" "Yourself?" "Yes, myself. This city is my city, and this tram is my tram." This citizen's consciousness is still missing in most of the new democracies. When it emerges it will be the strongest protection against corruption.

Corruption and Democracy

Focus group participants coming from local councils seemed to be at a loss to tell where the dividing line was between corrupt transactions and democratic maneuvering, or, more exactly, between corrupt transactions and: deals made within the context of democratic politics; compromises made by the mayor under various pressures; lobbying; "buying" the votes of a representative (offering, for instance, a new medical center, or a new school to his or her neighborhood). After discussing the issues, they came up with the following definition: if the mayor makes a deal, enters a compromise, yields to the pressure of lobby groups, "buys" votes in order to reach an optimal solution for the community as a whole, then this is not an act of corruption; it is part of the democratic game; it is a good decision. What if the same happens, but the resolution is sub-optimal? This, they said, is a failure, but not an act of corruption. What if the same happens, but the mayor personally profits from the decision? They answered that, if the profit is a gain in popularity, then this is still within the democratic game. If the gain in popularity is disproportionately great (and especially if we are in a pre-election period), however, then this transaction has a character of abuse of power. If the mayor financially profits from the decision, then this is a clear case of corruption, though the fact that his decision was optimal for the community becomes an extenuating circumstance.

So far so good, but in most cases, it is very difficult to exactly define what public interest, or the interest of the community, is, and this limits the practical application of the above distinctions.

Investigative Journalism

Investigative journalism could be one of the best weapons in the fight against corruption, but according to the journalist participants in the focus groups, the conditions for this type of journalism are not in place in Central European countries. Owners are not interested, or are even biased against, investigative journalism. The interests of companies advertising in the media may obstruct investigative journalism. Accurate investigative journalism is time consuming and expensive. Editors seldom support this type of journalism. There is a lack of peer solidarity among journalists. Journalists in trouble cannot expect support from their colleagues. There is also a lack of social solidarity: journalists in trouble cannot expect public support. Partisan politics are such that, in the jungle war of uncompromising interests, political parties are more interested in fighting each other than fighting corruption. They use cases or rumors of corruption for undermining each other's credibility and drop the issue as soon as they cannot politically capitalize on them any more. The law overprotects individuals, business, and public servants. An excessively large number of documents are "classified." There is a chronic lack of follow-up or consequences after exposures. Incriminating reports and materials published by journalists are often ignored by district attorneys and the police. Trials are infinitely delayed, there have been very few cases that led to a prison sentence. Journalists who lose their jobs because of having trodden on sensitive toes may have serious difficulties in finding a new job. Investigating journalists may be, and have been, threatened by affected parties. There are taboo topics that journalists carefully avoid (mafia issues, for instance).

The International Community

By helping build the institutions of democracy and market economy the Western world has helped also fight corruption, but its influence was not only positive. Corruption scandals in high-level western politics have strengthened skepticism, have disarmed anticorruption efforts and have served as an alibi for lenience towards corrupt practices. "If even they are corrupt, why should we be better?" With some important exceptions, Western companies coming to the region have been all too ready to offer "special commissions" to those (public servants) who had an influence on the allocation of public contracts.

Some of the business people participating in the focus group discussions argued that foreign (national and multinational) companies have seriously augmented corruption prices and have an unfair advantage over their Hungarian competitors even in this twilight zone of making business. Foreigners have much more money, Hungarian authorities are more lenient with them than with Hungarian companies, and besides money, the outsiders have a wide range of other means of influencing public decisions. Their governments lobby for them. They can tactfully blackmail Hungarian authorities by threatening to bring their investments somewhere else, or not supply some vital commodities, etc. Some of the business people argued that a crusade against corruption and Draconian rules forcing Hungarian companies to radically clean up their business would increase the competitive advantage of foreign companies. They propose, and would support, a consistent program for the gradual elimination of corruption.

In sum, corrupt practices have a strong survival potential. They have been present in all types of human societies (perhaps with the exception of prehistoric and early forms of tribal life). They are likely to stay with us in the emerging digitalized societies. This does not mean that we should not do everything in order to curb them, to minimize the social damage done by them. Wide-ranging social discussions, including public debates and focus group-type exercises, seem to be indispensable for better understanding the complexity of this social pathology and for carefully implementing the necessary remedies.

Corruption in Czech Privatization:
The Dangers of "Neo-Liberal" Privatization
Quentin Reed

[E]fficient capitalism needs financial market regulation, privatization
sets the tasks of regulators, and privatization establishes lasting
relationships between state regulatory authorities and owners . . .

Schwartz, 1999, p. 32).

What is happening now in front of the shocked gaze of the public is not only
a personal tragedy of individual politicians. Unfortunately, what is at stake is
the moral collapse of the entire political elite.

(Pavel Šafr, editor of right-wing Lidové Noviny, "Kalich hořkosti," LN 17/2/98)

Privatization and Political Corruption

Although this paper is about corruption in Czech privatization, its focus
is wider for two reasons. First, if the main motive for studying corruption
is to come up with effective anticorruption solutions, a narrow focus on
privatization is increasingly irrelevant. Second, corruption in privatization cannot be analyzed in isolation. Privatization is a founding political
act, and among other things, shapes the evolution of corruption control
frameworks and other regulatory frameworks.

This paper puts aside problems of defining corruption in post-communist societies. However, it is worth noting that the very frameworks
which standard political science approaches use to define corruption
are themselves in transition.[238] The Macek and Lizner scandals
described later show that definitions of corruption which rely on laws
and formal rules are simply too thin in postcommunist countries. This
contribution assumes that corruption is identifiable in Czech transition.[239]

Why Corruption Matters in Privatization: State Building and Hysteresis

Corruption in privatization matters for, at least the following four, different sets of reasons. First, the Czech experience indicates that corrupt

privatization decisions are more likely to be bad decisions. Second, corruption undermines regime legitimacy, especially if control mechanisms do not function. Levels of trust in Czech political institutions have not recovered since a corruption scandal brought down the Klaus government in 1997. Third, corruption compromises the task of state-building, and as Adam Przeworski notes, "[W]ithout an effective state, there can be no democracy and no markets." (Przeworski *et al.*, 1995, p. 11). If we accept the division of state-building into the tasks of vertical and horizontal consolidation as do Jon Elster, Claus Offe and Ulrich Preuss (Elster, *et al.*,1998, p. 28–31),[240] corruption clearly undermines both dimensions.

Corruption is also likely to have lasting effects on the quality of regulation. Andrew Schwartz argues in his study of Czech privatization that there is a clear causal relationship between the nature of privatization and the capacity and autonomy of the "state regulator" of financial markets. In particular, Schwartz makes the point that part of the privatization process itself is also the creation of laws and regulatory frameworks, and that,

> If the government institutionalizes its regulatory institutions reluctantly, then we would expect that many regulatory officials would tend to be either easily compromised or relatively inexperienced or obtuse. On the other hand, if the government begins to institutionalize its regulatory institutions with a high degree of independence and respect, then we might expect an autonomous and professional state regulatory administration to emerge. (Schwartz, 1999)

Part of the Czech privatization strategy itself was to weaken or even remove a number of key control mechanisms, and subsequent experience confirms that the country has fitted into the first of the above two categories.

Fourth and finally, as Jean Tirole has shown clearly (Tirole, 1993), corruption is characterized by hysteresis: not only is any corruption equilibrium unstable, but a corruption equilibrium tends to move upwards not downwards. The risk posed by hysteresis placing special demands on elites in post-communist societies. Hysteresis acts through knock-on incentive effects, under which we can loosely include example-setting by elites. Mark Granovetter (Granovetter,

1978) has shown how moral entrepreneurs—individuals who require only a small number of others (or even none) to act in a "virtuous" way so they too act virtuously—can have a radical effect on societal behavior where individual "thresholds" (the number of others who must behave virtuously so that any individual in question does as well) are stacked.

Thus, not only does corruption threaten the foundations of political and economic transition, there are also strong arguments for a "zero tolerance" approach to corruption and, by contrast, arguments for placing special demands on post-communist elites.

The Inherent Vulnerability of Privatization to Corruption

Although there are good reasons for restricting corruption in the post-communist privatization process, it would appear to be one of the most difficult areas in which to do so. The problem is one of strategy dependence, where elites are exposed to severe temptations to structure the rules to advantage themselves, and also to maximize their own initial endowment in the course of economic transition. Second, post-communist privatization is to a significant extent path-dependent (Stark, 1993). Privatization is a founding political act implemented by a post-communist state which itself suffers from a rich historical legacy of corruption (Reed, 1996). This is a context that is severely vulnerable to corruption, and the incentives facing potential claimants in privatization fuel this.[241]

Factors Conditioning the Level of Political Corruption in Privatization

The following discussion is based on the assumption that six main structural factors determine the "political opportunity structure" (Kitschelt, 1986) forming the environment for corruption in privatization: the strategy of privatization adopted by the governing regime; the distribution of political power within the state; the amount of discretion officials wield with respect to the method, conditions and price under which assets are privatized; whether the decision-making process is "sequential," "fragmented," "hierarchical" or "disorganized," following Susan Rose-Ackerman's analysis of the vulnerability to corruption of various types of bureaucracy (Rose-Ackerman, 1978, Ch. 9); the nature of control mechanisms; and the degree of transparency within the privatization process.

The upshot of Rose-Ackerman's analysis is that all bureaucratic forms are vulnerable to corruption, and which forms are less vulnerable depends upon assumptions about the characteristics of applicants (in particular, whether they are legally entitled to the permission in question or not) and the characteristics of bureaucrats (in particular, whether higher- or lower-level officials are more corrupt). As a quick glimpse of the analysis of Czech privatization below, the first of these factors presupposes a set of clear criteria of "legal entitlement" which was increasingly absent from the Czech privatization process as time went on. The second factor recalls the earlier point that corruption with a big 'C' is more damaging than corruption with a small 'c', and finally, as Rose-Ackerman notes in a citation, which is hauntingly relevant to both Czech privatization and Czech market regulation.

"The greater the volume of work the agency head faces and the poorer the quality and the larger the volume of the information available, the greater the incentive to let bribes determine outcomes."[242]

The Czech Privatization Strategy

The most important principles followed in Czech privatization were the following:

1. *A high degree of decentralization in preparation of privatization projects, but an increasingly centralized process of approval.* The basic link in Czech privatization was the privatization project, which once approved, became binding for the institutions implementing the process. The management of every company included in the large privatization process had to formulate a "basic" privatization project. However, any other entity could also submit a project to the enterprise's founding Ministry. The approval process started with the enterprise's founding Ministry and ended with approval by the Minister of Privatization, or in certain more important cases, by the government. The process of privatization from state enterprise to private company is summed up in the six stages in Figure. 1, and the

process of approval of privatization projects is summarized in
Figure. 2

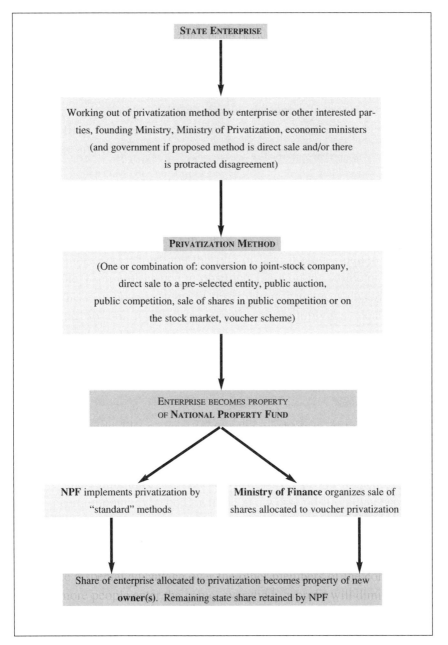

Figure 1. The Czech Privatization Process

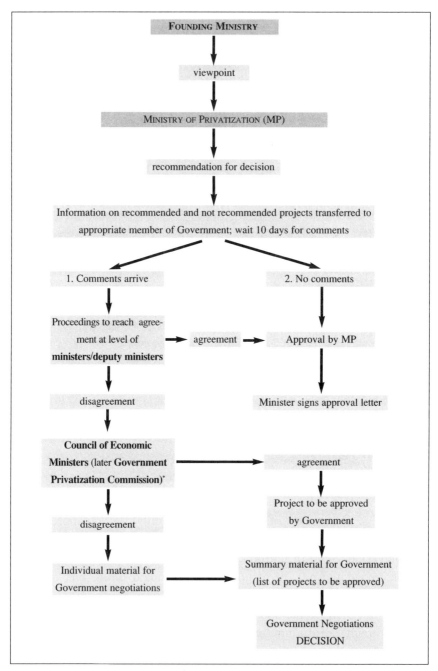

Figure 2. The Procedure for the Approval of Privatization Projects

* *The Council of Economic Ministers was replaced in July, 1992 by the Government Privatization Commission.*

Three main loci for corruption in privatization existed: the approval of privatization projects, the implementation of standard privatization methods by the National Property Fund, and the implementation of voucher privatization by the Ministry of Finance.

2. *Preference for voucher privatization.* Although the Ministry of Industry prepared privatization projects for around 50 key enterprises in 1991, envisaging their sale to foreign investors, the neo-liberal camp around then-Minister of Finance Václav Klaus won the day—and the June 1992 elections—on a policy of mass privatization by vouchers "sold" to Czech citizens for a symbolic price. Forty percent of assets privatized in the main waves of privatization—including the most productive assets—were distributed through the voucher process. However, "standard" methods of privatization were also used for a large part of privatized property. With very few exceptions, the most important Czech companies were either 100% voucher privatized, or privatized by a mixture of vouchers and sale.

3. *Aversion to foreign investment.* Part of the justification for voucher privatization was that it would create a class of domestic capitalist owners faster than any other legitimate privatization method. Notwithstanding the sale of Škoda Auto to Volkswagen in 1991, sales to foreign investors were largely rejected, with "family silver"—traditional Czech companies such as porcelain manufacturers and engineering companies—reserved for domestic buyers.[243] These buyers were usually vehicles of company management, as in the case of Škoda Plzeň and ČKD Praha, the country's two largest engineering companies. This way of selling companies combined with voucher privatization gradually earned the nickname "The Czech Way."

4. *Speed: "economists before lawyers."* A striking aspect of Czech privatization is the systematic neglect of control mechanisms. The guiding philosophy is summarized by Roman Frydman and Andrzej Rapaczyinski as follows:

"Rather than delaying privatization to carefully prepare enterprises and build institutions for the market, the Czechoslovak strategy has been to plunge ahead to change the ownership structure as quickly as possible, leaving most restructuring to the new, private owners and developing new legal frameworks and institutions only when the need becomes pressing" (Frydman and Rapaczynski 1993, p. 70).

Tomáš Ježek, Czech Minister for the Administration of National Property and its Privatization from 1990 to June 1992 and thereafter chairman of the National Property Fund until June 1994, summarized the dominant privatization philosophy as follows: "The application of normal laws to the privatization process is impermissible. Privatization is here so that normal laws can apply after it is finished."[244] Not only were control mechanisms given little priority and even rejected during the privatization process itself; aversion to regulation *per se,* especially of new capital markets, persisted long after the main waves of privatization.

5. *Continued state control.* Although Czech privatization was extremely rapid, it was not—despite the country's reputation in the West as a neo-liberal reforming country—comprehensive. About 60 strategic enterprises remained in state hands, as well as stakes in hundreds of other companies. Most importantly, the government deliberately avoided privatization of the four largest state-owned banks, with the first privatized in 1998. When combined with the Czech variant of voucher privatization, the result was an economy where 80 percent of assets were formally privatized, but where the role of the state remained dominant. Banks extended politically motivated loans to finance sales to Czech entities, a policy which led to a disastrous proportion of classified loans at the banks.[245] More importantly, in voucher privatization the majority of voucher holders entrusted their voucher points to investment funds owned by state-controlled banks. To complete an unhealthy circle, the funds then invested in companies whose main creditors were the same banks. As one analyst from Creditanstalt put it in 1998, "There is only quasi-privatization here. If the companies privatize through the banks that pump funds into them, ultimately the economy is still totally in the hands of the state."[246]

Corruption in Privatization: Beware of the Evidence

Former Czech Prime Minister Václav Klaus has asserted that the evidence for corruption in Czech privatization is insignificant. However, even if this were true, to infer that there has been little corruption is unjustified. Firstly, the amount of direct evidence of corruption may be negatively correlated with the real incidence of corruption. Both corruption and evidence of corruption are variables, which are determined to a greater or lesser extent by the strength and effectiveness of control mechanisms: the more effective the control framework, the less corruption, and probably the more evidence there is of corruption. Conversely, if control is weak then corruption may be rampant, but there may be little specific evidence of it. Second, the importance of the cases where corruption appears is probably more stressed than their number. For example, there is limited evidence of corruption in voucher privatization in quantitative terms, yet the arrest in October, 1994, and conviction of— Jaroslav Lizner—the most influential individual in the whole process— suggests serious problems of corruption, as does privatization of the steel mill *Třinecké železárny* mentioned below. Finally, earlier cases of irregularity in privatization indicate that control mechanisms were removed in response to evidence of surfacing irregularities.

The Approval of Privatization Projects
The Law on the Transfer of State Property to Other Persons

Law no. 92/1991 (hereafter the "large privatization law") established the framework and decision-making process for extensive privatization as outlined earlier. However, it did not lay down criteria for officials to choose winners in privatization. Although some vague criteria emerged in the course of privatization—such as a preference for voucher privatization or for selling to Czech entities—they were never clearly defined. Moreover, the sheer speed with which the Ministry of Privatization dealt with projects in the first wave of privatization—the Ministry began in the summer of 1991 with 20 employees and six computers, and in January 1992, 65 Ministry officials retreated to a government castle for two months to review around 11,252 competing projects for 2,727 companies being privatized—encouraged the development of what Andrew Schwartz terms the "honor system." Based on the philosophy that "Privateers asked society to trust them to privatize the economy expeditiously," this consisted in four rules (Schwartz, 1999, p. 129–131):

Ministry of Privatization decisions were secret.

The Ministry could, and did, adjust privatization projects, although this was against the privatization law. Then-Minister of Privatization Tomas Ježek estimated in various interviews that only 5–10 percent of projects were approved as written.

The Ministry lacked the authority and resources to police privatization, initially due simply to the sheer mountain of work, later due to deliberate policies to weaken control. Losing claimants lacked recourse, independent of the decision of the Ministry.

According to Eva Klvačová, former spokeswoman at the privatization ministry, "The absence of rules has regular results: a perpetual state of siege for everyone who reviews, and decides about, projects; continuous persuasion of decision-makers by arguments and promises of future advantages; evident desperation and arrogance of decision-makers in dealing with authors of projects and their spokesman; escapes of authors of projects to less accessible places and locked doors; the fulfillment or non-fulfillment of attempts at corruption; and, court disputes."[247]

Nonetheless, a caveat to the framework outlined by Schwartz is that, during the initial period of privatization, a degree of external control over privatization decisions existed. The approval process was not kept systematically secret, decisions could be challenged in court, state prosecutors retained the function of supervising the state administration and a degree of independent supervision was performed by the Ministry of State Control and the Supreme Audit Office.

Legal Challenges Muted: Karlovarský Porcelán[248]

A flavor of what was possible under the framework put in place in 1991 is provided by the privatization of the state porcelain company *Karlovarský Porcelán,* the largest manufacturer in the famous Czechoslovak porcelain industry. The privatization of the Karlovy Vary porcelain factory in 1992 produced one of the first major scandals of Czech privatization.[249] In October 1991 the management of *KP* submitted its basic privatization project, prepared in collaboration with several Western consulting firms, proposing to keep the company's 14 plants as one unit except for three to be sold separately. Although the Ministry of Industry recommended a slightly altered version of the basic project, the Ministry of Privatization decided that eight of the most profitable plants would be separated from the state enterprise and sold directly to selected parties for book value, and the remainder privatized by vouchers.[250] In April, 1992, the Czech Government approved this decision.

At that time, the approval process at the Ministry of Industry was based on Minister Jan Vrba's philosophy that, "[O]nly a quite open, transparent process could eliminate corruption—because the corrupt have to influence several different people."[251] The process included an independent commission composed of parliamentary deputies, representatives of employees and management and independent experts, and the press was often invited as well. According to the head of the Privatization Section of the Ministry at the time, "In this way we wanted to bring the conclusions of the assessment process under public control."[252]

Following the government decision, company management lodged legal complaints to the Supreme Court and Regional Commercial Court in Prague, on the basis that the large privatization law had been broken. Several privatization projects were not seen by the founding Ministry, the Ministry of Privatization changed the *KP* project when it was authorized only to approve or not approve projects,[253] and several of the eight "lucky" factories were undervalued in violation of National Property Fund regulations.

The response of those in power was indicative of the future direction the privatization process was to take. Vladimír Dlouhý, Minister of Industry in Václav Klaus's new Czech government after the June 1992 elections, sacked the managing director of *KP* and abolished the Ministry commission mentioned earlier. Only after firing another managing director did the third appointee withdraw the complaints in October 1992, whereupon the NPF transferred the eight factories to the new owners. This took place despite the fact that the Czech Minister for State Audit warned the Ministry of Privatization not to allow the transfer until an inspection of the privatization was completed.

At the end of 1992 the Czech Attorney-General ruled that since the privatization of *KP* was approved by a government resolution, state prosecutors did not have any authority to intervene—even though, in his own words, "[I]n the application of legal regulations in force, a somewhat free interpretation of . . . [the privatization] law . . . obviously occurred in the transfer of the property of *Karlovarský Porcelán.*" According to Libor Kudláček, who later became deputy-minister of Privatization, the privatization of *KP* was "probably quite typical" of the process of approval of privatization projects during the first wave.[254]

Books Galore: The Macek Scandal

The porcelain scandal was overshadowed in the second half of 1992 by a scandal around the privatization of the state book wholesale company *Knižní Velkoobchod*. In a process marked by numerous irregularities *KV* was acquired by a company named *Telegraf Praha*, which was part-owned by Miroslav Macek, then vice-chairman of the Czech Government and executive vice-chairman of the Civic Democratic Party.[255] The irregularities included the sale to a different company than the one stated in the winning privatization project (*Telegraf Ltd*); the intervention by the Minister of Culture Milan Uhde (ODS) who asked Ježek in a letter to follow the project "from a distance" so that it could be discussed and "implemented quickly"; the removal from the projects after its approval of a commitment to continue in the main subject of business for ten years; and numerous other tamperings with the project found by the Supreme Audit Office. The official at the Ministry of Privatization, who was responsible for the privatization of *KV*, left the Ministry at the time of the project's approval and became Commercial Director at the daily newspaper *Telegraf* owned by *Telegraf Ltd*.

Telegraf Praha (renamed *J.R. Vilimek Ltd.* in August 1992) purchased *KV* in October 1992 for Kč23m, while independent real estate agents were cited in the press estimating the market value of the company at around Kč500m. During 1993 Macek's company sold most of *KV*'s best assets, despite continuous attempts by the company's creditors to prevent it (the criminal law forbade the sale of property of an indebted firm without using the proceeds to pay creditors first). Although in 1993 the Prague City Prosecution Office began criminal proceedings for suspicion that the law was violated during and after privatization, the investigation ended in politically motivated disciplinary proceedings against one of the prosecutors.

The final twist in the affair is that some of *KV*'s creditors turned to the National Property Fund to claim their debts. Under the privatization law the NPF was the guarantor of debts of companies taken over in privatizations if the new owner proved unable to pay them. Whilst legal proceedings were going on, the Government amended the large privatization law three times in order to remove the NPF's obligation to meet such debts.

Although Macek failed to be re-elected executive vice-chairman of the ODS in November 1992, neither Klaus nor other key members of the government came out clearly against his actions. Macek's message to the public was unequivocal: in a famous statement he claimed that he had only done what any Czech citizen over the age of eighteen would have done. He also labeled efforts to reveal the facts around the privatization of *KV* as "an attempt to attack the policy of the ODS and its representatives, and at the same time to discredit privatization and economic transformation." Macek is now again vice-chairman of the ODS.

The Control Framework after the June 1992 Elections:
Politics Takes Precedence over Law

The porcelain and book scandals reflected a qualitative change in the privatization approach adopted by the Klaus government after it took power in July 1992. First, obstacles to privatization—or rather, obstacles to the government doing whatever it wanted in privatization—were progressively swept aside, as can already be seen in these cases. Second, over time corruption appears to have spread to take an institutionalized form, financing whole political parties.

The new government passed a series of amendments to the law, the most important in June 1993.[256] The amendment:

- removed privatization decisions from judicial review entirely, stating that, "Regulations concerning administrative proceedings do not apply to privatization decisions. These decisions are not subject to review by a court." In other words, state institutions could make whatever privatization decisions they liked, provided they did not break the criminal law;
- stated that, "Organs responsible for privatization decisions may change the conditions, scope and method of privatization contained in a proposed privatization project.";
- allowed the same organs to alter projects already approved, provided the property had not yet been transferred to the NPF;
- encoded secrecy in the process, stating that, "Privatization decision-making is not public . . ."; Submitters of unsuccessful projects had to be informed only about their project being unsuccessful, the method of privatization approved, and had no chance to see the privatization file.
- During the first year and a half of the Klaus government's term the chances of anybody being caught being corrupt in the course of privatization were reduced virtually to zero, as mechanisms of external supervision and control were—in the words of the vice-president of the Supreme Audit Office— "brutally removed." In addition to the changes in the privatization law already mentioned, control was blunted or removed in a number of other areas.

In 1993 the Supreme Audit Office was stripped of the power to choose where to audit, and henceforth could only carry out audits on the basis of initiatives from Parliament, the Government or the President of the Republic or initiatives that arose from audits it had already carried out.[257] Ineffective external auditing has been compounded by the fact that the government henceforth ignored SAO audits, and it completely failed to improve internal control in ministries.[258]

The operation of institutions of criminal investigation and prosecution was hindered by a number of changes. In the words of the chief of the Prague Bureau of Investigation department dealing with economic crime, "Since the Velvet Revolution, mechanisms for controlling economic criminality have been basically eliminated."[259] Since 1993 investigators have been unable to investigate an economic crime until they file a specific accusation, and have had to prove criminal intent to an unusual extent. The police Service for the Uncovering of Corruption and Serious Economic Criminality suffered, according to its former chief, Jan Šula, "because of a not-too-great will of politicians to see doubts cast on the privatization process." The Czech system of prosecution offices, for its part, was transformed and renamed in January, 1994. Significantly, the changes removed prosecutors' former duty and ability to supervise the legality of activities of the state administration. These changes prompted critics of corruption in privatization process to comment that "[W]here there is no prosecutor there is no judge."[260]

Czech courts have been hampered by two main problems. Court reform has stagnated since 1991, and rules of court proceedings have only changed slightly since the 1960's, allowing defendants to prolong cases virtually indefinitely. Second, the court system is overgrown and desperately underfunded. The result is a lack of quality judges, entire courts without computers in some locations, and, according to business sources, a significant problem of corruption in the judiciary itself. All this resulted, quite simply, in almost no cases of conviction for corruption in Czech privatization.

The freedom of officials to abuse their positions was also encouraged by the entirely ineffective regulation of conflicts of interest, both for politicians and public officials. In a similar fashion as the book wholesaler case, in 1992 the *Tesla Přelouč* electronics factory was sold to two former managers, who were shortly thereafter joined by the official responsible for the sale at the privatization ministry. The sale price has never been paid. A general conflict of interest law was passed in 1992 the and tightened in 1995, imposing duties on members of parliament, members of the government and heads of other central state institutions to declare interests to a parliamentary committee, disallowing government members from carrying on any business activity. However, the law contains no sanctions except publication at the discretion of parliament.

The Implementation of Privatization Projects
The National Property Fund: "Idiotic, Clumsy and Stupid Mistakes"?

The National Property Fund was originally designed as an institution, which yields no significant decision-making power, but "merely" implements the will of the government as expressed by approved privatization projects. In practice the NPF has not always behaved in exactly this way. For example, between the end of the first wave of voucher privatization (October, 1992) and the issuing of the shares allocated by it (May, 1993), the NPF called "shareholder meetings" in 458 of the 943 companies which went through the voucher scheme without informing participants, and approved changes in their share capital, increasing it overall by a total of Kč5.7bn.[261] By this step the NPF lowered the value of the shares for which funds and small investors had bid in the first wave, and often decisively altered the structure of ownership determined by the approved privatization project.[262]

A well-publicized example of what could happen at the NPF was the privatization of *Čokoladovny Praha,* the largest confectionery producer in Central and Eastern Europe.[263] In 1992 the NPF sold shares worth around Kč270m to *První Investiční,* an investment fund owned by *IPB,* for around one-third of this value, in contradiction of the approved privatization project. The NPF also swapped shares in 25 companies, which had remained unsold after the first wave of voucher privatization, for an *IPB* building, into which the fund moved. Less than a year later the shares were worth more than double the value of the building.[264] The *Čokoladovny* privatization was one of the few audited by the SAO, and was used as a political weapon to oust Ježek as Chairman of the Fund in June, 1994. In a third case of alleged collusion with *IPB,* in March, 1994, the head of the NPF Securities Department was removed by Ježek on suspicion that he provided information to *První Investiční* on bids for shares in three companies in the middle of a public tender, enabling the investment fund to change its offer accordingly and win.[265]

Another major problem at the NPF was its failure to screen winning parties to verify their ability to pay the price they offered, resulting in numerous sham tenders which caused direct damage to the companies privatized: winners used money from the company being privatized to pay overblown prices to the NPF rather than investing in the company.[266] Classic examples are the privatizations of *Poldi Kladno* and *Třinecké Železárny* described below.

Poldi Kladno: How not to Privatize[267]

The most famous case of bad privatization in the Czech Republic was the sale of the *Poldi Kladno* steelworks, one of the main steel plants in former Czechoslovakia. The Czech government ignored advice to restructure the industry prior to privatization and sell *Poldi* to a foreign investor, and in 1993 agreed to sell it to *Bohemia Art*, a company with little capital and no background in the industry. The privatization project submitted by *Bohemia Art* was prepared by Ivan Ježek, brother of the NPF Chairman. The price offered—Kč1.75bn—was more than double the nearest offer from foreign steel companies.[268]

Bohemia Art paid part of the price for *Poldi* using funds from the company itself, and never paid anything itself. Three years later *Poldi* was bankrupt, and the owners of *Bohemia Art* were being prosecuted for fraud, non-payment of social insurance, and the illegal transfer of *Poldi* assets to other companies. At the time of writing, court proceedings were expected to take place.

Voucher Privatization: Institutions, Individuals and Information

The voucher scheme was used to privatize a larger portion of the Czech economy than by any other method. It took place in two "waves" of rounds of bidding for the shares of enterprises being offered under the scheme. Any Czech citizen over 18 who purchased a voucher booklet for a nominal price of Kč1,035 (around $30) could participate, and over the two waves shares in 1,664 Czech enterprises with a book value of Kč355bn were distributed to 6 million Czechs (60 percent of the population).

The marked unexpected development in voucher privatization was the massive participation of investment privatization funds which, led by Viktor Kožený's *Harvard Capital and Consulting*, offered huge percentage returns in one year (1000 percent in the case of *HC&C)* to individual voucher holders who entrusted their booklets to the funds. 429 funds took part in the first wave and 353 in the second, and in total 68 percent of voucher books were entrusted to them. The overall result of voucher privatization was that the investment funds established by the top five banks, plus *HC&C*, which was the only one of the major funds not to be established by a bank, controlled 40 percent of the shares of enterprises which went into voucher privatization.

Although the voucher process began in October, 1991, a law to regulate investment funds was not passed until February, 1992. Neither then nor subsequently were funds required to provide sufficient information about themselves or their activities, nor were they sufficiently obliged to act in shareholders' interests. A substantial proportion of funds was founded by people who later turned out to be simply scoundrels and did not honor their commitments.[269]

The voucher bidding process was supposed to eliminate corruption and give an equal chance to all participants. Each voucher booklet contained 1000 "points" used to bid for shares in individual enterprises. The bidding process worked as a series of iterated rounds: all shares had the same "price" in the first round, but prices of shares in different companies were adjusted to reflect supply and demand as rounds progressed.[270] Price adjustments were suggested by a computer program simulating a market process.

However, precise information on the price-setting mechanism was not public,[271] and price adjustments were actually decided by a Price Commission at the Ministry of Finance.

Information on the likely prices of shares in given rounds, and on the structure of ownership of enterprises at any given stage, was clearly useful, and it was crucial who had access to this information. In fact,

> The prices of shares offered to citizens were created by a narrow group of experts, who at the same time controlled the sale of shares . . . Moreover, too many voucher experts have close ties to private firms which secured the implementation of voucher privatization, or are even co-owners of companies through which they deal in shares.[272]

After the Ministry of Privatization approved of what stakes in which companies were to be privatized via vouchers, the Ministry of Finance Center for Voucher Privatization (CKP) implemented the bidding process. The Ministry of Finance Securities Bureau (SCP) recorded all sales and purchases of shares and kept (and still keeps) the accounts of shareholders. The Ministry of Finance Price Commission actually decided the prices of shares in individual rounds of voucher privatization.

From the beginning of the privatization process the head of the first two of these institutions was Jaroslav Lizner (see below), and he was also a member of the third. The other members of the Price Commission were Roman Češka, Chairman of the NPF; and Vladimír Rudlovčák, Deputy Minister of Finance. On 3 June, 1993, the middle of the second wave of voucher privatization, Rudlovčák was elected Chairman of the Supervisory Board of *Češká Spořitelna*, the country's largest commercial savings bank, which owned the country's largest investment fund, *SIS.273*

Prices in individual rounds were proposed by the company *POSTPOsoft*, which employed Dušan Tříska, a former deputy minister of Finance and one of the main authors of the voucher privatization legislation.[274] Tříska also founded *RM-System*, one of the three trading systems at the Prague Stock Exchange. The company *Zlatý Klíč*, also founded by Tříska, shared with *HC&C* in providing advice on the software used for the *RM-System*, and probably in the software used for voucher privatization itself. The software for voucher privatization was provided by the company *Podnik Výpočetní Techniky (PVT)*, whose shareholders included the investment fund *Zlatá Brána*, *Komerční Banka* (the country's second largest bank, which owns one of the biggest investment funds), and *HC&C*. *První Investiční* (see under the NPF above) also had a stake in *PVT*.

The prices of shares were thus determined predominantly by people who had access to information on the demand for shares in the middle of the process, and who had private interests in business entities, which benefited from the process. The technical basis for suggesting the prices was provided by companies who either directly or through their shareholders participated in the purchase of shares themselves.

In June 1994, the Supreme Audit Office produced a damning audit of the CKP and SCP,[275] which concluded that information which could significantly influence the price or profitability of shares was being transferred from the SCP to the *RM-System*. The other main criticism provided by the report was that, in the words of Jana Krejčová, the SAO official responsible for the audit,

> Lizner was actually the head of both organizations—the Center [for Voucher Privatization] and the Central Securities Exchange. Normal employees were similarly 'two-faced': those who worked in the CKP had adjoining ties to the SCP and vice-versa. So most of them knew the structure of buyers and the strategies of investment funds, and at the same time could influence a thing or two." [276]

The reaction of Lizner to the SAO report was to threaten the SAO with legal proceedings, and the government did not react. A few months later (October, 1994) the biggest privatization scandal since the Velvet Revolution broke out when Lizner himself was arrested. He was caught, leaving a restaurant, carrying Kč3.8m that had been paid to him to facilitate the sale of shares in a large dairy company by a fund participating in the voucher process.[277] The affair became public before prices were announced for the sixth and final round of the second wave—at which point the fund in question already owned 40 percent of the shares in the company. a

Lizner's arrest, trial and conviction—he is the only Czech public official to have been so convicted—was the biggest Czech privatization scandal and appeared to mark a turning point in public perceptions of Czech privatization.[278] Lizner was convicted in October 1995 for bribery and abuse of power by a public official, and sentenced after appeal to six years plus a Kč1m fine. His main defense was that he took the money as a commission, and that he was not, in fact, a public official.

The question left by the scandal was to what extent Lizner had been an isolated case, or to what extent the voucher privatization framework had been abused. Abuse of the system could take place in two main ways. First, those with access to the SCP database could provide information on who owned shares after individual rounds to an IPF wanting to acquire shares, and, according to the investigation, Lizner several times requested a complete list of shareholders in certain enterprises during the voucher process, and had, in fact, already helped *CSF* to acquire shares previously. Second, those with access to information during the bidding process could inform external parties of the likely outcome of the rounds of bidding, allowing them to adjust their own bids accordingly to maximize their shareholding. As a member of the price commission, Lizner could look at the orders of individual funds, and he reportedly boasted of his ability to create an "overhang" of orders in individual rounds.

Circumstantial evidence that these activities helped funds is provided by the fact that through voucher privatization, *HC&C* gained very close to the legally permitted maximum of a 20 percent share in a number of key enterprises,[279] an unlikely event if *HC&C* possessed only the same information as other participants. Moreover, in a number of key enterprises the total orders for shares in the very first round of the second wave were at, or very close to, the ratio to supply of 1.25:1, the maximum ratio at which shares would actually be sold in the round.[280]

Privatization and Party Finance

The distribution of political power that emerged under the Klaus coalition was combined with an almost total absence of control of party finance to provide fertile ground for institutional corruption. The 1991 Law on Political Parties obliged parties to submit to parliament an annual financial report for the previous year stating all income and sources of all donations over certain amounts, and, from 1994, to submit the report to the Supreme Audit Office for audit. However, compliance with the reporting requirements was abysmal, sanctions for non-compliance were absent, and in October, 1995, the Constitutional Court invalidated the provision for audit by the SAO on the basis that it did not have the authority to audit political parties.

Attention first centered upon links between privatization and the financing of the Civic Democratic Alliance (ODA), which controlled the key industry and privatization ministries. Although the "privatization link" to the ODA has never been proven, scandals started in late 1996 when it was revealed that the party's biggest donor in 1994 bought one of the country's largest department stores in a public tender organized by the Ministry of Industry and Trade after coming third, and for half the price originally offered.[281]

In the run-up to the May, 1996, parliamentary elections important donors to all three coalition parties receded into anonymity.[282] The ODA did not provide the identity of its biggest foreign sponsor in 1995, and the Christian Democratic Union–Czechoslovak Peoples' Party's biggest donation, which came from the *Coutts and Co. Bank* in Liechtenstein, was similarly anonymous.[283] In the ODS's annual report for 1995 two of the biggest sponsors named in the report, each of whom sent Kč3.75m, were not sponsors at all (one was even dead). All three parties claimed that they had not even known the identities of these sponsors.

Institutionalized Political Corruption: Trinecké Zelezárny Steelworks

A year and a half later the identities of at least some of the anonymous donors to the ODA and ODS were revealed. The most famous example is former international tennis player Milan Šrejber, whose anonymous Kč7.5 million donation to the ODS shortly after his company *Moravia Steel* purchased the country's third-largest steel mill *Třinecké železárny* was the trigger for the fall of Klaus' government in November 1997. Although analysts were shocked by *Moravia Steel*'s Kč2.6 billion bid for the 51 percent stake, they should not have been: *Moravia Steel* proceeded to pay for a substantial proportion of the stake using money from *TŽ* itself. The case indicates that institutionalized corruption was a key factor in the privatization of at least one of the country's largest companies.[284] The scandal assumed unprecedented dimensions when several media claimed the ODS had at least one secret Swiss bank account.[285] This was the immediate reason for the collapse of the Klaus government in November, 1997, as a number of senior ODS figures jumped ship, followed by the withdrawal from the government of the two junior coalition parties.

In the months following this revelation, a number of secret donations to the ODS were uncovered, as well as a loan from *Škoda Plzeň* on very favorable terms. The ODS attempted to clear its name by ordering a "forensic audit" from *Deloitte and Touche*, the publication of which in May 1998 only confirmed newspaper allegations of murky financing and tax evasion while leaving more questions unanswered than answered.[286] Accounts by former ODS employees, and even former ministers, suggested that the ODS and ODA received Kč100m in secret contributions in connection with the privatization of *SPT Telecom* to the Dutch–Swiss *Telsource* consortium. The existence of the Swiss account, however, has never been proven. Documents from the police investigation state that the

ODS spent Kč80–90m more on the 1996 parliamentary election campaign than the Kč127m it declared in its annual report, and that much of the money came from accounts in various foreign locations. The only result of the investigation was the prosecution of a former ODS employee for tax evasion, which was in court at the time of writing.

As far as the ODA was concerned, the emergence of allegations in February 1998 that *Philip Morris* (which bought the Czech cigarette company *Tabák* in 1991), *Železárny Vítkovice* (the country's second-largest steelworks) and *PPF* (an investment fund) stood behind, or mediated, some of the party's anonymous donations in previous years led to the resignation of Chairman Jiří Skalický, the departure of many of the party's founding personalities, and almost the end of the party itself.[287] In an analysis of the privatizations of crystal manufacturer *Crystalex, Investiční a Poštovní Banka* and spirits producer *Becherovka*—three key privatizations which took place in 1997 and were accompanied by doubtful tenders—a commentator at weekly *Týden* wrote that

> [R]ather than . . . specific arguments about the needs of the companies being sold, what takes place in the cabinet are struggles based on the sphere of influence of this or that coalition party . . . [and] it is the government itself that produces privatization scandals. Through its mistaken decisions the government in most cases does not even respect the agreed rules of coalition communication, let alone the approved conditions of privatization. The result is distrust from the public, opposition attacks and shattered illusions of investors.[288]

The Aftermath: Political and Economic Stagnation

Although the collapse of the Klaus government in December, 1997, cannot be attributed to corruption alone, the steel privatization corruption scandal was the immediate reason. Moreover, the increasing animosity within the coalition which had built up over the previous 2–3 years is strongly linked to struggles over the parceling out of resources between parties on a basis that was often more-or-less corrupt.

Proponents of the privatization strategy pursued by the Klaus government argued that the disadvantages of such a strategy—including increased corruption—would be offset by the economic advantages flowing from the rapid privatization of assets. In the first half of 1997 the

Czech Republic experienced a currency crisis caused by a burgeoning trade deficit, combined with growing realization among investors that the Czech market was one best given a wide berth.[289] In the same year the economy fell into a recession that did not end until the second half of 1999, and now appears to suffer from lower growth potential than the neighboring Polish and Hungarian economies. The Social Democratic government, which took power in 1998, has ironically found it necessary to re-nationalize a number of large companies in order to privatize them effectively.

The main reason for this is a combination of bungled privatization and severe neglect of the regulatory role of the state.[290] The privatization of most large Czech companies was followed by wholesale asset-stripping and outright theft of company assets, taking place in an impotent legal environment, under the noses of state regulators and in some cases with their apparently active consent. The scale of the problem even gave rise to a new expression in Czech, "tunneling" *(tunelování)*. The biggest capital market fraud to take place, where Kč2bn in assets of CS Fond were stolen and moved abroad, was allowed by the Ministry of Finance even after the ministry's analytical section responsible for monitoring money laundering was warned about the transaction.

Regarding the role of the state, Andrew Schwartz sums up the situation neatly:

> The wholesale movement of assets could not have happened without the Czech state's acquiescence . . . [S]tate officials abetted tunneling and the associated market abuses. Co-opted government officials blocked legislation designed to make markets more honest, such as shareholder rights, investment fund regulation, conflict-of-interest and disclosure requirements. More importantly, they undermined efforts to enforce the market laws that did exist. The major reward for the corrupted state officials was wealth for themselves and for their political party . . . (Schwartz, 1999, p. 190)

Although the Czech Social Democratic Party (ČSSD) won parliamentary elections in June, 1998, largely on a platform of "Clean Hands" against economic crime and corruption, "Clean Hands" has been little more than a political campaign, and its main institutional consequence— a government committee to review suspicious privatization cases from the past—was abolished in April, 2000. Moreover, it has become clear that the ČSSD itself suffers from a degree of murky financing that places it in a difficult position to criticize other parties.[291] Finally, the government commands only a minority in parliament and relies on an "Opposition Agreement" with Klaus' ODS, which has guaranteed not to topple the government in return for important parliamentary and state functions and policy influence. Although the arrangement has not prevented the government from taking major reform steps (for example to complete bank privatization), it has become increasingly clear that an unwritten part of the agreement is that the parties do not air each other's dirty laundry,[292] and the likelihood of any effective anticorruption effort is doubtful.[293]

Corruption and the Lessons of Czech Privatization: Were Alternatives Possible?

One of the most important questions raised by this contribution is whether a better and less corrupt Czech privatization strategy has been possible. Clearly, for reasons of strategy dependence and other factors touched on in this contribution, relatively high levels of corruption should be expected during the postcommunist privatization process. However, this does not mean that those who shrug their shoulders and ask "What did you expect?" are right. Corruption is, by all accounts, widespread in all postcommunist countries, yet its depth and breadth vary widely, and policy decisions are surely a major factor determining the extent of the problem.

The Czech privatization strategy was based on a variant of neo-liberal philosophy where the main priority was to privatize fast, which exposed the state to the risk of severe regulatory incapacity. This risk became reality due to a second priority, which was opposition to market regulation as such. This opposition was partly sincere but increasingly self-serving as the interests benefiting from lax regulation co-opted those in power. The Czech experience, in fact, proved wrong the assumption that private ownership would spontaneously give rise to the institutions necessary for the economy to function efficiently.

The strategy outlined above was pushed most strongly by Klaus' ODS, the dominant party in the coalition, which took power in June, 1992. The government reversed a number of key policies of the previous Civic

Forum government that would have better contributed to an effective transformation.[294] Although the influence of domestic industrial and financial interests on the changes was undoubtedly present, the ODS was not captured at the time by such interests and had considerable autonomy to choose policies. Although the public mood in 1991–1992 was strongly in favor of the radical transformation slogans used by Klaus, this did not necessarily imply the privatization strategy that was chosen. Indeed, in the case of voucher privatization—which did much to win Klaus the 1992 elections—the public did not articulate any wish for a legal framework that would allow the assets they acquired to be stolen with ease. Moreover, the experience in neighboring Poland and Hungary indicates that even in countries which did not experience a government which was relatively united ideologically for a number of years, and indeed in which elites changed much more regularly, corruption was better controlled[295] and structural reforms advanced further.

In short, the autonomy of Klaus' team to pursue strategies it thought fit was wider than inevitability theories would assume. The indifference of that team to corruption and corruption control mechanisms in the period from 1992 to 1997 was a major factor facilitating the scale of the corruption problem,[296] let alone an important factor preventing the building of mechanisms of market regulation. It was not inevitable.

Note
Until October 1992 1 pound = approx Kč50; from October to April 1997 1 pound = approx Kč42; since April 1997 1 pound = approx Kč50–55.

Corruption and Administrative Barriers for Russian Business[297]
Vadim Radaev

Introduction

Corruption increasingly attracts the attention of experts and officials today. New programs and conventions are elaborated with the aim of combating corruption (OECD, 1997; Stapenhurst and Kpundeh, 1999, pp. 1–2). It has become a subject for international scandals, such as the Bank of New York in 1999. Still many things remain unclear in the discussion of the issue. We do not have fully satisfactory definitions of corruption and ways of measuring its level. It is certainly not a task of this paper to review the field of numerous concepts (for example, see: Noonan, 1984; Rose-Ackerman, 1978, 1999; Shleifer and Vishny, 1993), althongh, it is necessary to define the main elements of corruption, which, in our opinion, are the following: The Principal (a legislative body or a property owner) establishes formal rules of activity. The Principal delegates the rights of control over implementation of these formal rules to the Agent (a civil servant or a manager) who is fully aware of these rules and is not authorized to change them. There is the Client (a third party) interested in getting some benefits through the infringement of formal rules. Existence of these three actors is necessary for corruption to emerge (Gambetta, 1999). Practically, corruption presumes the following actions: Exchange of benefits between the Agent and the Client is arranged as a precondition of action. The Agent for the Client who gets a private or a public gain consciously violates the formal rules established by the Principal. The Agent gets a private gain from the Client. Let us sum it up in a general definition: Corruption is the use of office for private gain among individual and corporate actors by purposeful deviation from the formal office rules in favor of these actors.

Corrupt practices can be framed in different ways. For example, Shleifer and Vishny have suggested three models of corruption. In the first *monopolist model* the supply of public goods is concentrated in the hands of one bureaucratic agency. In the second one (let us call it *deregulated model*) bureaucratic agencies are acting relatively independently, each in their own field. As for the third competitive model, it presumes that every public good is delivered by more than one bureaucratic agency. The authors believe, and rightly so, that in postcommunist societies there has been a significant shift from a monopolistic to a deregulated model that is associated with the increasing level of corruption (Shleifer and Vishny, 1993, pp. 604–607). We will consider this statement from the viewpoint of the Russian entrepreneur in this paper.

This paper focuses on the micro-level relationships of Russian entrepreneurs with the state agencies in the late 1990s. Special attention is given to the practices of administrative control over the enterprise and corruption. The study is based on data of two 1997–1998 surveys. A standardized survey including 227 questionnaires of entrepreneurs from 21 regions of Russia and a set of 96 in-depth interviews with the entrepreneurs have been conducted by the author and research team of the Center for Political Technologies (Moscow). Regional evidence comes from the 1997–1999 study conducted by the author in Tomsk oblast. The paper concludes with a set of provisions for administrative restructuring.

Relations with officials present a painful problem for the entrepreneur in the case of Russia. Bureaucratic procedures are numerous, complicated, and costly. A principal point is that administrative barriers and the lack of information on formal rules are not just outcomes of the "inefficiency" of state authorities. They are caused by the willingness of the officials to maintain bureaucratic control over enterprises under the new conditions.

Turning to our micro-level empirical data, we treat the three following questions: What are the institutional preconditions for corruption in the relationships between civil servants and entrepreneurs? What is the spread of corruption in these relationships? How is corruption enforced through entrepreneurial strategies? We start with the market entry problems caused by the administrative barriers. Then we proceed to the issues of administrative control over the enterprise activity and practices of bureaucratic extortion. Finally, we turn to the entrepreneurial strategies in respect to the state authorities.

Data Sources

Data come from a number of our research projects including national and regional studies of Russian entrepreneurs. Our analysis is based on data collected in the course of two main 1997–1998 surveys of non-state enterprise managers and entrepreneurs (we do not make a distinction between "entrepreneurs" and "managers" here). These include a standardized survey and a set of in-depth interviews. The surveys have been conducted by the author and research team of the Center for Political Technologies (Moscow) (head—I.Bunin). The U.S. Center for International Private Enterprise (CIPE) funded the research. Apart from quantitative data you will find some brief quotations from the in-depth interviews below (for a detailed description of research outcomes see: Radaev, 1998b).

Sampling characteristics. A standardized survey was conducted in November 1997–January 1998. Exactly 227 completed questionnaires were collected from the heads of non-state enterprises in twenty-one regions (mainly in the Central European parts of Russia). All the main areas of economic activity were represented. You will find selected basic parameters of enterprises and entrepreneurs below:

Privatized state enterprises	18%
Non-state enterprises from the start	82%
Small firms	79%
Large and medium-sized firms	29%
Male entrepreneurs	75%
Female entrepreneurs	25%
Have a university diploma?	83%
(One of the) owners of the enterprise	79%
Members of business associations	28%
Moscow entrepreneurs	19%

In-depth interviews were conducted from May 1997 to April 1998. Ninety-six interviews were recorded in total. The sample includes 27 interviews which were conducted with respondents questioned for the second time after the Center for Political Technologies survey in 1993. The main focus was upon the emerging areas of non-state businesses. The sample also includes several leaders of the firms providing various market services.

We also also should note the outcomes of two studies conducted by the author in Tomsk oblast (one of the Siberian regions) in 1997 and 1999. They were initiated by the Organization for Economic Co-Operation and Development (for the outcomes of the first study see: Radaev, 1998a). The data were collected from the interviews with officials of regional and municipal administrations, heads of development agencies supporting small business and entrepreneurs. Regional legislative documents, official statistics, survey data and analytical papers have also been used.

The most recent data are supplemented by the outcomes of the surveys conducted before, namely: a survey of 277 Moscow entrepreneurs conducted in 1993 by the author and a research team of the Institute of Economics (Radaev, 1997); and a survey of the heads of 887 small enterprises and 210 medium and large enterprises, which was conducted with the participation of the author at the First Russian Congress of SME representatives (supported by the Russian Federation Chamber for Commerce and Industry) (Radaev, 1996).

Administrative Barriers and Market Entry

A challenging problem concerns the administrative barriers and transaction costs caused by these barriers. Both entrepreneurs and experts frequently raise the problem of painful bureaucratic intervention to economic activities. Considering the outcomes of the last decade, we can postulate that the situation is not getting better for the Russian entrepreneur. Economic barriers to market entry have been raised significantly within the last decade while the administrative barriers remain high. Let us analyze this in more detail.

a) *Registration*. The problems begin at the very first point of the registration of the enterprise. The entrepreneur is still supposed to spend a great deal of time visiting many agencies, though these problems can be easily avoided: There are a large number of firms, ready to register one's enterprise within two to four weeks or to sell an already registered firm with legal address and bank account within a couple of days. They are quite open in advertising their activity and charge from $300 to $700 for their services (at least in Moscow).

What services do they provide? They do the following: check the name of the firm; get a legal address for the firm; write a Statute for the enterprise; prepare official papers nominating the director and chief accounting officer; open a bank account and issue a stamp; fill numerous official forms; arrange all payments, including those to the Registration Chamber, Tax Inspection, State Committee on Statistics and Social Security Funds. The entrepreneur surely can try to cope with these problems on his/her own, but it would take much effort. Here is the view of a professional in the field of registration: "Just a common man . . . would never register his/her enterprise because it is impossible for a normal being. It is possible only in case if he/she will treat registration as an ultimate goal of his whole life" (head of a firm registering enterprises).

Unsurprisingly, many entrepreneurs look for the services of these special firms today, with transaction costs not being very high. Everyone is happy in the end: the entrepreneur gets registered, the intermediary firm gets a commission, and the bureaucrats keep their jobs and enjoy fees for their services.

This field is, no doubt, a good playground for semi-legal and illegal activity. Though the entrepreneur does not have direct contact with the officials when dealing via the middlemen, corruption looms as an in-built element of the whole system. Apart from corruption, administrative barriers lead to many awkward outcomes. For example, the registration of firms was prohibited at a home apartment addresses (the city of Moscow has become an exception to this). As a result, a large number of firms are registered at false addresses. Some cases are known when tens and even hundreds of enterprises were registered in one tiny room, which belongs to the non-apartment fund.

We can conclude that formal procedures of market entry not only raise many administrative barriers but also lead to significant transaction costs. The latter are not confined to mere registration payments. Let us illustrate these issues with a case from the Tomsk region in 1997.

Total costs of market entry were estimated at the level of 10 million rubles (then $2,000) at the beginning of 1997, if the newly established enterprise did not intend to deal with an activity which is subject to expensive licensing (trade in spirits, etc.). It would cost about 50 million rubles (then $10,000) to build up a trading stall (kiosk) in the city of Tomsk.

Payments to the numerous state institutions were measured by a multiple of minimum wages fixed at the level of 76,000 rubles a month ($15) at the beginning of 1997 (revalued to 83.5 rubles later in 1999). One had to pay the following sums (which may differ for different enterprise categories):

Equity capital (for Ltd. Company)	100-min. wages ($1,500)
Registration Chamber	10-min. wages
Notary office	0-min. wages
Bank account	1–1.5-min. wages
Registration at Goskomstat	5-min. wages

It is remarkable that exit from the market may be even more complicated than market entry. At least, to close down the enterprise in an official way presents much more of a problem than its registration. The entrepreneur is supposed to go through numerous check-ups, and transaction
costs are also relatively high. It costs about $1,000 to get the firm closed.
In the end a large number of enterprises are just left with zero balance to
avoid difficulties.

b) *Licensing*. Many areas of economic activity are subject to licensing
which may be very troublesome. In order to get a license from the State
Licensing Chamber, one has to submit a great deal of documents from a
dozen institutions: Fire Surveillance, Sanitary Surveillance, Standardization Committee, State Committee on Statistics, Architectural
Department, Communal Service and many specialized branches responsible for certain economic activity.

Let us turn back to the case of the Tomsk region in 1997. To license
activities one had to pay from 8- to 15-min. wages ($90–150) to a num-
ber of state-run controlling bodies: Licensing Chamber, Fire Inspection,
Sanitary Inspection and Standardization Committee. To build up a regular trading stall (kiosk), one must pay about 3 million rubles ($600) a year
for land if it is municipal property and up to 12 million rubles ($2,400)
for land if it is non-state property. More than 1 million rubles for the
"architectural project" was required by the Municipal Department of
Architecture; 500 thousand rubles for a three-month license for trading
spirits and 200 thousand rubles for trading cigarettes (this is doubled for
the night hours) (Radaev, 1998a; for more details at the regional level,
see: Loskutova, 1998, p. 3).

The range of activities which are subject to licensing is defined by
Federal legislation. However, this number is extended continuously by
two bureaucratic methods. The first method is to divide one area of activity into several products and establish a rule according to which the production of every single product is subject to special licensing. The following statement, on the example of insurance business illustrates the
point: "Officially we have 16 types of insurance. There are also so-called
insurance products in each type of insurance . . . Every small insurance
product is subject to a long long [licensing] procedure" (head of an insurance company). A second method is the following. Regional and municipal authorities introduce procedures of accreditation, which are compulsory for some areas of activity. Actually, it becomes a slightly camou-

flaged form of additional licensing, which is beyond existing legislative documents (Tsyganov, 1997).

Now let us have a look at our quantitative data. According to our 1997–1998 survey outcomes, one-fourth of entrepreneurs pointed to registration and licensing as one of the most serious issues faced by them during the start-up. More complaints come from those who started in 1989–1991 at the beginning of active privatization process, and those who have entered the markets most recently and have fresh memories of the entry procedures.

Privatized enterprises had fewer difficulties in this respect if compared to the newly established non-state firms (Table 1). There are differences across the areas of activity. The enterprises dealing with retailing, catering and, consumer services were facing serious problems more frequently (35 percent). The firms in science, health care and culture (31 percent) accompanied them. Those specializing in construction, transportation and communications find it relatively easier (only 16 percent of them pointed to serious problems of this sort).

Overcoming administrative barriers is closely linked to corruption. Let us mention that almost two thirds of our respondents claim that, apart from official payments, it is necessary to pay in non-official ways for getting permission for economic activity. It is even more so in case of new non-state enterprises, especially those that were established most recently (Table 1). Demands for bribes were reported more frequently by the firms in the wholesale trade (70 percent) and less frequently by those in industrial production (56.5 percent), science, health care and culture (50 percent).

Table 1. Problems with Bureaucracy by Type of Enterprise (Percent)

	TYPE OF ENTERPRISE	
	PRIVATIZED	NON-STATE
Serious problems with registration and licensing	11	27
Bribe-taking for the permission on economic activity	56	64

The situation is not becoming easier for the entrepreneur today. Most probably it is getting worse.

Institutional Preconditions for Corruption

Special firms can resolve the issues of licensing for the entrepreneur along with the registration problems. However, complaints on the side of small entrepreneurs are many. What lies at the bottom of the licensing issue and similar problems from the institutional angle? In many cases it is not so much connected with the policy of regional and local administrations, but with the activity of a different set of state institutions. Over thirty federal ministries and state committees still have branches in all regions of Russia. These branches are supposed to pursue an integral state policy and carry out control in their areas. They also have prerogatives of licensing and certification of certain activities.

This huge bureaucratic system has faced dramatic changes in recent years. Federal authorities often do not have enough funds to maintain their regional departments. However, they are reluctant to close them down. They provided their branches with the "freedom" to survive on their own instead. It is known that the worst elements of bureaucratic systems come from state institutions which act in a deregulated way and, above all, on a self-financing basis. No surprise, these numerous departments and controlling agencies have built up a lot of administrative barriers and started to live on their formal rent and informal bribes. They invent new requirements and "co-ordinate" their activity for the aims of mutual enforcement of their rights and positions. This means that the lists of requirements are extended in such a way that, in order to get a permission from one controlling agency, one must first seek permissions from the other agencies, and vice versa. Being in the position of a "state monopolist" in their specific areas, these agencies price their "services" in a rather arbitrary way. This also creates opportunities for bribery. At the same time these agencies do not implement regulatory control aiming to eliminate the causes of possible violations. Thus, they do not fulfil their principle functions.

In sum, we have a case of the deregulated model of corruption, as pointed out by Shleifer and Vishny, in a rather extreme form.

The long awaited Federal Law "On Licensing of Certain Activities" (adopted by the State Duma on September 16, 1998) have not improved matters. The list of activities subject to licensing was not reduced. On the contrary, it was extended from 88 to 110 types. Altogether, the list contains 208 activities, and it tends to get even longer. For example, three new types of activity were made subject to licensing in a special Law "On

Additions to the Federal Law on Licensing of Certain Activities" (adopted by the State Duma on November 4, 1998).

The Law on Licensing contains serious controversies. Formally, the minimum period of licensing was extended from one year to three years. At the same time a statement was included which allowed the authorities to confine it to one year if the entrepreneur "applies for it." This tricky statement is now efficiently used for putting pressure on firms. The Law also defines the list of documents which are necessary for submission to the Chamber for Licensing, and puts limits on the licensing fees. At the same time it includes the following principal statement: "Depending on a specific character of the activity, submission of other documents proving that the applicant meets licensing requirements can be introduced in the special provisions on licensing of certain activity." No doubt it leaves the door open for any sort of bureaucratic voluntarism.

What measures should be taken to diminish these damaging practices of bureaucratic extortion? The changes must be rather radical in this case to change the situation. At the federal level it is unrealistic to fight for removing the individual kinds of activity from the licensing list. It would be more effective to carry out an inventory of federal institutions having their branches in the regions, and to reduce their number.

At the regional level, the main instrument is to shift from authorization (*razresheniye*) to notification (*uvedomleniye*) of licensing procedure. It would allow the controlling bodies to check the activity of the firms and entrepreneurs. However, they would be cut off from the licensing process. This would make possible the centralization of numerous payments in the Chamber for Licensing, decrease their total amount, and make the start-up process easier. In all cases the practice of establishing "contract prices" for administrative services must be completely squeezed out.

These measures are really important but their implementation is by no means easy, because all the controlling bodies will oppose them in any possible ways. Apart from a clear understanding of the situation, manifestation of a strong political will is required.

c) *Access to premises and material resources.* The lack of access to premises and material resources is also an important problem when starting up (34 percent of entrepreneurs emphasized that in our 1998 survey), though there are shifts over time. It is easier to find rental space today, and the prices decreased after the 1998 crisis.

The most frequent difficulties appeared in the years 1989–1991, since the major proportion of premises and material resources were still state-owned property. Forty-two percent of the heads of firms which were created in those years report that these difficulties were experienced at the start-up stage. Of the new enterprises established in 1996–1997 this group makes up only 28 percent (Table 2).

Table 2. Access to Material Resources and Premises by Start-up Year (Percent)

	BEFORE 1991	1992–1993	1994–1995	1996–1997
Faced a severe deficit of material resources and premises when starting up	42	37	33	28
Point to a necessity of bribes for getting premises	13	25	24	25

The enterprises in industrial production (52 percent), science, health care and culture (46 percent), finance and market services (44 percent) face the lack of access to premises and material resources more often. The difference between small and large units is negligible here.

We asked the question whether the entrepreneurs were supposed to give bribes to the officials for getting premises: 22.5 percent of them said "yes." It is noteworthy that one group of entrepreneurs pointed at the serious problems with the leasing of space, while another group claims the necessity for bribing the officials; these two groups are largely separate (Table 2). A possible conclusion is the following: those who bribe the officials do not have problems with facilities.

The managers of firms working in retailing, catering, and consumer services find it necessity to "stimulate" the officials more often (32 percent). Those follow in science, health care and culture (27 percent). This problem is much less demanding for the firms in construction, transportation and communications (6 percent). The difference between small and larger enterprises is virtually absent again. There is a little doubt that space rental relationships are deeply connected with corruption. It is especially so in the case of sub-leasing. This is a regular practice when minimal payment rates are declared in formal contracts while 50 percent of payments and even more is delivered in "black cash."

A special Decree of the Russian Federation President "On Measures for Abolishing Administrative Barriers for the Development of Entrepreneurship" was issued on June 29, 1998. It prescribes the decreasing of the number of authoritative bodies involved in licensing of economic activities and the imposing of strict divisions of functions of licensing, control and state regulation among different state executive bodies. The Decree recommends that the regional and municipal authorities provide the following benefits to SMEs and individual entrepreneurs in cases when the outcomes of their own production amount to no less than 75 percent of sales: to give priority to these entrepreneurs in leasing of state and municipal property; to fix the rate of payment for space rental and communications which do not exceed payments for budget institutions; to introduce privileged schedules of payments when buying state and municipal property.

The Presidential Decree touched upon very important problems. However, it did not point to solutions and, therefore, did not change the situation in the area of administrative barriers.

Administrative Control over Enterprises

After the start-up new problems mount. Formally a significant part of property rights have been transferred from the state to the enterprises in the course of liberalization. However, state agencies still keep their formal and informal control over the firms in the day-to-day economic activity. Officials conduct numerous, spontaneous controlling surveys and are capable of destroying even a prosperous firm. To evaluate the scale of this control we have asked the entrepreneurs how often the administrative inspections of their firms took place on behalf of the state authorities. These are presented in Table 3.

Table 3. Administrative Inspections of Enterprises (per Month)

NUMBER OF INSPECTIONS	SHARE OF ENTERPRISES
< 1	26%
1	25%
1.5-2	22%
3-5	21%
>5	6%

Given that these inspections can bring serious distortions to enterprise activity, this element of the regulatory environment is not very favorable for business development in Russia. Let us add that a comparative survey of small shops conducted by Frye and Shleifer (1997, p. 357) in Moscow and Warsaw demonstrated that the number of inspections in Russia exceeded that in Poland by double, i.e., 18.5 vs. 9 check-ups per year.

What is also disturbing for firms, administrative inspections are largely carried out without any predetermined schedule. This sort of complaint was mentioned by 42 percent of the respondents. 7.5 percent of entrepreneurs claim that checking goes with serious infringements of schedule, and only 26 percent of them admit that inspections are accomplished more or less according to some schedules (hard to say— 25 percent).

Which regulatory bodies are the most frequent visitors to the enterprise? The absolute champion is the State Tax Inspection pointed out by 70 percent of respondents in an open-ended question. Medical Surveillance (22.5 percent), Fire Inspection (21 percent), social security funds (8 percent), and more than a dozen other controlling organizations follow the tax officials.

Intensity of control varies across the markets. Tax Inspectors, are most interested in checking up the firms dealing with finance (74 percent) and market services (70 percent). Medical Surveillance is most active in the areas of retailing, catering and consumer services (32 percent), health care, science and culture (28 percent), while Fire Guards watch more closely over retailing, catering and consumer services (26 percent), construction and transport (23.5 percent).

Relations with state agents go far beyond the formal rules. We have statistical evidence that the number of administrative inspections correlates with the amount of transaction costs the firm spent for "informal business services." The share of firms having significant expenditures of this sort increases from 7 to 31 percent with the increase of inspection numbers. At the same time, the share of enterprises having no expenditures of this sort declines from 43 to 23 percent with the increase of the number of check-ups (Table 4). There is very little doubt that corruption does take place here. We have to mention also that the number of inspections correlates with all major indicators of bureaucratic extortion at the enterprise level, which is the next point of our empirical analysis.

Table 4. Enterprise Expenditure on Informal Business Services and the Number of Administrative Inspections (Percent)

ENTERPRISE EXPENDITURES ON INFORMAL BUSINESS SERVICES	SHARE OF FIRMS %	NUMBER OF INSPECTIONS (PER MONTH)					AVERAGE NUMBER OF INSPECTIONS
		< 1	1	1.5-2	2.5-5	> 5	
Significant	14.5	7	17	13	21	31	2.4
Insignificant	46	50	41.5	49	43	46	1.9
Absent	39.5	43	41.5	38	36	23	2.2
Total	100	100	100	100	100	100	2.1

Spread of Extortion and Corruption

It is not easy to find a good way of measuring corruption. Direct questions such as "how much do you normally spend on bribes and gifts to the officials?" would not work. First, it is a rather delicate issue. Second, even being quite open and sincere, the entrepreneur often is not able to make reasonable calculations because the bribery is not confined to make monetary gifts (we will revert to this issue below). Measures based on expert estimates such as the corruption perception index (CPI) of Transparency International are also laden with many biases (Sík, 1999).

In our 1997–1998 survey we decided to put a number of indirect complementary questions approaching the subject from different angles. These include questions, regarding corruption perceptions; necessity to stimulate officials for some of their services, expenditure on informal business services and the existence of conflict with state agents. Let us start with a group of perception questions, which includes the following: What is the spread of bureaucratic extortion in Russian business in general? How often does the entrepreneur confront this extortion in his/her own day-to-day activity? Have bureaucratic pressures been changing within the last two to three years? Is it possible to run an efficient business without giving bribes to the officials under existing conditions in Russia?

According to our standardized survey data, the spread of bureaucratic pressures in Russian business is estimated by the entrepreneurs as follows: 87 percent of entrepreneurs claim that such pressures do exist in Russian business today, including 38.5 percent of them who report that extortion happens frequently (48.5 percent—from time to time). General estimations strongly correlate with the personal experience of confronting the extortion by the entrepreneurs, though the latter is certainly less frequent. Nearly two-thirds (65 percent) of respondents report that they used to be subject to extortion. It includes one fifth of entrepreneurs who face it frequently and 45 percent who face it from time to time (Table 5).

Although extortion does not necessarily end in bribe taking, we have sufficient evidence to conclude that corruption is a widespread phenomenon in Russian business. For which "services" do the entrepreneurs have to pay officials under the table? These bureaucratic services are listed below:

Issuing licenses and permissions	47%
Providing premises	36%
Giving access to loans	24%
Ensuring business protection	14%

According to the in-depth interview data, unprecedented openness of bureaucratic services (both voluntary and compulsory) is striking today in comparison with the Soviet era. The scale of bribery has obviously increased within the last decade. The following statement of our respondent illustrates this: "Unfortunately, in the recent years many [officials] do not take [bribes] but if they do, they take a great deal" (head of a multi-profile firm).

In the interviews opinions on the spread of corruption look rather diverse. Some entrepreneurs express their strong belief that there is no way to avoid bribery in Russian business nowadays. The others are very persistent in claiming that they do not give bribes at all. Personal emotions may certainly influence both radical views. However, the main explanation has to be seen in the segmentation of markets in terms of relations between entrepreneurs and officials. In some segments the informal exchange of bureaucratic services is more active; in other segments it is less regular or even negligible. This segmentation can be described by the following standard variables: size of firm (large businesses are normally more involved in dealing with state officials though their relative transaction costs are low if compared to small enterprises, for which it may be a heavy burden); area of activity (areas with high capital turnover and use of cash in transactions, including finance, wholesale trade, retailing, catering and consumer services attract more attention from the controlling bodies); type of activity (necessity to obtain and renew licenses and permissions).

What can we say about the dynamics of bureaucratic pressures on the enterprises? The majority of entrepreneurs tends to think that their level has not changed at all over the last two to three years. Some 28 percent of them complain that extortion has become even more frequent. Comparing our data with those from previous surveys, we can conclude that bureaucratic pressures are not decreasing at least (Radaev, 1996).

As for the principal possibility to avoid bribery in economic activity, only 20 percent of respondents believe that it is possible while 38 percent of entrepreneurs are certain that bribing is "unavoidable" (42 percent "difficult to avoid") (Table 5). Thus, successful economic activity without bribery seems unrealistic today to a majority of Russian businessmen.

Table 5. Bureaucratic Extortion in Russian Business (Percent)

BUREAUCRATIC EXTORTION	FREQUENT	FROM TIME TO TIME	ABSENT
In Russian business in general	38.5	48.5	13
	Frequent	From time to time	Absent
In one's personal experience	20	45	35
	More frequent	No change	Less frequent
Changes in the last 2–3 years	28	60	12
	Impossible	Difficult	Possible
Possibility to avoid bribing	38	42	20

Corruption imposes additional transaction costs paid for bureaucratic services. The latter vary from "small presents" of several hundred U.S. dollars to 10 percent of a subsidy or a contract provided by the official. You can see the links between bureaucratic extortion and expenditures on informal business services, which most probably includes bribes, in Table 6.

Table 6. Personal Experience of Confronting the Bureaucratic Extortion and Expenditure on Informal Business Services (Percent)

EXPENDITURES ON INFORMAL BUSINESS SERVICES	BUREAUCRATIC EXTORTION		
	FREQUENT	FROM TIME TO TIME	ABSENT
Significant	33	13	8
Non-significant	48	52	37
Absent	19	35	55
Total	100	100	100

Corruption and Entrepreneurial Strategies

It would be unfair to blame officials alone for their corrupt behavior. The corrupters often take a large part of the initiative. Entrepreneurs also try to mobilize state-owned resources or get individual privileges.

From Primitive Bribes to Relational Contracting

The choice of strategy in relations with the authorities plays an important part in making the profile of the Russian firm. On one side, we have "passive" business strategies, when the entrepreneur pays off the officials, trying to minimize this kind of transaction cost and have no extra benefits. On the other side there are "active" business strategies when bribing is used for getting individual privileges and competitive advantage. In the latter case transaction costs are higher, but they are covered by the additional benefits. It is noteworthy that only 28 percent of Russian entrepreneurs accuse the civil servants as the main or only party who initiates bribery. More than one-third (34 percent) of entrepreneurs considers that both businessmen and officials are equally responsible for these practices, while 13 percent of them lay the responsibility on entrepreneurs alone ("hard to say"—25 percent). Thus, the spread of corruption is, no doubt, stimulated by certain competitive strategies of entrepreneurs.

"According to experience, there is no way of doing business without people linking you to the regulatory bodies. It is possible to work without it but impossible to raise big money" (head of a real-estate firm). Nevertheless, it would be a mistake to present the entrepreneur and the civil servant as equal agents of "bureaucratic markets." So many administrative barriers surround entrepreneurs. Their institutional dependency on bureaucracy is still very high and their choice of strategy is far from being voluntary.

"Corrupt officials, seeing the financial benefits of accepting bribes, frequently have the discretion to redesign their activities. They create scarcity, delay, and red tape to encourage bribery" [Rose-Ackerman, 1999, p. 26]. The entrepreneur has relative freedom to choose initially after starting up. Then path dependency is increasing. As was said by our respondent: "If you compromise with the officials once it will never end" (head of tourist firm). Economic action builds up structural constraints of its own.

Additional difficulties for the entrepreneur have originated from serious changes in the bureaucratic order during the last decade in Russia. First, there was a large-scale redistribution of functions among different authorities and within bureaucratic hierarchies. Second, Soviet-type bureaucratic conventions defining the rules and methods of "shadow" remuneration of civil servants have become blurred. The lack of these conventions (to take "according to rank" etc.) leads to uncertainty and voluntarism most painful for the entrepreneur. Now these rules of a bureaucratic code are being established anew, though it is not easy to say how fast this process is.

We have evidence that some other elements of a new bureaucratic code are brought to life. According to the opinion of some entrepreneurs, at the early reform stages there were many officials seeking their "administrative rent" without taking much responsibility for the outcomes of their activity. Now we have more officials who may be involved in bribery but who are also taking care of the public good. They are becoming more professional and selective and want to ensure positive outcomes of the public projects together with their private gain. Bribes are considered as a "commission" and a legitimate way to raise the low official income of civil servants.

"It was pretty simple before: you were supposed to pay for everything. You came to the official, made promises, gave money and got access to a land plot or to some other resources. There were plenty of such examples and many of those firms disappeared long ago. After these years civil servants seem to have learned to treat the entrepreneurs in selective ways" (head of a construction firm).

Corruption is not confined to mere bribe taking. Bribing is an initial and most primitive form of corruption. It mediates rather the short-term relations and single transactions. Mainly low- and middle-rank bureaucrats apply it. For higher-rank officials the scale and scope of these relationships may look very different. First, "elementary" bribery develops into the exchange of services, which are not confined to cash and personal gifts. There are many more sophisticated ways to pay back. For example, the entrepreneur can employ a bureaucrat's relative or sign a contract with a firm which is under his/her patronage. We have a clear case of corruption here if reciprocity is expected by the parties as a precondition of the exchange of services.

"Officials at high level are not paid back with ordinary bribes but with services such as building a summer house, buying a new car, sending relatives for vacations abroad, etc. Cash has stopped being the main instrument for solving issues: alternative mechanisms have appeared" (head of a wholesale trading firm).

Second, with the strengthening of mutual trust the links between the entrepreneurs and officials may gradually transfer into relational contracting (O. Williamson), in which exchange of services does not necessarily presume an immediate reciprocity. It could develop into personal friendships or into the system of clientelism, which are not necessarily linked to corruption in the strict sense.

"There are always some informal relationships between the authorities and the enterprises (especially, the large ones). We ask for their support. They also ask for our support and we are trying to meet their requirements. Sometimes it concerns works, which cannot be paid for from the municipal budget (to repair a church, etc.). Sometimes you have to install a telephone in an official's summer house" (head of a construction firm).

We face mutual long-term support and partnerships here. In this way the mixture of economic interest and coercive pressures is enforced by social norms.

State Patronage

A very important condition for successful business development is linked to informal state patronage when an authoritative state body or an influential civil servant protects the firm. Apart from the protection of business it provides something even more important, i. e., state contractual orders. The latter creates an area in which bribery flourishes. "The main bribes are given to have guaranteed sales. It is not bribes for tax evasion but bribes for getting contracts which are most important. It is fantastic to get contracts providing a stable guaranteed profit" (head of holding company). Or: "It is one case when the bribe is offered for services which should have been done for free. It is completely another case when the bribe is given for getting a big contract. The mechanism of bribery is most powerful here" (head of a production enterprise).

Representatives of the state authorities allocate contracts among "their own" firms and protect them from the controlling bodies. Simultaneously, they create the official channels for their own institutional and material support. "If everyone knows that some firm belongs, or, indirectly, is connected with, the interests of a high-level official . . . naturally there will be no check-ups, no militia, no sanitary control" (head of firm dealing with fuel supply). Dependence on authoritative structures can be very significant in some areas of business. In a radical way this statement is expressed as follows: "No business is possible if you do not have a lobby in the corridors of power, and the rotation of business leaders is going along with the rotation in the power corridors. It is true for all levels" (head of a trading firm).

One of the main conclusions of our study is that from the very start of reform, emerging Russian entrepreneurship was divided into two distinct groups. One group of entrepreneurs decided to appeal for the support of the authorities. They invested their "political capital" and pursued their interests through the corridors of power. The other group preferred their independence and contacted bureaucrats only in cases of emergency: they tried to rely more on their human and cultural capital. We have to conclude that, after the last decade, at least in case of large businesses; the first strategy has become as more successful in economic terms despite our personal likes and dislikes. Additional "political" transaction costs have brought significant economic revenues.

"The role of the state is crucial today. Those who benefit from the [state] budget have much better chances to survive" (head of investment corporation).

In conclusion, let us mention that, by means of cluster analysis, we determined four major groups of entrepreneurs divided by their relationships with officials, namely:

Loyal to officials	15%
Aiming parity with officials	36%
In Conflict with officials	28%
Paying off officials	21%

A detailed description of these groupings is given in the Appendix below.

Conclusions and Policy Lessons

Economic barriers for market entry have risen in Russia over the last decade. New businesses are increasingly evolving as a result of spin-offs from large companies, which are able to provide necessary resources and protection. At the same time, many administrative barriers have not been removed during these years and still remain a serious obstacle for the entrepreneurial activity. Bureaucratic procedures have not been simplified. They demand much time and significant transaction costs. An environment for bribery and favors is maintained.

Numerous administrative barriers are not merely an outcome of "poor performance" of state authorities. They are maintained for keeping control over enterprises under conditions when many formal property rights have been transferred from the state to the enterprises. These barriers push the entrepreneurs into "gray" market segments and produce their subordination in two ways. First, given that it is impossible to follow all the formal rules, nearly everyone is subject to selective bureaucratic control and sanctions. Second, many economic agents have to start negotiations with the authorities for getting individual privileges.

Dependency on the authorities' decisions led the entrepreneurs to corruption-prone activity, which has become an important element of successful market strategies. Entrepreneurs seek the informal state patronage and opportunities to get contracts allocated by the state bodies. As a result, many Russian entrepreneurs could not imagine a Russian economy without bribery today.

Is corruption beneficial for the state agent and the client-entrepreneur involved? In the short run both of them can be better off. In the long run corrupt relationships block development and all actors may eventually lose. However, given the dominance of short-term strategies, no actors are interested in fundamental changes. Everyone complains but almost no one is ready to take on the costs of fair play. This maintains the status quo and provides the stability of the whole system.

Both Russian and Western experience demonstrate clearly that periodical campaigns of combating corruption lead to rather insignificant short-term outcomes and focus predominantly on narrow political targets. The widely advertised punishment of some corrupted officials achieves evident populist goals without any serious changes to the situation in general. Periodical campaigns for administrative apparatus curtailment normally try for similar populist effects. In our opinion, to chase individual bribe-takers is not the most efficient policy. Apart from the insignificant outcomes it is not easy to prove that it was bribery from technical and legal viewpoints. According to official data, only 5–8 percent of those accused of bribe taking in Russia are normally imprisoned.

In order to fight the deregulated character of corruption we should start from the federal level. It is necessary to carry out an inventory of federal institutions having branches in the regions, and to reduce their number. At the regional level, the main goal should be to move from authorization (*razresheniye*) to notification (*uvedomleniye*) in case of start-up procedures. This would allow the centralization of fragmented payments. The practice of establishing free "marked prices" for administrative services must also be eliminated.

In broader terms, the measures of administrative restructuring aimed at weakening the dependency on bureaucrats look more promising than police measures against corrupt officials (though the latter can be useful as well). We would define the following principles of this restructuring: intensive curtailment of various bureaucratic permits, which are connected with the registration and accreditation of enterprises and licensing of their activities; decrease of the number of economic activities which are subject to restrictions; extension of the time for which the administrative certificates are issued; unification and abridgement of formal administrative rules for economic activity; diminishing the practice of under-law administrative restrictions imposed by the authorities at all levels; institutional centralization of the bureaucratic functions instead of existing practices when the economic agent is supposed to submit dozens of documents to many official bodies and give many small payments to a great number of bureaucratic offices; the number of institutions carrying out their immediate control over economic activity has to be cut down; the introduction of elements of competition among bureaucratic bodies may come as a remedy, which gives an opportunity to the economic agent to obtain permission in different branches of a single bureaucratic office; raising the personal responsibilities of the officials for the ultimate outcomes of their decisions.

Apart from administrative measures, it is necessary to extend the programs of professional training of civil servants in various fields of social administration. These training programs may be carried out on a non-departmental basis by borrowing much from international experience.

Transformation of administrative relations within the state and strengthening of "control over controllers" are not sufficient in themselves. There is a call for independent (non-governmental) institutions carrying out extensive public control over the activity of authorities, which produce multiple administrative restrictions. Voluntary associations and unions of entrepreneurs as well as consumer associations have to play an important part in this process.

Appendix. Entrepreneurial Groups and Relations with State Authorities

We have worked out a typology of entrepreneurial groups based on a number of key indicators reflecting the relations of the entrepreneurs and officials. By means of factor analysis we have revealed six factors describing 70 percent of variance. Then we took the two main factors (34 percent of variance) for clustering procedures. These factors include: spread of bureaucratic extortion and involvement in informal dealings; type of enterprise by size and ownership status. Let us turn to a brief description of these four groups.

Group 1. Loyal to Officials (15 Percent)

The entrepreneurs in the first group rarely encounter the bureaucratic pressures. They also do not have much expenditure on informal economic dealings; 54 percent of them claim that these expenditures are virtually absent in their case. At the same time the entrepreneurs do have evident problems with the authorities here. For instance, the average number of administrative controlling visits to the enterprise is among the highest. Besides, one-third of the enterprise leaders evaluate their relationships with the officials as having tensions or even conflict (Table 7).

In sum, we define this group as loyal to the authorities. Despite the pressure of bureaucratic problems, as many as 43 percent of entrepreneurs believe that the attitude of the authorities towards the entrepreneurs is becoming better. A minimum group of 25 percent backs the necessity of active influence on the state authorities. They are also loyal to formal rules. Compared to all other groups, they have the largest number of those who would obey the law under any conditions. Only 11 percent of them tend to ignore "inconvenient" laws. More than half (54 percent) of the entrepreneurs in this group considers the risk of law violation as high (it is much more than in all other groups).

Let us add that four-fifths (82 percent) of the first group consists of the heads of privatized enterprises with the highest share large and medium-sized businesses—46 percent.

Group 2. Aiming Parity with Officials (36 Percent)

Bureaucratic extortion is not widespread in relation to this group and none of the entrepreneurs seems to face it frequently in their personal experience. The combination of a low level of administrative pressures and loose external control makes a specific feature of this group. The number of inspections of the enterprise is minimal. As a result, the representatives of the second group do not spend much on the informal business services; about a half of them (51 percent) claim that they spend nothing on these purposes. The risk of law violation is considered as relatively high. All in all, there is a remarkable intention not to break the borders of the formal economy.

A minority of entrepreneurs here has obvious problems in their relations with the officials—21 percent. The share of those who view their relations with officials as "tense" and "in conflict" is at minimum among all the groups—17 percent. At the same time we have a maximal representation of those who estimate these relationships as "mutual non-interference" here—47 percent (Table 7).

By and large, the situation in this group looks the most favorable. The entrepreneurs try to avoid confrontation with bureaucrats and their frequent controlling inspections. They do not spend much on bureaucratic services but manage to keep relations of mutual neutrality and parity with the officials.

The major part (94 percent) of this group consists of new non-state business heads. Their firms are predominantly small—91 percent. There is an even representation of all main areas of activity.

Group 3. In Conflict with Officials (28 Percent)

The spread of bureaucratic extortion in the third group is estimated much higher (66 percent) than in the previous two groups. There is also the highest number of those who face bureaucratic pressures frequently in their personal experience—4 percent. The share of entrepreneurs considering that bureaucratic extortion is becoming more frequent in the course of time is also at maximum level. Coercive pressures lead to additional costs: 70 percent of entrepreneurs have expenditures on informal business services; for 21 percent of them such expenditures are significant.

Informal dealings, in their turn, are often connected with the infringement of laws, and so it is no surprise that the level of law observance is low in this group if compared to the first and second groups. A majority (82 percent) of entrepreneurs would follow the law "when it is possible." 17 percent of them think that the risk of law violation is practically absent (Table 7).

The third group blames the bureaucrats as the initiators of bribery more often. It does not seem a big surprise given that the number of external controlling visits to each enterprise is at maximum point here (four times a month, on average). As for the main distinction of this group, 55 percent of its representatives evaluate the relations of business and authorities as tense and conflicting ones (Table 7). Aggravated tensions struggle for a way out. Thus, this group is relatively active in claiming the necessity to influence the authorities—53 percent.

The major part of the third group is made up of small enterprises, though 19 percent of firms are large and medium-sized. We have a significant share (56 percent) of firms created in the last four years of 1994–1997. The enterprises are concentrated more in wholesale trade, retailing, catering and consumer services, i.e. in areas most attractive for the controlling bodies, though a group of industrial production enterprises is also represented.

Group 4. Paying off Officials (21 Percent)

The last group is also subject to intensive coercive pressures. Two thirds of entrepreneurs point to the frequent practices of bureaucratic extortion in Russian business, 34 percent of them face it often in their personal experience. As many as 29 percent of entrepreneurs have significant expenditures on informal services. We also have a maximum of pessimists here: 73 percent of them think that bribery is unavoidable today (Table 7).

It is worth mentioning that administrative control over enterprises is not very tight and the number of inspections is fairly small here. How is it possible, given the reports of bureaucratic pressures? The point is that, most probably, the entrepreneurs of this group manage to pay off the officials. It is supported by the fact that they are not so scrupulous about law observing: 21 percent of them would ignore an "inconvenient" law; 25 percent of them claim that in their opinion the risk of systematic law violations is virtually absent today.

Their relations with the authorities are rather tense (39 percent) though the presence of open conflict is lower than in the third group. These entrepreneurs express no optimism concerning pro-business attitudes of the officials. At the same time, only 23 percent of them would like to influence the authorities by political means. It is certainly easier for them to pay off than to pursue a political voice strategy.

Non-state businesses make up 100 percent of the fourth group. There are many start-up firms established in 1996–1997—39 percent. Thus, it is largely new small business. Apart from wholesale trade, retailing, catering and consumer services, it concentrates more in the fields of finance and market services.

Table 7. Bureaucratic Extortion and Types of Entrepreneur (Percent)

	TYPES OF ENTREPRENEURS			
	LOYAL TO OFFICIALS	PARITY WITH OFFICIALS	IN CONFLICT WITH OFFICIALS	PAYING OFF OFFICIALS
Number of enterprises	28	70	53	41
BUREAUCRATIC EXTORTION				
Frequent in Russian business in general	11	11	66	68
Frequent personal experience	4	0	45	34
More frequent for the last 2–3 years	11	12	45	42
Impossible to avoid bribing	7	11	64	73
Have significant expenditures on informal business services	4	4	21	29
ATTITUDE TO THE LAW				
Better to ignore inconvenient law	11	14	12	21
Risk of law violation is high	58	58	35	23
RELATIONS WITH OFFICIALS				
Tensions and conflicts with officials	32	17	55	39
Get financial support from the state	15	4.5	2	3
Necessary to influence the authorities	25	42	53	23
TYPES OF ENTERPRISE				
Privatized state enterprise	82	9	11	0
Small enterprises	54	91	81	98

The Impact of Corruption on Legitimacy of Authority in New Democracies

Lena Kolarska-Bobińska

Many elements affect political legitimacy, among them the question of corruption. Any relation between corruption and legitimacy, however, is difficult to establish empirically, especially in countries where the political system and associated norms and principles are still developing. There is an observable clash between the acceptance of effective "coping strategies" (in the former system) which included corruption, and the developing, often ill defined, rules of the new system. This is one of the reasons the degree of consent regarding corruption in Central and Eastern European countries may differ from that in mature democracies that have clear norms defining acceptable behavior for persons holding public office. It is also possible to postulate that somewhat different factors influence the legitimacy of democracy in states ridding themselves of authoritarianism and simultaneously introducing capitalism, than, say, in states in which such a system evolved over a long period of time. The sources of legitimacy in the former will differ from the pillars of legitimacy in stable democracies and can change along with the consolidation of the new system. Such factors make it difficult to assess, concretely, the influence of corruption on the legitimacy of authority in emerging democracies.

In the first part of my paper, I aim to answer the question whether there has been progress in legitimizing authority in Poland and whether there has been an increased awareness of corruption. I point to their eventual convergence or divergence at a given period of time. In the second part, I aim to discuss the areas of public life affected by corruption and perceived mechanisms of corruption, which may have an influence on the legitimacy of authority.

Legitimacy of Democracy in Poland: 1989–1999

The liberation that came in 1989 sparked off hope for a higher standard of living, freedom and better government. This meant a better "quality" of government than that under Communism, greater professionalism and efficiency, representation of various social and group interests and, finally, confidence in the moral dimension of authority, the conviction that honest and law-abiding people would govern. "Our" people were in gov-

ernment and were, almost by definition, honest, trustworthy, and competent; they raised hopes for a quick transition to a better Poland. A great
deal was expected from the new elite and expectations were based on the
idea that the new system was the antithesis of the old discredited practices.

However, because expectations regarding the new system were, to a
large extent, of an economic nature, the short period of euphoria that followed the initial system change quickly gave way to disappointment,
already by 1991. Balcerowicz's shock therapy was perceived to be behind
a sharp decline in living standards, a rise in unemployment and fear about
what the future have keep in store for families, bringing about a sense of
bitterness at the transition. Also significant were the weaknesses of the nascent party system: political in-fighting, which caused confusion among voters, while various political divisions among parties, so natural in a democracy, seemed a negative phenomenon. As a result, there was a growing conviction that democracy was not capable of solving the country's principal
problems, economic inefficiency and growing foreign debt.

Following a period of severe economic recession, however, 1992 saw
the beginning of economic growth. GDP grew by 5 percent in 1994, by
7 percent in 1995 and by 6 percent in 1996. Consumer confidence and
the standard of living of many individuals also rose. Economic factors
were thus favorable for democracy to take root, all the more so because
they had a positive influence on public opinion. The growing optimism
over the economic situation of the country boosted views on the material situation of family households. Over time, social acceptance of
democratic procedures also increased independent of economic factors
(Table 1).

Table 1. Attitudes toward Democracy 1992–1999

Do you agree or disagree with the following statements?	PERCENTAGE OF POSITIVE RESPONSE ACCORDING TO POLLING PERIOD						
	'92	'93	'93	'95	'95	'96	'99
Democracy is better than any other form of government	57	62	61	66	71	67	64
Sometimes undemocratic governments can be better than democratic ones	34	45	45	47	35	46	41
For people like me it makes no difference whether a government is democratic or not	41	44	40	45	38	40	41

Source: CBOS opinion polls.

The increase in acceptance of the new democratic system did not, however, coincide with approval of the specific way that the political system functioned.

Table 2. Evaluation of the Functioning of Democracy

Generally Speaking are you Satisfied with the Way in Which Democracy Functions in our Country?	XI '93	V '95	XI '96	X '97	V '98	III '99
Satisfied	36	24	44	40	41	28
Dissatisfied	52	67	47	50	46	62
Difficult to say	12	9	9	10	13	10

Source: CBOS opinion polls.

The most common reasons mentioned by respondents for dissatisfaction with the operation of the political system were ineffective government and infighting among the elite. Such conflicts were perceived by the public as signs of the immaturity of the system, rather than as those of normal behavior in a democratic state. Half of those dissatisfied with the ways, in which democracy functioned pointed to "chaos," disorganization, and the free reign enjoyed by criminal activity.[298] Almost as often, respondents said that the government did not address the problems of "average" people. Only a small minority of respondents agreed with the statement that civil rights and freedoms were being violated in Poland. Respondents dissatisfied with the ways in which the democratic system functions seemed to think that there was an excess of freedom, rather than too little democracy (Table 2).

It is worth underscoring the increase in negative responses that took place at the end of the 1990s. Negative evaluations of the situation in the country and of the government in 1999 were higher than in previous years. There has, however, not been a drastic drop in support for democracy. One must stress that negative perception of the government is common in all new democracies. In Hungary, for example, 36 percent of respondents evaluated their government well, in the Czech Republic 19 percent, and in Poland 32 percent.[299]

The growing acceptance of democracy and its norms remains in contradiction to the negative evaluations of the political situation and the work of the government. Current events shape the norms, and negative evaluations of these events can precipitate rejection of not only democratic norms, but also of the entire system. This seems likely, especially in periods of transformation, when attitudes toward the new system are being formed. However, research conducted in the early 1990's indicated that something rather different was taking place. Political conflicts and the public's frustration with politicians did not undermine support for the democratic system.

Here two questions arise. First, does this divergence suggest an ability to disassociate attitudes toward the system itself from evaluations of the current situation and the work of the government? Or, rather, does it suggest a new definition of the role of politics in social life and along with this, new expectations? The second question, which I will answer in the latter half of my paper, concerns the reasons behind the extremely low public approval rating for the government in 1999, and the relation between this rating and public perceptions of the honesty of senior state officials.

In order to determine whether Poles have displayed a tendency to separate evaluations of the democratic system from evaluations of current events, I analyzed a series of polls conducted by the CBOS polling institute between 1992–1996. The surveys indicate that, contrary to what one might expect over time, the correlations between the general evaluation of the situation in the country as well as particular evaluations of the economic and political situation and attitudes toward democracy were not weaker, and, indeed, in some cases they were stronger. For example, in 1992 there was no relation between the general evaluation of the situation in the country and the opinion that "democracy is better than other forms of government." In 1993, however, the result was V' Cramer = .11, in 1995 V' C = .16, and in 1996 V' C= .15. The same tendency arose in connection with evaluations of the current economic and political situation and the acceptance of democracy (as quoted above) or its rejection ("sometimes undemocratic governments can be preferable to democratic governments" or "for people like me it makes no difference whether a government is democratic or not"). In 1992 the strength of the relation of the evaluation of the political situation and the attitude "democracy is better than other forms of government" was defined by the Cramer coefficient V' Cramer = .21, 1993 V' Cramer = .13, in 1995 V' Cramer = .21 and in 1996 V' Cramer = .23. A stronger relation was evident between attitudes toward democracy and forecasts concerning the future situation. However, the strongest relations occurred between evaluations of the development of the situation in Poland and satisfaction with the functioning of democracy in the country: 1995, V' Cramer = .22, in 1996 V' Cramer = .26.

These statistics indicate that attitudes toward democracy and evaluations of how the democratic system functions were closely tied to the evaluation of current events in the country. Further analysis indicated equally strong relations between attitudes toward democracy and opinions about its functioning with the evaluations of the government. For example, people who negatively evaluated the government had a tendency to evaluate democracy in the same way and had an over-all lower approval rating of democracy (V' C =.30). Moreover, the strength of these relations in 1996 was greater than in 1995.

Overall, then, in Poland there is no empirical proof to support Huntington's theory that the key to the stability of democracy is the ability of society to distinguish between evaluations of the overall system and evaluations of the political situation or the government at any given time.[300] As a result, society can be dissatisfied with elected elites, but not with the system overall, which allows it to make new choices. Over time in Poland no distinction emerged between evaluations of the functioning of government and those of the system as a whole. One can hypothesize that the perception of high levels of corruption among highly placed state officials should have contributed to negative evaluations of the government, and this in turn should have brought about the low legitimacy of authority and democracy. Before I present the data on corruption I will indicate the factors that modify this simple and clear formula in new democracies. Significant in this regard are changing perceptions of the role of politics and politicians in public life and changing expectations.

Perceptions of the Role of Politics and Politicians in New Democracies

In the initial period of transformation, the role of politics and politicians was shaped by a clash of conflicting tendencies. Democratic and market-oriented transformation limited the influence of politics on the economy and on society, but at the same time the political authorities were in charge of introducing the new system from "above." The role of the government and politicians in creating the new system, its rules and institutions was central.[301] These contradictions were the source of confusion in the perception of the role of politics. Initially many people did not know what role politics and politicians should play in the new democratic system or in the period of transformation. Neither the old system nor the models of developed western democracies could be entirely adopted in the new situation.

In the democratic system politicians are dependent on the evaluations and the will of their electorate. The focal point for the representatives of the new elite who took power in 1989 was the implementation of the transformation of the entire system and society. They defined their role as the "great builders," introducing reforms often against the will of voters. The reformers did not have to adapt to norms and rules—indeed, they made up the new norms. Politicians were convinced that their role was legitimized by the "building of a new system," which included the creation of new laws and principles, rather than bureaucratic adherence to established norms and rules.

This manner of thinking—i. e., justifying their own role on the basis of the great endeavor of systemic transformation—led to much behavior that would be judged unacceptable and politically suicidal in western democracies. In Poland this was accepted because no clear norms and expectations had developed to govern politics and the behavior of politicians. For example, the majority of respondents in a poll taken prior to the 1995 presidential election accepted highly placed, apolitical civil officials running in the elections—the head of the National Bank, the head of the Supreme Court and the Ombudsperson—who then returned to serve in their original capacity following the election.

It seems that, along with a in Poland's economic and political situation, a change also occurred in the public's expectations of politicians. The image of great reformers who were building a better Poland thanks to their moral and professional qualifications, was replaced by the impression of individuals constantly consumed by political wrangling, representing only particular interests, far removed from the concerns of the vast majority of the public. This change in perception, which resulted from the deep disillusionment following the initial period of enthusiasm and great public confidence in the Solidarity elite, had many causes. It was associated, among other factors, with the various negative effects of the formation of the new political system (i. e., a lack of clear programs, a plethora of small parties and pointless debates) and with disillusionment in the democratic system, which did not guarantee equality, justice and well-being.

The change also resulted from the perception that the elite was dishonest and did not abide by the law. A large portion of those polled were inclined to think that senior officials are always corrupt regardless of whether they worked in the old communist or new democratic system—40 percent.[302] However, in democratic Poland honesty has been the characteristic that voters demanded most from politicians,[303] and this in itself implied a perceived deficit of honesty. In October of 1995 77 percent of the public thought that politicians often took advantage of their contacts and office for personal gain.[304] In 1999 61 percent of those polled said they did not trust officials in charge of managing public funds, while 75 percent were of the opinion that dishonest people were getting rich (*Rzeczpospolita*, January 1999). I will return to this matter later, but here the following question arises: why have negative evaluations of politicians not undermined the nascent democracy?

One of the reasons may be the fact that citizens have, over time, begun to assign less importance to politics and political authorities. Privatization and a stronger market economy decreased the public's feeling that everyday life was dependent on politics and the behavior of individual politicians. Politicians began to be perceived as people who, although they did not do much good, "can't do much harm." Economic growth also led to a feeling of increased stability in the country, which could not be easily undermined by political quarrels and conflicts. Politics ceased to be the sole allocator of goods and wealth and became, instead, a forum for general policy or debate. Social expectations decreased because many came to feel that politics did not have a decisive influence on concrete matters associated with everyday life. Also, as mentioned, according to the vast majority of the populace, parliamentary discussions concentrated on lofty matters of worldview or on utterly banal arguments.

This change in social expectations meant that politics and the actions of politicians were regarded as being less and less significant. We can assume that, the smaller the feeling of dependence on political decisions and the smaller the degree of importance assigned to them, the lower the expectations and the less harsh the evaluations. Indeed, only 40 percent of the public assigned importance to the type of government (see Table 1), while nearly 50 percent did not vote and took no interest whatsoever in politics.

This matter takes on considerable importance when analyzing the influence of corruption on the legitimacy of authority. One can postulate that

decreased expectations with regard to politics and politicians and the growing conviction that the two have little influence on the economy, which
develops autonomously, contributed to greater tolerance of corruption. The
reasoning among a majority of citizens may have been that "even corrupt
government can't harm us, because the scope of its decision-making is
smaller than it was previously, and all authorities steal anyway." This kind
of perception, symptomatic of alienation and withdrawal from public life,
increased acceptance of (or indifference toward) corruption. In effect, even
increased perception of corruption did not automatically result in lower
approval ratings for those in government—a remarkable finding, given the
experience of Poland's eastern neighbors, Ukraine, Belarus, and Russia.

Perception of Corruption

The system change did not eliminate corruption—far from it; it seems to
have precipitated the perception that corruption became greater. I use the
term "perception" because there were no hard data that could be used to
gauge the actual scope of corruption in public life. On the one hand, the
number of people who admitted to having given bribes over the last few
years has not increased; on the other, the areas most often affected by corruption have changed, as have perceptions of the mechanisms governing
public and social life. Greater visibility of politically based corruption at
the "top" and perceived corruption in the judiciary system—which is supposed to be the guardian of lawfulness—heightened the perception of
corruption in Polish public life.

The number of Poles who admitted to giving bribes, either cash or a
gift, in the second half of the 1990s, in order to speed things up or to
clinch a deal, was very high—about one-fifth of all adults.[305] If we factor
in those people who would "rather not speak about it," we end up with a
figure of 25 percent of the population. It is interesting to note that despite
the strengthening of the market economy and democratic institutions, the
number of people who have given bribes has not decreased—it was still
the same in 1997. What did change, however, were the areas in which
corruption cropped up most often and the perceptions of the mechanisms
governing public and social life.

From the very beginning of the period of transformation the state
administration has been perceived as an area subject to corruption: in

1994 and 1997 the state administration was the first place on a list of the fourteen most corrupted areas.[306] In 1999 the health sector jumped to the number one slot, ahead of the state administration. This is interesting because of the fact that recent reforms in the health sector were designed to root out corruption. It is worth noting that the sharp increase (30 percent) of perceived corruption in the health sector was likely to be associated with the reform's ill-defined new rules and regulations governing medical services and government obligations. When introducing the reform with the goal of increasing efficiency, the government did not clearly define the medical services that citizens could obtain with their national health insurance.

It is also worth noting the role of the courts and prosecutor's offices in the perception of corruption-prone institutions. In 1994 the courts ranked second in the public's perception (44 percent) of institutions susceptible to corruption, in 1997 this sector fell to third place (25 percent), while in 1999 it rose again to second place (49 percent). The courts were perceived as being even more susceptible to corruption than the state administration. It is difficult to provide a comprehensive explanation for this state of affairs and equally difficult to assess whether the perception of increased corruption in the courts was justified in reality. However, one reason is certainly the underfunding of the justice sector, which has been closely covered in the media. If the public made a connection between the low salaries of judges and the low prison terms they meted out, it automatically concluded that criminals get low prison sentences because judges were taking bribes. However, regardless of the reasons behind perceived high levels of corruption in the justice sector, the sharp increase in the perception of corruption (from 25 to 49 percent) posed a significant threat to the legitimacy of authority.

It is interesting to note that in 1999, when the new term "local administration" was introduced into the quoted opinion poll, that category ranked third (39 percent of respondents) on the list of most corrupt sectors. It was perceived as being even more corrupt than the central administration. However, local government also enjoyed a relatively high degree of public confidence: aside from the President, it was the most trusted level of government. The rating of local authorities was not only high, but also stable; from 1992 it has enjoyed a steady level of confidence. The question arises why perceived high levels of corruption in local government have not precipitated lower public confidence in these institutions? Does the legitimacy of local government depend only on the belief that this institution is effective, and that it serves local residents well? Would such efficacy also guarantee legitimacy for corrupt central government authorities?

The behavior of civil servants as well as of highly placed government members plays a key role in the perception of corruption. As I have already mentioned, the image of politicians changed very quickly after Poland won its freedom: the picture of noble, uncompromising and honest people was quickly replaced by the conviction that "politicians always steal" regardless of the kind of system they serve in, and that the abuse of public office was rampant. Moreover, the perception that high-ranking officials abuse their posts for personal gain rose from 42 percent in 1995 to 55 percent in 1997 and 61 percent in 1999. Simultaneously, the public was less and less inclined to believe that there were only a few rotten apples; in 1995, 43 percent of those polled believed that dishonest officials were the exception rather than the rule, as compared to 24 percent in 1999. Also, between 1994 and 1997, negative opinion concerning corruption in political institutions rose—especially corruption at the highest levels of state. Corruption in high political office (27 percent) came only second to corruption in the central administration. Although we do not have up-to-date data on this topic, the results of other surveys indicate ever-greater public perceptions of informal arrangements, contacts and murky deals. There was also a general belief that nepotism played a key role in the filling of highly placed posts (from 78 in 1997 to 84 in 1999). According to 64 percent of those polled in 1999, high-ranking civil servants often took bribes, while 58 percent thought that they used public funds to the benefit of their own political party.[307]

Perceptions of nepotism and abuse of public office for personal gain led to a greater role being prescribed for mechanisms of social mobility, which are in contradiction to the logic of the market. Among the perceived mechanisms of the accumulation of wealth at the close of the 1990s, the role of hard work decreased, while the importance of connections and political acquaintances increased.[308] It is encouraging to see that the mechanisms of accumulating wealth most often cited in the early 1990s, such as breaking the law, taking advantage of loopholes and bribing officials, were being viewed as being less and less important. The role of professional qualifications and education was also increasing. However, belief in the key role of informal arrangements was similarly increasing. Research concerning the perception of opportunity also confirmed these observations. According to respondents, connections and patronage as well as professional qualification and education were the key to success.[309] According to Macieja Falkowska, the public was convinced that professional qualifications were very important, but that in order to succeed informal arrangements were crucial. Hence, the "arrangements" typical of the old system were beginning to be perceived as one of the key mechanisms of social and economic mobility in the new system, which was supposed to be the antidote to "shady deals."

In conclusion, despite the strengthening of democracy, there has not been a decrease in the perceived high levels of "small" corruption among political and state sector authorities. There has, however, been a change in the character of corruption. In addition to perceptions of corruption among civil servants, there was now also the perception of the increased politicization of the state of the abuse of public office for personal and political gain. According to Aleksander Smolar, "in local government there has appeared the disturbing phenomenon of a political consensus between those in government and the opposition. This is an agreement to plunder Poland. The government and the opposition do battle, but one is left with the impression that this is nothing more than political theatre, because when it comes to serious matters—money, ownership, influence—there is a great silence and a spirit of agreement predominates."[310] The reaction to this, on the part of society, has been moral revolt, as Smolar writes, and a loss of confidence in the entire political class. However, was it really the case that a moral and honest society looked on at the sinful elite whose behavior undermined their moral legitimacy to rule? In answering this question, it is worth taking a look at society's attitudes toward corruption. Society's acceptance of corruption, i.e., recognizing it as a necessary evil, has led to the delegitimation of authority, but only indirectly so.

Acceptance of, or Consent for, Corruption?

The attitude of Poles toward corruption could be described as inconsistent: moral condemnation coexisting with resignation (consent). The vast majority of those polled agreed with the statement that bribery everywhere and anywhere was immoral (83 percent), and that both those giving and receiving bribes were morally repugnant (73 percent).[311] However, a majority was also of the opinion that the current situation forced people to give bribes (64 percent) and that gifts given in return for favors were only tokens of respect and good manners (55 percent). Moreover, half of those polled thought that giving bribes in certain situations was justified *(op. cit.)*. Only 36 percent of those polled held the uncompromising view of, "even if circumstances would force me to give a bribe, I would not do so." Moral disapproval did not exclude tolerance for bribery when circumstances called for its use.

Two basic factors that served to justify corruption under communism were still present in the mentality of Poles a decade later. They were effectiveness and efficiency as well as poverty and insufficient financial resources. At the beginning of the period of transformation 61 percent of those polled thought that bribes were often the only efficient way of getting even the simplest of things done. One could postulate that the importance and the role of this reasoning decreased as institutions became stronger and the administration became more efficient. In time the reform of the health sector should also minimize corruption in the medical services sector. However, justifying corruption by pointing to underfunding in a given area of the public sector was still prevalent, and has only been strengthened by continued underfunding in the new system. The term "sponsorship" (derived from English) was coined to describe the private funding of state institutions. The lack of resources for the police, hospitals and schools, which resulted in low wages in these sectors, also became a justification of the growth of corruption at lower levels. Attitudes of social solidarity—i. e., "one must give doctors presents, because they earn so little"—were still prevalent and lent legitimacy to petty corruption. The elite, for their part, justified political corruption by citing a lack of funding for party activities. In this context any moral considerations were merely an afterthought.

Corruption thus took on a snowball effect: "If others are taking bribes and getting rich, why shouldn't I?" served as the reasoning of many. This absence of moral condemnation gave rise to acceptance and this, in turn, aided the growth of corruption in young democracies.

Perception of Corruption and the Legitimacy of Authority

In 2000, two tendencies were evident in Poland: a severe drop in public confidence in the government and an increased belief that high-ranking officials abuse public office for personal gain and that there was greater nepotism and politicization of the state. It is difficult to establish a direct and unequivocal connection between the two phenomena.

The Solidarity Electoral Action–Freedom Union (AWS–UW) coalition government introduced four very large and difficult reforms of the welfare state during a period of decelerating economic growth. Simultaneously, it was trying to restructure the coal mining, steel and arms sectors. The government's negative opinion poll ratings were not only a consequence of the politicization of the state, but also of the uncertainty precipitated by the often ill-conceived and ill-executed reforms, as well as the fact that the public had not been properly informed about their effects. The question arose as to whether greater government efficiency would mitigate the loss in public confidence and thus legitimacy that resulted from society's heightened perception of the abuse of public office. In other words, if the government were more efficient, would society turn a blind eye to the abuse of public offices? Or, perhaps officials would not be perceived as abusing their posts if they were more efficient in their official capacity. According to Aleksander Smolar, the center–right AWS–UW coalition promised honest government, which would be in contrast, it claimed, with the previous, postcommunist government. The public's disillusionment with the realities of public life, which has diverged very far from its initial promise, has become very great indeed.

Perhaps even more disturbing than the low public confidence in government was the increased perception of corruption in the system of justice and in local government. The first should be synonymous with the "rule of law," while the second, with grassroots democracy is, the institution closest to citizens. They were key to the efficient functioning of democracy and the legitimacy of the new system. The government and corrupted elites could be replaced in elections, but the institutions would remain. Such a loss of confidence in public institutions and democratic structures results in increased cynicism and withdrawal from participation in public life.

Structural Corruption of Party-Funding Models: Governmental Favoritism in Bulgaria and Russia
Daniel Smilov

Modern parties and political actors are financed from two main sources—private (essentially corporate) donations and public subsidies. Nowadays membership dues play a secondary role in political finance. The same could be said about foreign donations although their importance varies from system to system: for instance, in the countries in transition in Eastern Europe, financial resources, channeled through western organizations (such as the German political foundations, the U.S. International Republican Institute, or the Westminster Foundation), have substantially helped in the establishment and the entrenchment of the party systems in the region.

Globally, the professionalization of politics and the democratic competition among parties and candidates for elected positions constantly increase the demand for financial resources. The results are skyrocketing campaign expenditure and ever-growing costs for the maintenance of parties. The pressure on political actors to find sources of funding is one of the major features of modern liberal democracy. This pressure creates an enormous temptation to avoid and break the rules of party funding in order to get an advantage over competitors. Also it creates the temptation to bend the rules of the democratic process in such a way as to reduce competition by preventing or hindering the participation of some competitors. These temptations, in my view, explain the motivation behind most forms of structural corruption of party-funding models.

Corruption in the area of political finance is a common, but multifaceted phenomenon difficult to conceptualize. In this paper, I will not attempt to suggest a definition of political corruption, which will be considered in its various forms in the area of party funding. Rather, I will focus on the two temptations mentioned above, and on two particular problems they are likely to lead to. Firstly, party-funding rules are often violated in developed Western democracies: until quite recently, in countries like France and Italy, party finance has been an area of systematic violations of the law. Secondly, in other countries the existing rules have arguably exhibited a strong bias in favor of particular political actors (for instance, the parliamentary-represented political parties in Germany, big corporate business in the United States). In these cases, "corruption" of political finance has involved violation, not so much of particular legal rules, but of major constitutional principles concerning the democratic process, such as equality of opportunity, transparency of governmental activities, and lack of favoritism. With this in mind, for the purposes of the present paper, under "structural corruption" of party funding I cover either systematic violation of existing legal rules, or the introduction of rules and practices contradicting major constitutional principles of liberal democracy.

Under a "party-funding model" it will be understood that the rules and the practices of party funding in a given country form a more or less coherent system having two major integrative dimensions. On the one hand, from an ideological point of view, party-funding models tend to have either a libertarian or an egalitarian bias, depending on their capacity of restricting the influence of private financial resources in the political process and equalizing the chances of political actors. The egalitarian models are based on the assumption that the civil society's status quo (in terms of wealth distribution) should not determine the chances of political competitors in the democratic process. Therefore, these models try to eliminate a possible dependence of parties and candidates on private funding. This goal may be achieved by limiting political expenditure and contributions, or by the introduction of substantial public support in election campaigns and other political contests.

This rationale is foreign to the libertarian models, for which the civil society's status quo (wealth distribution) should be reflected by the democratic process. According to this view, it is illegitimate for the state to interfere and change the political prospects of competitors through financial subsidies or expenditure and contribution restrictions. Most of the debates in party funding today are centered on the legitimacy of each of these two models and on their capacity to work against the circumstances of modern politics: the increasing demand for financial resources.

The second major debate in political finance concerns not so much the ideology (theories of legitimacy) of liberal democracy, but its basic institutional arrangements: after all, there are a number of models of separation of power and party systems, each of which satisfies the legitimacy requirements of democracy. For instance, party-funding rules vary with the rationale of the separation of power model and the party system in the different countries. In parliamentary regimes, these rules favor the major parties represented in the legislature, and, as a rule, attempt to consolidate and strengthen them (Germany, the UK). This is so, because political parties play a central role in parliamentarianism: their factions in the legislature form the cabinet that depends on their continuous support. In other words, the parties are not only electoral associations but are semi-constitutionalized state bodies, performing important functions between elections as well.

In presidential regimes this is not necessarily the case—political parties are mobilized essentially for electoral purposes. Once the president and the members of the legislature are elected, the parties' role is not indispensable for the operation of the government. On the contrary, the existence of organized and cohesive political parties may sometimes lead to an institutional deadlock between the president and the legislature. In presidential systems, therefore, institutional rules (party-funding rules included) are essentially candidate-centered: they either help to weaken and fragment the party system (Russia), or promote intra-party pluralism and decentralization (the United States). In both cases, the general goal is to dilute the political strength of the parties, and to enhance the chances of individual candidates and other forms of political alliances (groups of representatives in the legislature, voter alliances, PACs, etc.)

On the basis of this brief typology, I propose four general models of party funding (Table 1):

Table 1. Models of Party Funding[312]

INSTITUTIONAL DIMENSION	IDEOLOGICAL DIMENSION	
	LIBERTARIAN	EGALITARIAN
Presidentialism	Libertarian-presidential model	Egalitarian-presidential model
Weak parties	(United States)	(Russia)
Parliamentarism	Libertarian-parliamentary model	Egalitarian-parliamentary model
Strong parties	(UK)	(Germany, Nordic Countries)

In what follows I argue that Bulgaria's party-finance rules fall into the egalitarian-parliamentary category, while Russia is closest to the egalitarian-presidential model. I will examine the forms of structural corruption that have emerged in the area of party funding in each of the two countries, and will suggest that the existence of the most important among them is explained by the substantial opportunities for governmental favoritism. In the parliamentary model of Bulgaria, it is majority-party favoritism, while in Russia there is a variation of the same phenomenon, characterized by favoritist constellations of "oligarchs" and big business around the president and the regional governors. These constellations, called "clans" by Virginie Coulloudon, bypass the democratic process, and, in a sense, engage in unfair competition with the political parties proper.[313]

In brief, the argument will be that the egalitarian party-funding rules adopted in Bulgaria and Russia do not adequately take into account the circumstances of modern politics and the growing demand for financial resources. The two models feature quite restrictive expenditure and contribution limits and not sufficient state financial aid for parties and candidates. As a result, the political actors systematically violate the rules and rely on illegal forms of funding in order to compensate for the financial shortages. In this situation, however, the political actors in control of the government enjoy substantial advantages. In the first place, they can use state assets and resources (as the publicly owned media, for instance) in reducing their campaign and party expenditure; in both of the countries, there are no established democratic principles of political fairness, the lack of which makes these practices possible. Secondly, the transition period gives to the government enormous possibilities of granting favors to its clients; therefore, businesses tend to align themselves with the parties in power. Thus, the "clanism" (Russia) and the "circle of PM's friends" (Bulgaria) phenomena emerge. In contrast to classical clientelistic regimes (like South Korea, for instance), the relationships between patrons and clients are not deeply entrenched, and seem to be much more temporary in Bulgaria and (to a lesser degree) in Russia. Therefore, I prefer to refer to the developments in both of the countries as "political favoritism," stressing the origin of the problems with the structural corruption of their party-funding models.

Party-Funding Models
Bulgaria's Egalitarian-Parliamentary Model

After the democratization of the regime in 1989, Bulgaria, like most Central European countries, became a parliamentary republic and a party-dominated state. The new Constitution of 1991 entrenched the dominance of the parties in the political process by the adoption of techniques from the toolbox of rationalized parliamentarism, designed to stabilize the majority faction in parliament, and to ensure its firm grip over the government and the administration. These trends, embodied in the Constitution, permeated the rest of the legal system as well and, most importantly, the electoral law and the rules on party funding.

In this respect, firstly, the political parties are granted a monopoly over participation in elections and other forms of political activities. Secondly, the electoral system for general elections is a pure proportional one, which eliminates the competition of independent candidates, and contributes to the centralization and consolidation of the major political parties.[314] Against this background the rules on funding further strengthen the positions of the parties. Public subsidies for elections are distributed exclusively through the national party leaderships; the same is true of the in-kind public support, coming mainly in the form of free airtime on the national TV and radio. Furthermore, the parliamentary-represented parties enjoy special privileges—they receive the lion's share of state aid (both financial and in-kind) which is distributed among them proportionally to the parliamentary seats they control. Last but not least, the central leadership controls the income of the party, and collects most of the contributions, which is additional to the centralization of the party structure.

The other major feature of the funding rules, apart from their tendency to strengthen the party state, is their largely egalitarian rationale. In the first place the 1990 Law on Political Parties, which set out the general principles of political finance, specifically provided that the "state may subsidize political parties in elections for representative bodies, as well as their other activities in proportion to their seats in parliament, and according to the appropriations of the budget law."[315] The public subsidies for the parties come mainly in the form of no interest loans and reimbursement of part of their election campaign costs—up to now, there has been no general financial aid for the operational costs of the parties (although adoption of a new law is considered, which will envisage annual state subsidies for the parties). State financial support was most significant in the first years of the transition period. It was gradually scaled down, and in the last general election became largely symbolic.[316] This is partly explained by the financial collapse of the state at that time (Spring 1997). However, there are various other forms of public support as well. For instance, the leadership of the political parties rent office buildings from the state and local government at preferential, non-market prices. Also, there is a significant amount of free airtime on the public electronic media (especially during elections), which is meant to prevent the escalation of campaign costs.[317] Having in mind that there is still no private national TV, the access to the public channels is of special importance.

Another major form of public assistance for the funding of the parties was the (temporary) permission for them to own firms, and to engage in business activities (technically, the "permission" was a loophole in the law rather than an explicit authorization). The rationale of such a solution is well demonstrated by the Israeli party-funding model, as well as by the practice of the communist parties in France and Italy, where major political actors control substantial satellite business communities.[318] In Bulgaria, most controversially, the law envisaged possibilities of tax and customs relief for non-profit organizations. On the basis of this authorization, in 1991 the Council of Ministers granted customs exemptions to the non-profit organizations, which were taken to include the firms of the political parties and their foundations. These exemptions became the object of systematic abuse, which led to the revocation of the permission to run businesses altogether. Some of the scandals from that period still linger, however, and due to poor legal arrangements there are still possibilities for the parties to run disguised businesses.

The third major feature of the party-funding model of Bulgaria, which underlines its egalitarian rationale, is the existence of various forms of expenditure and contribution restrictions during and between election campaigns. The 1990 law on elections for the Grand National Assembly introduced both expenditure and contribution limits, while subsequent legislation has provided only for overall expenditure ceilings in parliamentary polls. In presidential elections both expenditure and contribution limits were included in the 1991 law: the same rules were used in the 1996 elections as well. The local election laws follow similar patterns in terms of restrictions on expenditure and contribution, although they do not provide for state aid for the parties.

Thus, in summary, it is clear that the party-funding rules in Bulgaria generally follow the logic of the egalitarian-parliamentary model. The law provides for some public support and, most importantly, severe restrictions on political expenditure. Moreover, there is no challenge to the constitutionality or the legitimacy of the "egalitarian" principles of equalizing the chances of the major political actors through state intervention. Still, the efficacy of the system is problematic, as it shall be argued below. Public aid to the parties has been systematically scaled down, and some of its forms (e.g. custom relief) have been abolished. Also, the enforcement of expenditure restrictions has been highly problematic. I will suggest that this is a result of the structural corruption of the model, rather than of its development towards a more libertarian rationale.

Russia's Egalitarian-Presidential Model

From the point of view of separation of powers, Russia is a "superpresidential" regime, in which the directly elected chamber of the legislature, the Duma, plays a limited role in the governing of the country. To a large extent this determines the restricted role played by political parties in Russia as long as the Duma is their major forum. Since the shooting at the parliament in 1993 the dominance of the President has been firmly constitutionalized. Nevertheless, the Duma is the main counterbalance and rival of the President in the constitutional structure; therefore, each of these two actors tries to gain ground against their major competitor, and the party-funding rules are one of the most visible examples of this confrontation. The strategy of President Yeltsin, instead of attempting to create his own majority faction in the legislature, has been to weaken and fragment the parties as much as possible, in order to render the Duma inoperative.

In terms of party funding, this presidential strategy has been exhibited by the following legislative measures. Firstly, in sharp contrast to Bulgaria, not only political parties are allowed to run in elections, but also various sorts of *ad hoc* electoral associations and blocs.[319] The real hurdle which the competitors have to pass in order to put their name on the ballot is the collection of signatures (or the submission of cash deposit in the 1999–2000 election cycle), in which, however, the lack of stable and established party structures could be compensated for by superior financial resources or control over the media and the administrative apparatus.[320] Secondly, the electoral system (for Duma elections) is a mixed one and half of the deputies in the lower chamber are elected in single member districts. In addition, the parties do not enjoy any substantial privileges concerning the nomination of candidates, and in general, the majoritarian part of the elections has been either non-party or anti-party in certain cases, although this trend has weakened since the 1995 Duma elections.[321] The lack of a monopoly position for the parties in the electoral process has been of crucial importance for the character of the party-funding mechanisms. The parties neither control the whole flow of money in the campaign process, nor do they attract the total state aid.[322] When election time comes, as a rule, there is a wild coalition and electoral-bloc making process, which waters down the boundary between the "established" parties and *ad hoc* electoral alliances. This was particularly visible in the 1993 Duma elections, but the trend continued in 1995, and marked the 1999 campaign process as well.[323] Furthermore, there is no state aid for the operational costs of the parties between elections. In general, the primary subjects of state aid programs are the individual candidates but not the parties. Only the proportional part of the Duma elections constitutes an exception to that principle.

To be sure, the parties have managed to score some points against the all-powerful presidency as well. Most importantly, they managed to preserve the proportional quota in legislative elections in 1995, despite Yeltsin's plans to skirt it. In terms of funding, the most significant privilege that the parties have managed to obtain is the public subsidy for their factions in the Duma.[324] The subsidy allows the deputies to keep a team of advisers, which in practice alleviates the problem of maintaining a party apparatus. The main beneficiaries are, of course, the most cohesive parties, in which the identification between the party and its Duma faction is unproblematic. However, apart from the communists, most of the parties exist mainly as parliamentary factions, and the party-funding rules, in fact encourage such a development. This is revealing of the general rationale of the system—the parties are important players almost exclusively within the Duma. Once it comes to the real governing of the country, once it comes to presidential elections, the importance of the parties is strongly reduced. Therefore, in terms of funding, everything is centered on individual candidates.[325] They may be supported by a party or not—this does not bring any significant institutional advantages to them. As a device underlining the relative autonomy of the individual competitors in elections, there are restrictions on the amount of financial support a party or an electoral association can give to its candidates.[326] This measure seems specially designed for a president who is not bound by loyalty to a particular party—and, in fact, this has been the favorite role of President Yeltsin during his years in power. In the same vein, there are restrictions on the amount of individual funds which an association can use in the campaign[327]—a measure aiming to reduce the importance of developed and well-funded party structures, or, in the Russian context, directed against the CPRF and the LDP (to an extent).

The other major feature of the Russian party-funding model, its egalitarian rationale, is clearly visible in many of its rules and procedures. There are various forms of state aid (especially in electoral campaigns), and, most importantly, numerous restrictions on contributions and expenditure for political purposes. There are four major forms of public subsidies. Firstly, during elections the candidates and the parties receive campaign grants, which, however, are enough to cover only a small fraction of the expenditure ceilings.[328] Secondly, there is a tax exemption for donations to individual candidates and electoral alliances during electoral campaigns.[329] Thirdly there are various forms of in-kind support as free airtime,[330] free use of facilities (halls for meetings with supporters) and public transport.[331] Also, the candidates (the President excepted) are supposed to take leave from office during the campaign, for the duration of which they are reimbursed from the state budget. Finally, as already mentioned, the factions in the Duma receive considerable public funding, which helps towards the maintenance of a party apparatus.

Another major group of egalitarian features of the Russian party-funding model includes the restrictions on donations to individual candidates and electoral alliances.[332] Yet the limits are set rather high, and there is no prohibition against private corporate funding (by contrast, contributions from public enterprises are prohibited).[333] The feature that really determines the egalitarian rationale of the model, however, is the overall expenditure ceiling.[334] It is set low, making most of the parties and candidates able to meet it. The existing restrictions on the purchase of additional airtime during campaigns have a similar equalizing potential.[335] Together with the already mentioned substantial in-kind support, the tax exemptions for political donations, and subsidies for the factions of the parties in the Duma, they form the backbone of the Russian party-funding model. All the measures aim to equalize the chances of the participants in the campaign process from a financial point of view, and to restrict the influence of big money in the political process. Thus the major problem of the party-funding model in Russia has not been so much the lack of egalitarian potential in the rules, but rather the enforcement of these rules (Table 2).

Table 2. Comparison of the Party-Funding Models of Bulgaria and Russia

	BULGARIA EGALITARIAN-PARLIAMENTARY MODEL	RUSSIA EGALITARIAN-PRESIDENTIAL MODEL
Ideological dimension Measures endorsing egalitarian values	State aid: loans and reimbursements during elections; subsidized offices; free airtime Overall expenditure restrictions Prohibition of donations from public corporate bodies	State aid: electoral grants; free airtime; other forms of in-kind electoral support; financial support for the factions in the Duma; tax exemptions for electoral contributions Overall expenditure restrictions during elections Prohibition of donations from public corporate bodies Restrictions on contributions from individuals and corporate bodies
Institutional dimension Strong and cohesive parties v. weak and fragmented party system	Monopoly position for the political parties in the electoral process Party-centered, pure proportional electoral system; parliamentary elections of primary importance Fund raising and expenditure is centered on the parties. State aid disbursed through the party leadership Special electoral privileges for parliamentary-represented parties in terms of registration of candidates, state aid, access to the media. Privileges dependent on the parliamentary seats controlled by a party	The parties are on equal footing with other organizations in the electoral process Candidate-centered, mixed electoral system; presidential elections of primary importance Fund-raising and expenditure centered on the individual candidates and their electoral accounts ("funds"). State aid disbursed mainly through individual candidates *No* electoral privileges for parliamentary-represented parties. The number of parliamentary seats controlled irrelevant from the point of view of state aid and non-financial privileges Restrictions on the use of party's own funds in campaigns Restrictions on the contributions of the parties to their candidates during campaigns

Structural Corruption of Egalitarian Party-Funding Models— Governmental Favoritism

In this section I aim to examine the symptoms of structural corruption which can be detected in the party-funding models of Bulgaria and Russia. As argued above, both of these models feature mechanisms with very strong egalitarian potential. My argument will, however, be that this potential has never been realized in practice, because of systematic violation of certain rules and constitutional principles. In general, the structural corruption of the party funding models in these two countries affects mainly their ideological dimension. As far as the institutional dimension is concerned, both of the models have operated largely in accordance with their underlying rationale. In Bulgaria the party-funding rules have helped to strengthen and consolidate the major parties, while in Russia they have contributed to the establishment of a weak party system in which the borderline between political parties proper and *ad hoc* electoral alliances is rather vague.

If the Bulgarian and Russian party-funding models have failed in their egalitarian ideological ambitions, would it not be more appropriate to categorize them, respectively, as libertarian-parliamentarism and libertarian-presidentialism? Is their egalitarian façade not misleading? In fact, no. There are at least three reasons for presenting them as structurally corrupted egalitarian models, rather than as camouflaged libertarian ones. In the first place, sincerely or not, the legislators in these two countries have intended to restrict the influence of big money in the political process. Moreover, no important political actor in these countries has seriously challenged the legitimacy or the constitutionality of the egalitarian rationale behind the party-funding rules. Neither has any such actor defended systematically the superiority of libertarian party-funding principles in local public debates.

Secondly, and more importantly, the state and its apparatus in Bulgaria and Russia have sufficient legal means to legitimately restrict the influence of big money in elections and the political process in general. It is largely up to those controlling the state apparatus to activate the egalitarian potential of the party-funding rules. In this sense the failure of the party-funding models is a failure of certain officials to act. In what follows I will argue that this is revealing of rampant governmental favoritism and patronage practices. The failure of the state apparatus to restrict the influence of big money in politics is clearly a pattern that favors the governing party/president and their clientelistic entourage. Therefore, the most important justification of libertarian party funding models, i. e., that they allow the contender to outspend the incumbent and thus to neutralize his or her advantage in terms of popularity, does not apply to the situation in Bulgaria and Russia.

Thirdly, the corruption of libertarian models usually involves the dependence of political actors on influential economic pressure groups, which undermines the democratic process. In my understanding, what is going on in Bulgaria and Russia is, in part, the opposite process. Political elites energetically reshape the economic landscape of the countries and form "circles of friends," groups of supportive "oligarchs," "clans," and so forth. This is the background against which governmental favoritism becomes the dominant factor for the structural corruption of the party-funding models in both of the countries.

Probably, there will come a time when the clients will try to emancipate themselves from the patrons—then they will become a serious political threat to these patrons. Putin's march against the "oligarchs" in Russia in the first half of 2000 coincided with a wave of scandals in Bulgaria, which were perceived as an attempt by the ruling party to shake off particular patron–client relationships, but it is still unclear whether these processes are just reprisals against recalcitrant clients or the beginning of a radical reform of the system itself.

Bulgaria: A Case of Majority Party Favoritism

The two most important structural failures of the Bulgarian party-funding model concern its reporting and transparency procedures, and the enforcement of expenditure limits. In general, the biggest shortcoming of the 1990 Law on Political Parties is the lack of an adequate enforcement mechanism. All the restrictions and prohibitions of this piece of legislation are not accompanied by sanctions in cases of violation. Article 21 of the law established the principle of transparency of the financial activities of the political parties, which is the primary purpose of any similar document. The law envisages an annual report of the income and the expenditure of the political parties to be submitted to a standing parliamentary committee composed of parliamentarians and independent experts. On paper, reports have to be produced and submitted within two months after every election as well; the reports of the parties must be published in the Official Gazette.

In reality, however, a similar committee, with the participation of extra-parliamentary representatives, has never been established. There has only been one report on the financial standing of a political party published in the Official Gazette.[336] The practice of the parties that developed during the period 1991–1995 was to submit a report to a committee in Parliament—the so-called Committee on the Control over the Income, Spending, and the Property of the Political Parties. However, many of them (especially the extra-parliamentary parties) have failed to produce any report at all. In 1996, partly because of the political and economic turmoil in the country, which led to the fall of the Videnov government, the reporting practice was discontinued. In 1997 the newly elected parliament abolished the control committee altogether. In the beginning of 1998 a new half-hearted attempt to bring some transparency into party funding was made: the chairman of the parliamentary faction of the UDF, Ekaterina Mihaylova, advanced the idea that the Commission on budget, finance, and financial control should be responsible for receiving party reports.[337] This *ad hoc* solution, however, did not inspire enthusiasm in any of the other parliamentary-represented parties. For instance, the Euroleft party flatly refused to report to the Commission.[338] The avalanche of corruption allegations against the government in the spring of 2000 spurred the debate on the adoption of a new party law providing for annual party reports examined by the State Audit Office. At the moment of writing, the bill has passed only its first reading in the National Assembly.

The reporting of party income and expenditure is crucial to the operation of any egalitarian model. If an adequate disclosure mechanism is not in place, the observance of expenditure and contribution limits cannot be controlled. Thus, the failure of the overall expenditure limits in Bulgaria is an automatic consequence of the reporting failures, but there is an additional element that makes the systematic violation of restrictions possible. The issue of independent political spending in general, and in electoral campaigns, is not regulated at all in Bulgaria. In fact, it is not perceived as a problem at all. In practice, nothing prevents a political party from co-ordinating in advance with its supporters and "clients" the direct purchase of services such as advertising, printing of materials and so on. The law does not provide a strict doctrine of "electoral agents" responsible for all political expenditure. Therefore, the reporting mechanisms, even if successfully enforced, would give a picture only of a limited area of the process of party funding, the area which concerns the registered accounts of the parties.

The last systematic reports on the financial standing of the political parties date back to 1995 and are revealing, if not of the parties' real financial situation, at least of the way the disclosure rules attempt to monitor their financial affairs.[339] The parties are not obligated to reveal the names and addresses of their donors, neither are they supposed to disclose the sum of donations per donor. The reports reflect only the total sum of donations and the major sources by type (membership fees, private donations). The same system of reporting was preserved in 1997 and 1998, when some of the parties, the ruling Union of Democratic Forces in particular, resumed the practice of submitting annual reports.[340]

Despite the patchy character of the available information, one conclusion seems to be sufficiently warranted. There is a substantial disproportion in the financial resources of the governing party and the opposition. In 1995 the ruling BSP raised and spent four times more money than the major opposition party—the UDF; the difference was even more pronounced in 1994. Both of these were electoral years in which the BSP first won an absolute majority of the seats in the National Assembly, and then took over more than 80 percent of the local governments.[341] The period 1994–1996 was characterized by fragmentation of the opposition, and serious problems with the publication of the UDF (the Christian-Democrats) daily *Democracy*, which was constantly on the edge of bankruptcy. Especially revealing of the financial situation of the party is the fact that it relied substantially on foreign sources, donated by the American Republican Institute, for the organization of the primary presidential elections in 1996.[342] This trend was dramatically reversed within a year. The reports from 1997 show that the UDF, which came to power that spring, was flourishing financially. The debts of the daily were promptly paid, or at least reduced to a manageable level, and there was a substantial surplus in the party balance at the end of the year. Simultaneously, BSP, already in opposition, was struck by serious financial misfortune. It is hard to diagnose precisely the extent of BSP's financial difficulties in the period 1996–1997, because the party refused to file any annual reports. However, the symptoms were pretty obvious: the party daily, *Duma*, incurred debts and even stopped publication for a week and eventually changed its publisher in the summer of 1999;[343] also the party leadership had recurring difficulties in paying the rent and the bills for heating and electricity for its headquarters. Furthermore, the paid staff of the party was, reportedly, dramatically reduced,[344] there were constant complaints that the party has insufficient resources to fund the 1999 local elections campaign, and, last but not least, there were obvious trends of fragmentation within the party, similar to those experienced by the UDF two years before that.[345]

How is this bias in favor of the governing party, which the Bulgarian party-funding model demonstrates, to be explained? At first sight, it is normal for the party in government to attract more donations from private donors, because of the "incumbency bias," and the hope for direct clientelistic benefits. However, in comparative terms, the extent of the "funding gap" between governing parties and opposition in Bulgaria seems striking, although this point should not be overemphasized because of the unreliability of disclosed data. More importantly, the "gap problem" cuts across the left–right division. Both leftist (as a rule labor oriented), and rightist (presumably business-friendly) parties have enjoyed the benefits of the party-funding model when in government.[346] When we recall that the policies of the governing BSP in the period 1994–1996 stalled the economic reforms, which ultimately led to the 1996 financial collapse of the country due to uncontrolled public spending, the private donors' bias in favor of BSP during the period needs a more detailed explanation— after all, the party attracted close to three times more donations from private (essentially corporate) donors than the pro-business UDF. This fact could hardly be accounted for by a "normal incumbency bias" theory.

In order to throw light on the "gap" problem during the first ten years of the reform in Bulgaria, it is necessary to look more closely into some specific features of the Bulgarian transition. These features, I will argue, create the necessary environment for widespread governmental favoritism.

In the first place, the slowness of the privatization process preserved enormous economic powers for the government throughout the transition period. The factors for the privatization delay are numerous, and not in the focus of the present paper. The direct consequence in terms of political funding was that every government was able to reshape the economic landscape and to create its own clientelistic groups. It suggests that every change of government leads to a change of the financial fortune of particular private business groups. Thus, the fall of the 1992 UDF government spelled economic troubles for the "Tron" corporation, which was allegedly close to the UDF leadership. The 1992–1994 Berov coalition government brought the rise of the Multigroup holding as the major private business corporation in the country. The 1994–1996 BSP government was marked by numerous scandals around the "Orion" business group—or, as it was dubbed in the press, the "circle of Prime Minister's friends." The fall of the Videnov government led to the start of criminal proceedings against "Orion" firms, a prolonged war between the government and Multigroup over gas imports from Russia, and a relative stabilization of the financial situation of the "Tron" corporation and its leader. Subsequently, there have been numerous allegations in the press about relations between the present government and a business group called "Olympus." Although this is an oversimplified picture of the trends in the Bulgarian business climate, it is indicative of the reliance of major private groups on governmental favors and protection.

Secondly, there are significant possibilities of political control over the public electronic media in the hands of the government. Having in mind that private national TV has become operative only in June 2000, and that, at the time of writing, national public television is still the major source of opinion formation, the importance of this instrument for the exercise of government pressure becomes clear.[347]

In the third place, there were ample possibilities for governmental control over the public administration in terms of appointment, promotion, and staying in office: laws on public officials, and the public administration were adopted only in 1998–1999. This gave an opportunity to all governments to change key public officials and to put political pressure on them. This was true of managers of state-owned companies as well. In general, every new government attempted to replace the managers with loyalists. There were numerous allegations, as well, that governments had pressed managers of enterprises to contribute funds to party coffers.[348]

Fourthly, the lack of adequate conflict of interest laws gives an opportunity to the government to staff the governing bodies of state-owned enterprises and organizations with their MPs, party members, and, generally, loyalists. Thus, control over key state assets is in practice exercised by the governmental parties. This principle is valid not only at the central but also at the local level of government.[349]

Finally, the relative international isolation of Bulgaria, mainly because of the Balkan wars and the embargo against Yugoslavia, had numerous negative effects conducive to governmental favoritism. There is no significant foreign investment and foreign business presence in the country, and this lack turns the government and the state into the major source of credit and investment for the economy. Such isolation makes the success of private business dependent on preferential credits or other state-granted benefits and privileges. In addition, the isolation dramatically increased the corruption of the state apparatus; together with the Yugoslav embargo, this accounted for the expansion of a homegrown Bulgarian mafia.[350]

These factors, in my view, and the reality of governmental favoritism behind them, help to explain the funding gap between the governing party and the opposition that occurs, despite the superficially egalitarian rules of party funding. Thus, the party-funding model of Bulgaria is structurally corrupted essentially by means of governmental favoritism.

Quite simply, if public support is not provided in the form of direct subsidies for maintenance costs or tax-deductibility of donations, the major parties in the legislature do find informal (and sometimes illegal) ways of using the state apparatus to compensate for the lack. The most important among them are: a) ensuring control over the public electronic media, b) adopting tax and customs exemptions for party firms, c) toll-gating and kick-backs from government projects and privatization deals and various forms of customs evasion and tax law. All of these forms have been used in Bulgaria or there have been serious allegations to that effect: at present, the first and the last one are of primary importance.

Big private business in Bulgaria could hardly exist without the protection of a major party in power. In contrast to libertarian models, where financially strong actors from civil society threaten to reshape the political realm by buying political parties or candidates, in Bulgaria political parties in government are able to reshape the economic landscape in the country. The change of party in government entails indicative changes in the financial fortunes of private businesses and the management of big state-owned enterprises.

Some smaller parties in Bulgaria, such as the MRF and the BBB, seem to evade the logic of financing of the major parties. The firm electorate of the Turkish minority party, together with the possibilities of foreign support, create a cushion against financial difficulties. The BBB, on the other hand, according to the claims of its leader, is fully funded by him. Nevertheless, if these parties aspire to reach beyond their small electorate, they will be forced to adopt the practices of the major parties.[351] In turn, the control of the parties in government over the state apparatus (and the major means of political profiteering) leads to financial crises of the major opposition parties; these crises are sometimes overcome by the help of foreign financial sources.[352] In general, there has been a huge disparity in the funding of the governmental and the opposition parties. Finally, it is obvious that the major sources of financing of the parties in Bulgaria verge on the illegal. In order for this to be possible, the enforcement mechanisms of restrictive laws are very weak or non-existent. The same is true of the disclosure provisions. Therefore, the model closely resembles corrupted egalitarian-parliamentary models before the introduction of radical reforms (such as Italy and France, before the reforms of the late eighties).

Russia: "Clanism" or Executive Favoritism

In contrast to the Bulgarian case where annual party reports were discussed, I focus here on the available data from electoral campaigns in the Duma and presidential elections. This is justified, because the parties in Russia are for the most part loose electoral alliances, and, with few exceptions, hardly exist outside the Duma at all. Furthermore, there is no systematic information on the financial standing of the political parties, since there is no special law regulating this matter.[353]

The major structural failures of the egalitarian mechanisms of the Russian party-funding model consist in violation of the expenditure restrictions and the restrictions on the purchase of airtime in the public media. These have been endemic problems characteristic of all elections since 1993. The enforcement mechanism of the expenditure and contribution restrictions is based on the so-called "electoral fund" or a special purpose account, which every candidate and electoral association must open at the beginning of the campaign in one particular bank. All payments for electoral purposes, as well as all funds raised, should go through these accounts. The bank is obligated by law to disclose information about the accounts at the request of the electoral commissions. Why does this solution not work in the Russian context? First of all, there were some design flaws. Thus, in the 1993 Duma elections, the opening of an electoral account was not obligatory; this provision was interpreted by the candidates and parties as an authorization to use other accounts and ways of payment.[354] The "electoral funds" were primarily used for the collection of the financial state aid. This flaw was mended, and in the 1995, 1996 and 1999–2000 elections the use of "funds" was mandatory. There was no dramatic improvement of the situation, however, because the problem of "independent" spending persisted. It is close to impossible to prevent non-candidates from paying directly for campaign-related expenses; nothing in the Russian legislation addresses this problem. While it is clear that airtime in the public electronic media cannot be purchased for a candidate or association by someone else, most of the other campaign-related expenses remain a grey area, susceptible to "independent spending."

It is difficult to demonstrate conclusively the failure of the disclosure mechanism and of the expenditure restrictions. Nonetheless, we can note a manifest disparity between the official reports of expenditure, reflecting equality of resources, and the results of independent surveys and the impressions of independent commentators. According to the official reports most of the major parties and candidates are able to raise and spend funds up to a limit prescribed by the law.[355] Independent surveys and commentators paint a completely different picture, however. Most telling in this respect are the findings of the European Institute for the Media about the disproportion in the media coverage of the campaign efforts of the different electoral contenders.[356] Parties close to the presidency have received considerably more airtime and media coverage than their opponents. Closeness to the president is the decisive factor in the distribution of airtime; thus, in 1993 Russia's Democratic Choice was the beneficiary,[357] while in 1995 it could not pass the five percent threshold, being replaced by Our Home Is Russia as a presidential favorite. In 1999 the Unity alliance, and Putin in particular, got extensive favorable coverage, while their main rivals—Fatherland–All Russia—were at the receiving end of editorial criticism.[358] Market orientation and business-friendliness seem to be factors of secondary importance, which is demonstrated by the electoral fate of other liberal and pro-market formations (Yabloko, Forward Russia, etc.), and their leaders (Yavlinskii, in particular). The dominance of the President and the parties close to him in the media, which has been noted by other observers as well,[359] reveals an "expenditure-gap" problem, cutting across the party spectrum in a similar way to the one discussed in the case of Bulgaria. Again, formations close to the President and the government are in a dominant position in financial terms where it most matters—within the Russian constitutional framework and in the electoral process. The control over the government and the administration systematically gives advantages to the President and its entourage. The magnitude of this advantage is difficult to measure— home independent observers speak of fantastic disparities in expenditure in presidential elections,[360] although disproportion exists in Duma elections too.[361]

Thus, although the general rationale of the campaign finance legislation is largely egalitarian, through evasion of rules the system has been changed into one favorable for candidates supported by big business; but ut the crucial factor is control over the state apparatus—this is what determines the success of electoral campaigns. Established presidential libertarian models (the United States) have extensive provisions ensuring the fairness of the competition and lack of administrative pressure. They provide possibilities for the challenger to outspend the incumbent or at least to spend comparable amounts of money in his campaign for the office. This is largely made possible by the pluralistic and very strong civil society, which is relatively independent of the government and the presidential administration, in particular.

The Russian political environment can hardly provide such levels of pluralism and independence of civil society from the government. On the contrary, the prolonged and hesitant Russian transition (just like the case in Bulgaria), granted tremendous powers to the government, through the process of privatization, power to shape the new financial elites and the financially strong centres of civil society. Therefore, financial elites gravitate around the executive, which in the Russian case is headed by the president. President Yeltsin has exploited very well this transition specificity and managed to consolidate the big business around him, at least for the duration of the electoral campaigns. Thus, massive resources became available to him and there was not even a theoretical chance of outspending the incumbent.

The gravitation of financial elites around the presidency is the cause of two phenomena: governmental favoritism and clientelism. Both of them are successfully captured by the term "political clan" used by Virginie Coulloudon.[362] The clan comprises politicians close to the presidency, some regional governors, private banks, and firms from the extraction industry, which in principle are on the borderline between private and public in Russia. Typical of Russian favoritism and clientelism, in contrast to the corresponding phenomena in Bulgaria and Central Europe, is the secondary role played by political parties. Parties are not the major instruments of creating clans and forming clientelistic relationships in Russia. On the contrary, the clans are sometimes formed against the parties and may be, in principle, mobilized against them, as happened in the 1996 presidential elections.

Let us now look more closely into the character of Russian "clanism" and compare it with the "majority party" favoritism that was discussed in the Bulgarian context.

The concentration of economic power in the government and essentially the presidency is a major characteristic of post-Soviet Russia.[363] In contrast to Bulgaria, however, not so much the slowness of privatization, but its arbitrary and informal procedures were the main cause of this development. The Russian monopolistic strategic oil exporting corporations are (semi)private, and heavily dependent on tax privileges and breaks. "Authorized" banking (banks carrying out transactions with federal budget funds) has created some of the most important private financial institutions. Finally, the so-called "oligarchs" owe much of their fortunes to their contacts with the presidency and the government.[364] Although, at different points in time different oligarchs (and clans) have enjoyed presidential favors, the pattern has essentially been one and the same. The coming to power of Putin was announced as an end to the era of the oligarchs, but the evidence up to now does not fully support such a statement. His measures against the "oligarchs" may just be aimed at disciplining the more high-profile ones, as is alleged to be the case with Berezovsky and Gusinsky, the former boss of Media-MOST.

As in Bulgaria, control over the public electronic media is a major lever of political pressure in the arsenal of the presidency. In fact, the situation in Russia is even more problematic than it is in Bulgaria. Russia has no publicly owned and independent media, regulated by an independent board. If the procedure of setting up independent boards is flawed in Bulgaria, in Russia there is no attempt at ensuring the independence of the media of this kind at all. This explains to a considerable extent how it is possible for the parties and candidates close to the presidency to violate flagrantly the rules on media campaigning or to bend them in their favor.[365] As far as the private media are concerned, most of them have been controlled by the oligarchs, or by members of the "clans."[366] Having this in mind, the monopolization by Yeltsin in 1996 and Putin in 2000 of the media not only seems possible but natural. (In this vein, the criminal prosecution of some oligarchs in 2000 may be interpreted as a reprisal for "non-co-operative" media policies.)

The control over the federal administration is in the hands of the President in Russia. Moreover, politics in this country is highly personalized. Rule of men rather than rule of law and procedure has won the day under the constitution of 1993. This is helped by the lack of laws meant to establish professional and independent public administration. In fact, during elections the whole administration, which is dependent on the President, is put at his service and works in his favor. There is a notorious lack of adequate conflict of interest legislation in Russia.

The international isolation of Russia has a different character from the isolation of Bulgaria. The latter, although temporarily cut off from western Europe by the Yugoslav crisis, is still on its way to integration within the EU and NATO. There is an enormous amount of western pressure for the improvement of government and the assurance of more transparency in public affairs. The EU integration process is a very efficient lever for the exercise of such pressure. Russia is a much more complex case. It does not feature even in the long-term plans for the expansion of the political and economic western alliances. Russia is open to the west mainly as a raw materials and resources provider. Furthermore, the policies of the West towards Russia are built on persons rather than on principles: the preservation of a particular political elite in power has been the paramount goal. No matter how justified by the conditions in the country, this strategy has not contributed to the improvement of government, the establishment of the rule of law and the general depersonalization of Russian politics. In short, in terms of standards of governance and prospects for the future, Russia is much more isolated from the West than Bulgaria, which helps to entrench local undemocratic practices, such as "clanism" and governmental favoritism.

In Russia, the longevity and, especially, the electoral success of pro-reform party formations depend almost exclusively on their relations with the presidency. (Yavlinsii's failure is instructive; although he and his party allegedly spent millions of dollars over the limits in the 1999–2000 election cycle, their performance was modest.) The longevity of opposition formations depends on their capacity to present themselves as antisystem and a radical opposition to the presidential policies (and the constitutional order). Usually, they capitalize on the "protest" vote. As a rule, the latter rely much more on their organizational potential (membership, party structures). Being successful, they receive a limited forum of expression in the Duma. (This helps to explain the "radicalization" of Russian politics in comparison to the countries of Eastern Europe.) The constitutionalized super-domination of the presidency creates a huge bias towards incumbents during presidential elections. This is especially evident in the behavior of public media, local elites, managers of state enterprises, etc. The financial disproportion between the pro-presidential and the opposition camp is much greater in presidential elections, although it exists in Duma elections, too.

Party regulation and legislation do not stimulate the parties to play a more extensive (for instance, educational) role in society outside the Duma. Public funding is guaranteed only for Duma elections and Duma activities. Only the CPRF and the LDP have claimed some extra-parliamentary activity and organizational structures, but they face severe financial problems in sustaining these claims. Legal regulation of campaign financing, although formally egalitarian, stimulates the skyrocketing of successful campaigning through vagueness and possibilities of avoidance.

Conclusion

The Bulgarian and Russian party-funding models are ripe for reform; there is extensive structural corruption, which undermines the egalitarian ideological commitments embedded in their rules and procedures. The source of structural corruption of the models is similar in the two countries: governmental favoritism. In a nutshell, the strength of the government during the prolonged transition encourages big business to form clientelistic circles around the political forces in control of the executive. The clientelistic relationships are not stable, and change dramatically with the change of government in Bulgaria and the President (and sometimes, the Prime Minister) in Russia. Superficially, the Russian "clans" have seemed more stable than the Bulgarian "circles of the PM's friends," but their structure is identical. It is this structure that creates a strong bias in terms of party funding in favor of the governmental parties in Bulgaria, and the President and his entourage in Russia.

The analysis presented in the paper is not meant to suggest that the structural corruption of the egalitarian models of party finance makes them inappropriate for the countries of Eastern Europe (Bulgaria and Russia in particular) during the transition period. The tendency of structural corruption into governmental favoritism is not a flaw that automatically renders egalitarian models inferior to libertarian ones in the context of the region. This is so because the libertarian models have nothing to offer against governmental favoritism. Even if all restrictions on expenditure and contributions are abolished, and the provision of state aid and free airtime are discontinued in Bulgaria and Russia, the problem of governmental favoritism will persist.

Thus, the major conclusion I draw is that a reform towards "libertarianization" of party funding in the discussed countries could be a waste of time. Nothing would change dramatically, and the core of the problems, governmental favoritism, would remain unaddressed. Therefore, a genuine reform must take a different, although much more difficult and unpredictable path. Three levels of reform concerns should be kept in mind:

1) *General constitutional level.* Governmental favoritism raises a broad range of separation of powers and freedom of speech issues. The over-majoritarian (or authoritarian) way of decision making in sensitive areas such as the media, interference with the work of the judiciary and the public administration, are problems manifestly present in Russia, and, in more subtle forms, in Bulgaria. No party-funding reform could be successful without first addressing these problems.[367]

2) *Party-funding rules.* Of course, reformers should look more closely into the work of the specific party-funding rules as well. In the first place, they should ask whether the level of state aid to parties and candidates is adequate, since it has been scaled down in both Bulgaria and Russia. Insufficient state aid leads to systematic abuse of rules and restrictions. Secondly, the overall expenditure limits seem to be set rather low, which inevitably encourages violations. Thirdly, the lack of contribution limits from corporate donors in Bulgaria, as well as the relatively highly set limits in Russia, raise difficult questions; in both countries corporate donations are the backbone of the party-funding system. Even if the problem of favoritism is eliminated, "corporatism" will have to be dealt with more carefully. The reformers in the two countries should think about strategies of increasing the role of small individual donations and party-mem-

bership dues. Finally, and most importantly, enforcement and transparency mechanisms should be tightened, and also the judiciary should be encouraged to interfere aggressively into "independent" expenditure problems.

3) *NGO and other forms of public control.* The reformers should attempt to institutionalize the "defense of the public interest" in matters of party funding. Organizations like Common Cause in the United States have been the driving force behind campaign finance reform in that country for the last four decades. Similar bodies could contribute tremendously to the establishment of democratic rules of government and transparency in the public sphere in both Bulgaria and Russia.

Campaign finance reforms proper seem to start at the second level, but this is just an illusion; the real difficulty is that in order to tackle successfully governmental favoritism, reforms have to start either at level one or level three.

Post-Soviet Corruption Outburst in Post-Conflict Tajikistan[368]

Tokhir Mirzoev

Background

After Tajikistan gained independence with the breakup of the Soviet Union, clan and regional rivalries, which have always been a feature of this region, became more open. The weakness of the central government led to the resignation of the President in 1992 and the creation of a short-lived coalition government, mainly controlled by Islamists. In May 1992, southern Hatlon oblast rose against the Islamists with the support of Russia and Uzbekistan. Intensive fighting between the two parties continued until the spring of 1993, when most Islamist armed groups were forced out of the country to Afghanistan. The subsequent session of Parliament and Presidential elections brought to power Imomali Rahmanov, representing the southern (Kulyab, Dangara) clan. In exile, banned Tajik parties formed the United Tajik Opposition (UTO), led by the Islamic Renaissance Party.

The civil war officially ended in June 1997 with the signing of the peace accord between the current Government and the UTO after several rounds of talks, mainly negotiated by the UN and Russia. A referendum on the Constitution and new Presidential and Parliamentary elections has been scheduled. The anniversary of Tajik independence on September 9, 1999, was celebrated together with the 1001st anniversary of the ancient "Samanids State." Many connect the celebration with the government's effort at nation building and overcoming the split arising from the civil conflict. Macroeconomic stability, sound fiscal and monetary policy, combined with price liberalization as well as a relaxed foreign trade regime after signing the peace accord, allowed for the first positive GDP growth of around 2 percent in 1997 and its increase to 5 percent in 1998. The growth was mainly driven by expansion of activities in agriculture, which employs about 60 percent of the nation's labor force, as well as trade and various services. Economic reforms at the macro-level in recent years have mainly been implemented with the technical and financial assistance of the World Bank and the IMF and have mainly focused on strengthening key institutions and changing legislation pertaining to fiscal and monetary policy as well as on privatization. First efforts to reform agriculture, education and health have been started recently.

There is still a long way to go in the transition process. Among the key goals of the transition is a comprehensive reform of the public sector, changing its functions and improving its efficiency. The latter is vital because: a) improved efficiency will allow economizing greatly in the budget; b) it will raise the effectiveness of the reforms implemented; and c) it will lead to a higher quality of public goods/services provided which is closely connected with overall economic efficiency both in the short and the long term. Inefficiencies in state institutions originate from many factors either inherited from the old system or acquired during painful transition. One of the major factors causing the government's failure to operate efficiently is corruption.

This paper tries to explain some of the causes, forms and economic consequences of corruption in Tajikistan as well as to outline several program ideas on how to fight corruption more effectively. The results presented are based on the survey "Corruption in Tajikistan as seen by the private sector."[369]

Defining Corruption

As put by Tanzi (1998): ". . . like an elephant, even though it [corruption] may be difficult to describe, it is generally not difficult to recognize when observed." There are several definitions of corruption. The most popular is the one used by the World Bank, which defines corruption as "the abuse of public office for private gain" (ADB, 1997). A more complete definition is provided by the Asian Development Bank: "Corruption involves behavior on the part of officials in the public and private sectors, in which they improperly and unlawfully enrich themselves and/or those close to them, or induce others to do so, by misusing the position in which they are placed."

Many associate corruption with bribes. Although most examples of corrupt behavior involve payments in one form or the other, not all acts of corruption involve traditional bribes. For example, a personnel department employee in a public organization may promote and support members of his tribe or native town without receiving direct payment. While some payment may come in the future in the form of services, presents or money from newly promoted staff, that is not always the case. Tanzi (1998) distinguishes several classifications of corruption: bureaucratic (or "petty") or political, i. e., corruption by bureaucracy or political leadership; cost-reducing (to the briber) and benefit-enhancing; briber-initiated and bribee-initiated; coercive or collusive; centralized and decentralized; predictable or arbitrary; involving cash payments or presents and future benefits. One could also add other classifications, such as corruption involving theft of public property or not (see Shleifer and Vyshny, 1993).

Corruption in Tajikistan
Factors, Triggering the Corruption Outburst

As in most other republics of the Soviet Union, corruption has long existed in Tajikistan in one form or another, such as cash payments, gifts, and contacts used to secure positions of power, or be admitted to a public university. Very little information is available on the scope of corruption in the Soviet times. The civil war brought the previously hidden corruption to the surface. The immediate consequences of the post-conflict situation were the promotion of new forms of corrupt behavior, such as open extortion by government militia and rent-seeking activities by armed guerrillas. The old forms became more apparent because of the weakness of the central government and of public opinion. Increased clan relations made the use of contacts more widespread. The factors behind corruption in Tajikistan include "decentralization," missing structural reforms, low wages and a poor regulatory base, poor law enforcement and slow liberalization on the micro-level.

Decentralization and weakening of the central government provided ministries in many PCE's with greater discretion over decision making. In general, the flux in many sectors of Tajikistan's economy was mostly characterized by a transition from centralized to decentralized corruption, i.e., multiple agencies take bribes where only one did before, leading to a much less efficient allocation of resources (see Box 1).[370] Many transition economies were quite successful in liberalizing economic activity at the macroeconomic level, but, as noted by Kaufmann (1997), "liberalization at micro-level (often) did not take place." Excessive taxation, unstable and complicated regulation and other constraints create a fertile ground for corruption and remain serious impediments for successful transition. Combined with decentralization in the sense described above, these constraints make the cost of operating enterprises legally extremely high. Faced with such constraint, some domestic enterprises may choose to move to the unofficial sector if the cost of operating legally is too high due to increased corruption, others may simply go bust and never start again. Johnson, et al. (1997) conclude that, in transition, the share of the unofficial economy is positively correlated with the level of corruption in the economy.[371] Those firms that decide to stay may try to bribe officials to lower effective tax payments.

Tajikistan, as other PCEs, is preoccupied with the problem of structural reforms (privatization, bank restructuring), which bring opportunities for extracting bribes. Among the reasons that contribute to a high level of corruption during structural reforms (especially at the early stages) are a lack of transparency, unclear regulations and the strong political power of former managers of state enterprises and other interested parties.

Box 1. Centralized vs. Decentralized Corruption

Private agents often have to obtain several permissions from various government offices in order to start or continue a new business operation. Shleifer and Vyshny (1993) suggest that the structure of the "market," selling such complementary government goods is very important in determining the final impact of corruption on the economy. One possibility is when government agencies collude and provide the goods jointly setting the prices and collecting bribes that are further divided between all relevant parties. In this case it takes only one payment to get things done. In the other extreme alternative each ministry and agency is a monopolist for its particular good, which is a necessary part of the total package of permissions required for project initiation, and sets prices and extracts bribes independently, each maximizing its own profits.

Let us assume that the there are two complementary government goods and two agencies providing them. The prices charged by each agency are $p1$ and $p2$, respectively. If $MC1$ and $MC2$ are marginal costs to each agency (prices set by the government), then $(p1 - MC1)$ and $(p2 - MC2)$ represent per unit bribes. Let the amounts of each good sold be $x1$ and $x2$. When the two agencies act jointly as a monopolist, they will set p1 at which: $MR1 + MR2 * (dx2/dx1) = MC1$, where MR stands for marginal revenue. When the goods are complements for the same project, then $dx2/dx1 > 0$, meaning that $MR1 < MC1$ (less then government's price). The same applies to $p2$. In other words, the monopolist would keep the price of each good low so as to ensure demand for the other good. When the agencies act independently, the latter considerations are irrelevant ($dx2/dx1 = 0$) and they set prices so that $MR1 = MC1$ and $MR2 = MC2$. Thus they hurt each other by acting independently and driving up the prices affecting total demand. As argued by Shleifer and Vyshny (1993), in a decentralized system with free entry, the total price of the package of government goods necessary for starting a project will be driven up to infinity, while the amount of packaged goods sold will approach zero. In the third scenario, "each one of the several complementary government goods can be sold by at least two government agencies." In this case various agencies will be involved in bribe competition, which will eventually drive the level of bribes to zero [assuming that collusion is difficult]. Thus, Shleifer and Vyshny (1993) conclude that: "Competition is the best; joint monopoly is the second best; and independent monopoly is worst for efficiency."

Low wages in the public sector are a common feature of most transition economies. Tajikistan has always been the poorest republic in the fSU and real wages even decreased after the civil conflict. While sometimes corruption may happen due to greed, in certain situations state employees may accept bribes due to simple need.

Poor regulations in general are more common in transition economies and lead to distortions in various sectors of the economy, making government policies and interventions less efficient.

Political instability combined with poor law enforcement, which are consequences of the civil conflict in Tajikistan create ample opportunities for extortion and warm nests for corrupt officials who will then slow transition.

Evidence of Increased Corruption and its Present Scope

When searching for evidence of a phenomenon, it is important to agree on a unit of measure. Corruption is, in general, difficult to measure. Some may prefer to evaluate the significance of corrupt behavior based on the economic losses it triggers, others develop indices based on various surveys.[372] In the present research an emphasis is placed on frequency, i. e., on how often do agents in the private sector face extortion or have to pay to resolve their problems?

Results of the "Corruption in Tajikistan as seen by the private sector" survey support the hypothesis on increased corruption in Tajikistan. An absolute majority of households agree that the use of money and presents has become more widespread today than in the Soviet period. Partly because of bad laws and a sophisticated bureaucracy and partly due to extortion attempts when trying to obey the established rules only, many in Tajikistan find it easier to use various forms of "additional instruments." As shown in Figures 1 and 2, more than half of the businesses surveyed find it either always or most of the time easier to use additional instruments to get things done, rather than to follow established rules. This figure for households is more than 70 percent, which signals real problems in the functioning of the public sector.

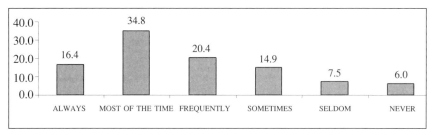

Figure 1. When Interacting with the Government Agencies, it is Easier for Firms Like mine to Use "Additional Channels" to Get Things Done Rather than to Follow Established Rules (Percent)

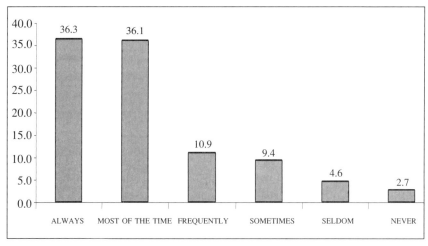

Figure 2. When Approaching Government Officials it is Easier for People to Use "Additional Channels" to Get Things Done Rather than to Follow Established Rules (Percent)

In the survey, businesses and households rated corruption as one of the most problematic factors for doing business/living and working in

Tajikistan among a set of nineteen factors. Surprisingly, despite post-conflict instability in the country, corruption was ranked by households as more problematic than political instability and equally with organized crime. That suggests that corruption is becoming more and more significant and the country is in danger of getting into a trap where development is simply blocked by inefficiency of the public sector caused by the corrupt behavior of civil servants.

Corruption in Tajikistan: Breakdown by Sector

Generally, corruption happens in the public sector. As noted by Lui (1996), ". . . if the resource allocation system is perfectly competitive, then corruption cannot exist . . . Deviations from the competitive market, caused by government regulations or interference is a major cause of corruption." Markets can never be perfectly competitive, however. A need for public goods, the presence of externalities in production activities and information deficiencies justify the existence of the public sector. The state plays its corrective role using the following tools: public spending for government consumption and transfers; taxation and public borrowing; various forms of regulations (including patents, permits, licenses, etc. in e. g., foreign trade, banking, foreign exchange, and other operations); lending activities and provision of some public goods, and other activities, which are less occasional and include privatization, nationalization and so forth.

Using the same principle of taking the frequency of acts of corruption as a measure, we aimed to find out the relative corruptness of various segments of the public sector. As table 1 shows, both businesses and households agree, in general, on the most popular situations where the use of money, presents, contacts or threats takes place. They are border crossing at customs, education and health institutions, as well as contacts with road police, obtaining export/import licenses, and tax and financial inspections. It is interesting to observe such situations as access to foreign exchange, public procurement and privatization rated relatively low—an indication of the government's progress in liberalizing activities at macro-level. Tax and customs authorities together with health and education facilities, all form the top five situations where corruption occurs most often.

Table 1. How likely is the Use of Money, Presents, Contacts or Threats (Corruption) to Occur in the Following Situations? *(1—Never, 2—Seldom, 3—Sometimes, 4—Frequently, 5—Often, 6—Always)*, Average Ratings

AVERAGE RATE	BUSINESSES	RANK	HOUSEHOLDS	AVERAGE GATE
4.79	Border crossing at customs	1	High schools, universities	5.03
4.76	High schools, universities	2	Health care institutions	4.98
4.66	Contact with road police	3	Border crossing at customs	4.84
4.61	Health care institutions	4	Export and import permits/licenses	4.53
4.29	Tax and financial inspections	5	Tax and financial inspections	4.39
3.90	Export and import permits/licenses	6	Property registration	4.36
3.81	State banking services	7	Contact with road police	4.36
3.51	Property registration	8	Privatization	4.34
3.39	Leases of state-owned real estate	9	Leases of state-owned real estate	4.28
3.38	Enterprise registration	10	State banking services	4.22
3.37	Privatization	11	Phone line installation	3.95
3.21	Phone line installation	12	Enterprise registration	3.93
3.07	Fire and sanitary inspections	13	Water and electricity services	3.88
2.85	Weights and measures inspections	14	Public procurement	3.87
2.79	Water and electricity services	15	Weights and measures inspections	3.72
2.78	Public procurement	16	Fire and sanitary inspections	3.45
2.50	Access to foreign exchange	17	Access to foreign exchange	3.41

It is plausible to hypothesize that corruption in tax/customs authorities has the greatest impact—at least in the short and medium term— on the fiscal deficit, GDP growth and macrostability overall. Uncollected taxes and customs fees that go into private pockets are a serious cause of fiscal deficits. On the other hand, extortion by inspectors and customs officers cuts the incentive to start new business operations or continue those started, having a direct impact on growth and speed of transition. Given the figures in table 1, reducing corruption in tax/customs services should be a top priority for reform.

The use of money, presents and the like in health and education institutions is subject to debate. In the Soviet era, when the provision of health and education services was more or less homogeneous across the country, corruption was much less observed. Today there is a "semi-market" system where assets still belong to the state, but public servants are free—at least in reality, due to the absence of any control or punishment—to charge for the services provided. One could argue that the use of payments for social services is a reflection of a need for privatization (or partial commercialization) of health and education. Since the government is no longer able to afford to subsidize these sectors, they have to become financially sustainable. Accepting money allows medical and educational institutions to survive in the absence of budgetary transfers. Since these payments are forbidden by law, they are legally considered as corruption. A natural remedy to the problem is to legalize commercial activities in these sectors. Another argument is based on the low level of wages in health and education. While the general level of wages in Tajikistan is fairly low, the salaries of teachers and medical doctors are almost three times lower than those in tax customs authorities and the police, the latter three having the highest salaries within the public sector. Thus, one may assume that most of corruption in the social sectors occurs due to need, while tax/customs and police officers have greed as a driving force.

One should exercise caution, however, before making a conclusion about the non-negative nature of corruption in health and education. Such a state of affairs may prevent the creation of private entities in these sectors. The reason is that de-facto commercial public hospitals pay no taxes (such as a normal clinic would pay) or any other form of rent for utilization of state assets, and are in a much more competitive position. Further harm from corruption in social services is in the limited access left to the primary target group—the poor (a rational profit-maximizing official is likely to first serve those who can pay and leave little time for the people with low purchasing power). Hence some of the corruption in health and education distorts the system and should definitely be fought, whilst additional measures are needed in order to curb greed where the use of money is unavoidable.

Factors Promoting Corruption

Besides the general features of the present system in Tajikistan, there are various factors that directly or indirectly promote corrupt behavior. In most cases they are closely linked to the structure of the public sector and sometimes can be eliminated or minimized through thoughtful government intervention. In principle, each area of government involvement contains something that the private sector might be interested in buying: government contracts (procurement, privatization, etc.), government benefits (transfers, privileged positions in the market, cheap credits, monopolistic positions through licenses, permits, etc.), public revenues (to avoid taxation or to reduce the amount to be paid), time (so-called "speed" money), changes in legal and regulatory provisions, positions in the government and so on. The existence of the public sector itself is not, however, a complete explanation of why corruption occurs. Many countries, such as Finland, the Netherlands, Sweden, Denmark and Canada, where the size of the public sector is among the largest in the world, are much less corrupt than many "more market-oriented" economies of Africa and Asia (Tanzi, 1998). The latter suggests that it is not the mere presence or size of the public sector, but the way it operates that largely determines the level of corruption in any given country. Thus, it is useful to take a closer look at the conditions that may or may not lead to corruption when various functions are performed by the state.

Issuing permits and authorizations. In many countries, permits, licenses and authorizations of one sort or another are needed to carry out certain activities (import/export, foreign exchange deals, driving, water/sanitation requirements, operations with land, international passports, etc.). These regulations secure a monopoly for the officers who have discretion over issuing authorizations and/or carrying out inspections. Table 1 shows that the use of money and gifts occurs frequently when obtaining export and import licenses. It is thus interesting to take a look at the conditions under which the existence of permits can result in corruption.

In many societies permits are issued only by a single office (or even a person). That is, there is no competition in the granting of these authorizations. Such a monopoly gives bureaucrats great power and opportunity to extract bribes. An example of a monopoly in granting permits is the Mayor's office in Dushanbe, which has to issue a permit for every citizen applying for a foreign passport to leave the country. Since the capacity of the issuing agency is limited and the number of applicants is large, paying extra is perceived to be a normal component of the fee.

The ability to extract bribes also depends on the degree of discretion that each potential bribee has and on his/her ability to deliver certain services in exchange. In cases where decisions are made collectively by several agents and discretion is limited, the cost of bribing is much higher and corruption is less likely to occur.[373]

The existence of regulations requires frequent contacts between managers and officials, taking a lot of the managers' time away from running their enterprises. According to Kaufmann (1997), in 1995 Ukrainian managers may have spent about 30 percent of their working hours with government officials, and up to 40 percent in 1996. It is obvious that many would prefer to save this time by paying bribes.[374] In our survey most businesses stated that they do not spend too much time with government officials. However, more than half of them spend over 10 percent of their sales to bribe corrupt tax/customs officials—an indication of successful "speeding."

Sometimes the price of certain permits may be so high that the private sector may find it more appealing to bribe officials to obtain authorizations at a lower price. Examples may include driving licenses, passports and export–import licenses. Buying the latter is even more attractive since it helps companies gain a better competitive position in the market. In this case it is not only the high price, but also the inefficient accounting system that promotes corruption. A lower price involves a simple theft of public property. Some other factors, including cultural particularities, low wages, punishment costs and control, that contribute indirectly to the corruption in all governments' activities, are discussed in further detail.

Low wages in the public sector. Many explanations of why corruption happens in certain countries (including Tajikistan) and sectors point to the low-wage problem. In many developing countries governments intentionally keep wages low in those sectors where officials are assumed to have additional sources of income (e.g., tax or customs authorities or police). Ul Haque and Sahay (1996) describe the relationship between wages and level of corruption as in figure 1 (see also Tanzi, 1998). Using cross-sectional data, Ul Haque and Sahay (1996) find statistically significant correlation between wage level and corruption. Curve CC in Figure 3 shows equilibrium levels of corruption corresponding to various sizes of wages in the public sector, when real wages are low.

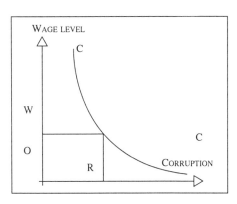

Figure 3. Corruption and Wage Levels

Tanzi (1998) drives a wedge between corruption due to need and due to greed. In the Figure, the current level of wages (OW) corresponds to the 'natural' level of corruption that is due to need, while anything beyond OR would be due to greed. A natural solution to the problem—if that were the case—would be to raise salaries of state employees (actually applied in Argentina and Peru). Ul Haque and Sahay (1996) argue that the measure need not be efficient. While the number of acts of corruption may decrease, the size of bribes may increase so that the total level of bribes paid remains unchanged. Moreover, it is not guaranteed that officials who accepted bribes prior to the salary increase will not be tempted to maximize their revenues afterwards. In Tajikistan, as in many other developing countries, revenues from bribes often by far exceeds the official salary and only a very significant increase can be of some help.

Taxation system. According to Tanzi (1998), corruption may be a major problem in tax administration and authorities when: " . . .the laws are difficult to understand and can be interpreted differently so that tax payers need assistance in complying with them; the payment of taxes requires frequent contacts between tax administrators and tax payers; the wages of tax administration are low; acts of corruption on the part of tax administrators are ignored, not easily discovered, or when discovered, are penalized only mildly; the administrative procedures (e.g. criteria for selecting companies for audits) lack transparency and are not closely monitored within tax or customs administrations; tax administrators have discretion over important decisions, such as those related to the provision of tax incentives, determination of tax liabilities, selection of audits, litigation, and so on; and more broadly, when state (the principal) control of the agents responsible for carrying out its functions is weak." On the contrary, taxes that are based on clear and transparent rules, not requiring frequent contacts between taxpayers and inspectors, are much less likely to lead to corrupt behavior.

To the list above, one can also add excessively high taxes, which make it profitable for most businesses to pay in cash to inspectors to avoid full payment. The latter is probably the case in Tajikistan (Figure 4). Besides, most businesses either always, or most of the time, expect tax inspectors to ask for additional payment to ease the process of inspection (see Figure 5). Most businesses simply find it too costly to refuse to pay when asked, since the inspection may become more lengthy and detailed (see Figure 6). An absolute majority of the businesses are likely to pay when dealing with tax inspectors or government officials in general (Figures 7).

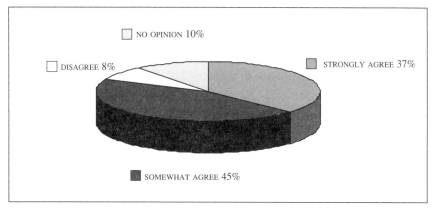

Figure 4. Taxes Levied on Business Activities in my Industry are so High that Most Businesses Prefer to Pay in Cash to Tax Inspectors to Avoid Full Tax Payments

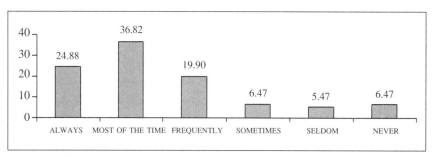

Figure 5. When Being Inspected by Tax/Customs Authorities, it is Likely that you Will be Asked for an Additional Payment to "Ease" the Inspection Process and/or Avoid Bureaucracy? (Percent)

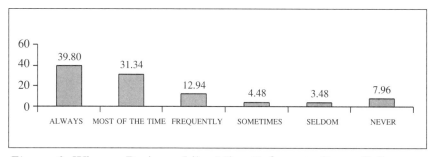

Figure 6. When a Business Like Mine Refuses to Pay a Bribe to a Tax/Customs Inspector and/or Reports the Extortion Attempt, it will Find it Even More Problematic to Go through the Inspection (Percent)

Figure 7. When Asked by a Government Official to Pay Some Extra to "Ease" the Process, is your Company Likely to Pay?

During the interview process many managers expressed their dissatisfaction with the lack of transparency in tax and customs authorities. Many do not even know about the exact rates of taxes and fees stipulated by law and operate on the basis of what inspectors are demanding. It is also not easy to find any documentation stating the exact amount of the various fees levied by both central and local governments. Some companies in Dushanbe were required to pay more than stipulated by law, and, after the "mistake" had been discovered, no reimbursement was provided. The bargaining power of inspectors is further strengthened by the importance of social capital and high personalization of relations in Tajikistan. Many managers are simply afraid to argue with tax/customs officials because of a fear of losing established connections and good relations with inspectors which usually results in unnecessary problems in future. Cultural factors such as social capital and public opinion are discussed below.

Cultural factors. Professor Prakash Reddy, a social anthropologist who spent a month in a Danish village studying the behavior of its inhabitants, was surprised to observe distant relations between neighbors and even members of the family. In an Indian village of a comparable size daily house visits would be common and everyone would be interested in the business of others (Tanzi, 1995). In communities with close family ties the idea of treating friends and relatives distantly would seem just immoral and strange. In such cultural environments the concept of "social capital," as used by Coleman (1990), is very important. Coleman criticizes the economic theory of perfect competition in that "individuals do not act independently" and that "personal relations and networks of relations" are important to achieve personal goals. He considers these relations and networks as a capital asset for an individual, a kind of personal social capital. Tanzi (1995) further develops this idea, noting the asset nature of social capital. "It is in essence a summation of 'I owe yous' that the individual has accumulates *vis-à-vis* others. Some of these may come from the family background, some developed at school or at work, some from past favors and so forth." However, social capital also implies certain liabilities: "While the individual can use this [social] capital to ask others to do things for him, others can draw from their social capital to ask him to perform tasks or to do other things for them. One could distinguish a gross from a net concept of social capital" (see Tanzi, 1995, pp.165–166). Using contacts is the most popular and effective instrument in influencing officials in Tajikistan (Figures 8 and 9).

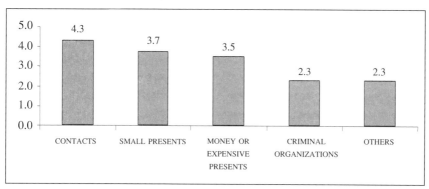

Figure 8. "Additional Means (to Influence Officials) are Most Likely to Take the Form of . . ." *(1— never, 6—always, averages),* Business

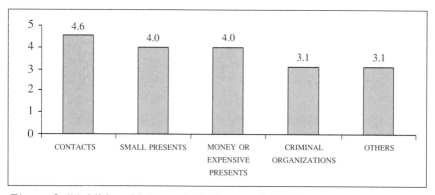

Figure 9. "Additional Means (to Influence Officials) are Most Likely to Take the Form of . . ." *(1— never, 6— always, averages),* Households

In many countries the importance of social capital can be even greater than other personal assets, such as money, education or experience, which naturally leads to higher levels of corruption, where bribes take the form of exchange of services with transactions often delayed in time.

Moreover, in such communities—Tajikistan is definitely one of them—the cost of reporting acts of corruption might be too high (reflected in the loss of social capital, i.e. lost friends, connections) securing a fertile ground for further corruption.

Another factor conductive to corruption is the public attitude towards it. Today many simply cannot imagine any activity without bribing someone and thus do not resist extortion. Figure 7 showed that most businesses are likely to pay extra when asked. Moreover, 61 percent of business managers believe that a possibility to pay to avoid unnecessary difficulties is helpful (see Figure 10), although an absolute majority of both businesses and households told us that corruption is bad for the country and for the people and should be prevented. Thus, although many would dislike corruption, very few are willing to resist it and many get along well with the present state of affairs, which creates favorable conditions for further extraction of bribes.

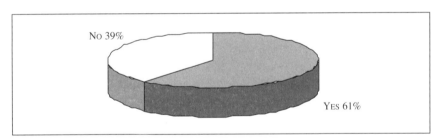

Figure 10. Do you Think that a Possibility "to Pay to Avoid Difficulties" Makes Life for a Business Like yours Easier, Despite the Probability of Being Caught and Punished?

Penalty and control systems. According to Becker (1968), the probability of a crime depends on the probability of being punished and the cost of punishment, given the probability of being caught. In countries where law enforcement is weak and punishment is unlikely or too mild, corruption is usually more widespread. Moreover, sometimes too sophisticated legislation impedes the quick application of penalties (too many requirements to prove that one is guilty). Control within institutions is also very important as a first defense line in the anticorruption combat. Efficient supervisors, good audit practice and sound and transparent accounting practice are often cited as factors that may prevent corruption from happening in many situations. In post-conflict situations, law enforcement is usually weak and many officials rely on the support of armed groups. A low probability of being caught and punished makes accepting bribes and extortions a very profitable occupation. As shown in Figures 11, 12 and 13, the latter factor is cited as the most probable reason of why tax and customs inspectors as well as employees in health and education facilities accept money and presents. Clan relations and the use of social capital are more widespread in tax and customs authorities than in social sectors, while poorly designed laws are a problem in both sectors. In support of our hypothesis about corruption due to greed and due to need in various sectors and households, confirming that medical and educational staff accept bribes due rather to low salaries than due to greediness. Businesses, on the other hand, rated these two almost equally.

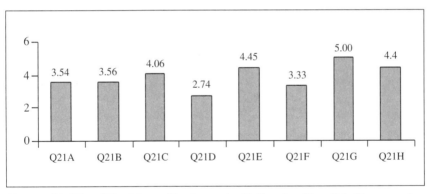

Figure 11. How Would you Evaluate the Following Possible Reasons for Why Tax/Customs Inspectors Take Money or Presents? *(1— not at all, 6— totally)*, Average Ratings. QA = They are too greedy, QB = Government does not pay them adequately, QC = Laws/rules are so poorly designed and difficult to follow that it is easier to pay to get things done, QD = This is a cultural tradition: people are used to taking money/presents, QE = Clan relations, QF = They have too much discretionary power, QG = Control over them is weak and punishment is unlikely, QH = Other

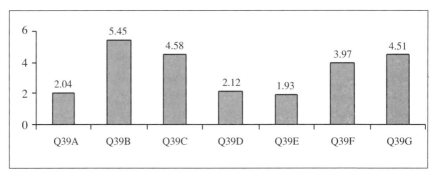

Figure 12. How Would you Evaluate the Following Possible Reasons for Why Doctors and Medical Staff Take Money or Presents? *(1— not at all, 6— totally)*, Average Ratings

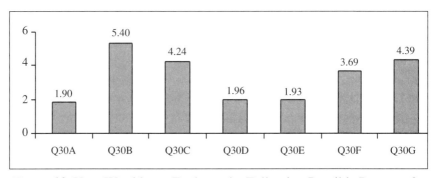

Figure 13. How Would you Evaluate the Following Possible Reasons for Why School Teachers/University Professors Take Money or Presents? *(1 – not at all, 6 – totally)*, Average Ratings

Forms of Corruption Prevailing in Tajikistan

When officials behave in a corrupt manner, most often they do so under the temptation to receive money or presents, delivering services to related parties or under threats from influential solicitors (criminal organizations). Among these tools and in support of our previous hypothesis about the decreased importance of political instability and of organized crime, households and businesses stated that the use of criminal organizations to influence decisions in government agencies takes place relatively seldom (see figures 8 and 9). The most frequently applied "additional instrument" is the use of contacts (friends, relatives or third parties), which largely reflects traditional values of the society that is predominant in Tajikistan. Many think of Central Asia as a region with strong traditions and cultural ties, where money is of little importance compared to observing customs. That is not true in many regions of the country, especially in major cities. Painful transition experience, rapid decrease in income, widespread poverty and the values that the capital accumulation phase of transition to market economy carries raised the importance of money for people in general and the younger generation in particular. As illustrated in figures 8 and 9, the use of presents and money happens quite often, although not as much as the use of contacts.

Corrupt behavior may take various forms. It is crucial to know the shapes it takes to have an efficient reform program in any given sector. Based on the survey results and numerous informal interviews conducted during the research period, we have found a set of ways through which corrupt behavior makes itself visible in tax and customs as well as health/education facilities.

Tax and Customs Services

Corruption in tax and customs authorities in Tajikistan takes various forms. Often inspectors extract bribes from businesses during the inspection to "ease" the inspection. The offer is usually made before starting the inspection and is more often made by inspectors themselves (see figure 5). Sometimes these types of offers are accompanied by a threat to create difficulties in the future. Also, the tax legislation in Tajikistan is not widely known, even by entrepreneurs. Officials can sometimes play on that and fool managers to extract payments. Such cheating more often occurs with small-scale firms.

Often inspectors in Tajikistan have enough authority to decide whether to inspect a subject or not and how detailed the inspection should be. Knowing this, businesses may offer, and/or officials may demand to enter into a sort of "agreement" when businesses pay a certain amount "to build good relations with inspectors to avoid difficulties." These payments may either occur in a single case or on a regular basis. We were told by an entrepreneur in Dushanbe that many clothes shops in the center of the capital prepare small bags with "presents" for tax inspectors. The presents may include food or other items and are collected daily or weekly.

Inspectors sometimes assist entrepreneurs in reporting lower figures on sales or hide illegal activities, which, again, implies sharing uncollected taxes.

When a violation of the rules is found by inspectors, it is considered an excellent opportunity to receive payment (see Figure 14). The size of these payments varies depending on how serious the violation has been. Further development of the situation usually follows one of two paths. Inspectors, who have found the violation, may receive payment and agree to let the entrepreneur correct his/her mistake. The other option, which has become more widespread recently, as we heard from entrepreneurs, is a joint extraction of a larger bribe by the inspector and a higher-level officer in the tax police/department. What happens is that the inspector does not agree to accept the payment and reports the case to a higher-level officer, providing him an opportunity to earn as well. The latter then negotiates with the entrepreneur to receive a larger bribe and pays a part of it to the inspectors for a job well done .

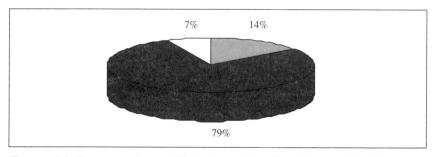

Figure 14. Encountering a Violation of the Tax Code, a Tax/Customs Inspector is Likely to:■ Report the Findings and Proceed in Accordance with the Rules, ■ Name the Price for "Correcting" the Violation, ▢ Other

Issuing authorizations and other permits required for starting new operations are often accompanied by a bribe to officials in local tax departments or the tax committee. Payment to the local committees are often made to speed up the process of granting a license/permit, while larger bribes are paid to the tax committee when a license is required for an illegal activity of one sort or another.

It is well known that in Tajikistan, as in most comparable countries, high-level officials in the tax authorities are among the richest people despite a relatively low salary. There are several ways the money is earned and some were described earlier. Sometimes businesses prefer not to deal with inspectors but to enter into contracts with their bosses—heads of tax departments or higher officials in the tax committee—to secure themselves. In this case inspectors are instructed not to inspect or to be mild during the inspection of the companies concerned. This form of corruption usually involves larger bribes.

The so-called "corruption ladder" also seems to work well in the tax authorities. Positions in tax administration are considered as the most profitable in terms of the potential to generate revenue. Thus, many are willing to pay to get this type of job. Payments are made not only when the employment decision is being made, but also afterwards on a regular basis. Promotion along the service ladder means a higher position on the "corruption ladder," and higher revenues, which has its price. We were told by many entrepreneurs that the structure of the tax authorities in Tajikistan is extremely hierarchical, so that higher officials exercise complete authority over their subordinates. This might be attributed to the higher than usual risk among top officials of losing their positions in these institutions.

Not all positions in the tax authorities are necessarily bought, however. Quite frequently social factors influence hiring decisions. Employing friends, relatives, etc. is very widespread in Tajikistan and is caused by social factors and by a need to have reliable assistants in hiding corruption more effectively.

There are companies in Tajikistan that pay fees or belong to criminal organizations or local field commanders. Many of the latter are very powerful and can directly influence decisions in government agencies. These companies are usually put in a privileged position compared to other firms, and this creates market distortions. These companies enjoy less frequent— or no—tax inspections, lower taxation, easy access to most permits/licenses and quick resolution of their problems in government offices. In the above-mentioned situations, payments by businesses is made in the form of money or, depending on the profile of the company in question, food, clothes for officials and their relatives, equipment for apartments, and they may, in principle, include anything that an official might need.

The forms corruption takes in Tajikistan's customs authorities are quite widespread across the developing world and include: harassment by customs inspectors at border crossings or at the airport. Tajik businesses believe that this is the most popular place where corruption is experienced (see Table 1). Inspectors demand money (without any justification), threatening to delay the inspection and/or create difficulties. Delaying inspections at the border can sometimes last for days and the entrepreneur has to pay the rent while the cargo is at the customs warehouse, not speaking of lost time. Often inspection of cargo is made only selectively, and thus some are willing to pay to avoid going through this lengthy process. Inspectors may accept bribes to oversee the transportation of illegal items (e.g. drugs or arms). It is widely known in Tajikistan that many new cars that appear on the roads in the capital were obtained in exchange for drugs in Russia and the other neighboring countries. Ironically, prices for cars in Dushanbe dropped in spring–summer 1999 as a result of a large supply of cheap cars. Customs officers often deceive entrepreneurs by asking more than stipulated by law since regulations and the precise amounts of duty are not well known. Bribes are often paid when receiving export/import licenses (see table 1), showing the inefficiency of the existing bureaucracy.

Almost all other forms described for tax authorities and including buying positions (positions in the customs are even more lucrative), hiring relatives and friends, providing privileges for companies that pay higher officials or pay/belong to influential commanders, the structure of the "corruption ladder," etc. are also valid in the case of the customs administration.

Health and Education Facilities

The use of payments of one sort or another in public schools and hospitals is a highly controversial issue. The government of Tajikistan, on one hand, is dedicated to build a socially oriented market economy (often heard in the speeches of top government officials), which means a guaranteed presence of the state in the provision of social services to protect poor and vulnerable groups of the population. The consequences of the war and the strained budget situation, on the other hand, will not allow (at least in the medium-term) these sectors to be brought to an adequate level—salaries are among the lowest in the country, the technical base depreciates rapidly, etc. Faced with this situation, many employees in public hospitals and schools/universities charge for their services to sustain themselves and their institutions. While in some sense the phenomenon is positive and allows these sectors to survive and to keep well-trained specialists from leaving the industry,[375] the primary target group (the poor) often suffers from being unable to use these services. The deteriorating quality of health care and education services was stated to be one of the most problematic factors for living and working in Tajikistan and corruption in these institutions occurs very often (see table 1). This part of the paper tries to describe various forms of corruption in the health and education sectors to offer some debate on how to deal with them more successfully.

High schools. When sending a child to a public secondary school in Tajikistan, parents may expect many additional expenses down the road. Payments may take various forms and can be either offered by parents themselves or required by the schools (see Figure 15). Most often, payment is asked for the reconstruction of the building, although other forms mentioned in the figure also appear quite often. When the school asks for payment, many find it difficult to refuse it since this may cause problems in academic achievement (see Figure 16). Payments, presents and contacts are also useful when accommodating a child to a better school, in order to build good relations with teachers, to have the teachers pay enough attention to the child at school, and to ensure the child's better grades regardless of his/her knowledge (Figure 17). Often parents have to hire private tutors for their children due to an insufficient quality of education in many public schools. Private tutors are mostly needed to prepare pupils for entrance examinations in colleges/universities or to simply ensure a better education for the child. Sometimes, teachers from the same school offer themselves as private tutors. If it works then teachers are much better off by providing poor education in class to generate revenues as private tutors.

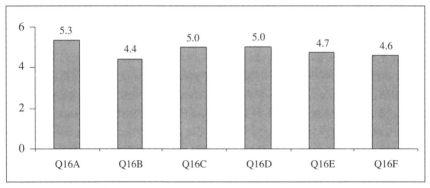

Figure 15. Additional Expenses are Most Likely to Take the Form of . . . *(1— never, 6— always)*, Average Ratings. Q16A = Extra payments for reconstructing of the school building, Q16B = Extra payments for accommodating children in the so-called "special cases," Q16C = Payments for festivities and other holidays held by the school, Q16D = Paying to buy textbooks recommended by the school, Q16E = Payments for new "prestigious" courses introduced by the school, Q16F = Direct payments/presents to teachers or directors to express "gratitude" and/or to build good relations

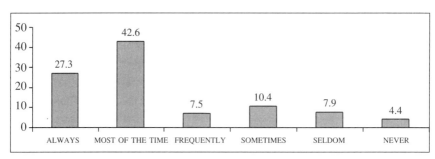

Figure 16. Refusal to Pay Additional Payments When Asked by a School Will be Negatively Reflected in a Child's Grades and in his/her Relations with the School Administration and Teachers (Percent)

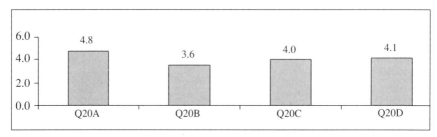

Figure 17. Please Evaluate How Likely is the Use of Money, Presents and Contacts to Occur in the Following Situations *(1— never, 6— always)*, Average Ratings. Q20A = In transfering a child to a better secondary school, Q20B = To ensure a child's better grades regardless of his/her knowledge, Q20C = To ensure that the child gets enough attention from the teacher, especially when the class is large, Q20D = To build good relations with teachers/directors in order to avoid possible unnecessary problems

Colleges and universities. The use of money, presents, contacts, etc. in public universities usually occurs in two situations: when entering a university and in the course of studies. When entering a public university students have to pass entrance examinations. This is probably the most profitable season for those employed in the admission service or for the professors who can influence admission decisions. About half of the households surveyed believe that the use of money, etc. always takes place during entrance examination, with another 30 percent stating that it happens most of the time (Figure 18). Corrupt professors frequently offer to facilitate admission and more than 80 percent of respondents are willing to pay (see Figures 19 and 20). Such willingness may be a result of poor chances of being accepted without paying extra. These figures can either be explained by the deteriorating quality of education or the total corruptness of the system.

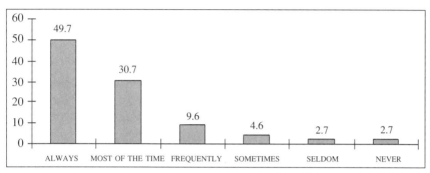

Figure 18. When Entering a University in Tajikistan, How Likely is the use of Money, Presents, Contacts or the Services of Criminal Elements to Influence the Decision of the Admission Service? (Percent)

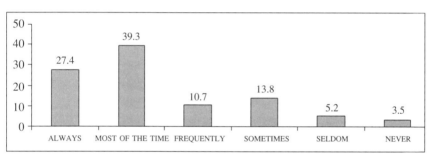

Figure 19. When Applying to a University, is it Likely that you Will be Asked (Informally) to Pay Extra to the University Staff to "Ease" the Passing of the Entrance Examinations? (Percent)

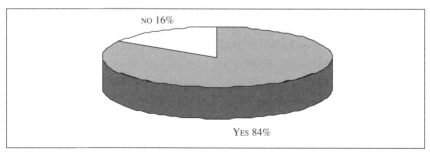

Figure 20. When Asked to Pay Extra to "Ease" Admission, are People Like you Likely to Pay?

Quite frequently the exact price of admission is widely known and even applicants with excellent knowledge may experience difficulties with admission unless some other ways are used.

Passing semester tests/examinations in the course of study in universities often involves payments of various sorts. When the student's knowledge is not adequate, exams can be passed with a moderate "facilitation." Often professors themselves offer such deals. In general, both students and professors might proffer deals during examination periods in universities with equal probability, but a student's refusal to pay, when asked by a professor could have negative consequences. Overall, more than 50 percent of respondents stated that they had been expected to pay money in public schools and universities (see Figure 21).

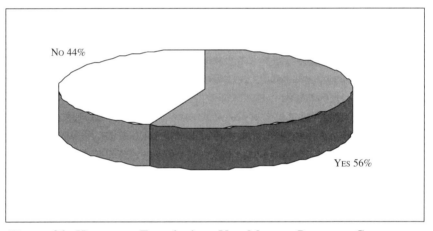

Figure 21. Have you Ever had to Use Money, Presents, Contacts or Threats to Influence Decisions in Schools/Universities?

Health-care facilities. More than 70 percent of the households surveyed believe that they will be asked to pay when requesting medical services that should be provided for free (Figure 22). Payment is often asked for when a patient has medicine prescribed (that should be provided by the hospital), when requesting surgery or other services in public hospitals, when preferring to be treated by a more experienced doctor within the hospital and when trying to avoid long lines, etc. (Figure 23).

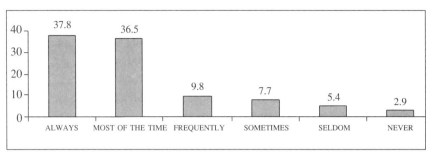

Figure 22. How Likely is it that a Person Like you Will be Asked to Pay When Asking a Doctor for a Service that Should be Provided Free? (Percent)

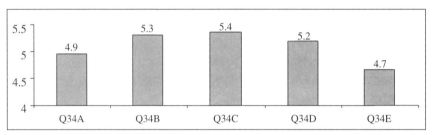

Figure 23. How Likely is the Use of Money, Presents or Contacts to Occur in the Following Situations? *(1— never, 6— always)*, Average Ratings. Q34A = When seeking a bed in a hospital and/or a better room for a hospitalized patient, Q34B = When requesting surgery or any other service that should not have been paid for, Q34C 7 = When requesting medicine for a patient even though it should be provided by the hospital, Q34D = When asking to be treated by a more experienced physician in the hospital, Q34E = When trying to avoid a long waiting time before consultation with a specialist

Another form of corruption widespread in the health care system in Tajikistan is buying positions, largely caused by the fact that the sector is in transition and has a long way to go before its reform is completed. This "semi-market" system, where doctors can freely accept or demand payments from patients, but use state-owned health care facilities and are appointed from the center, is attractive for both doctors and the senior administration in the system. The attractiveness for doctors lies in the fact that, when operating on a commercial basis using state-owned assets, they do not have to pay extra taxes such as a normal private clinic would pay. Thus, appointments to positions in a public hospital can sometimes provide excellent opportunities for revenue generation, especially those connected with surgery, international aid and the like. In an environment where competition in the labor market is intense—the state medical universities train far more doctors than are needed in the country—many are willing to pay to obtain a lucrative position in a hospital and/or to avoid losing it.

Concluding Remarks

This paper represents the first effort to systematize our knowledge about the outburst of corruption in post-conflict Tajikistan. Specific features of Tajikistan, such as the post-conflict situation, the slow transition towards market economy, deep-set cultural factors, low wages in the public sector, a poor regulatory environment and law enforcement, make it especially vulnerable to corruption.

The survey entitled "Corruption in Tajikistan as seen by the private sector," involving 201 business enterprises and 521 households throughout the country, provides some sense of the scope and causes of the problem in Tajikistan in general and, more deeply, in the four selected areas: tax and customs services, health and education institutions. Both businesses and households ranked corruption as the fifth most problematic factor for doing business/living and working in Tajikistan. Most often corruption happens at border crossings at customs, in the education and health sectors, when obtaining licenses for export/import activities, while in contact with road police and during tax and financial inspections.

Corruption in general diminishes the roles performed by the state. Corrupt behavior in the tax and customs authorities raises the cost of doing business legally, impedes private sector development, worsens tax collection indicators and leads to distortion of the market mechanism. When met in the health and education sectors, it makes living and working conditions more difficult, and, as the survey revealed, decreased the quality of health and education services, being the most problematic factors for households in Tajikistan.

It is crucial to realize the following about corruption in Tajikistan: it is not possible to eliminate the problem completely, given that some factors are simply too dominant. Thus, one should not be too ambitious, and should aim at minimizing the scope for corrupt behavior whenever possible. Efforts to combat corruption should be systematic and require a strong, true and long-term commitment on the government's side. The most important thing is to realize that fighting corruption calls for a long-term strategy with a great deal of technical work, aimed at improving the system, thereby making corruption less likely to happen. Experience worldwide shows that highly emotional hunting and punishment of individual bribers never helps, or may even worsen, prospects for reducing corruption.

It is obvious that a strategy to combat corruption is too costly for the government of Tajikistan or it is not within the technical capacities of the government to implement. Thus, broad financial and especially technical, assistance from the international community is the key to ensure progress in the area of improving governance. Only joint efforts of the government and the donors can result in reducing corruption and increasing efficiency in the country's economy.

AFTERWORD

The leitmotif of this handbook has been skepticism—skepticism about prevailing definitions of corruption, about the rumored incidence of corruption in transition countries, about the real uses and actual effects of anticorruption campaigns, about the scandal industry and about the international role in characterizations of entire countries as corrupt. With such skepticism, we have tried to offer a counterbalance to what may be regarded as a certain external prejudice and a certain misguided reformist enthusiasm on the question of corruption. If nothing else, our perspective might enliven the larger debate, which has been dominated by enthusiasm rather than skepticism. Our goal has not been to deny the existence of corruption in transition countries, or to exaggerate the corruption in Western countries, thereby suggesting some false equivalence or relativism.

Skepticism may seem like a defensive reaction, and perhaps it is, in part. Analysts of the economic success of Asia, however, are well aware that whatever the intentions of the IMF and other multinational agencies, their anticorruption crusades had the effect of achieving the long-sought, elusive goal of enabling U.S. firms to penetrate protected Asian markets.[376] In that vein it is also perhaps telling that the member states of the European Union became preoccupied with corruption in accession countries, so that anticorruption efforts became a benchmark criterion for accession. As demonstrated in OECD efforts (including the 1997 Paris Agreement), businesses oriented to foreign markets behave as a lobby, and from their collective perspective "corruption" networks are trade barriers. Corruption is described as a "threat" to both the country targeted for trade and to the "global economy," as if there were a complete confluence of interests rather than, at least, a partial conflict between them. Differentiating the interests at play, showing their operation and clashes and untangling the politics of both corruption and anticorruption, are prerequisites for effective measures to promote good government, economic performance, and the general welfare.

"Corruption is basically a political issue," writes the Bulgarian analyst Ivan Krastev. "It has to do with the nature of the 'political'. National anticorruption campaigns and the debate that they provoke are forms of redefining and renegotiating the borders between public and private."[377] Ultimately, the battles over corruption are, in no small measure, battles over market-centered definitions and public-interest-centered definitions. Such is the theme explored in this volume's afterword. We offer no conclusion. The debate goes on.

Liberalism, Geopolitics, Social Justice
Stephen Kotkin

> It would be impossible for an historian to write a history of polit-
> ical corruption in the United States. What he could write is the
> history of the exposure of corruption.
>
> *Walter Lippmann, Vanity Fair, 1930*

> Campaigns against corruption are hardly new. But this decade
> [1990s] is the first to witness the emergence of corruption as a
> truly global political issue . . .
>
> *Corruption and the Global Economy, 1997*

More than $1.3 trillion was spent in the U.S. on health care in 2000, com-
prising almost one-seventh of GDP. Government regulators in the mid-
1990s admitted that at least 10 percent of health care expenditures were
dubious or patently illegal. Independent experts estimate the cheating at
twice, or even thrice that amount, further noting that health care fraud is
very difficult to prove and expensive to combat: bogus medical bills often
look perfectly legitimate because they are backed by professionally falsified medical records. Also, claims reporting is done using automated
electronic submission, which perversely acts not to stem cheating but as
an instant and reliable test on the feasibility of getting away with specific kinds of fraud—"bill your lies correctly," is the motto. Even for otherwise law-abiding citizens, government programs and insurance companies are seen as "acceptable" targets for overcharging, and neither Health
Maintenance Organizations nor special investigative units have curbed
the ingenious array of fraudulent and illegal practices.[378] Here is corruption on a mass scale.

In the second half of the 1990s and through 2000, prosecutions for
health care over-billing significantly increased, resulting in billions of
dollars in collections and fines and yet such efforts served not to eradicate but instead to spotlight, the vast scope of the problem. It is clear to
anyone who has had direct experience of the U.S. medical system that the
amount of overcharges and fake charges is phenomenal. Using the
extremely conservative figure of 10 percent, one gets a total for questionable billings of $130 billion per year. This amount eclipses the entire
GDP of most countries in the world, particularly the ones highest on

Transparency International's infamous index of corrupt countries. Imagine what picture emerges when the more plausible 30 percent ratio is used: health care fraud in the U.S. is equal to the total GDP of the largest transition country, Russia. Thus, even if we limit ourselves to health care, we can see that the amount of *absolute* corruption, measured in dollars, is probably greater in the U.S. than in any other country. That conclusion should be no surprise, given the sheer size of the U.S. economy (around $10 trillion) and its federal budget (close to $2 trillion), not to mention the budgets of the fifty states and the many thousands of municipalities, making for a nonpareil scrum of petty and powerful interests, much of it questionable if not outright illegal.

Characteristically, endemic problems in the U.S. such as medical overcharging are not called corruption, but "fraud," "waste" or "abuse"—a conceit that gets to the heart of the matters addressed in this volume: corruption is in some ways a matter of definition, especially universalized American definitions. Whereas "fraud" in the U.S. is understood as intentional wrongdoing, and usually includes such practices as theft, kickbacks, embezzlement, false or illegal commissions, collusion and willful overcharging, "waste" means inefficiency or ineffectiveness, which may or may not be a result of fraud, but still produces avoidable expense and dissipation. "Abuse" often does not involve breaking the law, though it can entail violation of administrative rules or guidelines.[379] The term "corruption" implies much more: corruption is not a bad individual, a bad corporation, an illicit set of practices or circumvention of the rules, but a system as a whole, an entire country's reputation. (The TI index asks people with first hand experience, chiefly in doing business, not how corrupt a particular country is, but how corrupt they view it to be.) Corruption is a condition, and one out of which there usually appears to be no exit.

The United States was founded in the eighteenth century in an anticorruption crusade (against British colonial authorities), but throughout most of its history the U.S. was viewed both domestically and internationally as plagued by endemic corruption—the land of Teapot Dome and Tammany Hall. Today, that is no longer the case. The fact that the U.S. is no longer perceived as a corrupt country, and that other countries are so perceived, needs to be critically examined, if only because American definitions of corruption have come to dominate the thinking of the major transnational agencies. Countries labeled as corrupt (or as highly corrupt) may complain about such labeling, but they quickly discover that they cannot throw off "unfair" U.S. definitions of corruption any more than they can refuse world market valuations of their economies, currencies or stock markets. Power and geopolitics, not whim or conspiracy, stand behind the international definitions of corruption. Let me be clear: to plumb these definitions, and their implementation, is not to minimize the grave reality of corruption across the world, to equate the experience of the U.S. with that of other countries or to suggest that the U.S. is some kind of desirable standard.[380] Rather, my inguiry is aimed at providing a levelheaded perspective on the nature of the U.S. experience because of the ways this experience (especially recently) has come to shape the image and experience of other countries by virtue of America's undeniable cultural, economic, and political power. American-centered definitions can be decried, but they are not easily evaded, which renders highly apposite their examination.

Classic Liberalism and Corruption

One reason that the U.S. is no longer perceived to be corrupt is that it has a wide array of tools for combating corruption—indeed, as Jim Jacobs (and a co-author) have cogently argued, one might characterize the entire panoply of U.S. public administration rules and laws as a corpus of anti-corruption measures built up over a long time.[381] To enforce myriad laws and regulations (which bring significant costs), the U.S. has a well-funded and powerful judiciary and an extensive federal civil service (Treasury Department, Security and Exchanges Commission, Justice Department, General Accounting Office, etc.). To be sure, the jurisdiction of these and other federal agencies is restricted by the Constitution (and by the Constitution's interpretation); equally important, a great deal of government activity remains the prerogative of the fifty states or of county and municipal governments, meaning that much of what is called corruption in other countries takes place in the U.S. below the federal level, but this, too, has the effect of making "the U.S."—as opposed to "bad apples" in the states or cities—appear not to be corrupt.

A second distinguishing attribute of the U.S. is the predominance of a vast "private sector" in the economy. Public officials in the U.S. dispose of colossal resources and take decisions of life-or-death significance for enormous numbers of people and enterprises in the private sector, but remuneration in the public sector pales in comparison to that of the private sector. This relative enrichment difference between the private and public sectors is one source of the widespread belief that "privatization" decreases corruption. Of course it does not, but an extensive private sector does mean that officeholders cannot come close to dominating, let alone monopolizing, the avenues to enrichment. At the same time, activities within the private sector—the principal mode of transactions in the U.S.—are not generally analyzed in terms of corruption. Vast private sector fortunes that are made or transferred on the basis of patronage, old-boy networks, nepotism and other insider deals are, for the most part, seen as "private" affairs, even in publicly held (stock) companies.[382] Corruption would be an utterly different concept in the U.S. if it applied with equal force to transactions within the private sector—as it used to be, in previous epochs when corporate behavior came under far greater public criticism.

American democracy functions according to social science as a more or less transparent "market" for policy within existing laws and for new legislation; transparency does not mean equal access to the political process, which is impossible (though the degrees of differentiation in access can be reduced or increased). However, the illusion of equal access persists, leading to continued uneasiness about the connection between money and politics, and overall fairness. All the same, corruption and anti-corruption in the U.S. are not viewed as matters involving the basic exercise of power and the societal wide distribution of wealth and resources—though they were so viewed in the past. Instead, corruption is now generally defined narrowly in legal terms (fraud, bribery). At the same time, behavior patterns and practices that used to be acceptable (indeed, in some cases praiseworthy) have subsequently been re-defined as corrupt, meaning that much of what today is called corruption (in reference to other countries) was often not considered to be corrupt inside the U.S. in the not-too-distant past, which has been obscured. Even the now seemingly axiomatic distinction between private interests and public interests came about only after torturous battles, and as part of a long, continuous tussle over administrative practice, from processes of budgeting and auditing to appointments and training.[383] It is as if the great historical contest to combat corruption that once defined America has been defined out of existence, even as one of that long struggle's chief legacies—multiple layers and practices of anticorruption machinery in government—endures.

It is worth noting that many of America's manifold regulatory mechanisms have little to do with "democracy." The oversight agencies for regulation and fighting corruption are institutions of historic liberalism, which was anti-democratic (though forced to become democratic, allowing former slaves and women to hold property, join or form voluntary associations and vote). The confusion between democracy and historic liberalism is a commonplace in today's world, a form of ignorance or amnesia that distorts a wide array of policy debates. Simply put, it is not elections based on universal suffrage or multi-party systems, but powerful legal machinery to protect property and ensure contracts as well as regulatory bureaucracy that are simultaneously the key artefacts of the battles against corruption and the tools for continuing those battles. Of course, the press plays a decisive role in broadcasting allegations of corruption, but allegations in the media would be of limited effect had there not also existed a formidable legal apparatus to undertake investigations and prosecutions, an apparatus without which private and civic groups have little effective power, and third parties have no recourse against each other, or against the state itself, even when many public officials are freely elected. The empirically rooted distinction between historic liberalism (constitutionalism, rule of law) and democracy (a later transformation of liberalism) has major policy implications.

Communism and Corruption

There is an intriguing comparison with the Soviet Union. One scholar of the Soviet system argued, typically, that the opportunities for corruption are greater when "the state is the primary agent for employment, production, and regulation than when it is not." Since the state was a near monopoly employer in the Soviet Union, corruption there was considered to be universal.[384] At the same time, however, the term "corruption" as applied to the Communist context was often synonymous with the illegal private or shadow economy, which was seen as dynamic, innovative, and even corrective. Indeed, foreign scholars often designated this kind of corruption as entrepreneurial activity, whether undertaken for private gain or for achieving plan fulfillment.[385] Thus, corruption under Communism was viewed as more widespread because the state was more pervasive and because private activity was illegal. The definitions in the

U.S. that were applied to corruption under Communism were thus the mirror image of those used in the U.S. for analyzing domestic corruption in the post-WWII era.[386]

What of the official Soviet view? The *Great Soviet Encyclopedia* (New York: Macmillan, 1974), describing corruption as "characteristic of the bourgeois state," also defined it—as a liberal regime did—as "the direct use by an official of the rights granted to him by virtue of his office for the purpose of personal enrichment" (vol. 13:165). Moreover, entries for bribery and extortion made clear that corrupt practices were widespread under socialism, while the entry for embezzlement referred to "stealing state or public property" (vol. 20:84). The same entry noted that ten of the fifteen Soviet republic criminal codes also criminalized the embezzlement of someone's personal property, but this was not the case in the two largest republics, the RSFSR and Ukrainian SSR, with nearly 70 percent of the population. (Criminal codes were the prerogative of the republics, not the Union.) Thus, for the Soviet authorities, corruption, by and large, did not entail private activities, but access to, or use of, public positions of authority and resources.[387] The similarities between Western (liberal) and Soviet conceptions of corruption under Communism are striking.

There was another, popular conception of corruption under Communism predicated upon a deep-seated sense of social justice. Ordinary people often privately (and sometimes publicly) condemned the legal (if largely hidden) "privileges" of officials, particularly the access to better housing, medical care, consumer goods, resorts and trips abroad. These perquisites of office, like special higher pensions, chauffer-driven state vehicles, and higher salaries (with additional envelopes stuffed with cash), were often seen as illegitimate, and as "corrupt," even though their provision was foreseen in Soviet laws and regulations (albeit usually unpublished ones). Only when officials came under attack by rivals were their perquisites officially questioned (and thereby widely revealed), amid allegations that they had obtained them through connections, or that they had used state property for personal use. Of course, recourse to connections and the lack of differentiation between state matters and personal matters by officialdom were foundations of the Soviet system,[388] but elites who engaged in mud-slinging power struggles to undo their opponents and rivals counted on arousing public outrage, rooted in a sense of violated social justice.

Rarely were public debates sanctioned (until *glasnost*) over "legiti-mate" versus "illegitimate," or deserved versus undeserved, privileges, except in the case of workers in hazardous environments and remote regions, or war veterans, all of whom received publicly acknowledged privileges (modest though they were). By contrast, the reticence regarding benefits to functionaries pointed to the problem that the *very existence* of an elite under Communism was inexplicable. Soviet social theory recog-nized only two classes—peasants and workers—while a third group, the intelligentsia, was defined not as a class but as a "stratum" (*prosloika*). Conspicuously, there was no acknowledgment of party apparatchiks and state officialdom—what the apostate Milovan Djilas famously dubbed the "new class," but the people had their own categories, and, as a result, Soviet-style systems were internally subjected to conceptions and rhetoric of social justice that condemned legal perquisites for the powerful and privileged as "corruption." This critique was eagerly incorporated into the condemnation of the Soviet system during the Cold War by Western (lib-eral) commentary, which, however, generally tended not to recognize the same social justice concerns at home.[389]

Globalization and Corruption

In the 1990s, after the initial euphoria over the fall of Communism pre-dictably resulted in disillusionment, studies and reports on corruption poured forth, funded or carried out by multinational agencies like the Organization for Economic Cooperation and Development, the World Trade Organization, the International Monetary Fund, and the World Bank, as well as non-governmental groups like Transparency International. Suddenly, these cross-border actors redefined corruption as epidemic, particularly in so-called transition countries, which, it was argued, needed to adopt greater democracy as well as to liberalize (priva-tize and deregulate) in order to make their markets more functional and friendlier for foreign investors.[390] (Note that "liberal" here did not mean the creation of a strong judiciary and civil service, but the opposite—i. e., something akin to stateless markets, which are a captivating fantasy. That multinational agencies would deliver such prescriptions, sometimes in the form of ultimatums, to ostensibly sovereign countries, points to a key aspect of globalization—namely, the tension between globalization's (further) empowerment of transnational actors and disempowerment of national states which are then supposed to undertake prescribed actions when the idea of government itself is being devalued.

Sponsored studies of corruption during the 1990s begin with the premise that globalization has brought greatly expanded opportunities for corruption, but they take that to mean opportunities for state officials to demand bribes, not the increased degree to which ever-more foreign investors encourage bribery and kickbacks (a matter of "supply"). Nor does one find too much analysis of the ways that "democratization" and "liberalization" facilitate corruption by further weakening the machinery responsible (or potentially responsible) for oversight and regulation. Rather, it is indigenous, congenital corruption that is presented as a "threat" both to the global economy and to the transition countries that could be "bypassed" in international investment decisions (because of higher "transaction costs").[391] The possible negative impact of the international financial system, which greatly augments the rewards (and indeed the possibilities) for corruption in transition countries, is scarcely addressed.[392] On the contrary, the external environment appears primarily as a source of benefit whose full beneficence is being blunted by a lack of "vigorous" anticorruption campaigns. It is as if the international power hierarchy, known as the world economy, did not involve power at all.

Arguably, what distinguishes the varied transition countries is that in many ways they have become democratic, but generally they are not liberal in institutional terms (some far less so than others).[393] Each has universal suffrage, and some continue to have genuinely competitive elections, but few have a powerful judiciary or efficient regulatory agencies. In other words, these countries are being confronted by the strictures of liberal definitions of corruption largely without possessing the full array of liberal tools for implementing such strictures. Those liberal strictures, moreover, are predicated not merely upon the existence of well functioning public regulatory mechanisms, but on the existence of a large, thriving private sector, which these countries also do not have to the extent that Western countries do. Thus, liberal conceptions were, in effect, employed to condemn the absence of liberalism! Perversely, the exhortations to undertake still speedier transitions to liberal systems often take the form of blanket charges of corruption, which blacken the very governments that are supposed to institute, and thereafter act in accordance with, the liberal model.

One of the principal upshots of this linkage between globalization and corruption is that "corruption" became a broad-based collective characterization, even defamation, of the transition countries—the same countries that had been stamped as corrupt prior to 1989–91. This is a familiar, if generally unacknowledged Catch-22. Just as the emergence of more than seventy new states in the "third world" during decolonization in the period 1947–1975 gave rise to an expansive corruption literature, so the exit of the "second world" from Communism with the end of the Cold War certainties and the appearance of around twenty new states gave rise to a new wave of corruption studies. "First world" definitions and standards are again being applied, without recognition of the history of the transformations of those standards, let alone the extent to which practices differ from mythologies in the *first world* (as if globalization had completely transformed the possibilities for corruption only *outside* the first world—despite the manifest raucousness throughout the 1990s of Western capital markets, banking systems, accounting practices, and so on). For transition countries, just as for "developing" countries during decolonization, the drumbeat about corruption led to a backlash, and to assertions that corruption can often perform "positive" functions.

Still more fundamentally, in the 1990s' resurgence of indiscriminate charges of corruption, we can recognize the resurgence of the modernization theory, as well as a recurring resistance to the modernization paradigm,[394] and yet the battles against promiscuous applications of the term "corruption" for transition countries cannot be dismissed as a Western plot. Modernization is not a meta-historical process of change, but neither is it an optional policy agenda. The application of Western criteria for corruption in countries outside the G-7 follows the same merciless geopolitical pattern as the Western investors and multinationals which help determine prices for securities, currencies, and other not exactly sovereign elements of any given country's estimated wealth. Furthermore, inside these countries elements of the articulate public refuse to tolerate "excuses" and "different standards" for their own countries, which they measure against the contemporary West. Such internal constituencies may seem motivated by a neo-liberal worldview, but, once again, one can more often find in their views underlying assumptions about social justice. There is no small irony in the circumstance that deeply felt social justice concerns have greatly facilitated the blackening of transition countries.

Everyday Swindles, Illegalities, Tax Evasion

In U.S. public discourse and social science, explicit social justice concerns have greatly diminished, particularly since the 1970s. Yet a strong sense of violated social justice (or, at least, of basic fairness) can still be found, not in the academic or policy literature on corruption around the world to be sure, but in journalism and investigative reporting on the everyday operation of the U.S. system. Such unexceptional accounts offer a treasure trove of information about how power and influence work legally and illegally in the U.S., and thus they inadvertently offer a critical perspective on the narrow legalistic notion of corruption that dominates liberal rhetoric and programs directed at transition countries. This journalism rarely uses the vocabulary of corruption, at least for domestic reporting, and yet the huffing and puffing, indeed the indignation, expressed at the various pyramid schemes that emerged in the post-Communist world, can seem hypocritical if one follows reports on the swindles and bilking of people in the U.S., from phony land deals to pyramid-like chain letters, from "insurance" schemes to bogus charities to Initial Public Offerings (IPOs) of stock. American "scams" are nearly infinite, and the total sums involved astronomical.[395] And even though several public advocacy groups exist, such as the Better Business Bureau and the Consumer Protection Agency, the phrase "caveat emptor" is one of the first lessons one learns in American "civics."

Quotidian lawlessness is also prevalent in the U.S. A majority of U.S. inhabitants knowingly break the law in some fashion, whether that means exceeding the legal speed limit on roads or making payoffs to have a partly malfunctioning or polluting vehicle approved at Motor Vehicle Inspection. Employee skimming from cash businesses is extensive, as is employer non-reporting of cash income. Illegal sub-letting of apartments is widespread, and income earned from such leasing is frequently concealed. Mail order "degrees" and other sham credentials are more plentiful than ever. The number of fake social security cards in circulation, a principle form of legal identification, is not small. A very significant segment of the U.S. workforce consists of illegal aliens who are knowingly (and often preferentially) hired by employers, who can manipulate them more readily. The vast size of America's underground economy, including concealed parts of legitimate businesses, is unparalleled anywhere in the world. That remains true even though most forms of gambling are no longer illegal (indeed, gambling has become state-sponsored).[396]

To be sure, the use of state regulations to extort "fines" is far less widespread among U.S. bureaucrats and elected officials than it is in transition countries. (Extortion is, however, commonplace in the U.S. among private protection rackets that prey on businesses in immigrant and poorer neighborhoods. Extortion by state officials for personal gain defines daily existence in transition countries, from transit police and road inspection, safety and health inspection, to property registration, licensing, and tax inspection and collection. Problems in state tax collection, especially, get to the heart of the shortcomings in the civic order of transition countries (as elsewhere around the world, from Argentina to China). It is wrong to suppose that no taxes are collected in the transition countries—taxes and innumerable "fees" are endlessly collected from individuals and companies, but not always in such a fashion as to provide financing for road construction or schools, or to permit, let alone encourage, small business activity.[397] The illicit or questionable monies that change hands do sometimes finance socially important functions. Operationally, few distinctions are made between functional and non-functional forms of corruption, in part because many vested interests as well as ordinary people are not interested in such distinctions. Thus do Public services and corruption come to seem inseraparable.

In the U.S. the dominant arena of greatest extra-legal or illegal shenanigans is also taxes, though the problem is not state extortion but taxpayer dishonesty and the state's acquiescence therein. For example, in 2000, even as the taxes of individuals were rising, those of corporations were found to be falling—despite record corporate profits. Some of that decrease in corporate taxes reflected completely legal, though dubious, tax credits (such as deductions for stock options paid to management and favored employees), but more important was the resurgence in tax "shelters," accounting gimmicks, most of which are manifestly illegal, but few of which are ever investigated, let alone prosecuted. Even prominent companies known for guarding their public image, such as Colgate–Palmolive, Compaq Computer or United Parcel Service, are not being shy about recourse to the dodge, assisted by top-drawer investment houses like Merrill Lynch. The U.S. Treasury Secretary called corporate tax shelters our "No. 1 problem," and "not just because they cost money but because they breed disrespect for the tax system."[398]

Even as corporate tax avoidance and illegal evasion totaled many tens of billions of dollars, audits of corporations were way down, in part because during the 1990s the International Revenue Service (IRS) staff was cut by more than 15 percent (from 115,000 employees to 97,000). Staff cuts at IRS, which were ideologically motivated, took place even as government reports indicated that the total number of tax returns was increasing (reaching about 130 million). As a result, cheats and deadbeats among individuals were coming out on top, too. Enforcement actions against delinquent individuals fell by two-thirds for audits, and by 99 percent for property seizures. "No matter how they deploy their resources," one top accountant told a reporter, "the IRS just does not have a sufficient body of resources to enforce the law." He concluded that "as more and more people cheat and evade," knowing they can get away with it, "we, the honest taxpayers, are paying for this."[399] Taking a cue from the literature on transition countries, might we label such government-abetted tax evasion a form of corruption to promote "capital accumulation" and "economic development"?

U.S. Executives and Oligarchy

The foreign chorus of condemnation of "oligarchs," cronies, and insiders run amok in transition countries has been thunderous, yet such incantations can be directed inward. For example, in Sweden chief executives made 13 times their average worker's salary, while in German it was 15 times, and in Great Britain it was 24 times (the highest multiple in Europe), but in the U.S., corporate executives made 475 times their average worker's salary. What is more, executive pay was rising, and the differential with workers was growing, even though their companies were losing value. In fact, even companies that went belly up saw their chief executives receive substantial bonuses (and substituted cash payments for previously offered stock options when stock prices plummeted). "You don't even have to make your performance goals," commented one specialist on compensation to a reporter. "The board will pay you anyway." Indeed, what might look like an obvious conflict of interest—the fact that the members of "oversight" boards, which hand out colossal compensation packages regardless of performance to executives, themselves receive substantial fees for their "service"—is instead a hallowed element, if not the foundation, of American corporate "governance." When asked about the high payoffs to board members who set executive compensation packages, one executive told a reporter that, "you're not paying them for the time spent." Rather, "you're paying them for carrying the responsibility."[400] However, when the routine looting of a corporation by senior management becomes public, no board members are held accountable.

One would be hard-pressed to think of a more oligarchic system. It would, perhaps, be churlish to add that, unlike regular corporate employees, executives often do not pay for the food they consume, since they have so-called expense accounts (which are often at least partially deducted from revenues reported by the business, meaning they are essentially subsidized by taxpayers). Many companies maintain an airplane for executive travel (also a business expense "deduction"), and they pay for a wide range of costs incurred by their executives, from the schooling of their children to the preparation of their personal taxes. The higher up one goes on the corporate ladder, the more of an executive's daily life and personal expenses are usually considered a matter of the business, i.e., expenses to be paid by rank and file shareholders and ultimately, all taxpayers.

Indirect Pay-offs for Admission to Elite Universities

There are more than 3,000 institutions of higher learning in the U.S., with more than 14 million total students (a figure considerably greater than the number of farmers in the world's agricultural behemoth). Most U.S. universities do not have competitive admissions. For the handful of schools that are extremely difficult to get into, access is very far from being strictly merit-based, by the schools' own admission. For example, despite requiring that applicants sit for a standardized national test, the top universities in the U.S. offer admission to a far higher percentage of applicants whose parents attended the same institution. At Princeton University, where only about 10 percent of applicants are admitted annually, the success rate of family or "legacy" applicants is five times greater than for non-legacies. Princeton's experience is replicated at Harvard, Yale, Stanford and other highly prestigious U.S. universities and colleges. At least one aspect of the thinking appears to be that loyal families will donate relatively more money to the university than others might, though there is not supposed to be a quid pro quo in granting admissions;

future donations are voluntary (the solicitations, however, begin immediately, that is, even before graduation). Many applicants appear to be admitted to select schools not because of previous family ties, but simply because of their enormous wealth (though this is not publicly admitted), which is reported on their applications. In the European state education systems, those who seek to make "donations" to gain admission for their children are paying bribes; in the U.S., they are "developing" the university. Americans' more substantial payments to universities are transparent, there is no penalty for not paying (once the person has been admitted), and the funds go to the university budget rather than to the pockets of gate-keeping individuals.

Another group that receives preferential treatment for college admissions in the U.S. are athletes. Princeton University, like most small, elite U.S. schools, has more athletic teams (31 sports) than does the University of Michigan (21), even though Michigan is ten times the size of Princeton and considered to be an athletes' school. (It might be useful to recall that the term "Ivy League," which has come to connote academic excellence, refers to a sports league.) In 1951 20 percent of Ivy League students were athletes; fifty years later, that number has grown closer to 30 percent. Moreover, these are not academically qualified students who also happen to enjoy sports, but often students who are recruited primarily because of talent in sports—people for whom the universities are willing to lower academic standards (athletes' scores on national college entrance tests are significantly lower than the average at their schools). One might think that the exceptions are made because sports are moneymakers for the university; in fact, sports programs are extremely costly, taking budget funds away from academics. Preferential admission of athletes, at places that stress academic excellence, amounts to an arbitrary choice that benefits a select segment of the population.[401]

To the extent that one finds a debate in the U.S. about admissions to elite universities, however, it is not over the preferential admission of large numbers of academically less qualified athletes or children of alumni, but over the smaller group admitted on the basis of so-called affirmative action. In 1976 at twenty-eight predominantly white schools in one scientific study, some seven hundred black students were admitted who would probably have been denied admission if allowance for race had not been used in admission criteria. Twenty-four of those schools admitted about 2,600 athletes that same year, and the athletes' scores were also substantially lower than the average. In 1989 these same colleges admitted 3,300 athletes and the test score discrepancies were even greater. Meanwhile, as of 1992, of the seven hundred blacks admitted back in 1976 to selective schools on the basis of affirmative action, seventy had become doctors, about sixty were lawyers, one hundred and twenty five were business executives, and more than three hundred were said to be civic or community leaders.[402]

Whatever the criteria used for admission to selective schools in the U.S., there is no presumption of equal access—and hence, no violation of the law. Top universities are mostly private, not public, and though private universities must comply with U.S. laws against discrimination, there are no laws that mandate that a student with higher national test scores must be admitted over a student with lower scores and greater family wealth. The U.S. Constitution does not guarantee every one higher education, much less education at a prestigious university. What might be corruption in a fully state education system is, in the U.S. case, a matter of what is viewed as rational self-interest. Yet, however roundabout and sophisticated the mechanisms, there can be no question that money and connections buy access to elite higher education, and in turn, that elite higher education contributes mightily to the greater likelihood of career advancement.

Stock Market Manipulation

Stock "analysts," it turns out, are not analysts but salesmen, more akin to racetrack touts than to researchers, since they work for companies that also do underwriting for the companies' stocks they "analyze." Of 8,000 stock recommendations by analysts who cover the Standard and Poor's 500 stock index in late 2000, only 29 were "sell" orders. Many analysts issued buy orders to the public for stocks that their own investment bank was selling (top management of the companies often sold the stock as well, while continuing to tout it to the public),[403] but, instead of pursuing the manifest conflicts of interest among so-called analysts, the Securities and Exchanges Commission (SEC) made a scapegoat of a fifteen-year-old, hauled in for "pumping" stocks by sending out glowing reports on the Internet, and then, after the stocks rose, "dumping" or selling them at a profit—something that professionals had been doing far more successfully, with far larger amounts of money at stake, on cable television financial shows, right in the face of regulators.[404] (This conflict of interest among security firms, between their roles in investigating and reporting versus making profitable sales, became characteristic of the top five private accounting firms that form the backbone of the U.S. financial and economic system—a menace that may come to define America's first decade of the new millenium.)[405]

The SEC, which enforces laws and regulations that mostly date from the 1930s, when the market was last acknowledged to be fallible, successfully prosecuted an accounting fraud case in 2000 against Cendant Corporation for intentionally misreporting earnings, a circumstance that once it was revealed, caused company stock values to plummet. (Estimates of investor losses were $19 billion; consider that number against the total amounts involved in privatization in transition countries.) "The results of our cases," said Richard Walker, director of enforcement for the SEC, "show that financial fraud is not confined to very small and obscure companies, but is increasingly prevalent in large companies traded on major stock markets as well. Last year we brought more enforcement actions involving financial fraud and reporting abuses than ever before, and our inventory of such cases remains large."[406]

Even more significant are the cases of financial fraud that are not prosecuted. For example, prior to an IPO of a stock, large institutional investors, that shepherd the offerings to market, reserve quantities for themselves, favored clients, members of their board of directors and relatives, before the shares are made available to the rest of the public. In a "hot" market, such as existed in the second half of the 1990s, these stocks often rise quickly, especially on the first day, only to deflate when hard news about the new company becomes available, but in the meantime, insiders who have been given the privilege of buying on the first day, or simply been given stock for free, quickly "flip" their shares, meaning they sell and turn a substantial instant profit. The quick turnaround practice, which is also known as "puking" a stock back to the market, can be done more or less with every single IPO that a particular investment bank manages. Those non-insider shareholders, who bought into the rising stock that later deflates, pay the price for such commonplace manipulations.[407] Stringent new guidelines to disallow "flipping" were announced by one major brokerage (Merrill Lynch) in late 2001 and then quickly rescinded.

On Western stock markets, the incidences of manipulation may comprise a smaller portion of the overall trades than they do in transition countries. If that is true, it is partly because of the sheer size differential in respective bourses; at the same time, this also means that the total amounts of money involved in market manipulations are far, far greater in the West. Thus, as with all manner of corruption, there is either more, or less, stock market manipulation in the West than in transition countries depending on whether one measures absolutes or percentages. Bear in mind that the manipulation that becomes public in the West is only what is prosecuted—U.S. newspapers do not report corruption cases unless they have court documents. During any given year the SEC prosecutes fewer than fifty insider-trading cases. Germany, which established the first stock market in 1585, outlawed insider trading only in 1994, and has had a miniscule number of prosecutions since. Only one-third of the world's 103 stock markets have *ever* prosecuted an insider-trading case.[408]

"Moral Hazard"

In the 1990s, a "hedge fund" known as Long-Term Capital Management (LTCM), based in Connecticut, used approximately $3 billion in capital from investors as collateral to purchase $125 billion of securities, and then used those unsecured securities as collateral for a string of off-the-books global financial speculations (in derivatives and other hybrid instruments) valued at $1.25 trillion. All of this was legal. (LTCM's founder, John Meriwhether, founded the company after having been forced to resign from Salomon Brothers in August 1991 over a Treasury-bond bid-rigging scandal, which resulted in no prosecutions, though Meriwhether paid a "settlement" to the SEC.[409]) High-flying LTCM, employing two Nobel Prize economists and using powerful mathematical models, bet wrong across the board. In September 1998, the Federal Reserve Bank of New York orchestrated a private financial bailout of LTCM. This took place despite the fact that hedge funds, unlike chartered banks and brokerage houses, do not fall under laws providing for government regulation by the Federal Reserve or another agency.

A precipitous liquidation of the hedge fund would not have meant that its total exposure would have been lost, but bankruptcy, as provided by law, would have meant the sudden dumping of huge amounts of securities on the market across the world, depressing values. The race to get out faster than the other guy would have likely resulted in mass financial carnage. Instead, the bailout meant that the very lenders from the world's supposedly most sophisticated institutions which had provided money recklessly to the hedge fund were protected from significantly worse losses had the hedge fund not been prevented by government intervention from collapsing. "You had a very large entity," said the spokesman of the New York Federal Reserve about the measly capitalized hedge fund, "that was hemorrhaging, with very large exposures at stake."[410] Among those who gained protection were Merrill Lynch, whose clients and executives had enormous sums at stake in LTCM, and whose executives participated in setting the bailout terms. Substantial losses resulted all the same, but the added breathing room to "unwind" the hedge fund's position over a longer period of time saved everyone involved a lot of money.

"The financial system often operates as a club," Jeffrey Garten, Dean of Yale University's School of Management, told the *Wall Street Journal*. "Sometimes one of the members requires a very visible bailout from public authorities, but other times there's a lot of behind-the-scenes activity to shore up confidence and let it be known among the key players that there are backup lines of credit from other sources. That almost never makes the headlines, but this kind of support averts crises." What constitutes a "crisis"? The message seems to be: speculate and make money, but, if you make the wrong gamble and are threatened with big losses, and if you are in the "club," someone will come to your rescue, overtly or secretly. Indeed, examples of even the publicly acknowledged bailouts are very numerous.[411] When debated (but not prohibited), they come under the euphemism "moral hazard." That concept has become known internationally thanks to the IMF, which organizes last-minute packages to developing countries that, whatever their stated intentions, *in effect* bail out threatened foreign investors and indigenous insiders, protecting the privileged from the consequences of risk-taking in the market, in the name of averting "crisis."

Lobbying, Appropriations, Oil Money

During the annual federal budget preparation in Washington, the amount of plain-view skullduggery, let alone what goes on behind the scenes, is proportional to the staggering sums of money involved. The special deals won by lobbyists on behalf of "constituents"—mind-boggling giveaways that for the most part are legal—do not come under the rubric of "corruption," but are called the "appropriations process." What *is* called corruption in the U.S.—the financing of campaigns for public office—is also perfectly legal. Some $3 billion was spent on the presidential election in 2000 (not including the post-election monkey business in Florida). Unlike in transition countries, that election money did not go into the pockets of individual politicians or to journalists who were paid for favorable coverage. Almost $1 billion of U.S. presidential-race financing—fully one-third of total spending—did go to the bottom line of electronic media companies to pay for political advertising on what are, by law, public airwaves "leased" to for-profit corporations, such as ABC, CBS, and NBC.[412] These media decry the campaign financing system in the U.S. without explaining that they are at the heart of it. Another factor that makes for high costs is the inordinate length of American political campaigns, which, unlike in Europe, are not limited by law to specific time periods. Thus, compelling private corporations using public airwaves to broadcast political advertising without charge, as well as limiting the length of political campaigns, would go a long way to reducing the high costs of electoral politics in the U.S., but ultimately the big money would find its way to the politicians because of how much is at stake in the legislative process for the plethora of organized interest groups.

In the U.S. election campaigns are significantly more expensive than in any other country—there is just no comparison—but these campaigns are elaborately regulated in a vain attempt to prevent, or merely control, what is called the "influence of money on politics." Occasionally, the American press throws up examples of ludicrously crass, unsophisticated politicians who squeeze out finances in a manner reminiscent of what often takes place in many transition countries, but more often an observer can only be impressed at the multiple layers of precaution and the verbal gymnastics that are necessary to remain within the law, or at least very close to the edge of the law, in the financing of campaigns and the granting of favors to contributors. Beyond the financing of essentially never-ending electoral campaigns there is also the continuing financing of legislation by interested parties. A very instructive example of money-politics that encompassed an entire American state, Alaska, and that was redolent of transition countries, took place after oil was discovered in Prudhoe Bay in 1967. Within a few years the cash began to flow, and the state began to see what invariably accompanies such a sloshing of wealth.

At first, construction of a pipeline from Alaska's northern fields to the southern town of Valdez (an ice-free port) was estimated to cost $900 million. After the initial bidding, however, far higher costs were revealed. To cover the sudden cost differential, the city of Valdez was persuaded by the oil companies to float $1.5 billion (of a $2 billion bond issue) as a federally tax-free municipal bond—the largest-ever tax-free bond issue up to that time. One percent accrued to the city, a huge windfall for a tiny town of a few thousand people, so the oil company had little difficulty convincing them to do it. Work on the pipeline began in 1970, even though permits had not been issued. Then a series of environmental lawsuits halted construction, but a "special bill" expedited through the Congress in Washington cleared the way for resumption. On the job, goldbricking by contractors and by union laborers led to huge sums of money being gouged. The pipeline camps were also the site of mass theft, rape, gambling, prostitution, and murder. Construction was finally completed in 1977, at a cost of $8 billion, and influence peddling as well as quasi-legal profit skimming, took place on a colossal scale.

Oil money contributed to a jump in the Alaskan state budget from $368 million in 1978 to $4.5 billion by the beginning of the 1980s (the state only had about 250,000 residents). The oil companies picked the candidates to run for the legislature and prevented the ones they did not pick from getting on the ballot or getting known to the voters. Lobbyists were appointed, consultants were hired—friends, relatives, campaign contributors—and "commissions" were awarded on a range of contracts, virtually none of them put up for bid. Hundreds of projects were started, with no oversight or regard to specified procedures. There were contracts for schools, firehouses, health clinics, roads, incinerators, whether they were needed or not; an endless flow of "engineering studies," not necessarily connected to anything that might eventually be carried out, provided even more lucre. One tiny Alaskan municipality for a time was spending $1 million a day. The person designated by law to review contracts before they were sent to the mayor discovered that they arrived in the legal department already signed—so as to be "expedited." Public officials founded their own companies, and then awarded those companies big contracts—kickbacks in the grand style. Every final bill (for the few projects that were completed) came in far above original costs. Schools were built at a cost of $320,000 per student. One school library turned out to be the size of a small exercise room, and did not contain a single newspaper from the state capital, let alone any from out of state (or abroad). Audits were conducted, lawsuits threatened, and many "scandals" publicly revealed—mostly as a result of rival contractors who claimed to have been extorted for payment of bribes but lost the contracts anyway. Several people died under suspicious circumstances. Finally, the FBI came in and identified more than a dozen people linked to bribery, extortion, and tax evasion—the first white-collar corruption case prosecuted in Alaska. The trial was moved to Los Angeles; the most powerful defendants were acquitted.

However colorful this Alaskan example may be, it offers a variation on the links between money and power that cuts across and through the American political system. Unusually, instead of operating as the Alaskan constitution mandated, the Alaskan state senate, state house and state governor expediently agreed to divide the oil proceeds into thirds, and to do as each saw fit in the name of the greater public good. The unencumbered governor squandered at least $100 million on well-intentioned attempts to finance a dairy industry and barley harvesting. Legislators sank huge sums into an Alaska Renewable Resources Corporation that sought to establish fox farms, mushroom farms, and fish-processing plants, almost all of which went belly up. About $1 billion for public underwriting of housing was eventually written off as bad loans. Even more dubiously, some $350 million was spent on consulting fees for a dam that never got built. "Bribe-paying developers, greedy labor bosses, and professional racketeers thrived," wrote one author. "Corruption flourished, the rule of law suffered, and the wilderness shrank."[413] Environmentalists, meanwhile, demand prohibition of further drilling within Alaska, to protect its wilderness. Of course, without drastic reductions in U.S. consumption of fossil fuels—close to 25 percent for only 5 percent of the world's population—the agenda of "protecting Alaska" entails increased drilling in other countries, such as Russia or Kazakhstan, where environmental safeguards are less tough and less vigorously enforced.

Lingering Infamy of Public Contracts

Here we arrive at what, for the U.S., is the traditional area of corruption—government and private sector interaction—to discover, yet again, a 1990s twist: infatuation with privatization. "Privatization" of public serv-

ices—rubbish collection, fire protection, road maintenance, prison supervision—has become a passionate goal for many people in the United
States as a way to promote "efficiency," but current debates fail to note
that what is being called "privatization" of services used to be called
"public contracting," a practice made infamous, of course, by Boss
Tweed and his many imitators. Many years since Tammany Hall fell, the
results can still be eye-opening, even when public contracts are awarded
to private companies by tender. For example, a 1990s contract for private
highway maintenance in Massachusetts did not include in its tender and
signed contract any payment for state overhead to monitor financial
expenses or contract compliance. Nor did private contracts specify the
relationship of highway work to related activities still handled by state
agencies, making responsibility for problems and redress unclear. The
result was that profits accrued to the companies, while foreseeable costs
and problems were public responsibilities.

In Florida, one county in the late 1990s decided to experiment by "privatizing" ten of its bus routes, keeping another ten under state management as a control for comparison. The private contract did not cover
equipment maintenance, whose expenses would have exceeded revenues
from fares. So the buses on the private line were not fixed, and by the end
of the 18-month contract only one-quarter of the buses under private
'management' were in operation. The state inherited a huge repair bill,
which it could not avoid paying, unless it wanted to end bus services.
Elsewhere, corporations hired to do fire protection were found to have
"economized" on work crews, saving themselves money, which seemed
to work nicely when there were no fires, but when a large conflagration
broke out, the "lean" crews could not handle the blazes, and millions of
dollars' worth of private homes went up in flames. In that case costs were
picked up by insurance companies, and thus by future customers of insurance, not by the companies performing "private" management of public
services. These are just a few examples of the many dozens in a study of
the supposed panacea of "privatization" of public services by a diligent,
matter of fact urban planner.[414]

Empirically speaking, the upshot of public contracting (privatization of
services) is not generally better management—many private corporations
are run just as badly as, if not worse than, public agencies. Simply put, efficient management is an important goal but it should not be confused with
seeking help in the private sector. Moreover, most cost savings allegedly

attributed to a private firm probably derive from a narrower definition of "service," since for-profit companies, unsurprisingly, will frequently provide less public service, and seek to distribute costs to others, especially state agencies. Revenues from bus fares, sure; costs of maintaining overused buses, no thanks. Typically, however, this is not an issue of legal corruption, since there are ostensibly competitive bids and freely agreed contracts, but can there be any doubt about the resemblance to asset stripping? Consider as well the fact that public contracts are often not awarded by competitive bid in a transparent process. After a colorful career connected to handing out public contracts, for example, the mayor of Jersey City, New Jersey, on a salary of $9,000 a year, left office in 1956 and soon died, leaving an estate to his heirs valued at more than $5 million. In the ensuing decades, many anticorruption laws were passed, but the state's population grew rapidly, so that by 2000 New Jersey had acquired more than 560 municipalities, 600 school districts, 21 counties and the largest state government per capita in the U.S.—making for increased possibilities for corruption. One political scientist described New Jersey as chock full of "a lot of public expenditures, a lot of public contracts, a lot of opportunities for the public sector and a lot of temptations for the private sector."[415] Every American state is different, to paraphrase Tolstoy (somewhat liberally), but each is, in important ways, the same.[416]

Corruption and Power

Skeptical readers may interject that, although some of the above examples involved illegal behavior, most did not. That is true. However, keep in mind that the schemes for privatization in postcommunist countries were also, for the most part, legality and illegality distinctions and terminology matter. In the U.S., "fraud," "waste," and "abuse" are the preferred terms for questionable actions, but outside the U.S. "corruption" is the dominant category. Corruption is used with such wide application for transition countries that it becomes another name for the general distribution of wealth and power and the means by which such distribution occurs or does not occur—legal or illegal, transparent or opaque—in these societies. In such a way, the invocation of corruption has become a language of politics, indeed sometimes the only political language available.[417] Ideologically speaking, it is as if competing visions of "pure" or "free" markets versus social justice concerns have been recast as a contest between forces that are anticorruption and those that are pro-corruption, though rhetorically everyone is against corruption, and the politicians who are most effective at anticorruption campaigns are also often those most effective at skimming and graft.[418] What *is* the language of social justice in a politics of the market?

Our conclusion is a simple one: corruption and politics (or power) are inseparable. No one, however, should thereby be inclined to underestimate the differences not just in the public framing of the corruption problem but also in day-to-day practices between the well-off Western countries, including the U.S., and transition countries. The enormous differences between the U.S. and the transition countries consist primarily, but not exclusively, in the relative independence and strength of their judiciaries and civil service or regulatory agencies, on the one hand, and, on the other, in the overall scale of financial doings, whether in the expansive private sector or between private and public. Thus, transition countries have substantially less money sloshing around and, despite the very substantial variations among them, we can conclude that they, by and large, lack fully liberal institutions. Yet in the worldwide crusade against corruption which has enveloped transition countries, liberal definitions predominate. Ironically, these definitions of corruption are often made operative in transition countries by groups and individuals who hold potent expectations of social justice, which liberal definitions tend to overlook or even deny.

The dilemma of a corruption definition that for a variety of expedient and ideological reasons, holds little or no room for social justice concerns and yet is simultaneously dependent on expectations of social justice among indigenes, runs through the anticorruption prescriptions of the 1990s, just as it did during the previous boom in corruption studies accompanying decolonization twenty years ago. "Were it not for the fact that a host of government decisions represent valuable commodities to some citizens, there would be little corruption," concluded James Scott, in what remains one of the best comparative studies from the 1970s decolonization wave. "Nor," he added, "would there be much corruption if the valuable things a state had at its disposal was simply sold at auction to the highest bidder."[419] Perhaps, but even if state-provided services were made available to the highest bidder in auctions—assuming a Western level of interest-group competition or balancing—would we still not want to inquire of the bidders Whence their wherewithal to bid? That wherewithal, in many cases, would derive from privileged access to elite schools, golden job opportunities obtained through patronage and connections, fortunes amassed on the basis of insider information or other auspicious vantage points, regressive taxes as well as tax avoidance or illegal evasion, compounded by the authorities' discretionary (selective) prosecution of financial and tax irregularities, and a host of other factors involving the influence of power and wealth. The line between "corruption" and everyday politics by individuals and organized groups is blurry, not to mention subject to change.

It may seem like good public policy to define corruption in the U.S. in a limited, legalistic way, leaving out the vast majority of, mostly private, transactions as well as fully legal practices in the relations of power between the private and the public spheres. Such a definitional conceit, whatever else it does, helps to suppress elementary considerations of social justice in political discourse and practice. When applied abroad, it helps to insure that "corruption" becomes the primary or even exclusive vocabulary for framing discussions of the gaping inequalities in a given country—as well as the inequalities among countries—and it often further undermines the very mechanisms of regulation and oversight that are supposed to address corruption. The implication would appear to be a considerable broadening of the definition of "corruption" and its application in the U.S., a narrowing of the term and its usage in transition countries, or both. Then again, transition countries might prefer not just to define various forms of corruption out of existence but also to squeeze them out. We shall see.

Notes

1 Joseph LaPalombara "Structural and Institutional Aspects of Corruption, *"Social Research*, 61 (1994)

2 See e.g. Nathaniel H. Leff, "Economic Development through Bureaucratic Corruption," *Am. Behav. Scientist*, Nov. 1964, p. 8; J. S. Nye, "Corruption and Political Development: A Cost–Benefit Analysis," 61 *Am. Pol. Sci. Rev.* (1976) 417; Samuel P. Huntington, *Political Order in Changing Societies* (1968).

3 For a survey of these attempts see Omar Azfar, Yound Lee, Anand Swamy, The Causes and Consequences of Corruption, p. 573. *The Annals of the American Academy of Political and Social Science* 42 (January 2001).

4 The normalization of corruption in the public's mind has occurred in a number of Western countries too. In France 70 percent of the respondents of a survey taken by *L'Express internationale* in 1994 said that a certain measure of corruption is inevitable in a modern society.

5 Kaufmann, D., *Corruption: The Facts, Foreign Policy*, 1997 Summer, p. 114. The development is equally characteristic in transition economies and developing economies. In an account on Ugandan development, infrastructure projects are simply seen as opportunities for corruption. Ruzinanda, Augustine, "The Importance of Leadership in Fighting Corruption in Uganda," in *Corruption and the Global Economy*, ed., Kimberley Ann Elliot. Washington, DC: Insitute for International Economics, 1998.

6 Joel S. Hellman, Geraint Jones, Daniel Kaufmann, "Seize the State, Seize the Day: State Capture, Corruption and Influence in Transition," *World Bank Policy Research. Working Paper* No. 2444, 2000.

7 Clientelism has similar impacts on the state in Africa: "the . . . [d]evelopment of political machines and the consolidation of clientelistic networks within the formal political apparatus has been immensely advantageous. It has allowed them to respond to the demands for protection, assistance and aid made by the members of their constituency communities in exchange for the recognition of the political prominence and social status which, as patrons, they crave. The instrumentalization of the prevailing political [dis]order is thus a disincentive to the establishment of a more properly institutionalized state on the Weberian model. Why should African political elites dismantle a political system which serves them so well?" Chabal and Daloz, *Africa Works*, 14.

8 In Eastern Europe police may stop vehicles to carry out routine checks without any suspicion of illegality.

9 A. Schleifer and R. W. Vishny, "Corruption," *The Quarterly Journal of Economics* (August 1993), pp. 599–617.

10 John T. Noonan, Jr., *Bribes* (University of California Press, 1987), p. xi.

11 Stephen Holmes, "What Russia Teaches Us Now. How Weak States Threaten Freedom," The *American Prospect*, Vol. 8, Issue 33, July 1998.

12 Ironically, however, systemic corruption may develop in/may serve as support for, dictatorship. In a dictatorship the state seems to be strong, but this is true in terms of silencing social criticism and not in the sense of being able to sustain itself without corruption.

13 Jean Tirole, "A Theory of Collective Reputations (with applications to the persistence of corruption and to firm quality," *Review of Economic Studies* (1966) 53, 1, at 10.

14 Consider Edmund Burke's opening speech in the impeachment of Warren Hastings: "Your Lordship know that these gentlemen [Warren Hastings and his collaborators] have formed a plan of geographical morality by which the duties of men, in public and private situations, are not to be governed by their relation to the great Governor of the Universe, or by their relation to mankind, but by climates . . . latitudes, as if, when you crossed the equinoctial, all the virtues die . . . by which they unbaptize themselves of all that they learned in Europe . . . This geographical morality we do protest against: Mr. Hastings shall not screen himself under it . . . As quoted in Padideh Ala'I, "The Legacy of Geographical Morality and Colonialism: A Historical Assessment of the Current Crusade Against Corruption 33 Vand.," *Journal of Transnational Law*, 877, quotation at 888.

15 Walter Little and Eduardo Posda-Carbo, "Introduction," in W. Little and E. Posda-Carbo,eds., *Political Corruption in Europe and Latin America,* (Macmillan–St. Martin's Press, 1996), p. 2.

16 See e. g. Nathaniel H. Leff, "Economic Development trough Bureaucratic Corruption," *American Behavioral Scientist,* Nov. 1964. p. 8; J. S. Nye, "Corruption and Political Development: A Cost-Benefit Analysis," *American Political Science Review*, 61, 417 (1967); S. P. Huntington, *Political Order in Changing Societies* (1968).

17 G. Ben-Dor, "Corruption, Institutionalization, and Political Development: The Revisionist Theses Revisited," *Comparative Political Studies* 63, 65 (1974).

18 I. Krastev, "The Strange (Re)Discovery of Corruption," in Lord Dahrendorf et al.,eds., *The Paradoxes of Unintended Consequences* (Budapest, CEU Press), p. 35.

19 G. Moody-Stuart, *Grand Corruption: How Business Bribes Damage Developing Countries,* (Oxford: World View, 1997).

20 R. Klitgaard, *Controlling Corruption* (Berkeley: University of California 1988), p. 64.

21 A. J. Heidenheimer *et al.*, eds., *Political Corruption: A Handbook* (New Brunswick, NJ: Transaction Books, 1989), p. 3.

22 Gifts given to public officials in accordance with tradition may not amount to corruption if the amount is within the limits of the tradition because, among other consideration, these situations do not result in departure from the rules on behalf of the government agent. *Ex post* transactions (e.g. tips) that occur after the provision of services in accordance to rules may also be wrongly subsumed under the rubric of corruption. Yet both phenomena may play crucial roles in extortion. For these problems see Omar Azfar, Yound Lee, Anand Swamy, "The Causes and Consequences of Corruption," p. 573 *The Annals of the American Academy of Political and Social Science 42* (January, 2001); and Susan Rose-Ackerman, *Corruption and Government: Causes, Consequences, and Reform.* (Cambridge: Cambridge University Press, 1999) pp, 91–111.

23 An even closer look at the entry into the public services market will show that there are social services in high demand in advanced welfare states too (e. g., see certain professional schools). The system, however, does as much as possible to avoid opportunities for bribery, while in some other systems the institutional interest is to *keep* admissions, access to service within the institution's own decision which increases the local power of the local bureaucrats and inevitably increases the chances of corruption.

24 I would like to thank J. Cohen, J. Elster, I. Ermakoff, G. Mackie, M. Philp, A. Przeworski, J. Rohmer, and F. Varese for their helpful comments on earlier drafts of this essay. I would also like to thank the organizers of and the participants, in the Shelby Cullom Davis Center seminar, held in Princeton on 24–25 September, 1998, where I first presented this paper.

25 An example of the loose use of the term is in McKitrick (1968). A sense of the confusion can be derived from Gardner (1992). One of the most popular, if very congested, definition is by Joseph Nye (1967). Corruption, he wrote, is a "behavior which deviates from the normal duties of a public role because of the private-regarding (family, close private clique) pecuniary or

status gains; or violates rules against the exercise of certain types of private-regarding influence. This includes such behavior as bribery (use of rewards to pervert the judgment of a person in a position of trust); nepotism (bestowal of patronage by reason of ascriptive relationship rather than merit); and misappropriation (illegal appropriation of public resources for private-regarding use)." Most definitions tend to be sketchy, and I found no in-depth, sustained discussion of this concept, but see Philp (1997) for an interesting discussion of the pitfalls of trying to reach a viable definition.

26 I prefer this terminology to that suggested by Banfield (1975) and Rose-Ackerman (1978: 7–8) who call the truster "principal" and the trustee "agent"; this is partially misleading since a corrupt exchange does not exactly overlap with an instance of what in economics has become known as the principal-agent problem. The latter is, at the same time, broader, in that it deals with all those instances in which the principal needs to determine how much he should pay the agent to ensure his full co-operation when monitoring performance is costly, and narrower, in that a lack of co-operation on the part of the agent need not be of a corrupt kind.

27 Despite some differences (see fn. 26 above) the conceptual map developed here is indebted to the definition found in the principal-agent literature. First developed by Becker and Stigler (1974), it was then taken up by Rose-Ackerman (1978, 1998) (who crisply defines corruption as "an illegal payment to an agent to obtain a benefit which may or may not be deserved in the absence of payoffs"), and by E. Banfield, who provides an articulate version (1975): "The frame of reference is one in which an agent serves (or fails to serve) the interest of a principal. The agent is a person who has accepted an obligation to act on behalf of his principal in some range of matters and, in so doing, to serve the principal's interest as if it were his own. The principal may be a person or an entity such as an organization or public. In acting on behalf of his principal an agent must exercise discretion; the wider the range (measured in terms of effects on the principal's interest) among which he may choose, the broader his discretion. The situation includes third parties (persons or abstract entities), who stand to gain or lose by the action of the agent. There are rules (both laws and generally accepted standards of right conduct) violation of which entails some probability of a penalty (cost) being imposed upon the violator. A rule may be more or less indefinite (vague, ambiguous or both), and there is more or less uncertainty as to whether it will be enforced. An agent is personally corrupt if he knowingly sacrifices his principal's interest to his own, that is, if he betrays his

trust. He is officially corrupt if, serving his principal's interest, he knowingly violates a rule, that is, acts illegally or unethically albeit in his principal's interest" (pp. 587–8).

It is also indebted to elements suggested by Alatas (1990), with regard to the relevance of trust and the difference made by extortion. The World Bank Web site offers a good broad definition: "Corruption involves behavior on the part of officials in the public and private sectors, in which they improperly and unlawfully enrich themselves and/or those close to them, or induce others to do so, by misusing the position in which they are placed." (http://www.worldbank.org/)

28 He was not being extravagant but rather taking to the extreme an important Italian legal tradition first developed by S. Romano in the first half of the 20th century. Until well into the 1970s many Italian judges openly regarded the Mafia as an essentially benign institution, with which the state could co-operate rather than fight (see Gambetta, 1993, esp. Introduction). The Justice Minister in Silvio Berlusconi's 1994 cabinet, Filippo Mancuso, still publicly defended that view recently.

29 Here I assume that the motives that prompt F and C to enter a corrupt exchange are to safeguard and promote their own interests, broadly defined. A special category of self-interested motives, which bears some thinking about, occurs if agents have an interest in corruption per se, if, in other words, they derive pleasure from it, regardless of other payoffs. F may enjoy displaying one's power to C or pleasing C with a unique 'gift' that C could not otherwise obtain. Or both F and C may enjoy cheating T or C may derive special pleasure from showing that everyone has his price. While we may intuitively suspect that such corrupt personalities do exist, it is doubtful whether motives of this kind are of great social relevance.

30 Consider the following case that was put to me by A. Przeworksi. A woman in Mexico is stopped by a policeman and found with no driving license. She says her surname to the policeman who then apologizes and lets her go. Is this a case of corruption? No bribe was paid and yet the policeman acted against the rules. Does it follow that we have therefore a case of corruption in which no bribe is required? This example is interesting for it points to cases of *nested* corrupt relations, in which there are more than just three parties—the law, the policeman and the woman. The policeman acts on the expectation that the woman, who must have connections with powerful people, has the power to have him punished for doing his duty. He breaches the rules because of intimidation rather than corruption. The policeman's

expectation is based on the belief that his superiors are prepared to violate the rule and punish him if he observes the rules to please someone with whom they have an ongoing relation of sort, which may be corrupt.

31 For a discussion of the *positive* economic consequences of competition among corrupt agents, see Shleifer and Vishny (1993), p. 607.

32 Cf. MacRae (1982).

33 If there is a stream of rewards that F can deliver, a different solution opens to competing Cs. In Sicily, for instance, in order to avoid that unstable outcome, and also to avoid giving F the power to charge too high a bribe, many Cs have colluded with one another, often under Mafia protection (Gambetta and Reuter, 1995). They go forward one at a time, as it were, agreeing in advance who is to make the lowest bid and win the contract. Whoever's turn it is to get the contract also pays the bribe. In this case, however, the bribe buys F's silence over a violation rather than the contract as such. Collusion and corruption sustain each other. This case does approximate closely the standard case of corruption.

34 On the distinction between natural duties and positional obligations cf. G. Valdés (1995), pp. 111–3.

35 A collection of these practices is nicely illustrated by Lundahl 1997. On the differences between bribes and taxes see Shleifer and Vishiny (1993), pp. 611–2.

36 There are clearly extremes in which even the decisions by those who enjoy discretion do not look right, nonetheless, as when a new highway makes a long detour to by-pass the property of wealthy people while driving straight through a demolished neighborhood of ordinary folks. For all his grand vision and spectacular energy, Robert Moses, according to his biographer, was guilty of things like that (*The New Yorker* 1997), p. xx

37 I am grateful to M. Philp for suggesting this to me.

38 For how a culture of 'familism' can influence levels of corruption, see Banfield (1958). For a recent discussion and testing of Banfield's approach see Lipset and Lenz (1999).

39 Quoted by Alatas (1990, 176), who takes it from Landesco (1963, 213), who in turn took it from a magazine article.

40 See my 'Defining Political Corruption' *Political Studies* 45 (3) 1997, pp. 436–62; A. J. Heidenheimer, *Political Corruption: Readings in Comparative Analysis* (Holt, Reinhart and Winston, New York, 1970), and A. J Heidenheimer, M. Johnston and V. Levine *Political Corruption: Handbook* (Transaction Publishers, New Brunswick, N.J., 1989).

41 The three core elements of A, B, and C have been used by D. Gambetta as a way of identifying a consistent, cross-cultural account of corruption which identifies it as a trust relation between A and B which A violates to the benefit of C—where the commodity transferred to C is monopolistic and where A's motive to act in this way is C's bribe. This account allows the content of corrupt acts to vary across cultures and time, while the type of action remains constant. However, while he treats the triadic relation of trust as providing the core for a model of corruption (conditioned further by constraints on motive and on the presence of quasi-monopolistic rules regulating the distribution of the commodity in question), I would reverse the order, putting the concept of public office (which is closely connected to the presence of quasi-monopolistic rules) prior to, and not wholly reducible to, the concept of trust. That is, we need the concept of public office to identify which derelictions of trust are *politically* corrupt; but we also need it to identify which derelictions of trust are corrupt. That is, there are types of trust relationship (such as amorous relationships) whose subversion is not corrupt. For it to be corruption, the trust relationship must be a sub-set of such relationships where a set of publicly endorsed rules and norms identify the nature of the trust and its purposes (e.g., the rules and norms of public office, and the underlying principles which identify the point of that office), and which introduce of a separation within the individual between what is required of him in a public capacity and what he may wish to do as an individual agent with certain wants and preferences. It is a further move to resolve adjectival disputes as to whether the case of corruption is, for example, political or economic. The term corruption cannot be predicated of a relationship without reference to the particular set of rules and norms which turn a case of disappointed expectations into one of corruption.

42 Someone who is coerced into behavior which breaks the rules (the bank manager with a gun to his head), is not normally seen as corrupt. On the other hand, someone whose fears and weaknesses are exploited through threats may be regarded as corrupt: some forms of self-protection are regarded as legitimate self-defense, others are seen as moral weakness. On political gains—and 'institutional' corruption, see D. Thompson, *Ethics in Congress from Individual to Institutional Corruption* (Washington: Brookings Inst., 1995), p. 30.

43 Cf Alena V. Ledeneva, *Russia's Economy of Favours* (Cambridge University Press, Cambridge, 1998); S. N. Eisenstadt and L. Roniger, *Patrons, Clients and Friends: Interpersonal Relations and the Structure of*

Trust in Society (Cambridge: Cambridge University Press, 1984); and E. Gellner, 'Patrons and Clients', in E. Gellner and J. Waterbury, *Patrons and Clients* (London: Duckworth, 1977).

44 A. Przeworski, *The State and the Economy under Capitalism* (Harwood Academic, Switzerland, 1990), pp. 31–3. I introduce a further dimension at a later stage in the argument.

45 J. Linz. and A. Stepan (eds.), *Problems of Democratic Transition and Consolidation. Southern Europe, South America, and Post-Communist Europe* (Baltimore: Johns Hopkins University, 1996), p. 3.

46 On the account given here, the conception of public office cannot be distinctive to democratic states, nor can it involve a different conception of what it is or there to be political rule. Clearly, a democratized state may differ dramatically from the corrupt autocracy it replaces, but monarchical, aristocratic and various forms of constitutional rule which fall short of democracy, are, nonetheless, political forms of rule, with rules of public office and a conception of the appropriate parameters for political agency. Democracy changes issues of access and accountability, but its understanding of political office and rule is not *sui generis*.

47 J. Elster, C. Offe and U. Preuss, with F. Boenker, Ulrike Goetting, and F. W. Rueb, *Institutional Design in Post-Communist Societies: Rebuilding the Ship at Sea* (Cambridge: Cambrdige University Press, 1998), Chapter 1 (originally drafted by Offe), pp. 30–1.

48 Cited in Przeworski, *op. cit.*, p. 32.

49 In Elster, Offe, Preuss *et al.*, pp. 3–27.

50 On populism, its dangers and its relationship with corruption see Y. Mény, 'Politics, corruption and democracy', *European Journal of Political Research* 30, 1996, pp. 118–21. Nationalist agendas can themselves be the result of other forces, internal and external—as is graphically demonstrated in Susan L Woodward, *Balkan Tragedy: Chaos and Disintegration after the Cold War* (Washington, D C.: The Brookings Institution, 1995).

51 There are other ways of cutting this cake—for example, following Weber and Leslie Holmes, by distinguishing between different bases for legitimacy (charismatic, traditional and legal rational in the former case, and at least seven types in Holmes), but the distinctions drawn above are more pertinent for democratic states (which was the target of neither of these writers. See L. Holmes, *The End of Communist Power* (Oxford: Polity Press, 1993), chapter 1.

52 Note the potential restriction in scope. There may be an ideal of democratic legitimation, which is such that it encompasses all members of a state, but

political rule can be sustained with a much narrower band than this. What is most central, as Weber recognized, is that those who play a key role in supporting those in public office continue to accord them legitimacy and thereby help sustain stable and effective forms of political rule. In contrast, when those supporting do so wholly to serve their interests and secure spoils, they do not accord legitimacy, and the political character of rule becomes increasingly fragile.

53 On the international context see Y. Mény, 'Fin de Siecle' corruption: change, crisis and shifting values' *International Social Science Journal* 1996, 309–320. Should we, for example, hold that Mitterrand's donations to Kohl's electoral campaigns were corrupt, not just because of the failure of disclosure, but because of the creation of inappropriate types of influence between France and the German Chancellor.

54 At a lower than state level, for example, there is the covert funding for the PCI by the CIA in the aftermath of WW II.

55 See D. Thompson, *op. cit.* Also Mayor Daley of Chicago is reputed to have sought only the continuation and expansion of his control, and no private gain (unlike most of those he used to achieve his ends). We could redescribe political power as a private gain, but there is an important distinction between those who use corruption to gain and sustain political power and those who also use that power for private ends. The distinction becomes more difficult to sustain the greater the proportion of the resources which political office brings is invested in maintaining office.

56 See Elvira Maria Restrepo, *Corruption and the Judiciary in Colombia* (Oxford, D.Phil., 1999).

57 One example, it seems, of how it can be free standing is the case of the New South Wales police force, which was subject to a commission of inquiry in the mid-1990s. Neither the Independent Commission against Corruption nor, indeed, this subsequent commission, have proved able fundamentally to eliminate corruption from the force, but this seems more a function of the pattern of relationships between junior officers and the criminal fraternity than of any connection with the political system.

58 This is a complex issue which basically concerns the depiction of rational agency in economics and the understanding of what it is for there to be a rule. If rules have no salience for the individual except where following them maximises self-interest, then the character of a rule is not being recognized. For it to be a rule for an agent it needs to be recognized as a *prima facie* guide to conduct and/or as a way of initially framing a context. That a

rule may subsequently be violated to maximize self-interest does not mean that we should understand compliance, where it happens, as also self-interest maximizing. Given the chance, we might decide to cheat at chess, but to weigh every rule by the test of expedience would be to make the game itself unintelligible. Similarly, corrupt players, for the most part, want to cheat within a framework which identifies goals means and opportunities. To repudiate the framework entirely is to play another game, or to embrace nihilism. I take it that Olson's emphasis on rights as an implicit feature of market economies amounts essentially to this lack of opportunism with respect to the basic framework of the market—see M. Olson, *Power and Prosperity: Outgrowing Capitalist and Communist Dictatorships* (New York: Basic Books, 2000), esp. chapter 10.

59 As in shifting from a non-cooperative to a cooperative baseline. See Brian Barry, *Theories of Justice*, Vol. 1 (London: Harvester, 1989), part one.

60 We might try to treat these values as the expressed preferences of the agents, but doing so is either false since it fails to recognize the way that individuals may sacrifice their interests for other values, or is a case of definitional fiat (anything an individual does while not actually disturbed is counted as something done to further his/her interests), and thus true but trivial.

61 Education directed to clarity about margins can be important, since much public official corruption can begin on a small scale and then gradually escalate: as J. L. Burke's detective puts it: 'Seduction usually comes a teaspoon at a time . . . Sometimes a cop who won't take fifty grand will take two. Then one day you find yourself way down the road and you don't remember where you made a hard left turn.'J. L. Burke, *A Stained White Radiance* (New York: Hyperion, 1992), p. 105.

62 The evidence is that it is extremely difficult to change local police cultures—-short of sacking all the men and appointing only women—although it is not yet clear whether their hugely lower rates of corruption is a short term affair, perhaps resulting from their exclusion by male colleagues.

63 This discussion is influenced by M. S. Alam's discussion in 'A Theory of Limits of Corruption and some Applications,' *Kyklos* 48 (1995), pp. 419–35.

64 The paper covers only those corruption analyses which, while trying to estimate the level of corruption, provide any recoverable empirical methodology.

65 To describe the precise wording of the questions and alternative answers would take too much space. Those interested in the wording should check Rose (1998/b). Instead of this, I rather briefly characterize the respective situations: a clerk delays giving permission, to jump the queue, to get into hos-

pital, to get a public flat being ineligible, to get into the university unjustly, a clerk does not give unemployment benefit (unjustly), to get a doctor, to get the wage deserved, to make a shop assistant admit a mistake, and to get a job.

66 The precise wording of the corruption situations was the following:

receipt = An entrepreneur charges less for a job if he does not have to give a receipt;

gratuity = Health workers accept money for giving a patient a better treatment;

commission = An entrepreneur gives money to a civil servant to win a major state contract;

loan = A private individual gives money to the bank clerk to get a substantial bank loan;

fine = A policeman metes out a smaller fine if he is not asked to give receipt;

privatization = Officials dealing with privatization accept money from the bidders;

pension = A doctor accepts money for declaring someone eligible for pension;

greasing the wheels = Civil servants accept some kind of recompense to speed up the process;

permit = Civil servants accept some kind of recompense for giving a permission;

job = A private individual gives money to get a better job.

67 Earlier the minimum number of sources was 4 but this limited the number of countries covered to about 50, while in 1998 the CPI covered 85 countries.

68 Assuming of course that there is no change in the understanding of the same term and that the level of underestimation remains stable as well.

69 Based on school buddy-networks and previous job experiences, and thousands of expert meetings.

70 The major problems with local experts are that they are part of the system and, therefore, it is very difficult to believe that they are free from any vested interest and that they know "too much" but this "thumbnail knowledge" (often coming through personal networks) may be misleading and secret.

71 The dynamic version of this process would be the businessman who misunderstands a ceremonial gift and would give money as a reciprocal act. This, in turn, would be misunderstood by the recipient as a bribe and would be happily accepted, and this happy acceptance would reassure the businessman that the original gift was indeed a first stage of a corruptive transaction. The end of such a series of benevolent misunderstandings is a bad score for the country CPI.

72 Revised version of an article that first appeared in *Political Studies* 45/3
    (1997) under the title "The Politics of Privilege: Assessing the Impact of
    Rents, Corruption, and Clientelism on Third World Development." The
    copyright-holder of this article is the Political Studies Association; thanks
    to Blackwell Publishers for kindly granting permission to reprint.
    Thanks to D. Emmerson, J. K.S., Mushtaq Khan, A. MacIntyre, A. Mendoza,
    Jr., T .J. Pempel, A. Ramsay, T. Rivera, and J. Rocamora for offering comments
    that contributed to this article. I am also grateful for comments provided by par-
    ticipants in a panel of the Association of Asian Studies annual meetings, 11–14
    April, 1996, Honolulu, Hawaii; the "Rents and Development in Southeast Asia"
    workshop, 27–28 August, 1996, Kuala Lumpur, Malaysia; the Princeton
    University/Open Society Institute workshop on corruption, Princeton, New
    Jersey, 21 May, 1999; and the Princeton/Central European University confer-
    ence on corruption in East Europe and the former Soviet Union, Budapest,
    Hungary, 31 October 1999. All errors, of course, are mine alone.
73 A. Åslund, "The Russian Road to the Market," *Current History*, October
    1995, pp. 311–316 *(emphasis added)*.
74 K. Polanyi, *The Great Transformation: The Political and Economic Origins
    of Our Times* (Boston: Beacon Press, 1944), pp. 140, 139, 141 *(emphasis
    added)*. Many other economists, to be sure, very clearly highlighted the
    enormous political obstacles involved in the creation of a market economy.
    See M. I. Goldman, "Is This Any Way to Create A Market Economy?,"
    Current History, October 1995, pp. 305–310 (in the same issue as the
    Åslund analysis, cited above). Later in the decade, the central role of the
    state in development had been strongly acknowledged by the World Bank,
    most systematically in its *World Development Report 1997: The State in a
    Changing World* (Oxford: Oxford University Press, 1997).
75 In Transparency International's Corruption Perception Index for the year
    2000 Russia ranked 82nd and Nigeria 90th (with CPI scores—on a scale of
    1 to 10—of 2.1 and 1.2, respectively). See:
    http://www.transparency.org/documents/cpi/2000/cpi2000.html
76 J. M. Buchanan, "Rent-Seeking and Profit-Seeking," in J. M. Buchanan, R.
    D. Tollison and G. Tullock, eds., *Toward A Theory of the Rent-Seeking
    Society*, (College Station, Texas: Texas A & M Press, 1980), p. 9; Peter
    Evans, *Embedded Autonomy: States and Industrial Transformation*
    (Princeton: Princeton University Press, 1995), p. 24.
77 Margaret Levi, *Of Rule and Revenue* (Berkeley and Los Angeles:
    University of California Press, 1988), p. 24.

78 Evans, *Embedded Autonomy,* p. 25. Fortunately, as Evans demonstrates, use of a rent framework does not require that one adopt the anti-statist perspective of a neo-utilitarian.

79 Max Weber, *Economy and Society* (Berkeley and Los Angeles: University of California Press, 1978), p. 987; Jomo K.S. and E. T. Gomez, "Rents, Rent-Seeking and Rent-Deployment in Malaysia" (Kuala Lumpur: unpublished ms., 1995), p. 3.

80 Paul D. Hutchcroft, *Booty Capitalism: The Politics of Banking in the Philippines* (Ithaca: Cornell University Press, 1998).

81 See, for example, Anne O. Krueger, "The Political Economy of the Rent-Seeking Society," *The American Economic Review* 64, 3: 291–303.

82 Evans, *Embedded Autonomy,* p. 24.

83 As one scholar noted thirty years ago, "[e]stimates of the extent of corruption practices in underdeveloped countries are, expectedly, very imprecise. Rumor abounds, facts are scarce." David H. Bayley, "The Effects of Corruption in a Developing Nation," in A. J. Heidenheimer, M. Johnston and V. T. Levine, eds., *Political Corruption: A Handbook* (New Brunswick: Transaction Publishers, 1989 [1966]), pp. 935–52, at 939.

84 J. S. Nye, "Corruption and Political Development: A Cost-Benefit Analysis," in Heidenheimer *et al.*, *Political Corruption* 1989 [1967], pp. 963–83, at 966). Alternative definitions are based on notions of the public interest and public opinion, but by far the most widely accepted definitions are based on legal norms. See the discussions of J. C. Scott, *Comparative Political Corruption* (Englewood Cliffs, N.J.: Prentice-Hall, 1972), pp. 3–5; and R. Theobald, *Corruption, Development and Underdevelopment* (Durham: Duke University Press, 1990), pp. 1–18.

85 In 1965, Leys noted that "the question of corruption in the contemporary world has so far been taken up almost solely by moralists . . . Emotionally and intellectually, this seems to be in a direct line of descent from the viewpoint of those missionaries who were dedicated to the suppression of native dancing. The subject seems to deserve a more systematic and openminded approach." C. Leys, "What is the Problem About Corruption?," in Heidenheimer *et al.*, *Political Corruption*, 1989 [1965], pp. 51–66, at 52–53. The term "revisionist" is derived from Cariño, who argues the need to combine analysis with moral judgements. "Compare," she writes, "the outrage of American scholars against Nixon's indiscretions and their near-approval of more blatantly corrupt regimes in countries where they have worked." L. V. Cariño, "Tonic or Toxic: The Effects of Graft and

Corruption," in Cariño, *Bureaucratic Corruption in Asia: Causes, Consequences and Controls* (Quezon City: College of Public Administration, University of the Philippines, 1986), pp. 163–94, at 168. Among those who perceive, at least occasional, benefits to corruption are Nye, "Corruption and Political Development," and Scott, *Comparative Political Corruption*; more systematic benefits are asserted in the work of S. P. Huntington, *Political Order in Changing Societies* (New Haven: Yale University Press, 1968) and N. H. Leff, "Economic Development through Bureaucratic Corruption," in Heidenheimer *et al.*, *Political Corruption*, 1989 [1964], pp. 389–403. For additional analysis of costs and benefits, see Theobald, *Corruption*.

86 See, for example, Nye, "Corruption and Political Development"; J. Waterbury, "Endemic and Planned Corruption in a Monarchical Regime," *World Politics*, 25, 4 (July 1973): 533–55; and Theobald, *Corruption*.

87 See F. Riggs' analysis of how "the gulf between the study of politics and administration . . . became institutionalized" both in developed and in developing countries. F. W. Riggs, "The Interdependence of Politics and Administration," *Philippine Journal of Public Administration*, 31, 4 (October 1987), pp. 418–38, at 429.

88 Scott, *Comparative Political Corruption*, pp. 88–89, 6, and viii–ix; Waterbury, "Endemic and Planned Corruption," p. 555.

89 J. C. Scott, "Patron–Client Politics and Political Change in Southeast Asia," *American Political Science Review* 66/1 (1972): 91–113; Waterbury, "Endemic and Planned Corruption," p. 537.

90 See J. Th. Sidel, "Coercion, Capital, and the Post-Colonial State: Bossism in the Postwar Philippines," Ph. D., Cornell University, 1995, pp. 11–12; Scott, *Comparative Political Corruption*, pp. 34–35.

91 Weber, *Economy and Society*, pp. 240, 1095.

92 Lloyd I. Rudolph and Susanne Hoeber Rudolph, "Authority and Power in Bureaucratic and Patrimonial Administration: A Revisionist Interpretation of Weber on Bureaucracy," *World Politics* 31, 2 (January 1979), pp. 195-227, at 198; Scott, "Patron-Client Politics," p. 92.

93 Scott concurs that more predictable corruption is "less likely to seriously retard economic growth." Not only is the price more certain, but there is also greater "probability of receiving the paid-for 'decision.'" This type of corruption is more likely when: a) "The political and bureaucratic elites are strong *and* cohesive" and b) "Corruption has become 'regularized'—even institutionalized after a fashion—by long practice." *Comparative Political*

Corruption, pp. 90–91. These insights, I will seek to demonstrate, are strengthened by analysis of the relationship between power and authority.

94 J. L. S. Girling, *Thailand: Society and Politics* (Ithaca: Cornell University Press, 1981), pp. 37–38, 42. Anderson, similarly, speaks of the frequent standardization of "cuts and commissions" in post-independence Indonesia. B. R. O'G. Anderson, "The Idea of Power in Javanese Culture," in Claire Holt, ed., *Culture and Politics in Indonesia* (Ithaca: Cornell University Press, 1972), pp. 1–69, at 49.

95 Susan Rose-Ackerman, "Which Bureaucracies are Less Corruptible?," in Heidenheimer *et al.*, *Political Corruption* 1989 [1978], pp. 803–25, at 805, 816. Legal procedures, in fact, may be intentionally obscured in order to heighten the demand for illegal services. In such a system, moreover, those with specialized powers to interpret often-opaque rules (i.e., lawyers) will likely play a prominent role.

96 Leff, *Economic Development*, pp. 396–7, 393; Krueger, *The Political Economy of the Rent-Seeking Society*, pp. 292, 195.

97 A. M. Mendoza, Jr., *Notes for a Second Look at Rent-Seeking, Profit-Making, and Economic Change in the Philippines*, (Quezon City, unpublished manuscript, 1995), p. 13; J. E. L. Campos, *The 'Political Economy of the Rent-Seeking Society' Revisited: Cronyism, Political Instability, and Development* (Washington, D.C.: unpublished manuscript, 1992), p. 15. See also Krueger, *Rent-Seeking Society*, p. 301 and E. S. de Dios, "Parcellised Capital and Underdevelopment: A Reinterpretation of the Specific-Factors Model," *Philippine Review of Economics and Business* 30 (June 1993), pp. 141–55, at 154. Other neo-classical economists, notes Mendoza in his review of the literature, acknowledge that rent seeking is not always competitive yet nonetheless "assert that a more competitive situation will reduce wastes associated with rent-seeking" (p. 13).

98 Jomo and Gomez, *Rents*" pp. 3–4. Jomo and Gomez do not provide a definition for their passing reference to the term "rent deployment" (in their title as well as on pp. 21 and 22). I may be employing the term in a somewhat different sense than they originally intended, but I have taken the liberty to retain the term because it best suggests a systematic, purposive allocation of rents. The basic distinction between two types of rent allocation, however, derives from their discussion.

99 I am indebted to Jomo and Gomez for highlighting the important distinction between these two processes (*Rents*, p. 5). On corruption and capital accumulation, see Nye, *Corruption and Political Development*, p. 967.

100 Indeed, one could argue that an entrepreneur who benefits from a deployed rent (and is thus probably close to the regime in power) is likely more secure than an entrepreneur who has won out in a process of competitive rent seeking. If the regime as a whole is in danger of collapsing, however, neither category of entrepreneur is likely to have much sense of security.

101 R. F. Doner and A. Ramsay, "An Institutional Explanation of Thai Economic Success," a paper presented at the annual meetings of the Association for Asian Studies, Washington, D.C., April 6–9, 1995, pp. 3–4. See also R. F. Doner and A. Ramsay, "Competitive Clientelism and Economic Governance: The Case of Thailand," in Sylvia Maxfield and B. R. Schneider, eds., Business and the State in Developing Countries (Ithaca: Cornell University Press, 1997), pp. 237–276, at 248; and Scott, *Comparative Political Corruption*, p. 91.

102 R. H. Bates, *Markets and States in Tropical Africa: The Political Basis of Agricultural Policies* (Berkeley and Los Angeles: University of California Press, 1981).

103 World Bank, *World Development Report 1991* (Oxford: Oxford University Press, 1991), p. 9; Huntington, *Political Order*, p. 69.

104 Scott, *Comparative Political Corruption*, p. 67. Fegan offers a broadly similar distinction between "facilitative corruption" (in which the law is bent to the mutual benefit of both a bribing businessperson and a bribed bureaucrat, and neither has reason to complain to a third party) and "obstructive corruption" (in which legitimate applications are blocked until a bribe is paid, and the businessperson is likely to complain to a third party). The former is "probably a necessary lubricant to capitalist development," while the latter is an impediment. B. Fegan, "Contributions From Sir Arthur Conan Doyle and Mick Inder to a Theory of Bureacratisation and Corruption in Southeast Asia" (Sydney: unpublished ms., 1994), pp. 4–5.

105 Syed Hussein Alatas, *The Sociology of Corruption: The Nature, Function, Causes, and Prevention of Corruption* (Singapore: Times Books International, 1980), pp. 31–35.

106 Theobald, *Corruption*, p. 128, 131; Huntington, *Political Order*, p. 69.

107 Leff, *Economic Development*, p. 399.

108 R. Wade, "The System of Administrative and Political Corruption: Canal Irrigation in South India," *The Journal of Development Studies* 18, 3 (April, 1982), pp. 287–328, at 287–88.

109 Insights can also be drawn from comparisons of the incidence (and impact) of corruption at the national level versus the regional level, or Region A versus Region B. The more decentralized a polity, the more important such analysis would be.

110 Huntington, *Political Order*, p. 67, *emphasis in original*.

111 Evans, *Embedded Autonomy*, p. 61; Doner and Ramsay, *Thai Economic Success*, pp. 2–3. The relatively more efficient agencies may be more insulated from clientelistic pressures, but one should not presume that formal authority completely displaces informal networks of power. As Rudolph and Rudolph argue in their "revisionist interpretation" of Weber's work on bureaucracy, effective administration depends not only on rational-legal authority but also on the persistence of patrimonial features able to "[mitigate] conflict and [promote] organizational loyalty, discipline, and efficiency." *Authority and Power*, p. 196. Evans argues that informal networks within developmentalist states "reinforce the binding character of participation in the formal organizational structure rather than undercutting it in the way that informal networks based on kinship or parochial geographic loyalties would." *Embedded Autonomy*, p. 59.

112 Scott, *Comparative Political Corruption*, p. 94. I prefer the term "electoral system" to "party system," since (as discussed below) well-institutionalized parties may or may not play an important role within a system centered on competitive elections.

113 Wade, *Administrative and Political Corruption*, pp. 318–19, 288; Theobald, *Corruption*, p. 18. See also Riggs, *Interdependence*.

114 H. Crouch, *The Army and Politics in Indonesia* (Ithaca: Cornell University Press, 1988), pp. 40, 38. Overall, this period is, of course, known as one in which corruption in Indonesia lacked any real limits. Scott, *Comparative Political Corruption*, pp. 80–84. To the extent that institutionalization was taking place, it was seemingly almost entirely within a military that—after 1965—came to "backbone" the rest of the bureaucracy. D. K. Emmerson, "The Bureaucracy in Political Context: Weakness in Strength," in K. D. Jackson and L. W. Pye, eds., Political Power and Communications in Indonesia (Berkeley and Los Angeles: University of California Press, 1978), pp. 82–136; see also Crouch, *Army and Politics* and B. Anderson, "Old State, New Society: Indonesia's New Order in Comparative Historical Perspective," *Journal of Asian Studies,* 42, (May 1983), pp. 477–496.

115 Anderson, *The Idea of Power,* p. 49; Huntington, *Political Order,* pp. 70–71, *emphasis added*.

116 A. MacIntyre, "Clientelism and Economic Growth: The Politics of Economic Policymaking in Indonesia," a paper presented at the annual meetings of the Association for Asian Studies, Washington, D. C., April 6–9, 1995, pp. 10–16; Scott, *Comparative Political Corruption*, pp. 79–80.

117 In P. D. Hutchcroft, "Obstructive Corruption: The Politics of Privilege in the Philippines," in Jomo K.S. and Mushtaq Khan , eds., *Rent Seeking and Development in Asia* (Cambridge: Cambridge University Press, 2000). I apply the various elements of this framework to the Philippines, a notoriously skewed, irregular political economic landscape, long the playfield of both established oligarchs and favored cronies. The country's particular configuration of political power, I conclude, has nurtured types of rent-seeking, corruption, and clientelistic ties that have proven generally obstructive to sustained economic development.

118 See, for example, Nye, *Corruption and Political Development;* Scott, *Comparative Political Development*, pp. 90–91; and Theobald, *Corruption*, pp. 107–32.

119 Wade, *Administrative and Political Corruption*, p. 288.

120 U. von Alemann, "Bureaucratic and Political Corruption Controls: Reassessing the German Record," in Heidenheimer (1989).

121 For a provocative analysis of the history of economic growth, see Alice H. Amsden, *The Rise of "The Rest": Challenges to the West from Late-Industrializing Economies* (New York: Oxford University Press, 2001).

122 Doig indicates that the Korean pattern is typical for former Japanese colonial regimes. He concludes: "Political authoritarianism was combined with economic controls while indigenous businesses lacked political power and access and bribed elites for favours either in the form of capital allocation or administrative support. Business communities had to negotiate with state elites to gain access to resources, whilst state elites demanded general co-operation in economic policy and also pay-offs for this assistance. State elites could even govern the form business development took." A. Doig, "In the State We Trust? Democratisation, Corruption and Development." *Commonwealth and Comparative Politics*, 37/3 (November 1999), p. 19.

123 Heidenheimer (1989), pp. 719–20.

124 Parts of an earlier version of this contribution has been included in A. Heidenheimer *et al.* in their *Handbook on Political Corruption,* published by Transaction Publ., New Brunswick/ Oxford 2000.

125 C. J. Friedrich, *The Pathology of Politics: Violence, Betrayal, Corruption, Secrecy and Propaganda*, (New York: Harper & Row, 1972).

126 J. van Klaveren (1957–1960) Die historische Erscheinung der Korruption, Series of essays im *Archiv für Sozial- und Wirtschaftsgeschichte,* pp. 44–47.

127 For a survey of the scientific literature in those days compare the first edition of A. Heidenheimer (1970) *Political Corruption,* with his more recent documentation together with M. Johnston/Victor Levine *Political Corruption* (New Brunswick: Transaction Publ., 1998).

128 *La Repubblica* (April 14,1998).

129 See for all of the countries here compared C. Guarnieri/ Patrizia Pederzoli, *La Puissance de Juger,* (Paris: Michalon, 1966), ch.1, du 2.

130 See Violaine Roussel, "Les magistrats dans les scandals politiques," in: *Revue française de la science politique* 48,2 (1998) pp. 245–273 who bases her analysis on systematic interviews with some twenty judges and prosecutors.

131 Cf. D. Robert, *La justice ou le chaos* (Paris: Stock, 1996).

132 The instrumentalization of the press can be by *Il Mundo* as paper of the opposition against Gonzalez using investigatory information for scandalizing, just as *El Pais* is nowadays using them in opposition against Aznar.

133 See the documentation of Denis Robert, *op cit.*

134 The polemic *against* the increasing influence of judges as moral guardians is raised by E. Zemmour, *Le Coup d'Etat des Juges* (Paris: Grasset, 1997).

135 See my contribution together with R. Staudhammer and H. Steinert in: A. Heidenheimer *et al., Political Corruption* (New Brunswick: Transaction Publ., 1989), pp. 913–32.

136 The rumors about collusion and corruption in the course of the privatization of collective and state enterprises in Eastern Germany form a revealing example. Compare the 2nd Parliamentary Enquête on the Treuhandanstalt, 12. Deutscher Bundestag, Bonn (1994) which speaks of a multitude of suspicions and more than 70 investigations for which proof could not be made hard enough to warrant a judicial procedure.

137 Cf. W. Rügener, "Die deutsche Justiz und die Korruption," in: *Kritische Justiz* 30, (1997), pp. 458–474.

138 *Source*: H. Oversloot, *Rusland deze jaren: hervorming door corruptie* (RijksUniversiteit Leiden, 1996).

139 Vgl. B. Woodell, *Japan under Construction: Corruption, Politics and Public Works* (Berkeley: Univ. of California Press, 1996).

140 Cf. P. Eigen (1999) *Combatting Corruption in the Free World* (Berlin: Transparency International, 1999).

141 See L., J. Graf, "The TI Corruption Perception Index 1996," in: J.Pope and
    C. Mohn, eds., *Transparency International Report* 1997, pp. 61–66; also at:
    http://www.uni-goettingen.de/~uwvw

142 Charles deMontesquieu (1734), *Considérations sur les causes de la
    grandeur des Romains et de leur décadence;* J.J. Rousseau (1750) *Discours
    sur les sciences et les arts.*

143 See S. N. . Eisenstadt and Rene Lemarchand, eds., *Political
    Clientelism, Patronage and Development* (Beverly Hills: Sage
    Publications, 1981). A diverse literature exists on the origins of clien-
    telism.

144 Chie Nakane, *Japanese Society* 1–103 (Berkeley: Univ. of Calif. Press,
    1970); A. Yeo-chi King, "Kuan-hsi and Network Building: A Sociological
    Interpretation," *Daedalus* (Spring 1991), at 63.

145 B. Woodall, *Japan under Construction: Corruption, Politics, and Public
    Works (1996),* pp 9–11.

146 Shin Myung-soon, A Proposal to Prevent Power-Oriented Misconduct and
    Corruption, *Human Rights and Justice* 23, 25, 253 (Sept. 1997).

147 Shin, p. 25; Oh, p. 270.

148 *Id.*

149 Park Sang Chul, *Election Campaigns and Related Political Laws* (Hanjulgi,
    1995), p. 593.

150 According to one study, 70–80 percent of all government subsidies and 95
    percent of all political party contributions go to the ruling party. *Joongang
    Ilbo* (Dec. 6, 1990).

151 Tun-jen Cheng and B. Womack, "General Reflections on Informal Politics
    in East Asia," *Asian Survey* 1, 10, 320 (1996).

152 Cheng and Womack, see note 151.

153 Chong, p. 20.

154 The other major KCIA scandals include the Saenara Motors Scandal, the
    Walker Hill Hotel Scandal and the Pachinko Scandal.

155 Kim and Kim, pp. 567–568.

156 Yoo Young-Ul, "Political-Economic Collusive Offenses in Chun Doo-
    Hwan Regime," *Shindonga* (June 1988), pp. 387–388.

157 Kim and Kim, p. 568.

158 Nam, p. 365 (in particular emphasizing Roh's personal family ties with the
    Chairman of Sunkyong).

159 Kim Kwang-Woong, "The Ideology and Politics of Korea's Civil-Military
    Bureucratic Elites," *Kyegan Kyunghyang* (Spring 1998), p. 30.

160 A. Doig, *Corruption and Misconduct in Contemporary British Politics* (Harmondsworth: Penguin, 1984).

161 Kim and Kim (1997).

162 Peter Drucker, Innovate or die, *Economist* 25 (Sept. 25, 1999).

163 Kim Yong Hak (1999).

164 Martin Crutsinger, "Russia Urged to Attack Corruption," *Associated Press* (25 September 1999, 21:13 EDT).

165 Prime Minister Kasyanov's address was broadcast by Russia TV on May 17, 2000. Kasyanov then emphasized that "recent experience has shown that [Russia] cannot save on civil servants' payments. It inevitably results in corruption and expansion of the civil service. We should overcome these tendencies, these negative tendencies inherent in our state machine, increasing civil servants' salaries, creating an open and differentiated system of payments for private-honest labor and raising the moral authority of the civil service, as well as creating an atmosphere of intolerance to official corruption in society." See the text of the report reprinted by BBC Monitoring and accessible on *Internet Securities* at: http://www.securities.com/cgi-bin/

166 *Itar-Tass* (Febr. 27, 1999).

167 Susan Rose-Ackerman, *Corruption and Government: Causes, Consequences and Reform* (Cambridge: Cambridge University Press, 1999), p.114.

168 Stalin used to refer to "bureaucratic malfeasance" and to embezzlement. I am grateful to S. Kotkin for pointing this out to me.

169 For a description of political corruption under the Soviet regime, see J. M. Kramer, "Political Corruption in the USSR," *Western Political Quarterly,* 30/2 (June 1977).

170 Konstantin M. Simis, *USSR: The Corrupt Society; The Secret World of Soviet Capitalism* (New York: Simon and Shuster, 1982), pp.133–134.

171 The entire Soviet economy not being monetarized, industrial managers were not in a position to buy needed equipment or materials on the black market in return for cash and, therefore, were forced into multiple barter deals.

172 See, for exemple, A. Katsenelinboigen, "Tsvetnie rynki i sovetskaya ekonomika SSSR.Vnutrennie protivorechiya," 1981, cited in M. Heller, *Cogs in the Wheel: The Formation of Soviet Man* (New York: A. A. Knopf, 1988), p.139.

173 As a dysfunction, Clark points out that corruption entails the outflow of capital, distorts investments, decreases administrative capacity, and weakens

the legitimacy of the system. Clark, William A., *Crime and Punishment in Soviet Officialdom: Combating Corruption in the Political Elite, 1965–1990* (Armonk, N.Y.: M.E. Sharpe, 1993), pp. 208–214

174 For a description of political corruption under the Soviet regime, see J. M.Kramer, "Political Corruption in the USSR," *Western Political Quaterly,* 30/2 (June 1977).

175 L.Timofeyev, *Russia's Secret Rulers* (New York: A. Knopf, 1992), p. 56.

176 The authorization was given by presidential decree. A year later, in 1988, the Supreme Soviet (parliament) voted the Law on Cooperatives. See A. Jones, W. Moskoff. *Ko-ops. The Rebirth of Entrepreneurship in the Soviet Union* (Bloomington & Indianapolis: Indiana University Press, 1991).

177 On the role of the Komsomol, see S. L. Solnick, *Stealing the State: Control and Collapse in Soviet Institutions* (Cambridge, MA, London: Harvard University Press, 1998), pp. 60–124.

178 These banks are Menatep, Most Group, Kredobank, Mosbiznesbank and Inkombank.

179 Author's interview with Russian industrialist Kakha Bendukidze, 20 March 1998.

180 Author's interviews with former First Deputy Prime Minister Boris Nemtsov, 28 September, 1998, and 16 February 1999; former First Deputy Prime Minister Vladimir Shumeiko, 1 December, 1998; MP Sergei Yushenkov, 1 December, 1998; former Privatization Minister and Chairman of Montes Auri investment fund Alfred Kokh, 25 November, 1998; former Economics Minister and Chairman of the Board of the RFK State Investment Company Andrei Nechaev, 24 March, 1998 and sociologist and deputy chairman of the board of Unified Energy Systems, Leonid Gozman, 27 November, 1998.

181 In January 1998, the group—notably composed of Kakha Bendukidze and Vladimir Lopukhin—was considering running in the December 1999 legislative election to form an "anti-government parliamentary group." Interview with Grigori Tomchin, chairman of the All-Russia Association of Privatized and Private Enterprises, 12 January, 1998.

182 Russian scholars I. Klyamkin and Lilya Shevtsova compared the Yeltsin regime to an "elective monarchy," in which the president has "absolute powers," "Eta vsesil'naya bessil'naya vlast'," *Nezavisimaya gazeta* (24 June), 1998.

183 As J. Hellman has shown, leaders in postcommunist countries tend to insulate the state, favor arbitrage opportunities, and implement partial econom-

ic reforms "that generate concentrated rents for themselves, while imposing high costs on the rest of the society." J. S. Hellman, "Winners Take All: The Politics of Partial Reform in Postcommunist Transitions," *World Politics,* 50/2 (1998), 203–34.

184 These findings are based on 102 interviews conducted with elite represen- tatives in Moscow, Yekaterinburg, and Perm in the Urals, between March, 1998 and February, 2000. The research project, entitled "Elite and Patronage in Russia," is directed by the author, based at the Davis Center for Russian Studies, Harvard University, and funded by the Smith Richardson Foundation.

185 On January 20, 1993 the Finance Ministry decided to create a new bank, supposedly to increase Russia's hard currency reserves, stop capital flight, exert reliable control over the fiduciary circulation and, more importantly, "help the government implement its monetary policy toward privatized enterprises. *Kommersant* (Daily), 16 November 1995. OneksimBank—a short name for Obedinennyj Eksportno-Importnyj Bank—got its license from the Central Bank on April 20, 1993.

186 In 1995 it became the bank of the State Committees for Bankruptcy and Privatization. It was also authorized by the federal government to manage the funds allocated to the reconstruction of the war-torn breakaway repub- lic of Chechnya.

187 Under the various governments of Yeltsin's presidency, most senior gov- ernment officials have been at once co-opted officials and board members of private enterprises in various industrial sectors; they have served as the necessary liaisons between the financial-economic and the political worlds. There are numerous examples of such co-optations: Vladimir Kadannikov (Chairman of the Avtovaz automobile company appointed deputy Prime Minister in charge of Economy); Vladimir Potanin (Chairman of OneksimBank appointed deputy Prime Minister); Vitali Ignatenko (director of the TASS news agency appointed deputy Prime Minister in charge of the press); and Boris Berezovsky (Chairman of the Logovaz automobile com- pany appointed deputy chairman of the Russian Security Council).

188 The banks also wanted to restrict the involvement of foreign investors in buying up Russia's strategic enterprises. The members of this consortium were OneksimBank, Imperial, Stolichny, Menatep, Inkombank, *Kommersant* (Daily), 1 April 1995, *Segodnya* (6–18 May), 1995. Inkombank left the consortium in August 1995, *Kommersant* (Daily), (15 August), 1995.

189 In September 1995, a presidential decree made the existence of the consortium official. *Segodnya* (September 3), 1995.

190 See, for example, the interviews of Alexander Lyubinin, Rossiisky Kredit deputy chairman, who considered the deal to be "rather more political than economic;" and of Boris Sergeyev, member of the board of Tokobank, who thought that the consortium affair was ruining all kinds of honest competition on the market. *Kommersant* (Daily) (April 1), 1995.

191 In the Spring of 1997 then Defense Minister Igor Rodyonov summoned the country's leading bankers and asked them to finance short-term food supplies to the army's starving garrisons. Three banks—OneksimBank, Vozrozhdenie and Neftekhimbank—won a tender launched by the Finance Ministry to fund the Defense Ministry. OneksimBank offered Rodyonov a one trillion-ruble loan. To compete in the tender, the banks had to have capital equivalent to 200 billion rubles as of April 1, 1996, and have a network of regional agencies. OneksimBank had already offered a 725 billion-ruble loan to the Defense Ministry in December 1995. *Segodnya*, (May 7), 1996.

192 On March 18, 1998, then First Deputy Prime Minister Boris Nemtsov held a roundtable meeting entitled "Russia's Future: Democracy and Oligarchy." See his article in *Nezavisimaya gazeta* (March 17), 1998.

193 *Izvestiya*, (October 24), 1997, p. 1.

194 The new head of Transneft is Dmitri Vainshtok, the former head of LUKoil-Western Siberia. For more details on this scandal, see *Vremya-MN* (September 21), 1999, p.1; Tat'yana Malkina, "Prem'er teriayet priznaki," *Vremya-MN* (September 22), 1999; K Levi, "Neftyanoe pyatno na reputatsii Putina," Kommersant-Daily (September 22), 1999; interview with Pavel Bunich, chairman of the Duma privatization committee, Mayak radio station, program "Reportazh," (September 24), 1999, 11:15 a.m.

195 See, for example, Olga Kryshtanovskaya, "From Soviet Nomenklatura to Russian Elite," *Europe–Asia Studies*, 48 (July 1996), pp.711–734, and "Nomenklatura nashego vremeni," *Obshchaya Gazeta* (January 23–-29), 1997; Y. Burtin, *Novyj stroy. O nomenklaturnom kapitalizme: sta'ti, dialog, interv'yu* (Moscow: Seriya 'Mezhdu proshlim i budushchim,' 1995).

196 Visiting Washington D. C. during the fall of 1997, Yavlinsky, the leader of the Yabloko liberal group in the State Duma, noted that up to 82 percent of enterprises within the Russian Federation no longer belonged to the state, but he suggested that only a few of them were actually privately owned. P. Goble, "Russia: Analysis From Washington—The Paradoxes of Privatization" (September 9), 1997, RFE/RL Reports: http://www.rferl.org

197 Janine R. Wedel, *Collision and Collusion: The Strange Case of Western Aid to Eastern Europe (1989–1998)* (New York: St. Martin's Press, 1998).

198 See the definition of "ideological kleptocrats" in Rose-Ackerman, *Corruption and Government, op.cit.*

199 On this scandal see, for example, *Segodnya* (February 16), 1999, pp. 1,4; *Kommersant Daily,* (March 2), 1999, pp. 1,7 and (March), 1999, pp. 1–2; *Parlyamentskaya gazeta* (March 4), 1999, p. 4. See also the report of Price Waterhouse/Coopers, which was posted on the IMF web-site until September 4, 1999 at: http://www.imf.org

200 Interview with Alexei Mozhin, *Vremya-MN* (October 1), 1999.

201 Interview with Viktor Gerashchenko, *Kommersant-Daily*, (July 13), 1999, pp. 1–2. In this interview Gerashchenko also acknowledged that hard currency reserves were transferred in September 1994 to Fimako, a month before the October 1994 ruble crash, known as the "Black Tuesday" financial crash.

202 Theses of the CPSU Central Committee for the XIX All-Union Party Conference approved by a plenum of the CPSU CC on May 23, 1988 cited in J. L.Black, USSR Documents Annual, 1988: Perestroika, the Second Stage, (Gulf Breeze, FL: Academic International Press, 1989), p. 202.

203 *Ibid.*

204 On the Media-Group raid and its political consequences, see for example *Komsomolskaya Pravda* (May 13), 2000, p. 3.

205 See, for example, *Delovoy Mir*, 88, (May 8), 1992.

206 Yeltsin submitted several draft reports to the commission. Instead of proposing concrete measures to fight corruption, he suggested the creation of new organs, notably at the level of the Commonwealth of Independent States, *Kommersant-Daily* (April 2), 1993, p.10. On corruption under Yeltsin, see J. M.Kramer, "The Politics of Corruption," *Current History* (October), 1998, pp. 329–334.

207 See, for example, *Izvestiya* (May 25), 1993, p. 4; *Kommersant-Daily* (June 23), 1993, p. 2; *Nezavisimaya Gazeta* (July 14), 1993, p. 1.

208 *Izvestiya,*(February 10), 1993, p. 5.

209 See P. Ricoeur, "Force and Language" in M. Szabó, ed., *Az ellenség neve,* Budapest (1998). According to Ricoeur the language of force is the language of fear, anger, insulted honor, and shameless boasting. The state, giving form to the social body, speaks in this language in the legal order. At the same time, the state both overcomes of private force (inasmuch as the state subjects it to the legal order), and "power as well, overwhelming force,

which pushes its way into the arena of private force, and speaks the language of values and respect." Ricoeur, 129

210 In 2000 it will turn out whether the new government (emerging—bloody and dirty—from the oligarchic chaos of the Yeltsin-era), committed to a liberal market economy, will be able to avoid the traditional Russian formula of statism built on autocratic tyranny—the police state and economic re-nationalization—-in this time of restoring the authority and force of the federal state. We have no reason to doubt that Vladimir Putin and his political team *want* to build a constitutional state, democracy, and market economy, despite the ten-year long oligarchic chaos that has brought the whole region to the brink of collapse, but whether they are going to succeed seems very doubtful indeed. See, among others, Vladimir Putin "V kakuyu Rossihu mi' verim," Presidential message to the Federal Assembly: http://www.polit.ru (July 11), 2000. V. Putin, "Rossiya ne dolzhna bit' I ne budet' politseiskim gosudarstvom," Interview, *Izvestiya* (July 14), 2000. D. Kozak, "Ya ne vizsu seryoznih osnovanii boyatsa perevorot," Interview, *Nezavisimaya Gazeta* (July 15), 2000). G. Pavlovsky, "Biznes dachnoy appozitsii," *Nezavisimaya Gazeta* (July 15), 2000. G. Pavlovsky, "Rossiyu legko raskrit'it' na revolutsiyu," Interview, *Kommersant-Vlast'* 26 (2000).

211 See S. Korolyov, *Donos v Rossii,* Progress-Multimedia (1996), pp. 29–90.

212 See, among others, B. Kagarlitsky, "S terroristami ne razgovarivayem. No pomogayem?—Versii vzrivov domov v Rossii," *Novaya Gazeta* (January 24), 2000, p. 3. P. Voloshin, "Chto bilo v Razanii: Sakhar ili hexogen?" *Novaya Gazeta* (February14), 2000, p. 6.

213 Putin himself, interestingly, was never directly put under suspicion of being involved in the bombings by any of the publications of the Gusinsky media empire, although since summer 1998 he was the director of the FSB (the intelligence department). True, his disreputable friends—sometimes fighting a life-and-death battle against each other, and other times fighting shoulder to shoulder against a common enemy—Berezovsky and Chubais, the two "Putin-maker" clan leaders (or at least that is the name they would claim), cast a long and dark shadow over him as well. Yet for some reason no one wanted to notice this shadow. Just like none of those concerned ran to the courts to get satisfaction after any capital-offense kompromat. True, they only accused each other of such trivial matters as the bombing of Moscow apartment buildings, the ordering of Dagestan Chechen robberies, the financing of Chechen bandits, money laundering, assassinations, mafia connections

214 For example, the electoral cohesion of young reformers, Kiriyen-ko–Nyemtsov–Chubais–Hakamada, sang the tune of the pro-war party, The Union of Rightwing Forces [Soyuz Pravikh Sil'], and therefore gained ground in the elections; the Yavlinskii-led "Yabloko," on the other hand, was against the war and lost ground for that reason among others.

215 See, for more details: A. Galiyev, "Materialniye sekreti," 28 Ekspert (December 20), 1998.

216 The *Ekspert* article mentioned above gives this frank advice to its readers: "If you need kompromat or if you perhaps are afraid of kompromats, it is best to look around your circle of acquaintances and find yourself someone who worked or is still working for the secret services there today—there is no other way . . . However, no one can give you a hundred percent guarantee that someone won't incite a kompromat against you." Galiyev.

217 Galiyev.

218 *Ibid.*

219 I tried to analyze this formula in the concluding chapter of my book, *Borisz sztár és a sztárevicsek* (see *A nyolcadik főtiktár: Vlagyimir Putyin,* Helikon (2000), pp. 460–529). Also see the compilation "Putin's Russia," *East European Constitutional Review* (Winter/Spring), 9.1/2 2000, pp. 51–91.

220 First the Interior Ministry obtained the necessary licenses and instruments for independent wire-tapping and from then on all possible technology available in the West was brought into the country, both with and without authorization. Until recently the trade in technical spying equipment was unrestricted. In December, 1999, the first case occurred in which a sentence (one-year suspended imprisonment) was given for trading in technical equipment used for the gathering of secret information.

221 "We have had enough corruption," announced the editor-in-chief of *Versiya,* Rustam Arifdzsanov, and rushed to add, "Our task, above all else, is to increase circulation. It is rare that we pay for information. Like the old Soviet investigators, we also would rather use means of 'persuasion.' We try to find people who think like we do: who have had enough of the Russian corruption, but it happens sometimes that we are mistaken and such things cannot influence the person. In such cases we buy the information. The price varies: sometimes we pay 3000 dollars for something, but other times 10,000." (Of course the information referred to here is nothing more than kompromat itself. Since the sister-paper of *Versiya* is *Sovershenno sekretno,* in a certain sense it specializes in the communication of kompromat.) The interview appeared in the article of *Ekspert* (December 20), 1999, mentioned above.

222 A. Tsipko, "Beregit'e Putina," *Literaturnaya Gazeta* (October 20–26), 42,
1999,pp.1–2. Of course Putin has also received his share of kompromats (if
you don't have any kompromat, you aren't a politician in Russia!), but 99
percent of these were unfounded, of poor quality, or unverifiable; the
remaining one percent was simply "forgotten" by the oligarchs controlling
the media to be effectively publicized, stirred up and thrown before the
world. Who knows why.

223 Tsipko, "No one knows how this unprecedented kompromat war will end.
No one knows who will remain alive on the political stage and who will
remain in the people's consciousness if this total war, waged for "clean
hands," ever stops. At this time it is even possible that the kompromat war
will equally discredit both the current masters of the Kremlin and the cen-
trist coalition [i.e., Luzhkov and Primakov—author's note]. In this case,
however, it is also possible that under these scorched earth conditions a
third force would come into power in Russia—from outside the system.
People used to be afraid of the revenge of the communists. Now, however,
the danger is that the lords of the criminal world will come into power, with
Vladimir Zhironovsky at their heads." Tsipko.

224 See http://www.kompromat.com or http://www.kompromat.ru. Downloaded
on 10 January, 2000.

225 The Free Lance Bureau site, http://www.flb.ru, becoming famous in the past
six months, advertises itself as the Federal Investigation Agency (Agenstvo
Federalnih Rassledovanyii) and in June 2000 under the collective title "The
database of the MOSTsecurity service" began to put on the Russian web
this huge base of information (90 gigabytes, 600 files, and 20,000 typed
pages), presumably collected by private secret service agencies in the past
few years, with confidential tools, of course. According to speculations, the
information base is the result of the "corporate work" of security service
employees who were left without work in the wake of the series of bank
failures following the 1998 financial collapse. At the end of 1998 they tried
to sell it to the parties concerned, and in the fall of 1999 they began the
wholesale marketing of the information (200 dollars per file). As a result of
the kompromat inflation at the beginning of 2000, however, they quickly
got rid of it all: the FLB site bought the 90 gigabytes and put the most interesting megabytes on the web on June 6. Some suspect that the FSB (the
Federal Secret Service) was behind the flb.ru. activity. According to this
speculation, the action was directed towards discrediting Vladimir
Gusinsky's media holding company, MOST. Let us not forget that, during

a search of the company's headquarters in spring, they seized a database that had been amassed by the company's security service by illegal means and for illegal purposes. Yet, for that very reason it is supposed that Gusinsky and Philip Bobkov (Bobkov is a former KGB chief, who was once awarded "imperishable merits" for his persecution of dissenters; Gusinsky runs his own private secret service, for a monthly salary of 10,000 dollars) have at least that much interest in dumping the database on the web or withdrawing it from the market and, thereby, invalidating it. What kind of secret information base is it if everyone can read it? After this it will be truly difficult to initiate proceedings against those who created this huge kompromat library. The reason for these completely contradictory conjectures— and this is true of any situation analyzed today—is not a lack, but the abundance of information, the excess of information, and its incomprehensibility. The technological tools that came with the telecommunications revolution together with the misinformation technology of the old KGB have created a situation in Russia in which it is almost impossible to know anything for certain about the true motives of why they happen, as in spy stories, where at the end even the spy doesn't know whom he is working for. Information is the mystification of power—state power and private power. Information has been replaced by total misinformation; objective analysis by breath-taking or despairing speculation. No one knows anything, while at the same time everyone knows that everything is constantly being made known. New ignorance is in the making. "Do you need more information?" This question is like asking the bug drowning in the ocean if it needs more water. For information see S. Pluzhnyikov and S. Sokolov, "Spetssluzsbi olgarkhov": http://www.flb.ru (July 16), 2000, Olga Vandisheva, "Rossiyu zavalili kompromatom po samiye ushi," *Komsomolskaya Pravda* (June 6), 2000, and A. Soldatov, "Zatupivshiysa kogot," *Izvestiya* (July 8),2000.

226 Kopromat. ru is the invention of Sergei Gorshkov: "The Home Library of Internet Kompromat." Being of one year's standing, it is one of the oldest intellectual kompromat sites. For the purpose of entertainment, it posts information about backdated and up-to-date fresh kompromats, that is, about everything related to this topic which has been published in regional, national or foreign press or has been sent to the master of the site's "home library." According to other sources, Gorshkov's kompromat.ru opened at the beginning of December, 1999, at the end of the Duma elections. Whether this service is motivated by some kind of political interests or private interests will probably always remain a mystery (the site also includes

commercials and other services). The self-mystification employed for advertising purposes is no stranger to the site. For example, on 23 February 2000 the site was not accessible for an entire day, which its operator later claimed in the press, was the result of an attack by the FSB against the site—even though it turned out that one service provider simply wished to call attention to the site's outstanding debts. In any case, the scandal made Gorshkov's kompromat.ru famous with one stroke. Naturally, the site also publicized the kompromat that exposed the supposed FSB action as a false kompromat by the site's owner, Gorshkov. This proves that there is no longer any "truth" or "reality"; in the era of the information revolution the truth-value of information is equivalent to zero. People sitting in front of the screen can no longer *sense* that a piece of information is covering up the facts. The more amendments, exposures (including the exposure of the exposers), and possible versions, the less we are able to grasp what has actually happened. Who is telling the truth and who is lying? It is both likely that the "shutdown" of kompromat.ru was a PR-stunt by Gorshkov as that it was an attack by the secret service. It is just as possible that Gorshkov wrote an article against himself ("hey, this Gorshkov, this Gorshkov! He was capable of fooling the entire press, just to advertise his site!"), as also that someone else exposed him, like in a crime novel where the investigator puts together all the pieces. It could also be that the FSB wrote it, or had it written, or even that they blackmailed the site's owner ("if you don't write it, you can say goodbye to the Internet!"). We could go on listing possible versions. All information has become mystery on the virtual space and time of the information universe: you can only believe in it like ancient people believed in God, or be entertained by it, as by any work of art. It is pointless to try to figure out what is true and what is not. Believe in it, if you have enough strength to believe, or enjoy its absurdity, surprise, wit and humor. From this point of view, kompromat.ru is not a special information base and service but rather an unending soap opera.

227 Supposedly, sovesti.net would have been the snappy political answer to ovg.ru. But both the ideological justification for the opening of the site (the site of the true "patriots" fighting between the two pagans, i. e., between the "Kremlin family" and the "Moscow family,"for "one home") as well as its strange content (a restrained disparagement of Primakov and an exposure of the Kremlin's "cashier," the young financial executive Aleksandr Mamut, who has already been denounced in the press a thousand times) prove that this site is also the work of Pavlovsky. In any case it strengthened his Internet

"project" in two ways: on the one hand it made references to ovg.ru and pop-ularized it and stimulated political battles on the web; on the other hand the kompromat war against the OVR (Luzhkov–Yakovlev–Primakov block) could continue on the site of the alleged "patriots." Even the site's name— sovesti.net—is too witty to be a symbol of the "patriots." Sovesti.net is an ironic word game: it is built on the well-known Russian figure of speech "sovesti nyet," which means "there is no conscience" or "there is not an ounce of honor in you" and the English word "net," referring to the Internet. "They have no conscience" + "this is the net of conscience."

228 The social injustice of the system is obvious, although it may not funda-mentally differ from the injustices of market-based systems and systems that combine private and public health care. The rich will always afford spe-cial private health care, while those in the public social insurance system receive rationed care, and those outside the system very little care. Proportions are crucial here.

229 T. Frye and A. Shleifer, "The Invisible Hand and the Grabbing Hand," *American Economic Review, Papers and Proceedings*, 87/2 (1997), 354–358, cited by Radaev.

230 Maria Los and A. Zybertowicz, *Privatizing the Police State. The Case of Poland* (Hampshire–New York: Macmillan–St. Martin Press,. 2000), pp. 112–113.

231 Huntington argued that "to the extent that corruption builds parties, it under-mines the conditions of its own existence." *Political Order in Changing Societies* (Yale University Press, 1968), pp. 70–71. This might be true at certain levels of development (including, perhaps, England around the Reform Bill, 1832). The current media-dependent party politics is, howev-er, not proving that parties, once built, will not contribute to a new round of corruption.

232 On the strong-challenger issue, see, for starters, J. Krasno, *Challengers, Competition, and Reelection: Comparing Senate and House Elections* (New Haven, Ct., 1994).

233 Ph. Harling, *The Waning of "Old Corruption": the Politics of Economical Reform in Britain, 1779–1846* (Oxford: Clarendon, 1996).

234 E. Kheng-Boon Tan, "Law and Values in Governance: The Singapore Way." *Hong Kong Law Journal*. 30: 91, 2000.

235 Gallup Hungary, H-1033, Budapest, Fő tér 1. E-mail: robi@Gallup.hu

236 For a discussion of the role and interaction of organizing principles see: Polanyi, K.,. *The Great Transformation*. (Boston: Beacon Press; 1968) and

Hankiss, Elemér. *East European Alternatives* (Oxford: Clarendon Press, 1990).

237 Heidenheimer, A. J., *Political Corruption. Readings in Comparative Analysis* (New York. Holt Rinehart and Winston, 1970).

238 For standard approaches see Heidenheimer, Johnston and Levine (1989). As Yves Meny has noted, "The biggest bribes happen where old rules cease to apply and new ones are not yet established." (Quoted in J. Vítek, "Kdo maže, jede nìkdy až do vìzení," HN 19/2/96.) Yet, if as in conventional approaches we rely on rules to define corruption, then how can we talk of corruption under such circumstances?

239 For a fuller discussion of this issue see Reed (1996).

240 According to the authors, political systems need to be *vertically* consolidated in the sense that "[T]he . . . rules according to which political and distributional conflicts are carried out are relatively immune from becoming themselves the object of such conflict" (*ibid.*, p. 28) Systems need to be *horizontally* consolidated, ar rather differentiated where "a measure of such differentiation is the degree of insulation of institutional spheres from each other and the limited convertibility of status attributes from one sphere to another" (*ibid.*, p. 31).

241 Former Czech Prime Minister from 1990 to 1992, Petr Pithart, summarized the vulnerability of Czech privatization thus: "No country apart from Russia carried out such a complete nationalization as we: consequently, no country in the world has to . . . privatize such a huge amount of property in a short period. These facts, which are faced by both constitutional functionaries and officials of the state administration, are temptations such as which cannot exist anywhere else . . . [and] are succumbed to, not only by individuals, but also whole political parties." (P. Pithart, quoted in J. Muller, "Odvrácená tvář privatizace," *HN* 12/7/94.)

242 S. Rose-Ackerman, "Which Bureaucracies are Less Corruptible?" in Heidenheimer, Johnston and Levine, eds. (1989), p. 810.

243 V. Labuda (1995), p. 51; "Rodinné stříbro se neprodává" (interview with Minister of Industry Jan Vrba), *RP* 13/9/91.

244 *ČD* 15/10/93.

245 Indeed, the Czech policy of selling to Czech buyers probably *required* the state to maintain control over the banks, otherwise they would not have provided the necessary loans.

246 "Privatization in Hungary, Poland and the Czech Republic," K. Zijlstra, draft report for NATO sub-committee on East–West economic convergence, April 1998, p. 13.

247 *Ibid.*

248 *RP* 10/7/92, 20/10/92, 29/10/92, 4/11/92; *LN* 16/10/92, 21/10/92, 13/11/92; *MFD* 20/7/92, 22/9/92, 23/10/92, 29/10/92, 2/11/92, 7/11/92; *HN* 3/3/92, 5/5/92, 14/5/92, 13/7/92; *ČD* 10/10/92; *E* 44/1992; *Kvìty* 48/1992. Interview with former Managing Director of *KP* Miroslav Kaplánek, who provided various documents concerning the privatization, its legal blocking, and subsequent solution.

249 See Reed (1996) for a fuller account of the privatization.

250 It is worth mentioning that the Karlovy Vary Local Privatization Committee organized the preliminary stages of the privatization. The Chairman of the committee became a Deputy Minister of Privatization after leaving the committee in January, 1992, and was also a member of the Karlovy Vary Rotary Club, a group of local business people which at the time of the privatization included many of the managers who benefited from the privatization decision. According to KP managers at that time, he was also a member of the management and supervisory boards in the companies which bought three KP factories plants. His placement at the ministry coincided with the reversal of the Ministry of Industry's recommendation.

251 Vrba was also a proponent of case-by-case privatization, a role for the state in restructuring prior to privatization, and the sale of large enterprises to foreign strategic investors.

252 "Jde vlna za vlnou" (round-table discussion), *HN* 20/7/92. This approach seems to have been borne out by the fact that during Vrba's term of office (until June, 1992)—a period covering the approval process for almost the whole of the first wave of privatization—there was no scandal at the Ministry.

253 According to Tomáš Ježek, Minister of Privatization from August, 1990, to June 1992, at the beginning of the process only about 10 percent of projects were such that the MP could simply give a yes or no decision. Hence the Ministry did change projects itself, and this was later incorporated in an amendment to the law.

254 Interview with Libor Kudláček.

255 Labuda (1995), Ch. 1.; *RP* 2/9/92, 25/9/92, 2/10/92, 22/1/93, 7/5/93, 14/5/93, 18/5/93, 19/11/93, 24/3/93 1/4/94, 9/4/94, 16/4/94; *LN* 12/6/92, 23/9/92, 5/11/92, 9/11/92, 8/1/93, 28/1/93, 16/6/93, 16/7/93, 17/7/93, 11/9/93, 22/4/94 13/1/95; *MFD* 14/1/93, 15/4/93, 28/4/93, 21/5/93, 15/7/93, 25/8/93, 7/9/93, 19/4/94, 28/4/94; *ČD* 11/11/92, 26/1/93, 11/3/93, 14/9/93, 26/4/94, 21/6/94; P 22/10/93, 19/11/93; *SS* 21/5/93, 26/5/94; *Tel* 21/9/93; *E*

19/1994; *T* 7/1994; *Prosto*r 6/11/92; *Reflex* 43/1992; interviews with Pavel Rychetský (lawyer, Vice-Chairman of Federal Government 1990–1992), Vladimír Labuda (*RP* journalist), Ctirad Loffelman (Chief of the Central Bohemia Prosecution Bureau).

256 Law no. 210/1993.

257 Until November, 1995, the SAO also had the duty of auditing the annual accounts of political parties and checking their accuracy. However, the Constitutional Court then removed this function on the basis that political parties were private entities.

258 For example, a 1995 SAO audit of the Ministry of Industry and Trade's management of state enterprises falling under its competence concluded that, "[C]ontrol by the Ministry of Industry and Trade... has been completely ineffective" (SAO Audit Conclusion no. 33/1995).

259 Q. Reed and H. Lešenarová, "Negligence is no crime", *Prague Business Journal,* 34/1997.

260 V. Labuda, *"Tři* pravidla pro svatý klid," *RP* 3/12/93.

261 *RP* 7/9/93, 3/12/93, 3/3/94; *LN* 22/10/93; *HN* 8/9/93, 6/10/93, 7/10/93; *ČD* 18/10/93.

262 For a fuller account see Reed (1996).

263 Labuda (1995), Ch. 6; *RP* 27/4/94, 28/4/94, 11/5/94, 15/7/94, 22/7/94, 18/1/95; *LN* 29/4/94, 11/5/94; *MFD* 28/4/94; *HN* 20/5/94, 29/4/94; *ČD* 30/4/94; *Práce* 29/4/94, 20/5/94; *LD* 21/5/94; *Tel* 2/5/94, 5/5/94, 17/5/94, 15/6/94; *ZN* 29/4/94.

264 In an interesting twist, the shares included 3 percent of the shares of *Plzeňský Prazdroj* (Pilsen Breweries). After the privatization project for the brewery was approved in April, 1992, Minister of Privatization Ježek signed two letters with the same serial number: one, received by the management of *PP*, stated that 67 percent of the shares of *PP* would go to voucher privatization; the other, received by the Ministry of Agriculture, stated the figure of 70 percent. In the event, 67 percent was the correct figure, which resulted in 3 percent of the shares being unaccounted for in the privatisation project—the same 3 percent received by *Investiční Banka.*

265 Ravik (1995), *P.* 26; *RP* 28/2/95, 31/5/94; *MFD* 9/4/94, 15/4/94, 24/9/94, 26/1/95; *ČD* 13/4/94, 14/4/94, 18/4/94, 31/5/94; *Práce* 1/9/94; *LD* 14/4/94, 22/7/94; *ZN* 29/7/94; *R* 15/94, 19/94.

266 According to former spokesman of the NPF Miloš Růžička, "It has been a common practice here that you pay a deposit and then pay the rest through

the company." (H. Lešenarová, "Šrejber's grand scam," *Prague Business Journal*, 7/1998)

267 *RP* 24/2/93, 25/2/93, 18/6/93, 21/9/93, 25/9/93, 25/2/94, 29/8/94, 18/11/94, 3/1/95, 3/2/95, 28/6/94; *P* 7/2/96, 19/2/96; *LN* 17/2/93, 11/6/93, 22/6/93, 5/10/93, 25/8/94, 30/11/94, 7/2/95, 8/2/95, 9/2/95, 10/2/95, 21/2/95, 3/3/95; *MFD* 19/6/93, 13/11/93, 25/8/94, 9/2/95, 10/2/95, 11/2/95, 23/2/95, 20/2/96; *HN* 17/11/92, 24/2/93, 18/6/93, 28/11/94; *ČD* 4/1/92, 16/2/94; *Práce* 18/6/93, 22/9/93, 30/9/93, 8/2/95, 11/2/95, 13/2/95, 18/2/95, 22/2/95; *ZN* 14/11/91, 5/5/93, 17/2/95; *R* 10–16/8/92, 28/2-6/3/94; *T* 23/10/92, 18/11/92 30/9/93, 25/2/94, 9/2/95, 14/2/95, 4/3/95; *T* 9/1996; interviews with Pavel Rychetský, lawyer representing one of Poldi's creditors and 1990–1992 Vice-Chairman of the Federal Government, Václav Žák, 1991–1992 Chairman of the Czech National Council.

268 "We had our doubts when we saw the buyer was not qualified in the steel business," commented an official from the Swedish company, Inexa, which participated in the tender. Press reports indicated that the offer was so high because the director of *Bohemia Art* misread advice given to him by NPF officials.

269 Harvard, for example, never honored its promise of 1000 percent returns.

270 In each round, if supply exceeded demand, then demand was satisfied, and the shares not sold went back into the next round at a lower price. If the ratio of demand to supply exceeded 1.25:1 nothing was sold, and all the shares were entered into the next round at a higher price. If the ratio of demand to supply was between 1:1 and 1.25:1 the orders of participants were reduced automatically in the order that all the shares were sold, satisfying the demand of participants in the same proportion as their original orders implied.

271 Z. Bláha, O. Kýn, M. Mejstřík and J. Mládek, "Tři uzly na kuponové privatizace," R 5/1992.

272 J. Havligerová and R. Gallo, "Kuponové chyby nelze opakovat," *MFD* 14/11/94.

273 Livia Klausová, wife of Prime Minister Václav Klaus, also sat on the same board.

274 According to Vice-Chairman of the ODA Daniel Kroupa the privatization legislation was written in such a way that its authors could personaly benefit from the process.

275 SAO Audit no. 36/1993.

276 "Stát Ltd," *MFD* 16/5/96.

277 Sources for this case and the following information on shares gained by IPF's from voucher privatization were: *RP* 3/11/94, 4/11/94, 5/11/94, 7/11/94, 8/11/94, 10/11/94, 11/11/94, 12/11/94, 14/11/94, 15/11/94, 16/11/94, 22/11/94, 20/12/94; *P* 4/11/94, 13/9/95, 19/10/95, 20/10/95; *LN* 3/11/94, 4/11/94, 5/11/94, 14/11/94, 18/11/94, 2/12/94, 19/12/94, 24/1/95, 3/2/95, 22/2/95, 13/9/95, 19/10/95; *MFD* 3/11/94, 4/11/94, 5/11/94, 7/11/94, 8/11/94, 9/11/94, 12/11/94, 17/11/94, 24/11/94, 17/12/94, 30/12/94, 16/1/95, 20/1/95, 23/1/95, 31/1/95, 4/2/95, 7/2/95, 22/2/95, 12/9/95, 13/9/95, 14/9/95, 19/10/95; *HN* 4/11/94, 19/10/95; *ČD* 3/11/94, 4/11/94, 5/11/94, 7/11/94, 12/11/94, 17/11/94, 18/11/94; *ČT* 27–30/1/95; Tel 4/11/94, 10/11/94, 14/9/95, 20/10/95; 28/9/95, 12/12/95; *ZN* 4/11/94; *R* 7–13/11/94, 8/1995, 22/95, 26/95; *Dobrý večer* 3/11/94; *Prognosis Weekly* 10–16/11/94.

278 Lizner was the highest public official in Czechoslovak history ever to be convicted of corruption.

279 Including Plzeňské pivovary (19.9 percent), Sklo Union Teplice (19.11 percent), Energovod (19.7 percent), Pražská teplárenská, Komerční Banka (17.6 percent), Česká spořitelna, České energetické závody (the largest Czech company), and interestingly PVT itself (18.88 percent).

280 For example, *SPT Telecom* (1.24:1) or the country's biggest coal mining concern *Nová Huť* (1.25:1) and engineering giant *Škoda Plzeň* (1.25:1).

281 *RP* 10/1/95; *LN* 17/12/95, 9/1/95, 10/1/95, 11/1/95, 16/1/95, 27/1/95, 2/2/95, 14/2/95, 17/2/95; *MFD* 10/1/95, 15/2/95, 5/5/95; *ČT* 27-30/1/95. Minister Vladimír Dlouhý. Dlouhý defended the sale, saying his Ministry offered such reductions in price in tens of cases.

282 *P* 24/4/96, 25/4/96, 26/4/96, 29/4/96, 3/5/96; *LN* 29/12/95, 30/12/95, 9/1/96, 24/4/96, 26/4/96; *MFD* 12/4/96, 13/4/96, 23/4/96, 26/4/96, 27/4/96, 2/5/96; *R* 13/96, 9–15/6/96.

283 According to weekly *Respekt,* an investigation by the police anticorruption service and military intelligence service of contracts at the Ministry of Defense in 1995 mentioned a German firm with which defense company *Zenit* co-operated closely, and suggested that around Kč1m may have passed from *Zenit* through this firm to *Coutts and Co. Bank* in Liechtenstein, from which it was donated to the KDU–ČSL. Zenit won a contract connected with the modernization and sale of the T-72 tank.

284 H. Lešenarová, "Šrejber's grand scam," *Prague Business Journal*, 7/1998.

285 At the time of writing the Swiss anti-money laundering authorities were expected to release information confirming or rejecting the existence of the account.

286 "Audit hospodaření v ODS prokázal vážné machinace," *MFD* 14/5/98.

287 P 25/2/98.

288 Jiží Psenička, "Privatizace 1997: Zase už je zhasnuto," *T* 47/1997.

289 For example, investors often take minority stakes in Hungarian and Polish companies, but are now aware that to do so in the Czech Republic is in most cases an unjustifiable risk since minority shareholder protection remains almost non-existent.

290 Former privatization Minister and NPF chairman Tomáš Ježek, who apparently embraced the cause of regulation at some time in the 1995–1996 period, described the post-privatization atmosphere in the following way: "There wasn't disinterest [in regulation], there was active resistance. The period was driven by the false philosophy of *laissez faire*, of absolute liberalism." [Ježek cited in Schwartz (1999), p. 177.]

291 For example, one of the people being investigated in connection with the CS Fond fraud mentioned earlier was one of the ČSSD's most generous donors in 1998.

292 For example, at the time of writing, the trial of a former ODS employee for tax evasion in connection with corrupt party financing was taking place. Despite daily revelations of murky financing details, the ČSSD has not commented once.

293 For example, in February, 1999, the government approved a little-noticed policy document entitled "The National Fight against Corruption," a comprehensive and impressive initiative prepared over a long period by officials at the Ministry of Interior. However, little has been revealed by the document.

294 For example, projects to restructure and privatize the Czech steel industry and heavy engineering companies, both carried out in cooperation with the European Union, were both abandoned in favor of fast privatization to Czech interests.

295 This does not necessarily mean there was less corruption, but mainly that corruption control mechanisms functioned more effectively. However, the latter probably implies the former.

296 For example, recent survey research of businesses across post-Communist Central and Eastern Europe carried out by the World Bank and European Bank for Reconstruction and Development indicates that administrative corruption is significantly worse in the Czech Republic than in Poland and Hungary. (REF)

297 The paper summarizes the findings of a number of projects. We would like to thank many experts for their valuable comments and suggestions. Several

institutions have provided their organizational or/and financial support for certain parts of the study. Our special thanks are to A.Bayhan, M.Forst, and P.Paradis (OECD), I. Bunin, and N. Nazarova (Center for Political Technologies), V. Gubernatorov (Russian Federation Chamber of Commerce and Industry), V. Vlasov, L. Galkova, and M. Butova (Department for SME Support, Tomsk oblast administration).

298 "Społeczna ocena demokracji i instytucji politycznych," CBOS, 1996.

299 "Oceny sytuacji gospodarczej, warunków bytu i działalności rządu w Polsce, Czechach i na Węgrzech,"CBOS, 1996.

300 Huntington S. P. "The Third Wave. Democratization in the Late Twentieth" (University of Oklahoma Press, 1991).

301 "Aspirations, Values and Interests" (Warszawa: Wydawnictwo IFiS PAN, 1995).

302 "O społecznym postrzeganiu korupcji,",CBOS, 1997.

303 "Uczciwość w polityce," CBOS, 1995.

304 "Uczciwość w polityce," CBOS, 1995.

305 "Pinie o łapówkach," CBOS, 1999.

306 "O społecznym postrzeganiu korupcji," CBOS, 1997.

307 "O społecznym postrzeganiu korupcji," CBOS, 1999.

308 "Opinie o bogactwie i ludziach bogatych," CBOS, 1999.

309 "Oszczędności i lokaty," CBOS, 1999.

310 Smolar, A.,"Państwo grzesznych moralistów," *Gazeta Wyborcza* (September 25–26 September), 1999.

311 "Opinie o łapówkach," CBOS, 1999.

312 The general models should be understood as ideal types—real party-funding models will always deviate from them in one respect or another. For instance, public financing schemes in U. S. presidential elections run against the libertarian logic. See J. Nelson, "The Supply and Demand of Campaign Finance Reform," *Columbia Law Review*, 100/2 (2000). The U. S. Supreme Court in 1976 constitutionalized the libertarian logic of campaign finance in *Buckley v. Valeo*. Thus, not only does the U. S. model work in a libertarian fashion, but also it is ideologically supposed to do so. In the U. K., triggered by the report of the Neill Committee in 1998, the model of party funding is set to undergo a serious reform in an egalitarian direction (in the terms of this paper). As the rules stand at the time of writing, however, with the exception of the ban on paid campaign ads on public electronic media, the model fits the libertarian-parliamentary ideal type. See M. S. Shugart, "The Inverse Relationship between Party Strength and Executive Strength: A Theory of

Politicians' Constitutional Choices," *British Journal of Political Science*, (1998) 28, 1–29. Since the two case studies I am dealing with fit the general typology, I am not going to discuss possible deviant cases.

313 See Virginie Coulloudon, "The Criminalization of Russia's Political Elite," in *East European Constitutional Review*, 6/4 (1997).

314 Here, I am not challenging Duverger's rule, according to which the first-past-the-post electoral systems lead to stable two-party systems. I am calling attention to the fact that the pure proportional system *consolidates* internally the parties, by avoiding competition from individual candidates and ad hoc electoral blocs. In Bulgaria the first democratic elections in 1990 were carried out under a mixed electoral system, but all subsequent general elections have been under a pure proportional system, strengthened by the d'Hont formula for translating votes into parliamentary seats.

315 "Law on Political Parties," *Official Gazette*, No. 29, 1990, Art. 18.

316 The public support for the parties is regulated by the electoral law for every election. Since the first parliamentary elections in 1990 the parliamentary represented parties have been entitled to the lion's share of state support.

317 As a rule, free airtime is dependent on the seats in parliament that the parties control. Only in the first parliamentary elections, the rules for which were negotiated at the Round Table talks, all parties had equal access to the media, and most importantly, a right to make one presentation in the beginning and one at the end of the campaign. There were opportunities for the purchase of additional airtime. In subsequent parliamentary elections, there were more generous provisions of free airtime; in addition to the time for presentations, there were opportunities for so-called "thematic debates" in which the PRP had a separate quota larger than the others. In presidential elections, the candidates have the right to an opening and a closing address to the nation, as well as to several presentations during the campaign (each day three candidates make such presentations). In local elections, only the opening and the closing statements of the parties on the national media are free of charge. The parties have to pay for their participation in the "thematic debates" (90 minutes a week). Half of this time is reserved for the PRP, to be divided among them in proportion to the seats in the legislature. The paid access to the media is, however, at preferential prices set by the Council of Ministers.

318 See K. Z. Paltiel, "Campaign Finance: Contrasting Practice and Reform," in *Democracy at the Polls: A Comparative Study of Competitive National Elections,* eds., Butler, D., H. Penniman, A. Ranney, *American Enterprise Institute for Public Policy Research,* Washington, D. C., 1981, p. 140.

319 The concept "electoral association," introduced in the Duma elections of
1993, includes not only federal political parties but also, federal "movements" registered with the Ministry of Justice, and blocs of public associations created for participation in elections. See art. 5(2) of the *Polozhenie o
vyiborah deputatov Gosudarstvennoi Dumyi v 1993 godu,* adopted by
Presidential Decree of October 1, 1993, No. 1557, Moscow, Kremlin (here-
inafter "Rules 1993"). While the parties and movements could form electoral associations on their own, the other public associations (registered
with the Ministry of Justice) could participate only in electoral blocs. The
1995 Duma election law *(Federalnyi zakon o vyiborah deputatov
Gosudarstvennoi Dumyi, 1995,* art. 2) provided that the electoral associations have to be registered six months in advance of the elections: electoral
blocs, which are coalitions of associations, are exempted from this restriction. Individual candidates for the Duma may be nominated not only by
electoral associations and blocs, but by groups of voters as well.
Presidential candidates are to be nominated by electoral associations, blocs,
or directly by groups of 100 voters (Law on presidential election,
Federalnyi zakon o vyiborah presidenta Rossiiskoi Federatsii, 1995, No.
21, arts. 32 and 33).

320 In 1993 the electoral associations participating in the proportional elections
to the Duma were required by law to collect at least 100,000 signatures of
voters, out of which only 15 percent could be from a single member of the
Russian Federation. The threshold was raised to 200,000 signatures in the
1995 Duma elections, while only seven percent could come from a single
member of the federation. In the 1996 presidential elections, the threshold
for a presidential candidate was one million signatures. In 1999, there were
possibilities for submitting a cash deposit instead of collecting signatures.

321 In the 1993–1995 Duma, almost a third of the seats were won by "independent" candidates. See White, Rose, and Allister, *How Russia Votes*
(Chatam House Publishers., Inc., 1997), p. 125. In 1995 the share of inde-
pendents fell to 17.1 percent of the seats in the Duma.

322 Every electoral association and bloc, every registered candidate, is obligated by law to open a special electoral account (fund). Only these accounts
can be used for fund raising and electoral expenditures. Contributions to
these funds are tax exempt.

323 See White, Rose, and Allister, *op. cit.,* pp. 200–202.

324 Public subsidies are given both to the Duma factions and individual deputies
in the Duma and the Federation Council (the upper chamber of the Federal

Assembly). Each of the deputies of the Duma and the Federation Council has a right to hire up to five assistants. This subsidy is coupled with a subsidy to the factions in the Duma for the maintenance of faction apparatus. It is dependent on the number of deputies the faction has. (These subsidies were first introduced by the Standing Orders of the Duma, March 25, 1994, No. 80-1GD, art. 73, and Ordinance of the Federal Assembly, November 5, 1997, No. 378 SF.) There are also in-kind forms of support for the faction apparatus, as introduced by the Law "On the Status of the Deputy in the State Duma," May 8, 1994, No. 3- FZ. These include the right to free public transport, offices, office equipment, and communication services during their trips to their electoral districts for meetings with the voters. These forms of public support have played an important role for some of the parties. "With their salaries paid from the state budget, the 800-odd assistants to the communist deputies are effectively the organizational core of the party . . . Communist deputies, of course, have all the latest office equipment, and the twelve who head Duma committees and other Duma institutions have separate staffs of their own, government cars . . . Richard Sakwa, "Left or Right? CPRF and Democratic Consolidation," in *Party Politics in Post-communist Russia* (Frank Cass, London, Portland, 1998), p. 150.

325 Even the subsidies in the Duma are *mainly* distributed through individual candidates. Moreover, many of the Duma factions do not represent a single party, but are rather alliances of individual candidates; these loose alliances (deputies' groups) enjoy the same institutional advantages as the party factions. Despite Thomas Remington's conclusion that "party-based factions were considerably higher in cohesion that were deputies' groups," it will be far-fetched to claim that the Duma is structured along party lines, as the legislatures in parliamentary democracies. Remington, "Political Conflict and Institutional Design: Paths of Party Development in Russia," in *Party Politics in Post-Communist Russia, op. cit.*, p. 205.

326 The restriction on the contributions of associations to their candidates was introduced in the Duma elections in 1995, where it was set at 65.55 million roubles (then approximately US$ 15,000). In the presidential elections of 1996 the limit on contributions by an association to its candidate was set at 2,888,500 roubles or less than one-fourth of the total expenditure ceiling. 1999—1/2 of the maximum expenditure limit of a candidate for the Duma; 2000—2/3 of the maximum expenditure limit.

327 In the 1995 Duma elections, the limit on the use of candidates' own funds was 43.7 million roubles (then slightly less than US$ 10,000), while for the

alliances it was 4,370 million roubles (less than a half of the total expenditure limit). In the 1996 presidential elections the candidates were allowed to use up to 57.75 million roubles (around US$12,000) from their own money. 1999—a) individual candidates for the Duma—1/10 of the maximum expenditure limit from their own money; b) electoral associations—2/5 of the max. expenditure limit from their own money. 2000—1/150 of the max. expenditure limit.

328 In the 1993 Duma elections each electoral association and bloc received 50 million roubles, or around US$50,000. In the 1995 Duma elections, each of the electoral associations and blocs received 80 million roubles (or around US$18,000). In the 1996 presidential race the registered candidates received 300 million roubles (approximately US$ 60,000). 2000—US$ 14,000, a tiny portion of the expenditure limit.

329 This issue was regulated by a 1994 amendment to the Law on the Tax on Profits of Enterprises and Organizations, December 27, 1991, as amended. According to art. 6(1)/f/, tax exempt are donations to the electoral funds of individual candidates, not exceeding 100 statutory minimum monthly wages; according to the same provision, tax exempt donations to the funds of electoral alliances should not exceed 10,000 statutory minimum wages. Similar provisions were introduced in the Law on Income Tax of Natural Persons of December 7, 1991 (amendment by Federal Law of October 27, 1994 No. 29-FZ).

330 This is by far the most important form of public support for the parties. Its egalitarian effect is reduced (albeit restricted) by the possibilities of buying additional airtime during campaigns. In the 1993 parliamentary elections, all candidates were entitled to one TV and one radio appearance in the public media; the electoral associations had one hour of free airtime at their disposal. See Daphne Skillen, "Media Coverage in the Elections," in P. Lentini, ed., *Elections and Political Order in Russia* (CEU Press: Budapest, London, New York, 1995). In the 1996 Duma elections, the registered electoral associations used together one hour a day during the electoral campaign (the time was equally divided among them). The amount of additionally bought airtime could not exceed the amount of free airtime. See *Instruktsiya o poryadke predostavleniya efirnogo vremeni na kanalah gosudarstvennyih teleradiokompanii . . .*, issued by *Postanovlenie* No. 18/149-ii of the Central Electoral Commission of September 20, 1995. The *Instruktsiya* provided for free space in the public printed media as well (art. 3.1). Similar rules were applicable in the 1999–2000 elections.

331 These forms of support were entrenched in the Law on the Basic Guarantees of Electoral Rights (*Federalnyi zakon ob osnovnykh garantiyakh izbiratel- nyikh prav grazhdan Rossiiskoi Federatsii*, 26 October 1994), art. 24. The traveling privileges included a free plane return ticket (or three tickets by train) to the member of the federation where the candidate was registered, and free use of public bus and rail transport on the territory of the electoral district. See art. 44 (4, 5, 6) of the Law on Duma Elections 1995.

332 Restrictions on donations to candidates and associations were introduced for the first time in the 1993 Duma elections; subsequently, the limits were changed several times.

333 Donations and contributions from state owned and municipal enterprises are prohibited. The same applies to contributions from foreign sources. Russian corporate bodies with foreign participation of more than 30 percent are also covered by the ban. See the 1995 *Law on Duma Elections*, art. 52(7).

334 The overall expenditure restrictions were first introduced in the 1995 Duma elections.

335 The parties and candidates were allowed to buy additional airtime on the public electronic media, but not exceeding the amount of free airtime they are entitled to by law. See *Instruktsiya o poryadke predostavleniya efirnogo vremeni na kanalah gosudarstvennyikh teleradiokompanii . . .* issued by *Postanovlenie* No. 18/149-ii of the Central Electoral Commission of September 20, 1995.

336 In 1991 the Bulgarian Socialist Party Supreme Council published in the Official Gazette "Information on the Income and Expenditure of BSP in 1990, and about the Property of the Party until December 31, 1990." This report was a result of the heated debates during the "battle" for nationaliz- ing the property of BSP, and was not so much a demonstration of the enforcement of the law.

337 Lilyana Klisurova, "The Parties Did Not Fill in Their Tax Declarations and Violated the Law," newspaper *Kontinent*, May 4, 1997 (in Bulgarian).

338 Lili Lyubomirova, "Euroleft Will Not Report Their Income to Tsonev," newspaper *Kontinent*, May 5, 1998. Only five parties, out of the 39 par- ties registered for the April 1997 elections presented reports to the Commission. Out of all parliamentary-represented parties, only the UDF filed a report.

339 Sixty-seven reports were received by the committee controlling party fund- ing in 1996 (for 1995—a a record number for the four years after 1991. The reports are not publicly accessible.

340 In 1997, out of all parliamentary-represented parties, only the UDF filed a report. According to the disclosed information, the income of the party was some 921, 718, 000 Levs (exchange rate 1DM = 1000 Levs), while the expenses amounted to 282, 994,000 Levs. The party had been financed almost entirely by donations and sponsorship: out of the whole income, only 718,000 Levs were coming from membership dues and other sources different from donations. The salaries of the officials and the associates of the UDF amounted to 44 million Levs. (Immediately after the announcement of these figures, a number of opposition politicians commented that the reported income is understated.)

341 It is important to keep in mind that the BSP was a governing party in the 1992–1994 period as well, in coalition with the Turkish minority party.

342 This is interesting from the viewpoint of political finance regulation, because the law prohibits donations from foreign states and limits the amount of donations from foreign natural persons. However, this limit is easy to avoid in Bulgarian context, by channeling of the funds through specially registered foundations, like the foundation "Democracy" in the case of the UDF.

343 Officially, the party firm publishing the daily—*Duma Press*—went bankrupt in 1999. The trademark (the name of the newspaper *Duma*) was given to another company, which is currently publishing the daily.

344 In 1994–1995 the BSP spent over twenty times more on salaries for staff than the UDF. This trend was obviously reversed in 1997–1999.

345 In addition, the opportunities for foreign funding were significantly reduced because, obviously, the western European left, and especially the Greek socialists, made aid dependent on the unification of the Bulgarian leftist opposition.

346 This is in sharp contrast with the situation in Western Europe and Canada. There, the "funding-gap" problem concerns the privileged position in financial terms of the pro-business, rightist parties. Moreover, the closing down of the "gap" by leftist parties is due mainly to the adoption of business-friendly policies, something demonstrated by the Blair Labour Party in the U. K.

347 Initially, the media were controlled by a committee in parliament, dominated by the majority faction. The BSP majority parliament passed a law on the media in 1995, which created a regulatory body, appointed by the government and its majority in parliament: the law was struck out by the Constitutional Court, as violating the principle of political neutrality. In 1998 the UDF majority in parliament adopted a new law, which gave the right to the president to appoint some of the members of the regulatory

body, the rest being appointed by the majority in parliament. In essence, this formula again gave the opportunity for the government to exercise control over the media and did not contribute to the application of the principle of political neutrality in media regulation (especially, having in mind that the president and the government are from the same party at present). Paradoxically, the Constitutional Court upheld the law, and thus entrenched the structural governmental bias in the media.

348 The report of the Council of Europe discussed in the Parliamentary Assembly of the Council for 1998 contained criticisms against the policy of the government in personnel matters and media governance. The accusations against the government were along the lines of the above-discussed problems: non-independence of the public media and politically motivated appointments and dismissals. See, for instance, *PARI* daily, 23 September 1998, "Europe Expects Bulgaria to Comply with the Requirements within a Year," electronic edition, in Bulgarian.

349 For conflict of interest scandals and governmental toll gating see *Capital, 15 August, 1998,* "Vidin Directors Accuse UDF of Racketeering" (electronic edition, in Bulgarian). See also R. Emanuilidu, "The Blue Premyanov Implanted His Proteges in All Key Positions," *Kontinent*, 425 (15 October), 1998.

350 Recently there were major scandals concerning grand-scale customs violations with alleged involvement of high administrators and government officials. See *Sega Daily* 245 (October 23), 1998, "One Day at the Customs," in Bulgarian. For the relation between border control, criminalization, and governmental favoritism see Y. Nikolov, "Smuggling—the Backbone of the Mafia," *Capital* weekly (September 21), 1998, electronic edition. For recent allegations about the involvement of officials close to the former government in smuggling see "State Security Firms Direct Cigarette Smuggling Affair," *Demokratsiya Daily*, 286 (October 26), 1998.

351 This was shown by the creation of the coalition of the MRF with some liberal parties claiming the support of one big financial corporation, Multigroup. This strategy, however, failed because of the falling out of favor of the corporation with the new government of the UDF in 1997 and 1998. Commentators alleged that a condition for reconciliation between the government and Multigroup was the withholding of the funding of the coalition of the MRF. As far as the BBB is concerned, due to personal conflicts between its leaders, the bloc in practice fell apart, so it does not really present evidence challenging my model.

352 Such was the case of the UDF and the opposition parties in 1996, which received support from the American Republican Institute and other organisations. Also, the Euroleft (an offshoot of the BSP) allegedly relies on foreign donors, after the stepping down of the BSP government in 1996. The BSP is also allegedly resorting to the support of Greek socialist and communist parties. Allegations that the MRF relies on Turkish financial (private and state) support have also been common.

353 A draft law "On Political Parties" is pending in the Duma since 1995. It was never signed by the President or passed by the Federation Council.

354 White, Rose, Allister, *op. cit.*, p. 118. "Although the parties were meant to report their spending and keep within prescribed limits, some admitted that their real outlays were three or four times greater than the costs reported to the Central Electoral Commission, and "almost all" made use of sponsors paying advertising and other bills directly. The source of the funds on which the Liberal Democratic Party had drawn remained a mystery even after its accounts had been submitted."

355 In the 1995 Duma elections, according to the official reports, all the parties raised and spent comparable amounts of money. See V. Novikov, "Uprychte vashi dengi: Finansovyie krugi v vyiboryi ne veryat," *Moskovskii Komsomolets* 233 (December 6), 1995. For official reports concerning the expenditure of the major candidates in the 1996 presidential campaign—only Zyuganov was unable to raise and spend funds up to the limit, mainly because of the CPRF boycott of the electronic media and the refusal to have a strong media campaign—see CEC reports of the Russian Federation, published on the Internet by the National News Service: http://www.nns.ru. Similar patterns were observable in the 1999–2000 election cycle. See CEC report of November 15, 1999.

356 Concerning the 1995 Duma elections "[T]he European Institute for the Media, which monitored campaign coverage on behalf of the European Union, concluded that free time had been allocated "fairly and in accordance with the regulations," in spite of a "few minor complaints . . ." Unacknowledged advertising in the newspapers and on some regional channels, however, was "commonplace," and the volume of advertising on national radio and television was much greater than the total that all the parties had been allowed to spend on their campaigns. Several parties exceeded the legal limits by a considerable margin." White, Rose, Allister, *op. cit.* p. 213. Similar findings mark the report of the institute on the 1996 presidential election campaign, showing lopsided coverage of Yeltsin. *Ibid.*, p. 252.

357 White, Rose, Allister, *op. cit.*, p. 117. "Russia's Choice, for instance, bought 180 minutes on the first television channel, twice as much as any other group . . . The Liberal Democrats bought more radio advertising than any other party, but the disproportionate share of editorial time in favor of Russia's Choice gave it the largest overall share . . . "

358 This could be observed in the 1999–2000 electoral cycle as well, according to the findings of the EIM. See RFERL/Russian Election Report 8 (January 7), 2000. The bias in the public electronic media was in favor of the parties close to the presidency and against the Fatherland–All Russia alliance. The same bias was reported by the EIM after the 2000 presidential elections. It is striking that Putin's media domination took place despite his refusal to use free airtime. See RFERL/Russian Election Report 5(April 7), 2000 and especially Laura Belin, "How State Television Aided Putin's Campaign," in the same issue.

359 "Russia, Constitutional Watch," in *East European Constitutional Review,* Vol. 5, Nos 2, 3, p. 21. "Yeltsin's team managed to monopolize most of the Russian media, above all, television and radio. The overwhelming majority of liberal newspapers that had previously been critical of the president, but were now alarmed at the mounting communist threat, took an unequivocal pro-Yeltsin position."

360 "Russia, Constitutional Watch," *East European Constitutional Review*, Vol. 5, Nos 2, 3, p. 21. "[A]ccording to some estimates, about one billion dollars was generated primarily by Russian gas and oil companies, beneficiaries of handsome tax breaks, to help fuel Yeltsin's campaign." For slightly more modest estimates see White, Rose, Allister, *op. cit.*, p. 250. "Although there was an official limit of little more than $3 million on campaign expenditure, businesses contributed at least $100 million to finance campaign efforts, and some estimates put the total as high as $500 million . . . Business supporters were prepared to put their bankrolls where their mouths were . . . "

361 White, Rose, Allister, *op. cit.*, p. 117. On the financing of the Communists and other parties see Lentini, "Overview of the Campaign," in P. Lentini, ed., *Elections and Political Order in Russia* (Budapest, London, New York: CEU Press, 1995).

362 Virginie Coulloudon, *op. cit.*

363 President Yeltsin had enormous possibilities to shape Russia's economic landscape. Thus, as early as in 1991 "the deputies in the Congress of the People's Deputies of RSFSR passed an ordinance "On the Legal Guarantees of the Economic Reform." This Ordinance granted President Yeltsin excep-

tional prerogatives to carry out reforms, including power to issue normative acts with the force of law in the sphere of banking and finance." D. Galligan and D. Smilov, *Administrative Law in Central and Eastern Europe 1996–1998* (Budapest: CEU Press, 1999), p. 286. Although this authorization was temporary, it gave the President an opportunity to lay the foundations of the present-day business community of Russia.

364 For the ties between government and big business in Russia see Juliet Johnson, "Russia's Emerging Financial Industrial Groups," Post Soviet *Affairs*, 1997, 13, 4, pp. 333–365; D. N. Jensen, "The Abuses of 'Authorized' Banking," in *Russian Financial Empires*, Radio Free Europe/Radio Liberty (electronic newsletter), 1998. See also D. N. Jensen, "Rumors of Oligarch's Demise Greatly Exaggerated" (December 7), 1998 (RFE/RL).

365 The two major federal newspapers, *Rossiiskaya gazeta* and *Rossiiskie vesti* were openly pro-presidential in the 1996 campaign; their journalists opposed the the CEC Instruction on the campaigning in the media, because it endeavored to prohibit the expression of journalist opinion on the campaign on the pages of the publicly owned press. N. Vainonen, *Rossiiskie vesti* (March 2), 1996, p. 2, tr. by B. Collins, in Sarah Reynolds, ed., *Statutes and Decisions*, May–June 1996, p. 83.

366 For the relationship between private corporations and the media see the coverage of the problem provided by Radio Free Europe/Radio Liberty: http://www.rferl.org. See especially Floriana Fossato and Anna Kachkaeva, "Russian Media Continue to Change Shape and Influence Media," Moscow (May 19), 1998 (RFE/RL); Fossato, "Kremlin Steps up Pressure on The Media," Moscow (May 19), 1998 (RFE/RL).

367 Therefore, the *normative* integration of Bulgaria and Russia in the family of democratic states is crucial to the success of the reform. Bulgaria is in a much more favorable position in this regard, being a candidate for EU accession. The normative integration of Russia, however, may involve nothing less than rethinking the existing international order by creating institutional forms of interdependence between the main former rivals from the Cold War—U.S. and Europe and Russia. Whether this interdependence will have a military, political or economic character is beyond the scope of this paper.

368 This paper could not have been produced without the financial support provided by the Central European University. The "Corruption in Tajikistan as seen by the private sector" survey was sponsored by the Local Government

and Public Services Initiative of the Open Society Institute. I am thankful to my research group—Mr. Husrav Gaibullaev, Mr. Iskandar Samandarov, Mr. Abdurakhim Shodiev and Ms. Zarina Abdushukurova—for a professional job. Special gratitude to Mr. Mustapha Rouis, Resident Representative of the World Bank in Tajikistan, for moral and technical support as well as for valuable advice in the course of project implementation.

369 The survey of 201 businesses and 521 households was conducted between July and August, 1999, with the financial support of the Open Society Institute, Local Government and Public Service Initiative, H-1051 Budapest, Nádor utca 11, Hungary.

370 It should be noted, however, that not all corruption in communist times was centralized. While more important decisions (public housing, bank loans, etc.) were made centrally, petty corruption was present even then.

371 In fact, that conclusion undermines the belief that corruption in the presence of bad laws is good and facilitates development.

372 The most widely used is the Corruption Perception Index, produced by Transparency International.

373 In many cases there is a clear tradeoff between the level or, rather, the sophistication of bureaucracy and corruption. For a detailed discussion see Tanzi (1995).

374 Some may believe that the impact of bribes is positive in this case. In fact, many have argued that, when the laws are bad, corruption can be a good, since it plays the role of a lubricant and facilitates business activities whenever rules impose an obstacle. See, for example, Leff (1964). However, the rules are not exogenous. On the contrary, many government regulations have been designed specifically to generate bribes and thus are already a derivative of corruptibility and signal inefficiencies.

375 Many have left to work in new businesses.

376 Tat Yan Kang, "Corruption and its Institutional Foundations: The Experience of South Korea," *IDS Bulletin*, 27/2 (1996), pp. 48–55.

377 Krastev, "The Strange (Re)Discovery of Corruption," in Lord Dahrendorf *et al.* eds., *The Paradoxes of Unintended Consequences* (Budapest: CEU Press), p. 40.

378 M. K. Sparrow, *License to Steal: Why Fraud Plagues America's Health Care System*, updated edition (Denver, 2000). Sparrow points out that no other country spends more than 10 percent of its GDP on health care, and yet U.S. health indicators significantly trail those of other developed countries: life expectancy at birth is 17th in the world, and infant mortality is 19th.

379 For discussion of definitions, see J. B. McKinney and M. Johnston, *Fraud, Waste, and Abuse in Government: Causes, Consequences, and Cures* (Philadelphia: Institute for the Study of Human Issues, 1986).

380 For attempts to conceptualize corruption, and test those conceptions with analyses of recent experience in several countries, see P.l Heywood, ed., *Political Corruption* (London, Oxford: Blackwell, 1997).

381 F. Anechiarico and J. B. Jacobs, *The Pursuit of Absolute Integrity: How Corruption Control Makes Government Ineffective* (Chicago: The University of Chicago Press, 1996).

382 The "prevailing definition" of corruption, according to one of its leading scholars, involves the interaction between the public and the private, especially transactions converting public into private. A. J. Heidenheimer, preface, Heidenheimer, M. Johnston, V. T. Levine, eds., *Political Corruption: A Handbook* (New Brunswick:Transaction Publ., 1989), p. 6.

383 S. E. Finer, "Patronage and Public Service: Jeffersonian Democracy and the British Tradition," *Public Administration*, 30 (1952), 333–53; reprinted in A. J. Heidenheimer *et al.*, eds., *Political Corruption: A Handbook* (New Brunswick, 1989), pp.101–28. At the height of the British empire's power its government ministers made no distinction between the public purse and their private benefit. On the contrary, elites assumed that their financial management and their private firms were best for the country, thereby profiting substantially from their positions of public power while congratulating themselves on their act of public service. For choice examples involving the bond market, see N. Ferguson, *The Cash Nexus: Money and Power in the Modern World, 1700–2000* (New York: Penguin, 2001).

384 J. Kramer, "Political Corruption in the USSR," *Western Political Quarterly*, 30/2 (1977), 213–24 (quote p. 218). See also K. Simis, *USSR: The Corrupt Society. The Secret World of Soviet Capitalism* (New York: Simon and Schuster, 1982).

385 By contrast, rarely, if ever, do scholars celebrate "entrepreneurial" aspects of the illegal economy in the U. S., such as the huge illicit drug trade or the highly sophisticated schemes for tax evasion.

386 One could add that the existence of the Soviet Union as the quintessential corrupt system also helped deflect association with corruption from the U. S. The KGB's chief analyst wrote in his memoirs that the U.S. spared no resources in the discrediting of the USSR. "It is necessary to admit," he added, in an understatement, "that our reality gave them an enormous

amount of material for such work." Nikolai Leonov, *Likholet'e* (Moscow: Mezhdunarodnye ostnosheniia, 1994), p. 252.

387 Shadow economy practices among individuals fell within the category of economic crimes. In general, see G. Grossman, "The 'Second Economy' of the USSR," *Problems of Communism*, 26/5 (1977), pp. 25–40.

388 One expert wrote, during the Brezhnev era, that corruption in the Soviet Union served the regime as a preferred substitute for institutional reform, "which would involve shifting toward a more participatory, semi-authoritarian system with greater reliance on group and individual autonomy and on the market mechanism." Ch. A. Schwartz, "Corruption and Political Development in the U.S.S.R.," *Comparative Politics*, 11/4 (1979), pp. 425–43.

389 Social justice concerns within the U.S. were often championed by individuals and groups that frequently tended not to recognize the full depravity of Communism, though there were important exceptions, such as George Orwell in Britain.

390 J. W. Williams and Margaret E. Beare, "The Business of Bribery: Globalization, Economic Liberalization, and the 'Problem' of Corruption," *Crime, Law, and Social Change*, 12/2 (1999), 115–46. See also Kimberly Ann Elliott, ed., *Corruption and the Global Economy* (Washington, D.C.: Institute of International Economics, 1997).

391 By the end of the 1990s, the tide seemed to be turning. See, for example, J. Thornhill and Ch. Clover, "The Robbery of Nations: Billions of Dollars Are Flowing out of the Former Soviet Union," *Financial Times* (August 21), 1999; J. Kahn and T. L. O'Brien, "Easy Money: A Special Report," *New York Times* (October 18), 1998.

392 Also overlooked was the transparent use of IMF and other international mechanisms as vehicles for the U. S. government and business interests to complete their bilateral agendas and penetrate Asian markets. Tat Yan Kong, "Corruption and its Institutional Foundations: The Experience of South Korea," *IDS Bulletin*, 27/2 (1996), pp. 48–55.

393 Roughly speaking, it makes sense to distinguish Slovenia, Estonia, and Hungary in one group, Poland, the Czech Republic, Slovakia, Romania, and Bulgaria in a second, and most of the rest of the fourteen former Soviet republics in a third. (The statelets of the war-torn Caucasus, somewhat like the Balkans, probably ought to be in a separate category.) Russia's place is ambiguous. Removed from proximity to Germany or Scandinavia, the concentrated wealth and talent in the city of Moscow,

which is larger than all relatively 'successful' members of Central Europe other than Poland, makes Russia an exception in the East, and different from Ukraine.

394 See D. C. Tipps, "Modernization Theory and the Comparative Study of Societies: A Critical Perspective" and C. E. Pletsch, "The Three Worlds, or the Division of Social Scientific Labor, Circa 1950–1975," *Comparative Studies in Society and History*, 15/2 (1973), 199–226 and 23/3 (1981), pp. 265–90.

395 R. S. Rosefsky, *Frauds, Swindles, and Rackets: A Red Alert for Today's Consumers* (Chicago: Follett Publ. Co., 1973); D. W. Stewart and H. A. Spille, *Diploma Mills: Degrees of Fraud* (New York: Greenwood Publishing, 1988); M. A. Henderson, *Rip-offs, Cons, and Swindles: Money for Nothing* (Fort Lee, NJ., Barricade Books, 1992); M. Punch, *Dirty Business: Exploring Corporate Misconduct: Analysis and Cases* (London and Thousand Oaks, Calif.: Sage Publications, 1996); and S. L. Weisman, *Need and Greed: The Story of the Largest Ponzi Scheme in American History* (Syracuse, NY, Syracuse University Press, 1999).

396 T. L. O'Brien, *Bad Bet: The Inside Story of the Glamour, Glitz, and Danger of America's Gambling Industry* (New York: Times Business, 1998).

397 For the parallels with the experience of Latin America, see H. de Soto, *The Other Path: The Invisible Revolution in the Third World* (New York: Harper and Row, 1989).

398 D. C. Johnston, "Corporations' Taxes are falling Even as Individuals' Burden Rises" and "A Smaller I. R. S. Gives up Billions in Back Taxes," *New York Times* (February 20), 2000 and (April 3), 2001.

399 *Ibid.* See also D. L. Barlett and J. B. Steele, *The Great American Tax Dodge: How Spiraling Fraud and Avoidance are Killing Fairness, Destroying the Income Tax, and Costing You* (Boston: Little Brown and Co., 2000).

400 "Executive Pay: A Special Report," *New York Times* (April 1), 2001.

401 J. L. Shulman and W.G. Bowen, *The Game of Life: College Sports and Educational Values* (Princeton: Princeton University, 2001).

402 W. G. Bowen and D. Bok, *The Shape of the River: Long-term Consequences of Considering Race in College and University Admission* (Princeton: Princeton University, 1998).

403 For some choice examples, see "If Only You'd Sold Some Stock Earlier——Say $100 Million Worth," *Wall Street Journal* (March 22), 2001.

404 Gretchen Morgenson, "How Did So Many Get It So Wrong?" *New York*

Times, (December 31), 2000; M. Lewis, "His So-Called Life of Stock Fraud," *New York Times Magazine* (February 25), 2001. An utterly unconvincing effort to "clean up" the reputations of "analysts" led to the adoption in 2001 of "voluntary" guidelines for ethics, which have no teeth. See also *Fortune* (May 14), 2001.

405 On this and many other matters, see Th. Frank, *One Market under God: Extreme Capitalism, Market Populism, and the End of Economic Democracy* (New York: Doubleday, 2000).

406 F. Norris, "U. S. Accuses Former Cendant Chiefs of Fraud," *New York Times* (March 1), 2001. See also Kitty Calavita, H. N. Pontell, and R. H. Tillman, *Big Money Crime: Fraud and Politics in the Savings and Loan Crisis* (Berkeley: University of California Press, 1997); and I. Walter, *The Secret Money Market: Inside the Dark World of Tax Evasion, Financial Fraud, Insider Trading, Money Laundering, and Capital Flight* (New York: Harper & Row, Ballinger Divison, 1990).

407 M. C. Perkins and Celia Nunez, "Why Market Insiders Don't Feel Your Pain," *Washington Post* (March 15), 2001. To combat IPO abuse by company owners, the SEC does prohibit company owners from selling within 180 days of an IPO, but investment banks skirt the regulation by offering their company-owner clients the option of selling their stock back to the bank after 180 days at higher earlier prices, if the stock has declined, as the majority do. Company owners, of course, have paid the investment bank a handsome fee to manage the IPO.

408 See U. Bhattacharya and H. Daouk, "The World Price of Insider Trading," available at www.ssrn.com. On the grayness of legal issues governing stock trading, see also Elizabeth Szockyj, *The Law and Insider Trading: In Search of a Level Playing Field* (Buffalo: NY: W.S. Hein, 1993). Insider training seems to be a potencial crime largely in a town market.

409 Meriwhether figured prominently in the best-selling exposé by M. Lewis, *Liar's Poker: Rising through the Wreckage on Wall Street* (New York: Norton, 1989).

410 S. Lipin, M. Murray and J. M. Schlesinger, "Bailout Blues . . ." *Wall Street Journal* (September 25),1998; J. Kahn and P. Truell, "Troubled Investment Fund's Bets Now Estimated at $1.25 trillion," *New York Times* (September 26), 1998. See also N. Dunbar, *Inventing Money: The Story of Long-term Capital Management and the Legends Behind It* (Chichester, NY, John Wiley and Sons, 2000). Unlike an earlier fiasco at the long-standing British firm Barings, which went bankrupt, colossal losses at LTCM did not result from

"unauthorized" trades made by rogue employees of the firm but from normal operations. Cf. L. Hunt and Karen Heinrich, *Barings Lost: Nick Leeson and the Collapse of Barings Plc.* (Singapore: Butterworth-Heinemann Asia, 1996).

411 T. Herman, "Historians Marvel at Rescue's Size, Twists," *Wall Street Journal* (September 25), 1998.

412 It could also be noted that the 1996 Telecommunications Act gave away new public airwaves (digital frequencies), estimated in value at $70 billion, to private corporations. R. McChesney, *Rich Media, Poor Democracy* (Urbana: University of Illinois Press, 1999), pp. 64–65, 75, 151.

413 J. Strohmeyer, *Extreme Conditions: Big Oil and the Transformation of Alaska* (New York, Simon and Schuster, 1993), 10–1. In March 1989, in Valdez—site of a $12 million barley terminal that never held a grain of barley—a giant oil tanker operated by Exxon ran aground, spilling a quarter million barrels of crude oil, blackening more than a thousand miles of coastline, and decimating marine life and fisheries. It was the largest oil-spill disaster in U.S. history.

414 E. D. Sclar, *You Don't Always Get What You Pay for: The Economics of Privatization* (Ithaca: Cornell University Press, 2000).

415 D. Rebovich, quoted in D. Barry, "Different Era, Same Reputation," *New York Times* (March 25), 2001.

416 It might be noted that the career trajectory of President George W. Bush perfectly encapsulates the workings of money and influence in the U. S., from his preferential admission to Yale University and Harvard Business School and early oil businesses (which went bust), to his financial bailouts via family connections and his windfall enrichment through access to public monies. See L.-E. Nelson, "Legacy," *New York Review of Books* (February 24), 2000; and N. D. Kristof, "The 2000 Campaign: The Legacy; a Father's Footsteps Echo throughout a Son's Career," and "The 2000 Campaign: Breaking into Baseball; Road to Politics Ran through a Texas Ballpark," *New York Times* (September 11 and 24), 2000.

417 "In an ideological environment where there are no plausible alternatives to democracy and a free market, anticorruption rhetoric can, in a distorted way, occupy the place of a policy alternative." I. Krastev, "Dancing with Anticorruption," *East European Constitutional Review*, 7/1 (1998), pp. 51–58 (quote at 58).

418 For the voting public in transition countries, charges of corruption can often increase a politician's standing, just as they often do in the Philippines or India, where populists who campaign on behalf of the poor come under

attack for corruption. In transition countries, such redistribution concerns become the nominal goal of avowed neo-Communists, or transformed Communists who have assumed new political appellations. Western advocates of a "free" market who insist that policy-directed redistribution of wealth stifles economic growth fail to acknowledge the uncanny success of redistribution politics in the 1990s—that is, the massive redistribution of wealth upward, such as took place in the U. S.

419 J. C. Scott, *Comparative Political Corruption* (Englewood Cliffs, NJ: Prentice Hall, 1972), p. 21. Scott also noted that, "the dominant forces in a political system have no reason to resort to corruption . . . to make their influence felt, for the state is organized to serve their purposes" (p. 28).

Select Bibliography

Asian Development Bank, "Corruption" (1997):
http://www.adb.org/Work/Policies/Anticorruption/.

Alatas, S.H., *Corruption: Its Nature, Causes and Functions* (Aldershot: Avebury, 1990).

Alimova, T., and V. Buyev, *et al.*, "Kak reguliruyetsya razvitiye predprinimatelstva v Moskve," *Biznes dlya vsekh*, (1997), pp. 16–17.

Bacharach, M., and D. Gambetta, "Trust in Signs," in Karen Cook, ed., *Social Structure and Trust* (New York: Russell Sage Foundation, forthcoming).

Banfield, C.E., *The Moral Basis of a Backward Society* (New York: The Free Press, 1958).

——, "Corruption as a Feature of Governmental Organization," *Journal of Law and Economics*, 18/3 (1975), pp. 587–605.

Becker, G., 1968, "Crime and Punishment: An Economic Approach," *Journal of Political Economy* 76(2) (March/April), pp. 169–217.

Becker, G. and G. J. Stigler, "Law Enforcement, Malfeasance, and the Compensation of Enforcers." *Journal of Legal Studies* 3 (1974), pp. 1–19.

Bíró, A. Zoltán, "Mindennapi ellenfelünk a rend," in *Írások a korrupcióról* (Budapest: Helikon–Korridor, 1998), pp. 209–224.

Bognár, G. and Gál R.I.: *Hálapénz a magyar egészségügyben* (Budapest: TÁRKI, 1999).

Boo Sung Ok, *The Systematization of Political Contributions*, The Modern Society Institute (1991), pp. 90–7 (in Korean).

Bureau of Economic Analysis, *Ogranicheniye konkurentsii na regionalnykh rynkakh tovarov i uslug mestnymi organami vlasti i upravleniya* (Moscow, 1999).

Carothers, Th., "The Rule of Law Revival," *Foreign Affairs*, 95, (March 13, 1998), p. 77.

Cheng, Tun-jen, and B. Womack, "General Reflections on Informal Politics in East Asia (Informal Politics in East Asia)," *Asian Survey*, 320, 36 (March 1, 1996).

Chepurenko, A. *et al.*, "Malyi Biznes Posle Avgusta 1998 g.: Problemy, Tendentsii, Adaptatsionnye Vozmozhnosti," in Gorshkov, M.K., A.Yu. Chepurenko, and F.E. Sheregi, eds., *Osennyi Krizis 1998 goda: Rossiiskoye obschestvo do i posle* (Moscow: ROSSPEN, 1998), pp. 101–183.

Chong, Ku-hyon, "Business–Government Relations in Korea," in Kae-H Chong and Lee Hak-chong, eds., *Korean Managerial Dynamics* (New York: Praeger, 1989).

Chung In Moon, and Jongryn Mo, eds., *Corruption in South Korea: Its Costs and Countermeasures*, (Seoul: Oreum, 1999) (in Korean).

Coleman, J. S., *Foundations of Social Theory* (Cambridge, MA: Belknap Press, 1990).

Czakó, Ágnes, and E. Sík, "Managers Reciprocal Transactions," *Connections,* 9/3 (Winter 1998).

Eckert, C. J., *Offspring of Empire: The Koch'ang Kims and the Colonial Origins of Korean Capitalism, 1876–1945* (Seattle: University of Washington Press, 1991).

Elster, J., *The Cement of Society* (Cambridge: Cambridge University Press, 1989).

Elster J., C. Offe, and U.K. Preuss, *Institutional Design in Post-communist Societies* (Cambridge: Cambridge University Press, 1998).

Frequently Asked Questions and Answers on the TI 1998 Corruption Perceptions Index: http://www.transparency.de/documents/cpi/cpi-faq.html

Frydman, R. and A. Rapaczynski, *The Privatization Process in Central Europe* (Budapest: Central European University Press, 1993).

Frye, T., and A. Shleifer, "The Invisible Hand and the Grabbing Hand," *American Economic Review, Papers and Proceedings,*. 87/2 (1997), pp. 354–358.

Fukuyama, F., *Trust* (New York: Free Press, 1996).

Gambetta, D., *The Sicilian Mafia: The Business of Private Protection* (Cambridge, MA: Harvard University Press, 1993).,

——, "Comment on 'Corruption and Development' by Susan Rose-Ackerman," in B. Pleakovic and J. Stiglitz, eds., *Annual World Bank Conference on Development Economics 1997* (Washington, DC: World Bank, 1997), pp. 58–61.,

——, *Corruption. An Analytical Map*, Shelby Coullum Davis Center/Open Society Institute Workshop, May 21–22 (proceeds) (1999).

——, and P. Reuter, "Conspiracy among the Many: The Mafia in Legitimate Industries," in G. Fiorentini and S. Peltzman, eds., *The Economics of Organized Crime* (Cambridge: Cambridge University Press, 1995), pp. 116–139.

Gardner, J.A., "Defining Corruption," *Corruption and Reform* 7 (1992), pp. 111–124.

Garzòn, Valdés E., "Sul concetto di corruzione," *Ragioe Pratica* 3 (1995), pp. 108–131.

Goda, N. J. W., "Black Marks: Hitler's Bribery of his Senior Officers during World War II," Davis Center Seminar, Princeton University, Princeton, NJ, unpublished manuscript (1999).

Gombár Csaba, "A korrupció, mint közrossz," in *Írások a korrupcióról* (Budapest: Helikon–Korridor, 1998), pp. 47–87.

Granovetter, M., "Threshold Models of Collective Behavior," *American Journal of Sociology* 83/6 (1978).

Gray, Cheryl and D. Kaufmann, "Corruption and Development," *Finance and Development* (March 1998).

Heidenheimer, A. J., M. Johnston, and S. Levine, *Political Corruption: A Handbook* (New Brunswick, NJ: Transaction Publishers, 1989).

Hessel, Marek and Ken Murphy, "Stealing the State, and Everything Else" (1999) http://www.transparency.de/documents/workpapers/hessel/index.html

Johnson, S., D. Kaufmann, and A. Shleifer, "Unofficial Sector in Transition Economies," *Brookings Papers on Economic Activity,* 2 (1997), pp. 159–239.

Kaufmann, D.l, "Why is Ukraine's Economy—and Russia's—Not Growing?" *Transition* (April 1997).

Kim Hae-Dong, and Yoon Tae-Bum, *Bureaucratic Corruption and its Control* (Seoul, 1994) (in Korean).

Kim Kwang-woong, "The Ideology and Politics of Korea's Civil–Military Bureucratic Elites," *Kyegan Kyunghyang* (Spring 1998), p. 30 (in Korean).

Kim Taek, "The Corruption Collusion and Structure in Korean Society," (December, 1997) (in Korean).

Kim Yong-Hak, "The Origins of the East Asian Financial Crisis and Its Social Scientific Impact", *Sahwoe Bipyong* 19, (Seoul, 1999), pp. 175–183 .

Kim Joongi, and Jongbum Kim, "Cultural Differences in the Crusade against International Bribery: Rice-Cake Expenses in Korea and the Foreign Corrupt Practices Act," *Pacific Rim Law and Policy Journal*, 6/549 (1997).

Kitschelt, H. P., "Political Opportunity Structures and Political Protest: Anti-Nuclear Movements in Four Democracies," *British Journal of Political Science* 16 (January 1986).

Klitgaard, R., *Controlling Corruption*. (Berkeley: University of California Press, 1988).

Kurer, O., "The Political Foundations of Economic Development Policies," *Journal of Development Studies,* (June 1, 1996) p. 645.

Labuda, V., *Nejapné aféry aneb privatizace po Česku* (Prague: Periskop, 1995).

Lande, C., "The Dyadic Basis of Clientelism," in S. Schmidt, J. Scott, C. Lande, and L. Guasti, eds., *Friends, Followers, and Factions: A Reader in Political Clientelism* (1977).

Laothamatas, Anek, "From Clientelism to Partnership," in A. MacIntyre, ed., *Business and Government in Industrializing Asia* (Ithaca, NY: Cornell University Press, 1994).

Leff, N., "Economic Development through Bureaucratic Corruption," *American Behavioral Scientist* (1964), pp. 8–14.

Letowska, E., *Corruption: towards Greater Transparency? Ethics in the Public Sector: Challenges and Opportunities for OECD Countries* (Paris: Organization of Economic Co-Operation and Development, 1997).

Levin, M., and G. Satarov, "Yavleniye korruptsii Rossii," *Nezavisimaya* (October 2, 1997), pp. 1, 5.

Licandro, A., and A. Varano, *La città dolente. Le confessioni di un sindaco-corrotto* (Torino: Einaudi, 1993).

Lipset, S. M., and G. M. Lenz, "Corruption, Culture and Markets," (1999) unpublished manuscript.

Loskutova, L., "Gosudarstvenny racket, ili nepomernye pobory dlya malogo buznesa," *Predpriyatie*, (24 June 1998), pp. 174–175.

Lui, F., "An Equilibrium Queuing Model of Bribery," *Journal of Political Economy* (August 1985), pp. 760–781.

Lundahl, M., "Inside the Predatory State," *Political Economy* 24/1, (1997) 31–50.

MacDonald, S. B., "Transparency in Thailand's 1997 Economic Crisis: The Significance of Disclosure," *Asian Survey*, 38, 688 (July 1, 1998).

MacRae, J., "Underdevelopment and the Economics of Corruption: A Game Theory Approach," *World Development*, 10, (1982), pp. 677–687.

Martz, J. D., *The Politics of Clientelism* (New Brunswick, NJ; London: Transaction Publishers, 1996).

Mauro, P., "Corruption and Growth," *Quarterly Journal of Economics* (August, 1995), pp. 681–712.

McKitrick, E. L., "The study of corruption," in S.M. Lipset and R. Hofstadter, *Sociology and History: Methods* (New York: Basic Books, 1968).

Milhaupt, Curtis J., "Property Rights in Firms," *Virginia Law Review*, 84, (September, 1998).

Murphy, K. M., A. Schleifer and R. W. Vyshny, "The Allocation of Talent: Implications for Growth," *Quarterly Journal of Economics,* (May 1991), 106, 503–530.

Nakane, Chie, *Japanese Society.* (Berkeley: University of California Press, 1970).

Nam, Chang-Hee, South Korea's Big Business Clientelism in Democratic Reform. *Asian Survey* 35, (April 1995), pp. 357–366.

Noonan, J.T., Jr., *Bribes* (Berkeley: University of California Press, 1984).

Nye, J. S., "Corruption and Political Development: A Cost–Benefit Analysis," in A. J. Heidenheimer, M. Johnston, and V.T. Levine, eds., *Political Corruption: A Handbook* (New Brunswick, NJ: Transaction, 1967).

OECD, *Corruption: Towards Greater Transparency? Ethics in the Public Sector: Challenges and Opportunities for OECD Countries* (Paris: Organization for Economic Cooperation and Development, 1997).

Oh Kyung-Whan, "Those Who Touch Rice-Cakes Will Have Rice-Cake Powder on Their Hands," *Junggyun Moonhwa* 20, 268 (September 1984) (in Korean).

Oh Young-Keun, and Lee Sang Yong, *A Study on Bribery Offenses in Korea,* Korea Institute of Criminology (1996), pp. 94–25 (in Korean).

Park Sang Chul, *Election Campaigns and Related Political Laws* (Hanjulgi, 1995) (in Korean).

Philp, M., "Defining Political Corruption," in P. Heywood, ed., *Political Corruption* (Oxford: Basil Blackwell, 1997), pp. 21–46.

Przeworski, A., et al., eds., *Sustainable Democracy* (Cambridge: Cambridge University Press, 1995).

Radaev, V., "Maly Biznes i Problemy Delovoy Etiki: Nadezhdy i Realnost," *Voprosy Ekonomiki*, 7, (1996), pp. 72–82.

——, "Practicing and Potential Entrepreneurs in Russia," *International Journal of Sociology* Fall, 27/ 3, (1997), pp. 15–50.

——, *Formirovaniye novykh rossiiskikh rynkov: transaktsionnye izderzhki, formy kontrolya i delovaya etika* (Moscow: Center for Political Technologies, 1998a).,

——, "Regional Entrepreneurship: The State of Small Business," in *A Regional Approach to Industrial Restructuring in the Tomsk Region, Russian Federation*, proceedings (Paris: Organization of Economic Cooperation and Development, 1998b), pp. 275–319.

Ranking (1995): http://www.gwdg.de/-uwvw/rank-1995.htm

Ravík, S., *Latrina magika v Čechách, na Moravi a ve Slezsku* (Prague: Periskop, 1995).

Reed, Q., "Political Corruption, Privatization and Control in the Czech Republic: A Case Study in Problems of Multiple Transition," D. Phil. Thesis, Oriel College, Oxford University (1996).

Roh Byung-Man, "The Formation and Analysis of the Origins of Divisive Regionalism of the Political Structure," *Korea Political Scientist Association* 32, 59 (Spring 1998) (in Korean).

Roniger, L., and A. Gunes-Ayata (eds.), *Democracy, Clientelism, and Civil Society* . Boulder, Colo.: Westview, 1994.

Rose, R., "Getting Things Done in an Anti-Modern Society: Social Capital Networks in Russia," *Studies in Public Policy,* 304, Centre for the Study of Public Policy (Glasgow: University of Strathclyde, 1998a).,

—, Getting Things Done with Social Capital, *Studies in Public Policy,* 303, Centre for the Study of Public Policy (Glasgow: University of Strathclyde, 1998b).

—, and Ch.Haerpfer, "Adapting to Transformation in Eastern Europe," *Studies in Public Policy*, No. 212, Centre for the Study of Public Policy (Glasgow: University of Strathclyde, 1993).

—, "New Democracies Barometer V," *Studies in Public Policy,* 306, Centre for the Study of Public Policy (Glasgow: University of Strathclyde, 1998).

Rose-Ackerman, Susan, *Corruption: A Study in Political Economy* (New York: Academic Press, 1978).

—, "Corruption and Development," in J. Stiglitz and B. Pleskovic, eds., *Annual World Bank Conference on Development Economics 1997* (Washington, DC: World Bank, 1998), pp. 35–57.

—, *Corruption and Government: Causes, Consequences, and Reform* (Cambridge: Cambridge University Press, 1999).

Salbu, Steven R., "Are Extraterritorial Restrictions on Bribery a Viable and Desirable International Policy Goal under the Global Conditions of the Late Twentieth Century?" *Yale Journal of International Law* 24, 223 (Winter, 1999).

Schelling, T., *The Strategy of Conflict* (Cambridge, Mass: Harvard University Press, 1960).

Schwartz, A., *The Best-Laid Plan: Privatization and Neo-Liberalism in the Czech Republic*, PhD. Dissertation (Berkely: University of California at Berkeley, 1999).

Shin Myung-soon, "A Proposal to Prevent Power-Oriented Misconduct and Corruption," *Human Rights and Justice* 23, 253 (Sept. 1997) (in Korean).

Shleifer, A., "Government in Transition," *European Economic Review*. 41, (1997), pp. 385–410.

—, and R. W. Vishny, "Corruption," *The Quarterly Journal of Economics*, 108(3), (August, 1993), pp. 599–617.

Sík, Endre, "Some Thoughts about the Sociology of Corruption—from an East-European Perspective,"Proceeds of a Princeton University–CEU Joint Conference on Corruption, Budapest, Hungary (October–November, 1999).

——, "From Multicoloured to Black and White Economy: The Hungarian Second Economy and the Transformation, *International Journal of Urban and Regional Research*, 18/1, (1994a), pp. 46–70.

——, "Network Capital in Capitalist, Communist and Post-Communist Societies," *International Contributions to Labor Studies* 4, (1994b), pp. 73–93.

——, *Ellenőri korrupció*, manuscript, Budapest, Hungary (2000).

Stapenhurst, R., and S. J. Kpundeh, *Curbing Corruption: Toward a Model for Building National Integrity* (Washington, DC: World Bank, 1999).

Stark, D., "Recombinant Property in East European Capitalism," *Collegium Budapest and Cornell University Discussion Paper* (December 1993).

Szekely, A., "Democracy, Judicial Reform, the Rule of Law, and Environmental Justice in Mexico," *Houston Journal of International Law* 21, 385 (Spring, 1999).

Tanzi, V., "Corruption: Arm's Length Relationships and Markets," in G. Fiorentini and S. Peltzman, eds., *Economics of Organized Crime* (Cambridge: Cambridge University Press, 1995).

——, "Corruption around the World: Causes, Consequences, Scope and Cures," *IMF Working Paper,* WP/98/63 (1998).

Tirole, J., "A Theory of Collective Reputations with Applications to the Persistence of Corruption and to Firm Quality," *Insitut d'Economie Industrielle* (Toulouse: MIT, and Ceras, 1993).

Toinet, Marie-France, and I. Glenn, "Clientelism and Corruption in the "Open" Society: The Case of the United States," in Christopher Clapham, ed., *Private Patronage and Public Power* (St. Martin's, 1982).

Tóth, I. Gy. "Normakövetés és normaszegés a kilencvenes évek Magyarországán, Paper presented at the Rudolf Andorka Memorial Conference "Törések és kötések a társadalomban" (April 22–23, 1999).

Transparency International, "The Corruption Perceptions Index," (1998): http://www.transparency.de/documents/cpi/index.html., "TI Press Release: 1998 Corruption Perceptions Index," (1998): http://www.transparency.de /documents/press-releases/1998/1998.09.22.cpi.html.

——, "TI Activities Report in the CEE/FSU Region, November 1, 1998–June 10, 1999," Transparency International, Berlin.,

——, *Systemy obschegosudarstvennoi etiki povedeniya: Posobiye TI* (Systems of Universal State Ethics of Conduct: A TI Guide) (Moscow, 1999).

——, "The Role of the Corruption Perceptions Index," http://www.transparency.de/documents /cpi/cpi-role.html

Tsyganov, A., "Predprinimatel i vlast: problemy vzaimodeistviya," *Voprosy ekonomiki*, 6, (1997), pp. 97–103.

Ul Haque, Nadeem and Ratna Sahay, "Do Government Wages Cuts Close Budget Deficits? Costs of Corruption," *IMF Staff Papers*, 43, (December 1996) pp. 754–778 .

Vásárhelyi, Mária, "Public Opinion Regarding Corruption," *Review of Sociology,* Special issue, Budapest (1999), pp. 82–94.

——, "Rejtőzködés, önigazolás, hárítás és egymásra mutogatás," in *Írások a korrupcióról,* (Budapest: Helikon–Korridor, 1998), pp. 136–208.

Wallace, Claire and Ch. Haerpfer, "Democratization, Economic Development and Corruption in East-Central Europe," paper presented at the CPHR conference "Transparency in the Slovak Economy—III," Bratislava (25 June 1999).

Watson, Laura "Labor Relations and the Law in South Korea," *Pacific Rim Law and Policy Journal* 7, 229 (January, 1998).

Woodall, Brian, *Japan under Construction: Corruption, Politics, and Public Works (Berkely: University of California Press,* 1996).

Yeo-chi King, Ambrose, "Kuan-his and Network Building: A Sociological Interpretation," *Daedalus* (Spring, 1991).

Yeon Seong-Jin, and Kim Ji-Sun, *Corruption among Public Officials and Its Control*, Korea Institute of Criminology (1998), pp. 97–108 (in Korean).

Yoo Young-Ul, "Political–Economic Collusive Offenses in Chun Doo-Hwan Regime," *Shindonga* (June, 1988), pp. 387–388 (in Korean).

Yun, Daniel, "Bribery among the Korean Elite: Putting an End to a Cultural Ritual and Restoring Honor," *Vanderbilt Journal of Transnational Law* 29 (November, 1996).

Abbreviations for Publications Cited

ČD: Český deník (became Český týdeník 1/1/95)
ČT: Český týdeník
E: Ekonom
HaNo: Halo noviny
HN: Hospodářské noviny
LD: Lidová demokracie
LN: Lidové noviny
MFD: Mladá fronta Dnes
MS: Mladý Švìt
P: Právo
R: Respekt
RP: Rudé právo (renamed Právo in October 1995)
SS: Svobodné slovo
T: Týden
Tel: Telegraf
ZN: Zemìdelské noviny

INDEX